ART BOOKS

a basic bibliography
on the fine arts

ART BOOKS

A basic bibliography on the fine arts

E. LOUISE LUCAS

New York Graphic Society Ltd.

Greenwich, Connecticut

This book is based on the bibliographies previously
prepared by E. Louise Lucas under the title
The Harvard List of Books on Art, last published
in 1952 by the Harvard University Press.

Library of Congress Catalog Card No. 68-12364

Printed and bound
in the United States of America
by Vance Weaver Composition, Inc.
and The Colonial Press, Inc.
Design by Peter Oldenburg.

PREFACE

No true library develops in a vacuum. It grows as it fills needs, as students make requests and librarians anticipate needs and fill requests. The titles chosen for this bibliography do not constitute a buying list for a well-rounded collection, but rather they form a basic selection from which studies may expand in every direction. Many items are too expensive for the small library and many are in languages foreign to the American student, but they are fundamental and neither price nor language has been considered of importance. Many out-of-date as well as out-of-print titles are included because they are often quoted and are helpful in understanding the field. Sometimes picture books with texts of only slight value are included, for a good collection of photographs or other reproductions is not always at hand.

The criterion of selection has been that of usefulness to the four year college undergraduate working in the field of art history. Access to a good college library with facilities for reference in the study of history and literature has been taken for granted. If, at times, the choice seems to go beyond undergraduate needs it is with the hope that the list may encourage work at a more advanced level, and may even serve to refresh the memory of advanced students seeking a standard, but forgotten title.

Although museum and exhibition catalogues are one of the most important sources for studies in art history their number is so overwhelming as to make selection nearly impossible. This type of publication has, with few exceptions, been omitted from the list.

I realize fully that every selective list of books has a personal bias, and glaring omissions appear almost as soon as it is published. Therefore all users of the list are urged to follow, for further guidance, the bibliographies in the books noted here, the reviews in the best of the current journals, and the scholarly booklists issued by many dealers serving the specialized field of art history. The bibliography in every good text opens new and often exciting possibilities for further investigation.

To faculty and library colleagues and to the thousands of students who enriched my library experience by their comments and their questions I am ever grateful. Yet the choice of titles for inclusion, or for omission, is my sole responsibility. May this list prove helpful to them in their further studies.

E.L.L.

Rockport, Massachusetts
December 1967

TABLE OF CONTENTS

Dictionaries, Indexes, Encyclopedias   1

Iconography – Sacred and Profane   6

History and Theory   9
  General   9
  Ancient and Primitive   13
    Assyria, Babylonia, Chaldea   14
    Egypt   15
    Etruria   16
    Greece and Rome   16
    Far East   23
    Near East   25
  Medieval, Byzantine, Early Christian   29
  Renaissance and Baroque   35
  Nineteenth and Twentieth Centuries   36
  Canada   38
  France   38
  Germany, Austria, Switzerland   39
  Great Britain   40
  Italy   41
  Low Countries   43
  Mexico, Latin America   43
  Russia   45
  Scandinavia   45
  Spain   46
  United States   47

Architecture   50
    General   50
    France   53
    Germany, Austria, Switzerland, Low Countries   55
    Great Britain   56
    Italy   58
    Mexico, Latin America   59
    Russia   59
    Scandinavia   60
    Spain, Portugal   60
    United States, Canada   61

Sculpture   63
    General   63
    France   64
    Germany, Austria, Switzerland, Low Countries   65
    Great Britain   67
    Italy   67
    Spain, Portugal, Latin America   69
    United States   69

Painting   71
    General   71
    Technique and Theory   74
    Canada   76
    France   76
    Germany, Austria   78
    Great Britain   80
    Italy   81
    Low Countries   84
    Mexico, Latin America   86
    Russia   87
    Scandinavia   87
    Spain, Portugal   88
    Switzerland   88
    United States   89

Graphic Arts   91
    General   91
    Drawings   92
    Engravings   96
    Techniques   99

Minor Arts   101
   General   101
   Costume   102
   Enamels   103
   Furniture   103
   Glass   106
   Ivory   108
   Metals   108
   Mosaics   111
   Photography   111
   Pottery and Porcelain   112
   Tapestry and Textiles   114

Monographs on Artists   119

Index   207

NOTES AND ABBREVIATIONS

An asterisk (*) preceding an entry indicates that a paper back edition is available.

HMSO — His, or Her, Majesty's Stationery Office
NYGS — New York Graphic Society Ltd.
NYPL — New York Public Library
MIT   — Massachusetts Institute of Technology

Dictionaries, Indexes, Encyclopedias

Aeschlimann, Erardo. Bibliografia del libro d'arte italiano, v.1– . Rome, Bestetti, 1952– .

Aeschlimann, Erardo and Ancona, Paola d'. Dictionnaire des miniaturistes du moyen âge et de la renaissance. Milan, Hoepli, 1949. 2 ed.

American Art Directory. N.Y., Bowker, 1967. 43 ed.

Amsterdam. Rijksmuseum. Kunsthistorische Bibliotheek. Catalogus der Kunsthistorische Bibliotheek in het Rijksmuseum te Amsterdam. 4v. Amsterdam, Dept. van Onderwijs, 1934–1936.

Annuario Bibliografico di Archeologia. v–1. Modena, Societa Tipografica Modenese, 1954– .

Annuario Bibliografico di Storia dell'Arte. v–1. Modena, Societa Tipografica Modenese, 1954– .

Art Index. v.1– . N.Y., H. W. Wilson, 1929– .

Bénézit, Emmanuel. Dictionnaire critique et documentaire des peintres, sculpteurs, dessinateurs et graveurs. 8v. Paris, Gründ, 1948–1955. 2 ed. Reprint 1957.

Bessone-Aurelj, Antonietta M. Dizionario degli scultori ed architetti italiani. Genoa, Dante Alighieri, 1947.

____Dizionario dei pittori italiani. Milan, Albrighi, 1928. 2 ed.

Borroni, Fabia. Il Cicognara: bibliografia dell'archeologia classica e dell'arte italiana, v.1– . Florence, Sansoni, 1954– .

Bradley, John William. A dictionary of miniaturists, illuminators, calligraphers and copyists, with reference to their works and notices of their patrons, from the establishment of Christianity to the eighteenth century. 3v. London, Quaritch, 1887–1889. N.Y., Franklin, 1958 reprint.

Briquet, Charles M. Les filigranes. Dictionaire des marques du papier, dès leur apparition vers 1282 jusqu'en 1600. 4v. Leipzig, Heirsemann, 1923. Reprint 1966. 2 ed.

Bryan, Michael. Bryan's dictionary of painters and engravers. Rev. by G. C. Williamson. 5v. N.Y., Macmillan, 1925–1927. Port Washington, Kennikat, 1964 reprint.

Chamberlin, Mary W. Guide to art reference books. Chicago, American Library Association, 1959.

Chicago. Art Institute. Ryerson Library. Index to art periodicals compiled in the Ryerson Library.11v. Boston, Hall, 1962.

Cicognara, Leopoldo. Catalogo ragionato dei libri d'arte e d'antichità. 2v. Pisa, Capurro, 1821. Leipzig, 1931. Reprint.

Colnaghi, Dominic E. A dictionary of Florentine painters from the eleventh to the seventeenth centuries. London, Lane, 1928.

Columbia University. Avery Architectural Library. Catalog of the Avery Memorial Architectural Library. 12v. Boston, Hall, 1963.

Colvin, Howard M. Biographical dictionary of English architects, 1660–1840. London, Murray, 1954.

Comanducci, Agostino M. Dizionario illustrato dei pittori e incisori italiani moderni, 1800–1900. 4v. Milan, Patuzzi, 1962. 3 ed.

Cummings, Paul. Dictionary of contemporary American artists. N.Y., St. Martins, 1966.

Deutscher Verein für Kunstwissenschaft. Schriften zur deutschen kunst. v.1– . Berlin, Deutscher verein für kunstwissenschaft, 1933– .

Du Peloux de Saint Romain, Charles. Répertoire biographique et bibliographique des artistes du XVIII siècle français. 2v. Paris, Champion, 1930–1941.

Édouard-Joseph, René. Dictionnaire biographique des artistes contemporains, 1910–1930. 3v. Paris, Art et Édition, 1930–1934. Supplement, 1936.

Encyclopedia of World Art, v.1– . N.Y., McGraw, 1959– . Italian edition titled: Enciclopedia universale dell'arte. Florence, Sansoni, 1958– .

Erréra, Isabelle. Dictionnaire répertoire des peintres depuis l'antiquité jusqu'à nos jours. Paris, Hachette, 1913. Supplement, 1924.

_____Répertoire des peintures datées. 2v. Brussels, VanOest, 1920–1921.

Fielding, Mantle. Dictionary of American painters, sculptors and engravers. N.Y., Carr, 1965. Reprint of 1926 edition with an addendum containing corrections and additional material.

Florence. Kunsthistorisches Institut. Bibliothek. Katalog. 9v. Boston, Hall, 1964.

Forrer, Leonard. Biographical dictionary of medallists; coin, gem, and seal-engravers, mint-masters, etc., ancient and modern, with reference to their works, B.C. 500–A.D. 1900. 8v. London, Spink, 1902–1930. N.Y., Franklin. Reprint.

Foster, Joshua J. A dictionary of painters of miniatures, 1525–1850, with some account of exhibitions, collections, sales, etc., pertaining to them. London, Allen, 1926. N.Y., Franklin. Reprint.

Galetti, Ugo and Camesasca, E. Enciclopedia della pittura italiana. 2v. Milan, Garzanti, 1950.

Goldstein, Franz. Monogrammlexikon; internationales verzeichnis der monogramme bildenden künstler seit 1850. Berlin, deGruyter, 1964.

Graves, Algernon. Art sales from early in the eighteenth century to early in the twentieth century. 3v. London, Graves, 1918–1921. N.Y., Franklin. Reprint.

——A century of loan exhibitions, 1813–1912. 5v. London, Graves, 1913–1914. N.Y., Franklin. Reprint.

——A dictionary of artists who have exhibited works in the principal London exhibitions from 1760 to 1893. London, Graves, 1901. 3 ed. N.Y., Franklin. Reprint.

Groce, George C. and Wallace, David H. The New York Historical Society's dictionary of artists in America, 1564–1860. New Haven, Yale Univ. Press, 1957.

Gunnis, Rupert. Dictionary of British sculptors, 1660–1851. London, Oldhams, 1953.

Hall, H. van. Repertorium voor de geschiedenis der Nederlandsche schilderen graveerkunst. 2v. The Hague, Nijhoff, 1936–1942.

Hammond, William A. A bibliography of aesthetics and of the philosophy of the fine arts, 1900–1932. N.Y., Russell, 1934. 2 ed.

Immerzeel, Johannes. De levens en werken der hollandsche en vlaamsche kunstschilders, van het begin der vijftiende eeuw tot heden. 3v. Amsterdam, van Kesteren, 1842–1843.

Internationale Bibliographie der Kunstwissenschaft. 15v. Berlin, Behr, 1903–1920.

Internationales Kunst-Adressbuch. International directory of arts. Annuaire international des beaux-arts. 2v. Berlin, Deutsche Zentraldruckerei, 1965–1966. 8 ed.

Lami, Stanislas. Dictionnaire des sculpteurs de l'école française. 8v. Paris, Champion, 1898–1921.

Lancour, A. Harold. American art auction catalogues, 1785–1942. N.Y., New York Public Library, 1944.

Lugt, Frits. Répertoire des catalogues de ventes publiques. v.1– . The Hague, Nijhoff, 1938– .

Mallett, Daniel T. Mallett's index of artists: international and biographical. N.Y., Bowker, 1935. Supplement, 1940. Magnolia, Smith, 1948 reprint. 2v.

Mireur, Hippolyte. Dictionnaire des ventes d'art. 7v. Paris, Vincenti, 1911–1912.

Müller, Hermann A. and Singer, Hans W. Allgemeines künstler-lexikon. 6v. Frankfort, Rütten, 1922, 6 ed.

*****Murray, Peter and Linda.** Dictionary of art and artists. N.Y., Praeger, 1966.

Museums Directory of the United States and Canada. Washington, Smithsonian, 1965.

Nagler, Georg K. Neues allgemeines künstler-lexikon. 25v. Vienna, Manz, 1924–1925.

Netherlands. Rijksbureau voor Kunsthistorische Documentatie. Bibliography of the Netherlands Institute for art history. v.1– . The Hague, Nijhoff, 1943– .

New York. Metropolitan Museum of Art. Library. Catalogue of the library, v.1– . Boston, Hall, 1960– .

Pollen, John H. Universal catalogue of books on art, 1868–1877. N.Y., Franklin. Reprint.

Rave, Paul O. Kunstgeschichte in festschriften. Berlin, Mann, 1962.

Répertoire d'Art et d'Archéologie, v.1– . Paris, Morancé, 1910– .

Royal Institute of British Architects. Library. Catalogue of the library. 2v. London, R.I.B.A., 1937–1938.

Schlosser, Julius. La letteratura artistica. Trans. by F. Rossi. Appendix by Otto Kurz. Florence, Nuova Italia, 1964. 3 ed. Original title: Die kunstliteratur. 1924.

Schutz, Anton. Fine art reproductions, old and modern masters. Greenwich, NYGS, 1965. 6 ed.

Singer, Hans W. Allgemeiner bildniskatalog. 14v. Leipzig, Hiersemann, 1930–1936.

——Neuer bildniskatalog. 5v. Leipzig, Hiersemann, 1937–1938.

Thieme, Ulrich and Becker, Felix. Allgemeines lexikon der bildenden künstler. 37v. Leipzig, Seemann, 1908–1950.

UNESCO. Répertoire international des archives photographiques d'oeuvres d'art. International directory of photographic archives of works of art. 2v. Paris, Dunod, 1950–1954.

Vollmer, Hans. Allgemeines lexikon der bildenden künstler des XX jahrhunderts. v.1– . Leipzig, Seemann, 1953– .

Who's Who in American Art, v.1– . N.Y., Bowker, 1936– . Originally published in American Art Annual.

Who's Who in Art, v.1– . London, Art Trade Press, 1927– .

World Collector's Annuary. v.1– . Amsterdam, Minerva, 1950– .

Wurzbach, Alfred. Niederländisches künstler-lexikon. 3v. Vienna, Halm, 1906–1911.

The Year's Art, v.1– . London, Hutchinson, 1880– .

Iconography
Sacred and Profane

Aurenhammer, Hans. Lexikon des christlichen ikonographie. v.1– . Vienna, Hollinek, 1959– .

Barbier de Montault, Xavier. Traité d'iconographie chrétienne. 2v. Paris, Vivès, 1890.

Braun, Joseph. Tracht und attribute der heiligen in der deutschen kunst. Stuttgart, Metzler, 1943. Reprint 1964.

Bréhier, Louis. L'art chrétien, son développement iconographique dès origines à nos jours. Paris, Laurens, 1928. 2 ed.

Cabrol, Fernand. Dictionnaire d'archéologie chrétienne et de liturgie. v. 1–15, pt.4 (fasc. 1–176). Paris, Letouzey, 1907–1953.

Didron, Adolphe N. Christian iconography; or, The history of Christian art in the middle ages. Trans. by E. G. Millington. 2v. London, Bell, 1896. N.Y., Ungar, 1965 reprint.

Drake, Maurice and Drake, Wilfred. Saints and their emblems. London, Laurie, 1916. N.Y., Franklin. Reprint.

Goldsmith, Elizabeth E. Ancient pagan symbols. London, Putnam, 1929.

____Sacred symbols in art. London, Putnam, 1912. 2 ed.

Holweck, Frederick G. A biographical dictionary of the saints, with a general introduction on hagiology. St. Louis, Herder, 1924.

Jacobus de Varagine. The golden legend of Jacobus de Varagine, translated and adapted from the Latin by Granger Ryan and Helmut Ripperger. 2v. London, Longmans, 1941.

Jameson, Anna B. The history of our Lord. 2v. London, Longmans, 1881. 4 ed.

____Legends of the Madonna. Boston, Houghton, 1911.

____Legends of the monastic orders. Boston, Houghton, 1911.

____Sacred and legendary art. 2v. Boston, Houghton, 1911.

Kaftal, George. Iconography of the saints in central and south Italian painting. Florence, Sansoni, 1965.

———Iconography of the saints in Tuscan painting. Florence, Sansoni, 1952.

Künstle, Karl. Ikonographie der christlichen kunst. 2v. Freiberg, Herder, 1926–1928. v.1–Principien hilfsmotive. v.2–Iconographie der heiligen.

Mackenzie, Donald A. The migration of symbols. N.Y., Knopf, 1926.

Mâle, Émile. L'art religieuse de la fin du moyen âge en France. Paris, Colin, 1949. 5 ed.

———L'art religieux de la fin du XVI siècle et du XVII siècle et du XVIII siècle; étude sur l'iconographie après le Concile de Trent. Italie, France, Espagne, Flandres. Paris, Colin, 1951. 2 ed.

———L'art religieux du XII siècle en France. Paris, Colin, 1947. 5 ed.

*———The Gothic image: religious art in France in the thirteenth century. N.Y., Harper, 1958.

*———Religious art from the twelfth to the eighteenth century. London, Routledge, 1949. N.Y., Farrar, 1963.

Marle, Raimond van. Iconographie de l'art profane au moyen âge et à la renaissance, et la décoration des demeures. 2v. The Hague, Nijhoff, 1931–1932.

Millet, Gabriel. Recherches sur l'iconographie de l'évangile aux XIV, XV et XVI siècles, d'après les monuments de Mistra, de la Macédoine et du Mont-Athos. Paris, Fontemoing, 1916.

Molsdorf, Wilhelm. Christliche symbolik der mittelalterlichen kunst. Leipzig, Hiersemann, 1926. 2 ed. Reprint 1967.

Pigler, A. Barockthemen; eine auswahl von verzeichnissen zur ikonographie des 17 und 18 jahrhunderts. 2v. Budapest, Ungarischen Akademie der Wissenschaften, 1956.

Praz, Mario. Studies in seventeenth century imagery. 2v. London, Warburg Institute, 1939–1947. Rome, Ediz. di Storia e Letteratura, 1964. 2 ed.

Réau, Louis. Iconographie de l'art chrétien. 3v. in 6. Paris, Presses Universitaires, 1955–1959.

Ricci, Elisa. Mille santi nell'arte. Milan, Hoepli, 1931.

Roeder, Helen. Saints and their attributes; with a guide to localities and patronage. London, Longmans, 1955.

Rohault de Fleury. Archéologie chrétienne. Les saints de la messe et leurs monuments. 10v. Paris, Réunies, 1895–1900.

Schiller, Gertrud. Ikonographie der christlichen kunst. v.1– . Gütersloh, Mohn, 1966– .

Tabor, Margaret E. The saints in art. N.Y., Stokes, 1908.

Tervarent, Guy de. Attributs et symboles dans l'art profane, 1450–1600. 3v. Geneva, Droz, 1958–1964.

Webber, Frederick R. Church symbolism; an explanation of the more important symbols of the Old and New Testament, the primitive, the medieval and the modern church. Cleveland, Jansen, 1938. 2 ed.

HISTORY and THEORY

General

Abell, Walter. Representation and form; a study of aesthetic values in representational art. N.Y., Scribner, 1936.

Ackerman, James S. and Carpenter, Rhys. Art and archaeology. N.Y., Prentice Hall, 1963.

Antal, Frederick. Classicism and romanticism and other studies in the method of art history. N.Y., Basic Books, 1966.

*****Arnheim, Rudolf.** Art and visual perception. Berkeley, Univ. of California, 1954.

_____Toward a psychology of art; collected essays. Berkeley, Univ. of California, 1966.

Batchelder, Ernest Allen. Design in theory and practice. N.Y., Macmillan, 1925.

Baudelaire, Charles. The mirror of art. London, Phaidon, 1955.

Beam, Philip C. The language of art. N.Y., Ronald, 1958.

*****Bell, Clive.** Art. London, Chatto, 1949.

*****Berenson, Bernard.** Aesthetics and history in the visual arts. N.Y., Pantheon, 1928.

Bernheimer, Richard. The nature of representation. N.Y., New York Univ., 1961.

Cairns, Huntington. The limits of art. Princeton, Princeton Univ., 1948.

Chambers, Frank P. The history of taste; an account of the revolutions of art criticism and theory in Europe. N.Y., Columbia Univ., 1932.

Cheney, Sheldon. A new world history of art. N.Y., Viking, 1956.

*****Collingwood, Robin G.** Principles of art. Oxford, Clarendon, 1964.

Cossío, Manuel B. and Pijoán y Soteras, José. Summa artis. 10v. Madrid, Espasa, 1931–1946.

*Croce, Benedetto. Aesthetic as science of expression. Trans. by Douglas
   Ainslee. London, Macmillan, 1922. 2 ed.
*Dewey, John. Art as experience. N.Y., Minton, 1935.
Encyclopédie Photographique de l'Art. 5v. Paris, Tel, 1936–1949.
Faure, Élie. History of art. Trans. by Walter Pach. 5v. in 2. N.Y., Dover, 1948.
Fiedler, Konrad. On judging works of visual art. Berkeley, Univ. of California,
   1949.
*Focillon, Henri. The life of forms in art. Trans. by C. B. Hogan and G. Kubler.
   N.Y., Wittenborn, 1957.
Fry, Roger E. Transformations. London, Chatto, 1926.
*____Vision and design. London, Penguin, 1937.
Gardner, Helen. Art through the ages. Rev. by Sumner M. Crosby. N.Y., Har-
   court, 1959. 4 ed.
*Gaunt, William. The aesthetic adventure. London, Cape, 1945.
Goldscheider, Ludwig. Art without epoch. London, Phaidon, 1938.
____Five hundred self portraits from antique times to the present day in
   sculpture, painting, drawing and engraving. London, Phaidon, 1937.
Goldwater, Robert J. and Treves, Marco. Artists on art from the XIV to the
   XX century. N.Y., Pantheon, 1945. 2 ed.
Gombrich, Ernst H. Art and illusion. Princeton, Princeton Univ., 1961. 2 ed.
*____The story of art. N.Y., Phaidon, 1966. 11 ed.
Greene, Theodore M. The arts and the art of criticism. Princeton, Princeton
   Univ., 1940.
Hamann, Richard. Geschichte der kunst von der altchristlichen zeit bis zur
   gegenwart. Berlin, Knaur, 1933. N.Y., Rosenberg, 1945. Reprint.
____Geschichte der kunst von der vorgeschichte bis zur spätantike. Munich,
   Droemer, 1952.
*Hauser, Arnold. The philosophy of art history. N.Y., Knopf, 1959.
*____The social history of art. 2v. London, Routledge, 1951.
*Herbert, Robert. Modern artists on art. N.Y., Prentice-Hall, 1964.
Hildebrand, Adolf. The problem of form in painting and sculpture. N.Y.,
   Stechert, 1945.
*Holt, Elizabeth G. Documentary history of art. 3v. N.Y., Doubleday, 1957–
   1966. Original title: Literary sources of art history.
Janson, Horst W. History of art. N.Y., Abrams, 1962.
____Key monuments of the history of art. N.Y., Abrams, 1962.
Kallen, Horace M. Art and freedom; a historical and biographical interpreta-
   tion of the relations between the ideas of beauty, use and freedom in

Kallen (cont.)
    western civilization from the Greeks to the present day. 2v. N.Y., Duell, 1942.
Kepes, Gyorgy. The language of vision. Chicago, Theobald, 1945.
*****Kubler, George.** The shape of time; remarks on the history of things. New Haven, Yale Univ., 1962.
Lavalleye, Jacques. Introduction aux études d'archéologie et d'histoire de l'art. Louvain, Nauwelaerts, 1958. 2 ed.
Lavedan, Pierre. Histoire de l'art. 2v. Paris, Presses Universitaires, 1949–1950. 2 ed.
Lowry, Bates. The visual experience; an introduction to art. N.Y., Prentice Hall, 1961.
Malraux, André. The psychology of art. Trans. by Stuart Gilbert. 2v. N.Y., Pantheon, 1949–1951.
Michel, André. Histoire de l'art depuis les premiers temps chrétiens jusqu'à nos jours. 8v. in 17. Paris, Colin, 1905–1929.
Munro, Thomas. The arts and their inter-relations. Cleveland, Case Western, 1966.
Myers, Bernard. Understanding the arts. N.Y., Holt, 1963.
Newton, Eric and Neil, William. 2000 years of Christian art. N.Y., Harper, 1966.
Panofsky, Erwin. Idea. Ein beitrag zur begriffsgeschichte der alteren kunsttheorie. Berlin, Hessling, 1960. 2 ed.
*____Meaning in the visual arts. N.Y., Doubleday, 1957. Includes his History of art as a humanistic discipline.
Pepper, Stephen C. Principles of art appreciation. N.Y., Harcourt, 1949.
Pevsner, Nikolaus. Academies of art, past and present. Cambridge, Cambridge Univ., 1940.
Pijoán y Soteras, José. History of art. Trans. by R. L. Roys. 3v. London, Batsford, 1933. 2 ed.
Pliny. Chapters on the history of art. Trans. by E. S. Strong and K. Jex-Blake. N.Y., Argonaut, 1966.
*****Read, Herbert E.** Art and society. London, Faber, 1950.
____Education through art. London, Faber, 1947.
*____The meaning of art. N.Y., Pitman, 1951. 3 ed. Original title: The anatomy of art.
____The philosophy of modern art, N.Y., Horizon, 1952.
Richardson, Edgar P. The way of western art, 1776–1914. Cambridge, Harvard Univ., 1939.

Riegl, Alois. Historische grammatik der bildenden künste. Graz, Böhlau, 1966.

Robb, David M. and Garrison, J. J. Art in the western world. N.Y., Harper, 1963. 4 ed.

Roos, Frank J. An illustrated handbook of art history. N.Y., Macmillan, 1954. 2 ed.

Rosenberg, Jakob. On quality in art: criteria of excellence, past and present. Princeton, Princeton Univ., 1967.

*****Rowland, Benjamin.** Art in East and West, an introduction through comparison. Cambridge, Harvard Univ., 1954.

_____Classical tradition in western art. Cambridge, Harvard Univ., 1963.

*****Santayana, George.** The sense of beauty. N.Y., Dover, 1955.

Scott, Geoffrey. The architecture of humanism. London, Constable, 1924. 2 ed.

Sesonske, Alexander. What is art; aesthetic theory from Plato to Tolstoy. N.Y., Oxford, 1965.

Springer, Anton. Handbuch der kunstgeschichte. 6v. Leipzig, Kröner, 1923. 12 ed.

*****Sypher, Wylie.** Art history: an anthology of modern criticism. N.Y., Vintage, 1963.

Troescher, Georg. Kunst und kunstlerwanderungen in Mitteleuropa, 800–1800. Baden-Baden, Verlag f. Kunst u. Wissenschaft, 1953–1954.

UNESCO. World art series. v.1– . Greenwich, NYGS, 1954– .

Upjohn, Everard M. and others. History of world art. N.Y., Oxford, 1958. 2 ed.

*****Venturi, Lionello.** History of art criticism. Trans. by Charles Marriott. N.Y., Dutton, 1936.

Vermeule, Cornelius C. European art in the classical past. Cambridge, Harvard Univ., 1964.

*****Wölfflin, Heinrich.** Principles of art history. Trans. by M. D. Hottinger. N.Y., Dover, 1963.

_____The sense of form in art. N.Y., Chelsea, 1958.

Worringer, Wilhelm. Abstraction and empathy. Trans. by M. Bullock. N.Y., International Universities Press, 1963.

Zaidenberg, Arthur. The art of the artist; theories and techniques of art by the artists themselves. N.Y., Crown, 1951.

History — Ancient and Primitive

Adam, Leonhard. Primitive art. N.Y., Barnes and Noble, 1963.

Bacon, Edward. Vanished civilizations of the ancient world. N.Y., McGraw, 1963.

Bataille, Georges. Lascaux: pre-historic paintings. Trans. by A. Wainhouse. Cleveland, World (Skira), 1955.

*Boas, Franz. Primitive art. Cambridge, Harvard Univ., 1962.

Breuil, Henri. Four hundred centuries of cave art. Montignac, Centre d'études préhistoriques, 1952.

Byvanck, Alexander. De kunst der oudheid. 5v. Leiden, Brill, 1946–1965.

Carpenter, Rhys. The humanistic value of archaeology. Cambridge, Harvard Univ., 1933.

*Childe, Vere Gordon. The dawn of European civilization. N.Y., Knopf, 1958. 6 ed.

____Progress and archaeology. London, Watts, 1945.

*____What happened in history. N.Y., Penguin, 1946.

Christensen, Erwin O. Primitive art. N.Y., Crowell, 1955.

Curtius, Ludwig and Zschietzschmann, Willy. Die antike kunst. 2v. Berlin, Athenaion, 1923–1939.

Déchelette, Joseph. Manuel d'archéologie préhistorique, celtique et gallo-romaine. v.1- . Paris, Picard, 1908- .

Furtwängler, Adolf. Die antiken gemmen. 3v. Leipzig, Giesecke, 1900. Amsterdam, 1964. Reprint.

Graziosi, Paolo. Paleolithic art. N.Y., McGraw, 1960.

Griaule, Marcel. Folk art in black Africa. N.Y., Tudor, 1950.

*Kühn, Herbert. The rock pictures of Europe. London, Sidgwick, 1956.

Lem, F. H. Sudanese sculpture. Paris, Arts et Métiers Graphiques, 1949.

Linton, Ralph and Wingert, Paul S. Arts of the South Seas. N.Y., Museum of Modern Art, 1946.

Osborn, Henry Fairfield. Men of the old stone age, their environment, life and art. N.Y., Scribner, 1934. 3 ed.

Pauly, August F. von and Wissowa, Georg. Encyclopädie der classischen altertumswissenschaft. v.1- . Stuttgart, Metzler, 1894- .

Peet, Thomas E. The stone and bronze age in Italy and Sicily. Oxford, Clarendon, 1909.

Piggott, Stuart. The dawn of civilization. N.Y., McGraw, 1961.

Radin, Paul and Sweeney, James J. African folktales and sculpture. Princeton, Princeton Univ., 1964. 2 ed.

Raphael, Max. Prehistoric cave paintings. N.Y., Pantheon, 1945.

Rice, David T. The dawn of European civilization. N.Y., McGraw, 1965.

Schmalenbach, Werner. African art. N.Y., Macmillan, 1954.

*****Segy, Ladislaw.** African sculpture speaks. N.Y., Wyn, 1952.

Spearing, Herbert G. The childhood of art; or, the ascent of man. London, Benn, 1930.

Sweeney, James J. African negro art. N.Y., Museum of Modern Art, 1935.

Swindler, Mary H. Ancient painting from the earliest times to the period of Christian art. New Haven, Yale Univ., 1929.

Sydow, Eckart von. Afrikanische plastik. N.Y., Wittenborn, 1954.

_____Die kunst der naturvölker und der vorzeit. Berlin, Propyläen-verlag, 1927.

Tischner, Herbert. Oceanic art. N.Y., Pantheon, 1954.

Trowell, Margaret. Classical African sculpture. N.Y., Praeger, 1964.

Winckelmann, Johann J. Geschichte der kunst des altertums. 2v. Dresden, Walther, 1764.

Windels, Fernand. Lascaux cave paintings. N.Y., Humanities, 1949.

Wingert, Paul S. Art of the South Pacific Islands. N.Y., Beechhurst, 1953.

*_____Primitive art. N.Y., Oxford, 1962.

_____The sculpture of negro Africa. N.Y., Columbia Univ., 1950.

ASSYRIA, BABYLONIA, CHALDEA

Borovka, Grigorii I. Scythian art. Trans. by V. G. Childe. London, Benn, 1928. N.Y., Paragon, reprint.

*****Gurney, Oliver R.** The Hittites. London, Penguin, 1961.

Handcock, Percy S. P. Mesopotamian archaeology. N.Y., Putnam, 1912.

Harcourt-Smith, Simon. Babylonian art. London, Benn, 1928.

Perrot, Georges and Chipiez, Charles. Histoire de l'art dans l'antiquité: Égypte, Assyrie, Perse, Asie Mineure, Grèce, Étrurie, Rome. 10v. Paris, Hachette, 1882–1914.

Robinson, David M. Baalbek, Palmyra. Photography by Hoyningen-Huene. N.Y., Augustin, 1946.

Vieyra, M. Hittite art, 2300–750 B.C. N.Y., Transatlantic, 1955.

Zervos, Christian. L'art de la Mésopotamie de la fin du quatrième millénaire au XV siècle avant notre ère. Paris, Cahiers d'Art, 1955.

EGYPT

Aldred, Cyril. The development of ancient Egyptian art from 3200–1315 B.C. 3v. N.Y., Transatlantic, 1952.

Badawy, Alexander. Architecture in ancient Egypt and the Near East. Cambridge, M.I.T., 1966.

____A history of Egyptian architecture. Berkeley, Univ. of California, 1966.

Capart, Jean. L'art Égyptien. 4v. Brussels, Vromant, 1922–1947.

Drioton, Étienne. Egyptian art. N.Y., Arts Inc., 1951. 2 ed.

*****Edwards, Iowerth E. S.** The pyramids of Egypt. N.Y., Penguin, 1961.

Fechheimer, Hedwig. Kleinplastik der Aegypter. Berlin, Cassirer, 1923.

____Die plastik der Aegypter. Berlin, Cassirer, 1923.

Groenewegen-Frankfort, Henriette A. Arrest and movement. N.Y., Humanities, 1951.

Hayes, William C. The scepter of Egypt. v.1– . Greenwich, NYGS, 1953– .

Lange, Kurt. Egypt. Photography by Max Hirmer. London, Phaidon, 1961. 4 ed.

Lucas, Alfred. Ancient Egyptian materials and industries. N.Y., St. Martins, 1962. 4 ed.

Maspero, Gaston C. C. Manual of Egyptian archaeology and guide to the study of antiquities in Egypt. Trans. by A. S. Johns. N.Y., Putnam, 1926. 6 ed.

Mekhitarian, Arpag. Egyptian painting. Trans. by Stuart Gilbert. Cleveland, World (Skira), 1954.

Murray, Margaret A. Egyptian sculpture. London, Duckworth, 1930.

____Egyptian temples. London, Low, 1931.

Petrie, William M. F. The arts and crafts of ancient Egypt. Edinburgh, Foulis, 1923.

Ranke, Hermann. The art of ancient Egypt. London, Allen, 1936.

Ross, Edward D. The art of Egypt through the ages. N.Y., Rudge, 1931.

Smith, Earl B. Egyptian architecture as cultural expression. N.Y., Appleton, 1938.

Smith, William S. Art and architecture of ancient Egypt. London, Penguin, 1958.

____A history of Egyptian sculpture and painting in the old kingdom. N.Y., Oxford, 1949. 2 ed.

____Interconnections in the ancient Near East; a study of the relationships between the arts of Egypt, the Aegean and western Asia. New Haven, Yale, 1965.

Steindorff, George. Egypt. N.Y., Augustin, 1943.

*Steindorff, George and Seele, K. When Egypt ruled the East. Chicago, Univ. of
    Chicago, 1957.
Vandier, Jacques. Egypt; paintings from tombs and temples. Greenwich,
    NYGS, 1954.
____Manuel d'archéologie égyptienne. v.1– . Paris, Picard, 1952– .
Worringer, Wilhelm. Egyptian art. Trans. by B. Rackham. London, Putnam,
    1928.

ETRURIA

Beazley, John D. Etruscan vase painting. Oxford, Clarendon, 1947.
Bloch, Raymond. Etruscan art. Greenwich, NYGS, 1966.
Ducati, Pericle. Storia dell'arte etrusca. 2v. Florence, Rinascimento del librò,
    1927.
Giglioli, Giulio Q. Arte etrusca. Milan, Treves, 1935.
Goldscheider, Ludwig. Etruscan sculpture. London, Phaidon, 1941.
Lopez Pegna, Mario. Saggio di bibliografia etrusca. Florence, Sansoni, 1953.
Pallottino, Massimo. Etruscan painting. Cleveland, World (Skira), 1952.
____The Etruscans. London, Penguin, 1955.
Pallottino, Massimo and Hürlimann, Martin. Art of the Etruscans. N.Y., Van-
    guard, 1955.
Poulsen, Fredrik. Etruscan tomb paintings; their subjects and significance.
    Trans. by I. Anderson. N.Y., Oxford, 1922.
Randall-MacIver, David. The Etruscans. Oxford, Clarendon, 1927.
Riis, Poul J. An introduction to Etruscan art. Copenhagen, Munksgaard, 1941.
Weege, Fritz. Etruskische malerei. Halle, Niemeyer, 1921.

GREECE AND ROME

Anderson, William J. The architecture of ancient Rome. Rev. by Thomas
    Ashby. London, Batsford, 1927.
Arias, Paolo E. History of one thousand years of Greek vase painting. N.Y.,
    Abrams, 1963.
Arndt, Paul. Photographische einzelaufnahmen antiker skulpturen. v.1– .
    Munich, Verlags f. Kunst und Wissenschaft, 1893– .
Ashmole, Bernard and Yalouris, N. Olympia; the sculptures of the temple of
    Zeus. N.Y., Phaidon, 1967.

Baikie, James. The sea kings of Crete. London, Black, 1926. 4 ed.

Beazley, John D. Attic black figure vase painters. N.Y., Oxford, 1956.

____Attic red figure vase painters. 3v. N.Y., Oxford, 1963. 2 ed.

Beazley, John D. and Ashmole, B. Greek sculpture and painting to the end of the Hellenistic period. Cambridge, Cambridge Univ., 1965.

Bernouilli, Johann J. Römische ikonographie. 2v. Stuttgart, Spemann, 1882–1894.

Bieber, Margarete. Sculpture of the Hellenistic age. N.Y., Columbia Univ., 1961. 2 ed.

Blegen, Carl W. Troy and the Trojans. N.Y., Praeger, 1963.

***Boardman, John.** Greek art. N.Y., Praeger, 1964.

Boardman, John and others. Greek art and architecture. N.Y., Abrams, 1967.

Boas, George. The Greek tradition. Baltimore, Johns Hopkins, 1939.

Boethius, Axel. The golden house of Nero; some aspects of Roman architecture. Ann Arbor, Univ. of Michigan, 1960.

Bossert, Helmuth T. The art of ancient Crete. London, Zwemmer, 1937. 3 ed.

Bothmer, Dietrich von. Amazons in Greek art. Oxford, Clarendon, 1957.

***Bowra, Cecil M.** The Greek experience. Cleveland, World, 1958.

Brommer, Frank. Die metopen des Parthenon; katalog und untersuchung. 2v. Mainz, Zabern, 1967.

***Brown, Frank E.** Roman architecture. N.Y., Braziller, 1961.

Brunn, Heinrich. Denkmaler griechischer und römischer sculptur. 5v. Munich, Bruckmann, 1888–1947.

____Griechische und römische porträts. v.1- . Munich, Bruckmann, 1891- .

Buschor, Ernst. Greek vase painting. Trans. by G. C. Richards. N.Y., Argonaut, 1967.

____Griechische vasen. Munich, Piper, 1940.

***Carpenter, Rhys.** The esthetic basis of Greek art of the fifth and fourth and centuries, B.C. Bloomington, Indiana Univ., 1959.

Casson, Stanley. The technique of early Greek sculpture. Oxford, Clarendon, 1933.

Chamoux, François. Greek art. Greenwich, NYGS, 1966.

Charbonneaux, Jean. La sculpture grècque archaique. Paris, Cluny, 1938.

____La sculpture grècque classique. Paris, Cluny, 1943.

Corpus Vasorum Antiquorum, v.1- . Paris, Champion, 1922- . Konkordanz by J. W. Crous. Rome, Bretschneider, 1942.

Curtius, Ludwig. Die wandmalerei Pompejis. Leipzig, Seemann, 1929. Hildesheim, 1967 reprint.

Daremberg, Charles V. and Saglio, Edmond. Dictionnaire des antiquités grècques et romaines. 5v. in 10. Paris, Hachette, 1877-1919. N.Y., Argonaut, 1962. Reprint.

Daux, Georges. Les merveilles de l'art antique (Grèce-Rome). Paris, Nathan, 1946.

Deonna, Waldemar. Du miracle grèc au miracle chrétien. v.1- . Basel, Birkhaeuser, 1945- .

Desborough, Vincent R. d'A. The last Mycenaeans and their successors. N.Y., Oxford, 1964.

Dickens, Guy. Hellenistic sculpture. Oxford, Clarendon, 1920.

*__Dickinson, G. Lowes.__ The Greek view of life. Ann Arbor, Univ. of Michigan, 1958.

Dinsmoor, William B. The architecture of ancient Greece. London, Batsford, 1950. 3 ed.

Ducati, Pericle. L'arte classica. Turin, Ediz. Torinese, 1944. 3 ed.

_____L'arte in Roma dalle origini al sec. VIII. Bologna, Cappelli, 1938.

Evans, Arthur J. The palace of Minos at Knossos. 4v. N.Y., Macmillan, 1936. Biblo and Tannen, 1964. Reprint.

Fleischer, Robert. Die römischen bronzen aus Österreich. Mainz, Zabern, 1967.

Fowler, Harold N. and Wheeler, James R. Handbook of Greek archaeology. N.Y., American Book, 1909.

Furtwängler, Adolf. Masterpieces of Greek sculpture. Trans. by E. S. Strong. Rev. by A. L. N. Oikonomides. Chicago, Argonaut, 1964.

Furumark, Arne. The Mycenaean pottery; analysis and classification. Stockholm, Petterson, 1941.

Fyfe, David T. Hellenistic architecture. Cambridge, Cambridge Univ., 1936.

Gardner, Ernest A. Handbook of Greek sculpture. London, Macmillan, 1929. 2 ed.

Gardner, Percy. Archaeology and the types of Greek coins. Chicago, Argonaut, 1965. Reprint.

_____Greek art and architecture. N.Y., Oxford, 1922.

_____The principles of Greek art. N.Y., Macmillan, 1926.

Goldscheider, Ludwig. Roman portraits. London, Phaidon, 1940.

Goodenough, Erwin R. Jewish symbols in the Greco-Roman period. v.1- N.Y., Pantheon, 1953- .

Grinnell, Isabel H. Greek temples. N.Y., Metropolitan Museum, 1943.

Hall, Harry R. H. Aegean archaeology; introduction to archaeology of prehistoric Greece. N.Y., Putnam, 1915.

Hamberg, Philip G. Studies in Roman imperial art. Uppsala, Almquist, 1945.

Hanfmann, George M. A. Classical sculpture. Greenwich, NYGS, 1967.

———Roman art; a modern survey of the art of imperial Rome. Greenwich, NYGS, 1964.

Hawes, Charles H. and Hawes, Harriet A. Crete, the forerunner of Greece. N.Y., Harper, 1911.

Head, Barclay V. Historia numorum; a manual of Greek numismatics. Oxford, Clarendon, 1911. Chicago, Argonaut. Reprint.

Hege, Walter and Rodenwaldt, Gerhart. Olympia. London, Sidgwick, 1936.

Hekler, Anton. Greek and Roman portraits. London, Heinemann, 1912.

Hill, George F. Ancient Greek and Roman coins. Chicago, Argonaut, 1964. Reprint.

———Historical Greek coins. Chicago, Argonaut, 1966. Reprint.

———Historical Roman coins. Chicago, Argonaut, 1966. Reprint.

Hoppin, Joseph C. Handbook of Attic red figured vases. 2v. Cambridge, Harvard Univ., 1919.

———Handbook of Greek black figured vases. Paris, Champion, 1924.

Huish, Marcus B. Greek terra cotta statuettes, their origin, evolution and uses. London, Murray, 1900.

Kähler, Heinz. The art of Rome and her empire. N.Y., Crown, 1963.

Kraay, Colin M. Greek coins. N.Y., Abrams, 1966.

Lamb, Winifred. Ancient Greek and Roman bronzes. N.Y., Dial, 1929. Chicago, Argonaut. Reprint

Lane, Arthur. Greek pottery. London, Faber, 1948.

Laurie, Arthur P. Greek and Roman methods of painting. Cambridge, Cambridge Univ., 1930.

Lawrence, Arnold W. Classical sculpture. London, Cape, 1929.

———Greek architecture. London, Penguin, 1957.

———Later Greek sculpture and its influence on East and West. London, Cape, 1927.

Lehmann, Phyllis. Roman wall paintings from the Boscoreale in the Metropolitan Museum. Cambridge, Archaeological Inst., 1953.

Lullies, Reinhard. Greek sculpture. Trans. by M. Bullock. N.Y., Abrams, 1957.

MacDonald, George. Coin types, their origin and development, 700 B.C.–1604 A.D. Glasgow, Maclehose, 1905. Chicago, Argonaut. Reprint.

MacDonald, William L. The architecture of the Roman empire, New Haven, Yale Univ., 1965.

Maiuri, Amedeo. Roman painting. Cleveland, World (Skira), 1953.

Mattingly, Harold. Roman coins from the earliest times to the fall of the western empire. N.Y., Barnes, 1967. 3 ed.

Matz, Friedrich. Geschichte der Griechischen kunst. v.1- . Frankfurt am Main, Klostermann, 1950- .

Mau, August. Pompeii, its life and art. Trans. by F. W. Kelsey. London, Macmillan, 1904.

Menzel, Heinz. Die römischen bronzen aus Deutschland, v.1- . Mainz, Römisch-Germanische-Museum, 1960- .

Minns, Ellis H. Scythians and Greeks. Cambridge, Cambridge Univ., 1913.

Mylonas, George E. Mycenae and the Mycenaean age. Princeton, Princeton Univ., 1966.

Nilsson, Martin P. Minoan-Mycenaean religion and its survival in Greek religion. Lund, Gleerup, 1950.

Paton, James M. The Erechtheum. Cambridge, Harvard Univ., 1927.

Payne, Humfry and Young, G. M. Archaic marble sculpture from the Acropolis. Chester Springs, Dufour, 1950.

*****Pendlebury, John D. S.** The archaeology of Crete. N.Y., Biblo and Tannen, 1965.

Pfuhl, Ernst. Malerei und zeichnung des Griechen. 3v. Munich, Bruckmann, 1923.

_____Masterpieces of Greek drawing and painting. Trans. by J. D. Beazley. Chicago, Argonaut, 1967.

Picard, Charles. Manuel d'archéologie grècque. 4v. Paris, Picard, 1935–1954.

_____La sculpture. v.1- . Paris, Picard, 1935- .

Platner, Samuel B. A topographical dictionary of ancient Rome. Rev. by Thomas Ashby. London, Oxford, 1929.

Plommer, William H. Ancient and classical architecture. London, Longmans, 1956. Forms v. 1 of Simpson's History of architecture.

Pottier, Edmond. Douris and the painters of Greek vases. Trans. by Bettina Kahnweiler. N.Y., Dutton, 1917. 2 ed.

Randall-MacIver, David. The iron age in Italy. Oxford, Clarendon, 1927.

_____Italy before the Romans. Oxford, Clarendon, 1928.

_____The Villanovans and early Etruscans. Oxford, Clarendon, 1924.

Reinach, Salomon. Répertoire de la statuaire grècque et romaine. 6v. Paris, Leroux, 1920–1930.

Reinach (cont.)

____Répertoire de peintures grècques et romaines. Paris, Leroux, 1922.

____Répertoire de reliefs grècs et romains. 3v. Paris, Leroux, 1909–1912.

____Répertoire des vases peints grècs et étrusques. 2v. Paris, Leroux, 1899–1900.

Richter, Gisela M. A. Archaic Greek art against its historical background. N.Y., Oxford, 1949.

____Attic red figured vases. New Haven, Yale Univ., 1958.

____The craft of Athenian pottery. New Haven, Yale Univ., 1923.

____Furniture of the Greeks, Etruscans and Romans. N.Y., Phaidon, 1966.

____Handbook of Greek art. N.Y., Phaidon, 1967. 5 ed.

____Kouroi: archaic Greek youths. N.Y., Oxford, 1960. 2 ed.

____Portraits of the Greeks. 3v. N.Y., Phaidon, 1965.

____The sculpture and sculptors of the Greeks. New Haven, Yale Univ., 1950.

Riegl, Alois. Spätrömische kunstindustrie. Vienna, Staatsdruckerei, 1901. Reprint 1967.

Rivoira, Giovanni T. Roman architecture and its principles of construction under the empire. Trans. by G. M. Rushforth. Oxford, Clarendon, 1925.

Robert, Carl and Rodenwaldt, Gerhart. Antiken sarkophagreliefs. 7v. Berlin, Grote, 1890–1952. Vols. 1 and 6 never published.

Robertson, Donald S. Handbook of Greek and Roman architecture. Cambridge, Cambridge Univ., 1954.

____Greek and Roman architecture. Cambridge, Cambridge Univ., 1943. 2 ed.

Robertson, Martin. Greek painting. Cleveland, World (Skira), 1959.

Rodenwaldt, Gerhart. Die kunst der antike (Hellas und Rom) Berlin, Propyläen, 1927.

Rodenwaldt, Gerhart and Hege, Walter. Akropolis. Norman, Univ. of Oklahoma, 1958.

Rostovtsev, Mikhail I. Out of the past of Greece and Rome. New Haven, Yale Univ., 1932. N.Y., Biblo and Tannen. Reprint.

Schliemann, Heinrich. Mycenae. Darmstadt, Wissenschaftliche Buchgesellschaft, 1880. Reprint 1967.

Schoder, Raymond V. Masterpieces of Greek art. Greenwich, NYGS, 1965.

*Scranton, Robert L. Greek architecture. Braziller, 1962.

Scully, Vincent. Earth, the temple and the gods; Greek sacred architecture. New Haven, Yale Univ., 1962.

*Seltman, Charles T. Approach to Greek art. N.Y., Studio, 1948.

____Masterpieces of Greek coinage. Oxford, Cassirer, 1949.

Smith, William. Dictionary of Greek and Roman biography and mythology. London, Murray, 1919.

Smith, William and others. Dictionary of Greek and Roman antiquities. 2v. London, Murray, 1890–1891. 3 ed.

Strong, Donald E. Greek and Roman gold and silver plate. Ithaca, Cornell Univ., 1966.

Strong, Eugénie S. Roman sculpture from Augustus to Constantine. London, Duckworth, 1911.

_____La scultura romana da Augusto a Constantino. 2v. Florence, Alinari, 1923–1926.

Tarbell, Frank B. A history of Greek art. N.Y., Macmillan, 1927.

Toynbee, Jocelyn M. C. Art in Roman Britain. N.Y., Phaidon, 1962.

Tsountas, Chrestos and Manatta, J. I. The Mycenaean age; a study of the monuments and culture of pre-Homeric Greece. Boston, Houghton, 1897. Chicago, Argonaut. Reprint.

*****Vermeule, Cornelius C.** Bibliography of applied numismatics in the fields of Greek and Roman archaeology and the fine arts. Chicago, Argonaut, 196- .

Vermeule, Emily. Greece in the bronze age. Chicago, Univ. of Chicago, 1964.

Wace, Alan. Mycenae, an archaeological history and guide. N.Y., Biblo and Tannen, 1949.

Webster, Thomas B. L. Greek art and literature, 530–400 B.C. Oxford, Clarendon, 1939.

Wickhoff, Franz. Roman art. N.Y., Macmillan, 1900.

Wycherley, R. E. How the Greeks built their cities. N.Y., St. Martins, 1962. 2 ed.

Zervos, Christian. L'art de la Crète néolithique et minoenne. Paris, Cahiers d'Art, 1956.

_____L'art des Cyclades du début à la fin de l'âge du bronze, Paris, Cahiers d'Art, 1957.

_____L'art en Grèce des temps préhistoriques au début du VIII siècle. Paris, Cahiers d'Art, 1936. 2 ed.

_____L'art en Grèce du troisième millénaire au IV siècle avant notre ère. Paris, Cahiers d'Art, 1946.

FAR EAST

*Alex, William. Japanese architecture. N.Y., Braziller, 1963.

Ashton, Leigh and Gray, Basil. Chinese art. London, Faber, 1935.

Bachhofer, Ludwig. A short history of Chinese art. N.Y., Pantheon, 1946.

Binyon, Laurence. The flight of the dragon. London, Murray, 1935. N.Y., Paragon. Reprint.

*____Painting in the Far East; an introduction to the history of pictorial art in Asia, especially China and Japan. N.Y., Longmans, 1934. 4 ed.

*____The spirit of man in Asian art. Magnolia, P. Smith, 1935. Reprint.

Binyon, Laurence and others. Japanese colour prints. London, Benn, 1923.

Boerschmann, Ernst. Chinesische architektur. 2v. Berlin, Wasmuth, 1925.

*Bowie, Henry P. On the laws of Japanese painting. N.Y., Dover, 1951.

*Bowie, Theodore R. East-West in art; patterns of cultural and aesthetic relationships. Bloomington, Indiana Univ., 1966.

Bushell, Stephen W. Chinese art. 2v. London, Board of Education, 1924.

Cahill, James. Chinese painting. Cleveland, World (Skira), 1960.

Cohn, William. Chinese painting. London, Phaidon, 1948.

Drexler, Arthur. The architecture of Japan. N.Y., Museum of Modern Art, 1955.

Fenollosa, Ernest F. Epochs of Chinese and Japanese art. Rev. by Petrucci. 2v. London, Heinemann, 1921. Magnolia, P. Smith. Reprint.

Ferguson, John C. Chinese painting. Chicago, Univ. of Chicago, 1927.

Fischer, Otto. Die kunst Indiens, Chinas und Japans. Berlin, Propyläen, 1928.

Fry, Roger E. Chinese art. London, Batsford, 1946.

Giles, Herbert A. An introduction to the history of Chinese pictorial art. London, Quaritch, 1918. 2 ed.

Grousset, René. The civilizations of the East. Trans. by C. A. Phillips. 4v. N.Y., Knopf, 1931–1935.

Hackin, Joseph. Asiatic mythology. Trans. by F. M. Atkinson. N.Y., Crowell, 1963.

Harada, Jiro. The pageant of Chinese painting. Tokyo, Otsuka-Kogeisha, 1936.

Hobson, Robert L. Chinese art. N.Y., Macmillan, 1952. 2 ed.

____Chinese pottery and porcelain; an account of the potter's art in China from primitive times to the present day. 2v. London, Cassell, 1915.

Honey, William B. The ceramic art of China and other countries of the Far East. London, Faber, 1945.

____Corean pottery. London, Faber, 1947.

Jenyns, Soame. Chinese art. v.1– . N.Y., Universe, 1963– .

*****Kates, George N.** Chinese household furniture, from examples selected and measured. N.Y., Harper, 1948. Magnolia, P. Smith. Reprint.

Koechlin, Raymond and Migeon, Gaston. Oriental art; ceramics, fabrics, carpets. Trans. by F. Heywood. N.Y., Macmillan, 1928.

Koop, Albert J. Early Chinese bronzes. London, Benn, 1924.

Kuo, Hsi. An essay on landscape painting. Trans. by Shio Sakanishi. London, Murray, 1935. N.Y., Paragon. Reprint.

Laufer, Berthold. The beginnings of porcelain in China. Chicago, Field Museum, 1917.

——Chinese pottery of the Han dynasty. Rutland, Tuttle, 1962.

——Jade; a study in Chinese archaeology and religion. London, Routledge, 1946. N.Y., Kraus. Reprint. 2 ed.

Lee, Sherman E. Chinese landscape painting. Cleveland, Museum of Art, 1962.

——History of Far Eastern art. N.Y., Abrams, 1964.

Minamoto, Hoshu. An illustrated history of Japanese art. Trans. by H. G. Henderson. Kyoto, Hoshino, 1935.

*****Okakura Kakuzo.** The book of tea. Rutland, Tuttle, 1966.

——The ideals of the East. London, Murray, 1920.

Paine, Robert T. and Soper, Alexander C. Art and architecture of Japan. London, Penguin, 1955.

*****Rowland, Benjamin.** Harvard outline and reading lists for Oriental art. Cambridge, Harvard Univ., 1958.

Rowley, George. Principles of Chinese painting. Princeton, Princeton Univ., 1959.

Rudolph, Richard. Han tomb art of west China. Berkeley, Univ. of California, 1951.

Sakanishi, Shio. The spirit of the brush. London, Murray, 1957.

Schäfer, Heinrich and Andrae, Walter. Die kunst des alten Orients. Berlin, Propyläen, 1925.

Seidlitz, Woldemar. A history of Japanese colour prints. Trans. by A. H. Dyer and G. Tripler. Philadelphia, Lippincott, 1910.

Sickman, Laurence and Soper, Alexander C. The art and architecture of China. London, Penguin, 1956.

Silcock, Arnold. Introduction to Chinese art and history. N.Y., Oxford, 1948.

Sirén, Osvald. Chinese painting; leading masters and principles. 7v. N.Y., Ronald, 1956–1958.

Sirén (cont.)
____Chinese sculpture from the fifth to the fourteenth century. 4v. London, Benn, 1925.
____A history of early Chinese painting. 2v. London, Medici Society, 1935.
____A history of later Chinese painting. 2v. London, Medici Society, 1938.
Soper, Alexander C. The evolution of Buddhist architecture in Japan. Princeton, Princeton Univ., 1942.
Taki, Sei-Ichi. Three essays on Oriental painting. London, Quaritch, 1910.
Toda, Kenji. Japanese scroll painting. Chicago, Univ. of Chicago, 1935.
Tsuda, Noritake. Handbook of Japanese art. Tokyo, Sanseido, 1935.
Waley, Arthur. An introduction to the study of Chinese painting. N.Y., Scribner, 1923.
Warner, Langdon. The craft of the Japanese sculptor. N.Y., McFarlane, 1936.
*____The enduring art of Japan. Cambridge, Harvard Univ., 1952.
____Japanese sculpture of the Suiko period. New Haven, Yale Univ., 1923.
____Japanese sculpture of the Tempyo period — masterpieces of the eighth century. Cambridge, Harvard Univ., 1964.
Willetts, William. Chinese art. 2v. London, Penguin, 1958.
With, Karl. Buddhistische plastik in Japan bis in den beginn des 8 jahrhunderts n. Chr. Vienna, Schroll, 1922. 3 ed.
Wu, Nelson I. Chinese and Indian architecture. N.Y., Braziller, 1966.
Yashiro, Yukio. 2000 years of Japanese art. N.Y., Abrams, 1958.

NEAR EAST

Akurgal, Ekrem. Art of the Hittites. N.Y., Abrams, 1962.
*Albright, William F. The archaeology of Palestine. London, Penguin, 1960.
Andrews, Frederick H. Wall paintings from the ancient shrines in Central Asia, recovered by Sir Aurel Stein. London, Oxford, 1948.
Archer, William G. Indian miniatures. Greenwich, NYGS, 1960.
____Indian painting in the Punjab. London, HMSO, 1952.
*Arnold, Thomas W. Painting in Islam; a study of the place of pictorial art in Muslim culture. Oxford, Clarendon, 1928.
Arnold, Thomas W. and Grohmann, Adolf. The Islamic book; a contribution to its art and history from the VII — XVIII century. N.Y., Harcourt, 1929.
Bachhofer, Ludwig. Early Indian sculpture. 2v. N.Y., Harcourt, 1929.
Beckwith, John. The art of Constantinople. N.Y., Phaidon, 1961.

Bernet Kempers, August J. Ancient Indonesian art. Cambridge, Harvard Univ., 1959.

Bhattacharyya, Benoytosh. The Indian Buddhist iconography, mainly based on the Sadhanamala and other cognate Tantric texts of rituals. Calcutta, Mukhopadhyay, 1958. 2 ed.

Binyon, Laurence and Arnold, Thomas W. The court painters of the Grand Moguls. London, Oxford, 1921.

*****Binyon, Laurence and others.** Persian miniature painting, including a critical and descriptive catalogue of the miniatures exhibited at Burlington House, January – March, 1931. London, Oxford, 1933.

Blochet, Edgar. Musulman painting, XII-XVII century. Trans. by C. M. Binyon. London, Methuen, 1929.

Briggs, Martin Shaw. Muhammedan architecture in Egypt and Palestine. Oxford, Clarendon, 1924.

Brown, Percy. Indian architecture. 2v. N.Y., Tudor, 1965. 5 ed.

——Indian painting. Calcutta, YMCA, 1947. 5 ed.

——Indian painting under the Mughals, A.D. 1550–1750. Oxford, Clarendon, 1924.

Butler, Alfred J. Islamic pottery; a study mainly historical. London, Benn, 1926.

Childe, Vere Gordon. New light on the most ancient East. London, Routledge, 1952. 4 ed.

Codrington, Kenneth deB. Ancient India. London, Benn, 1926.

*****Coomaraswamy, Ananda K.** The arts and crafts of India and Ceylon. N.Y., Farrar, 1964.

——Elements of Buddhist iconography. Cambridge, Harvard Univ., 1935.

*——History of Indian and Indonesian art. N.Y., Weyhe, 1927. Magnolia, P. Smith. Reprint.

——Rajput painting. 2v. London, Oxford, 1916.

*——The transformation of nature in art. Cambridge, Harvard Univ., 1934.

Creswell, Keppel A. C. A bibliography of painting in Islam. Cairo, Inst. Fran. d'Arch. Orient., 1953.

——A bibliography of the architecture, arts and crafts of Islam to 1960. N.Y., Oxford, 1961.

——The Muslim architecture of Egypt. v.1– . Oxford, Clarendon, 1952– .

Diez, Ernst. Iranische kunst. Vienna, Andermann, 1944.

——Kunst der islamischen völker. Berlin, Athenaion, 1917.

——Die kunst Indiens. Berlin, Athenaion, 1925.

Ettinghausen, Richard. Arab painting. Cleveland, World (Skira), 1962.

_____Selected and annotated bibliography of books and periodicals in western languages dealing with the near and middle East. Washington, Middle East Inst., 1954.

Ettinghausen, Richard and others. Treasures of Turkey. Cleveland, World (Skira), 1966.

Fergusson, James. History of Indian and Eastern architecture. Rev. by J. Burgess and R. P. Spiers. 2v. London, Murray, 1910.

Filov, Bogdan D. Early Bulgarian art. Berne, Haupt, 1919.

_____Geschichte der altbulgarischen kunst. 2v. Berlin, deGruyter, 1932–1933.

_____Geschichte der bulgarischen kunst unter der turkischen herrschaft und in der neueren zeit. Berlin, deGruyter, 1935.

Firdausi. The Shah-namah. Described by J. V. S. Wilkinson. N.Y., Oxford, 1931.

Frankfort, Henri. Art and architecture of the ancient Orient. London, Penguin, 1963. 3 ed.

*_____The birth of civilization in the Near East. London, Williams, 1951.

Gadd, Cyril J. The stones of Assyria. London, Chatto, 1936.

Glück, Heinrich and Diez, Ernst. Die kunst des Islam. Berlin, Propyläen, 1925.

Goetz, Hermann. The art of India. N.Y., Crown, 1965.

Gray, Basil. Persian painting. Cleveland, World (Skira), 1961.

_____Rajput painting. N.Y., Pitman, 1949.

Groslier, Bernard P. The art of Indochina. N.Y., Crown, 1962.

Groslier, Bernard P. and Arthaud, J. Angkor; art and civilization. N.Y., Praeger, 1966.

Havell, Ernest B. A handbook of Indian art. London, Murray, 1927.

_____Indian architecture. London, Murray, 1927. 2 ed.

_____Indian sculpture and painting. London, Murray, 1928. 2 ed.

Herzfeld, Ernst E. Iran in the ancient East. N.Y., Oxford, 1941.

*Hoag, John D. Western Islamic architecture. N.Y., Braziller, 1963.

Kar, Chintamoni. Classical Indian sculpture. N.Y., Transatlantic, 1950.

Kramrisch, Stella. The art of India. N.Y., Phaidon, 1965. 3 ed.

_____The Hindu temple. Calcutta, Univ. of Calcutta, 1946.

_____Indian sculpture. London, Oxford, 1933.

_____A survey of painting in the Deccan. London, India Society, 1937.

Kühnel, Ernst. Islamic art and architecture. Trans. by Katharine Watson. Ithaca, Cornell Univ., 1966.

Lane, Arthur. Early Islamic pottery; Mesopotamia, Egypt and Persia. London, Faber, 1958. 4 ed.

_____Later Islamic pottery; Persia, Syria, Egypt, Turkey. London, Faber, 1957.

Lyons, Islay deC. and Ingholt, Harald. Gandharan art in Pakistan. N.Y., Pantheon, 1957.

Mackay, Ernest J. H. Early Indus civilizations. London, Luzac, 1948. 2 ed. Original title: Indus civilization.

Marcais, Georges. L'architecture musulmane d'occident: Tunisie, Algérie, Maroc, Espagne et Sicile. Paris, Arts et Métiers, 1954.

_____ L'art de l'Islam. Paris, Larousse, 1946.

Marshall, John H. Mohenjo-daro and the Indus civilization. London, Probsthain, 1931.

Martin, Fredrik R. The miniature painting and painters of Persia, India and Turkey, from the eighth to the eighteenth century. 2v. London, Quaritch, 1912.

Migeon, Gaston and Saladin, Henri. Manuel d'art musulman. 2v. Paris, Picard, 1927. 2 ed.

Millet, Gabriel. L'ancien art serbe: les églises. Paris, Boccard, 1919.

Mulk-Raj, Anand. The Hindu view of art. Intro. essay by Eric Gill. London, Allen, 1933.

Pope, Arthur U. An introduction to Persian art since the seventh century A.D. N.Y., Scribner, 1931.

_____Masterpieces of Persian art. N.Y., Dryden, 1945.

_____Survey of Persian art from prehistoric times to the present. 13v. London, Oxford, 1965. 2 ed.

Porada, Edith. The art of ancient Iran: pre-Islamic cultures. Trans. by R. H. Dyson. N.Y., Crown, 1965.

*Rice, David T. Islamic art. N.Y., Praeger, 1965.

Rivoira, Giovanni T. Moslem architecture. Trans. by G. M. Rushforth. N.Y., Oxford, 1918.

Ross, Edward D. Persian art. London, Luzac, 1930.

Rostovtsev, Mikhail I. The animal style in South Russia and China. Princeton, Princeton Univ., 1929.

_____Dura-Europas and its art. N.Y., Oxford, 1938.

_____Iranians and Greeks in south Russia. London, Oxford, 1922.

Rowland, Benjamin. The art and architecture of India. London, Penguin, 1953.

Rowland, Benjamin and Coomaraswamy, Ananda K. The wall paintings of India, Central Asia and Ceylon. Boston, Museum of Fine Arts, 1938.

Sakisian, Armenag. La miniature persane du XII au XVII siècle. Paris, Brussels, VanOest, 1929.

Schmidt, Erich F. Persepolis. 2v. Chicago, Univ. of Chicago, 1953–1956.

Singh, Madanjeet. India: paintings from the Ajanta caves. Greenwich, NYGS, 1954.

Smith, Vincent A. A history of fine art in India and Ceylon. Rev. by Karl Khandalavala. N.Y., Tudor, 1963. 3 ed.

Stein, Mark Aurel. Innermost Asia; detailed report of explorations in Central Asia, Kan-su and eastern Iran. 4v. Oxford, Clarendon, 1928.

____Serindia; detailed report of explorations in Central Asia and westernmost China. 5v. Oxford, Clarendon, 1921.

____The thousand Buddhas. London, Quaritch, 1921.

Wilber, Donald N. Architecture of Islamic Iran; the Il Khanid period. Princeton, Princeton Univ., 1955.

Wilson, Ralph P. Islamic art. London, Benn, 1957.

Woolley, Charles L. The development of Sumerian art. London, Faber, 1935.

*____Digging up the past. London, Penguin, 1954.

*____Ur of the Chaldees. N.Y., Norton, 1965.

Zimmer, Heinrich R. The art of Indian Asia, its mythology and transformations. Ed. by Joseph Campbell. 2v. Princeton, Princeton Univ., 1955. 2 ed.

*____Myths and symbols in Indian art and civilization. N.Y., Pantheon, 1946.

History — Medieval, Byzantine, Early Christian

Agnello, Giuseppe. Le arti figurative nelle Sicilia bizantina. Palermo, Ist. Siciliano di Stud. Biz., 1962.

Allen, John R. Celtic art in pagan and Christian times. London, Methuen, 1904.

Anthony, Edgar W. Romanesque frescoes. Princeton, Princeton Univ., 1951.

Artz, Frederick B. The mind of the middle ages, A.D. 200–1500. N.Y., Knopf, 1958. 2 ed.

Baum, Julius. Malerei und plastik des mittelalters in Deutschland, Frankreich und Britannien. Berlin, Athenaion, 1950.

Baum (cont.)

——La sculpture figurale en Europe à l'époque mérovingienne. Paris, Édit. d'Art et d'Hist., 1937.

*Beckwith, John. Early medieval art. N.Y., Praeger, 1964.

Boeckler, Albert. Abendlandischen miniaturen bis zum ausgang der Romanischen zeit. Berlin, deGruyter, 1930.

Boinet, Amédée. La miniature carolingienne, ses origines, son développement. Paris, Picard, 1913.

Boskovic, Durde. Medieval art in Serbia and Macedonia; church architecture and sculpture. Belgrade, Jugosl. Kujiga, 1951.

Breasted, James H. Oriental forerunners of Byzantine painting; first century wall paintings from the fortress of Dura on the Middle Euphrates. Chicago, Chicago Univ., 1924.

Bréhier, Louis. L'art byzantin. Paris, Laurens, 1924.

——La sculpture et les arts mineurs byzantins. Paris, Édit. d'Art et d'Hist., 1936.

Bunim, Miriam S. Space in medieval painting and the forerunners of perspective. N.Y., Columbia Univ., 1929.

Butler, Howard C. Early churches in Syria, fourth to seventh centuries. Princeton, Princeton Univ., 1929.

Byron, Robert. The birth of western painting. N.Y., Knopf, 1931.

Contenau, Georges. Manuel d'archéologie orientale depuis les origines jusqu'à l'époque d'Alexandre. 4v. Paris, Picard, 1927–1947.

Coulton, George G. Art and the reformation. N.Y., Knopf, 1953.

Dalton, Ormonde M. Byzantine art and archaeology. Oxford, Clarendon, 1911. N.Y., Dover, 1965.

——East Christian art. Oxford, Clarendon, 1925.

Délaissé, L. M. J. Medieval miniatures. N.Y., Abrams, 1964.

Diehl, Charles. L'art chrétien primitif et l'art byzantin. Paris, VanOest, 1928.

——Manuel d'art byzantin. 2v. Paris, Picard, 1925–1926. 2 ed.

——La peinture byzantin. Paris, VanOest, 1933.

Dupont, Jacques and Gnudi, Cesare. Gothic painting. Cleveland, World (Skira), 1954.

Ebersolt, Jean. Les églises de Constantinople. Paris, Picard, 1913.

——La miniature byzantine. Paris, VanOest, 1926.

——Orient et occident. 2v. Paris, VanOest, 1928–1929.

Evans, Joan. The flowering of the Middle Ages. N.Y., McGraw, 1966.

Focillon, Henri. L'art des sculpteurs romans; récherches sur l'histoire des formes. Paris, Leroux, 1931. Reprint 1964.

Focillon (cont.)

———Art of the west in the middle ages. Trans. by Donald King. 2v. N.Y., Phaidon, 1963.

Frankl, Paul. The Gothic; literary sources and interpretations through eight centuries. Princeton, Princeton Univ., 1960.

Freeden, Max H. von. Gothic sculpture, the intimate carvings. Greenwich, NYGS, 1962.

Gayet, Albert J. L'art copte; école d'Alexandrie – architecture monastique – sculpture – peinture – art somptuaire. Paris, Leroux, 1902.

Gerstinger, Hans. Die griechische buchmalerei. 2v. Vienna, Österr. Staatsdruckerei, 1926.

Golzio, Vincenzo. Architettura bizantina e romanica. Milan, Società. Edit. Libreria, 1939.

Grabar, André. L'art byzantin. Paris, Edit. d'Art et d'Hist., 1938.

———Byzantine painting. Cleveland, World (Skira), 1953.

———Martyrium; récherches sur le culte des réliques et l'art chrétien antique. 2v. Paris, Collège de France, 1943–1946.

———La peinture religieuse en Bulgarie. Paris, Geuthner, 1928.

Grabar, André and Nordenfalk, Karl. Early medieval painting. Trans. by Stuart Gilbert. Cleveland, World (Skira), 1957.

———Romanesque painting. Cleveland, World (Skira), 1958.

Grant, Michael. The birth of western civilization; Greece and Rome. N.Y., McGraw, 1964.

Grüneisen, Wladimir de. Les caractéristiques de l'art copte. Florence, Alinari, 1922.

Hamann, Richard. Deutsche und französische kunst im mittelalter. 2v. Marburg, Kunst. Seminar, 1922–1923.

Hamilton, John A. Byzantine architecture and decoration. London, Batsford, 1956.

Harvey, John H. The Gothic world, 1100–1600; a survey of architecture and art. London, Batsford, 1950.

Hauttmann, Max. Die kunst des frühen mittelalters. Berlin, Propyläen, 1957. 2 ed.

Hell, Vera and Hell, Hellmut. The great pilgrimage of the middle ages. N.Y., Potter, 1966.

*****Hinks, Roger P.** Carolingian art. Ann Arbor, Univ. of Michigan, 1962.

Hubert, Jean. L'art pré-roman. Paris, Edit. d'Art et d'Hist., 1938.

*****Huizinga, Johan.** The waning of the middle ages. London, Arnold, 1963.

Jacobsthal, Paul. Early Celtic art. 2v. Oxford, Clarendon, 1944.

Jantzen, Hans. Ottonische kunst. Munich, Münchner verlag, 1947.

Karlinger, Hans. Die kunst der gotik. Berlin, Propyläen, 1927.

*****Katzenellenbogen, Adolf.** Allegories of the virtues and vices in medieval art from early Christian times to the thirteenth century. N.Y., Norton, 1939. N.Y., Kraus. Reprint.

Kaufmann, Carl M. Handbuch der christlichen archäologie, einführung in die denkmälerwelt und kunst des urchristentums. Paderborn, Schöningh, 1922. 3 ed.

*****Kitzinger, Ernst.** Early medieval art in the British museum. London, Brit. Museum, 1955. 2 ed. Magnolia, P. Smith, 1963. Reprint.

Kleinschmidt, Beda. Geschichte der christlichen kunst. Paderborn, Schöningh, 1926. 2 ed.

Köhler, Wilhelm R. W. Die karolingischen miniaturen. 4v. Berlin, Cassirer, 1930–1958.

Kondakov, Nikodim P. Histoire de l'art byzantin considéré principalement dans les miniatures. 2v. Paris, Libr. d'Art, 1886–1891. N.Y., Franklin. Reprint.

Leclercq, Henri. Manuel d'archéologie chrétienne depuis les origines jusqu'au VIII siècle. Paris, Létouzey, 1907.

Lethaby, William R. Medieval art, from the peace of the church to the eve of the Renaissance, 312–1350. Rev. by D. T. Rice. N.Y., Philosophical Libr., 1950.

*****Lowrie, Walter.** Art in the early church. N.Y., Pantheon, 1947. Magnolia, P. Smith. Reprint.

——Monuments of the early church. London, Macmillan, 1923.

Mahr, Adolf. Christian art in ancient Ireland, v.1– . Dublin, Stationery Office, 1932– .

Michelis, P. A. An aesthetic approach to Byzantine art. Chester Springs, Dufour, 1954.

Millet, Gabriel. L'école grèque dans l'architecture byzantine. Paris, Leroux, 1916.

*****Morey, Charles R.** Christian art. London, Longmans, 1935. Magnolia, P. Smith. Reprint.

——Early Christian art. Princeton, Princeton Univ., 1953. 2 ed.

——Medieval art. N.Y., Norton, 1942.

*****Moss, Henry S. B.** The birth of the middle ages, 395–514. Oxford, Clarendon, 1935.

Müntz, Eugène, Les arts à la cour des papes pendant le XV et le XVI siècles. 3v. Paris, Thorin, 1878–1882.

———Les arts à la cour des papes: Martin V, d'Eugène IV, de Nicolas V, de Calixte III, de Pie II et de Paul II. Paris, Cuggiani, 1884.

———Les arts à la cour des papes: Innocent VIII, Alexandre VI, Pie III (1484–1502). Paris, Leroux, 1898.

Muratov, Pavel P. La peinture byzantine. Paris, Crès, 1935.

Omont, Henri A. Miniatures de plus anciens manuscrits grècs de la Bibliothèque nationale du VI au XIV siècle. Paris, Champion, 1929.

Paatz, Walter. Süddeutsche schnitzaltäre der spätgotik. Heidelberg, Winter, 1963.

*****Panofsky, Erwin.** Gothic architecture and scholasticism. N.Y., Meridian, 1964.

Peirce, Hayford and Tyler, Royall. L'art byzantin. 2v. Paris, Libr. de France, 1932–1934.

Porter, A. Kingsley. The crosses and culture of Ireland. New Haven, Yale Univ., 1931.

———Medieval architecture, its origins and development, with lists of monuments and bibliographies. 2v. N.Y., Baker, 1912. N.Y., Hacker, 1965. Reprint.

———Romanesque sculpture of the pilgrimage roads. Boston, Marshall Jones, 1923. 10v. N.Y., Hacker, 1965. Reprint. 3v.

Pugin, Augustus C. Examples of Gothic architecture. 3v. London, Pugin, 1831–1836.

Rey, Raymond. L'art roman et ses origines. Paris, Didier, 1945.

*****Rice, David T.** The art of the Byzantine era. N.Y., Praeger, 1963.

———Byzantine art. Oxford, Clarendon, 1935.

Rossi, Giovanni B. de. La Roma sotteranea cristiana. 3v. Rome, Cromo-lito. Pontifica, 1864–1877.

*****Simson, Otto von.** The Gothic cathedral. N.Y., Pantheon, 1962. 2 ed.

———The sacred fortress; Byzantine art and statecraft in Ravenna. Chicago, Univ. of Chicago, 1948.

Smith, Earl B. The dome. Princeton, Princeton Univ., 1950.

Stewart, Cecil. Byzantine legacy. London, Allen, 1947.

Stokes, Margaret M. Early Christian art in Ireland. 2v. Dublin, Stationery Office, 1928.

Strzygowski, Josef. Die baukunst der Armenier und Europa. 2v. Vienna, Schroll, 1918.

———Early church architecture in northern Europe. N.Y., Harper, 1928.

Strzygowski (cont.)

____Orient oder Rom. Leipzig, Hinrichs, 1901.

____Origin of Christian church art. Trans. by O. M. Dalton and H. J. Braun-holtz. Oxford, Clarendon, 1923.

Swarzenski, Hanns. Monuments of Romanesque art; the art of church treasures in north-western Europe. Chicago, Univ. of Chicago, 1967. 2 ed.

Swift, Emerson H. Hagia Sophia. N.Y., Columbia Univ., 1940.

____Roman sources of Christian art. N.Y., Columbia Univ., 1951.

Sybel, Ludwig von. Christliche antike. Marburg, Elwert, 1906–1909.

Taylor, Henry O. The medieval mind. 2v. Cambridge, Harvard Univ., 1959. 4 ed.

Theophilus (called Rugerus). An essay upon various arts, forming an encyclopedia of Christian art of the eleventh century. Trans. by Robert Hendrie. London, Murray, 1847.

Underwood, Paul A. The Kariye Djami. 3v. Princeton, Princeton Univ., 1966.

Van Millingen, Alexander and Traquair, Ramsey. Byzantine churches in Constantinople. London, Macmillan, 1912.

Volbach, Wolfgang F. Art byzantin. Paris, Lévy, 1933.

____Early Christian art. N.Y., Abrams, 1962.

Weitzmann, Kurt. Die byzantinische buchmalerei des 9 und 10 jahrhunderts. Berlin, Mann, 1935.

Wessel, Klaus. Coptic art; the early Christian art of Egypt. N.Y., McGraw, 1965.

White, John. The birth and rebirth and pictorial space. London, Faber, 1967. 2 ed.

Whittemore, Thomas. The mosaics of Santa Sophia at Istanbul. v.1– . Paris, Byzantine Inst., 1933– .

Wilpert, Josef. Die malereien der katakomben Roms. 2v. Freiberg, Herder, 1903.

____Roma sotterranea; le pitture delle catacombe romane. 2v. in 3. Rome, Desclée, 1903.

____I sarcofagi cristiani antichi. 3v. in 5. Rome, Ist. di Archeol. Crist., 1929–1936.

*Worringer, Wilhelm. Form in Gothic. Edit. by Herbert Read. N.Y., Schocken, 1964.

Wulff, Oskar K. Altchristliche und byzantinische kunst. 2v. Berlin, Athenaion, 1918.

Bibliographisch-kritischer nachtrag, 1939.

History — Renaissance and Baroque

Adama van Scheltema, Frederick. Die kunst der renaissance. Stuttgart, Kohlhammer, 1955.

Barocchi, Paola. Trattati d'arte del cinquecento fra manierismo e contrariforma. 3v. Bari, Laterza, 1960–1962.

Benesch, Otto. The art of the renaissance in northern Europe. N.Y., Phaidon, 1965. 2 ed.

Brinckmann, Albert E. Kunst des barocks und rokokos. Berlin, Athenaion, 1923.

*Castiglione, Baldassare.** The book of the courtier. Trans. by T. Hoby. N.Y., Dutton, 1956.

*Clark, George N.** The seventeenth century. Oxford, Clarendon, 1947. 2 ed.

Cox, Trenchard. The renaissance in Europe, 1400–1600. London, Methuen, 1933.

Fokker, Thomas. Roman baroque art, the history of a style. 2v. London, Oxford, 1938.

Frey, Dagobert. Gotik und renaissance als grundlagen der modernen weltanschauung. Berlin, Filser, 1929.

*Friedrich, Carl J.** The age of the baroque, 1620–1660. N.Y., Harper, 1952.

Gengaro, Mario L. Umanesimo e rinascimento. Turin, Unione Tip. Edit. Torinese, 1953. 3 ed.

Glück, Gustav. Die kunst der renaissance in Deutschland, den Niederlanden, Frankreich. Berlin, Propyläen, 1928.

Gombrich, Ernst H. Studies in the art of the renaissance. v.1– . N.Y., Phaidon, 1966– .

Haskell, Francis. Patrons and painters; a study in the relations between Italian art and society in the age of the baroque. N.Y., Knopf, 1963.

Hess, Jacob. Kunstgeschichtliche studien zu renaissance und barock. 2v. Rome Ediz. di Storia e Letteratura, 1967.

Kimball, S. Fiske. The creation of the rococo. N.Y., Norton, 1964. Reprint.

Landsberger, Frantz. Die kunstlerischen probleme der renaissance. Halle, Niemeyer, 1922.

Magni, Giulio. Il barocco a Roma nell'architettura e nella scultura decorativa. 3v. Turin, Crudo, 1911–1913.

Mahon, Dennis. Studies in seicento art and theory. London, Warburg Inst., 1947.

Novotny, Fritz. Painting and sculpture in Europe, 1780–1880. London, Penguin, 1960.

Osborn, Max. Die kunst des rokoko. Berlin, Propyläen, 1929.

Paatz, Walter. Die kunst der renaissance in Italien. Stuttgart, Kohlhammer, 1953.

***Panofsky, Erwin.** Renaissance and renascences in western art. N.Y., Humanities, 1965. 2 ed.

——Studies in iconology; humanistic themes in the art of the renaissance. N.Y., Harper, 1962.

***Pater, Walter.** The renaissance. N.Y., Meridian, 1961.

Salis, Arnold von. Antike und renaissance. Zurich, Rentsch, 1947.

***Seznec, Jean.** The survival of the pagan gods; the mythological tradition and its place in renaissance humanism and art. Trans. by B. Sessions. Princeton, Princeton Univ., 1953.

Soehner, Halldor and Schönberger, Arno. The rococo age, art and civilization of the eighteenth century. N.Y., McGraw, 1960.

***Stechow, Wolfgang.** Northern renaissance art, 1400–1600; sources and documents. N.Y., Prentice Hall, 1966.

Steegmann, John. The rule of taste from George I to George IV. London, Macmillan, 1936.

***Sypher, Wylie.** Four stages of renaissance style. N.Y., Doubleday, 1955.

Weisbach, Werner. Die kunst des barock in Italien, Frankreich, Deutschland und Spanien. Berlin, Propyläen, 1924.

***Willey, Basil.** The seventeenth century background. N.Y., Columbia Univ., 1950.

Wind, Edgar. Pagan mysteries in the renaissance. New Haven, Yale Univ., 1958.

***Wölfflin, Heinrich.** Renaissance and baroque. Trans. by K. Simon. Ithaca, Cornell Univ., 1966.

History — Nineteenth and Twentieth Centuries

Breton, André. Les manifestes du surréalisme. Paris, Pauvert, 1962.

——Le surréalisme et la peinture. N.Y., Brentano, 1945.

***Brion, Marcel.** Art since 1945. N.Y., Washington Sq., 1962.

Brizio, Anna M. Ottocento, novecento. Turin, Unione Tip. Edit. Torinese, 1945.

Brown, Milton W. The story of the Armory Show. Greenwich, NYGS, 1963.

Canaday, John. Mainstreams of modern art. N.Y., Holt, 1959.

Cheney, Sheldon. The story of modern art. N.Y., Viking, 1958.

Einstein, Carl. Die kunst des 20 jahrhunderts. Berlin, Propyläen, 1951, 3 ed.

Focillon, Henri. La peinture aux XIX et XX siècles du réalisme à nos jours. Paris, Rénouard, 1928.

_____La peinture au XIX siècle; le retour à l'antique, le romanticisme. Paris, Laurens, 1927.

Gascoyne, David. A short history of surrealism. London, Cobden, 1936.

*****Gleizes, Albert.** Le cubisme, 1908–1914. N.Y., Wittenborn, 1957.

Gray, Christopher. Cubist aesthetic theories. Baltimore, Johns Hopkins, 1953.

Grohmann, Will. New art around the world. N.Y., Abrams, 1966.

Haack, Friedrich. Die kunst des XIX jahrhunderts und der gegenwart. 2v. Esslingen, Neff, 1922–1925. 6 ed.

Hildebrandt, Hans. Die kunst des 19 und 20 jahrhunderts. Berlin, Athenaion, 1924.

Jaffe, Hans. De Stijl, 1917–1931. Amsterdam, Meulenhoff, 1956.

Klingender, Francis D. Art and the industrial revolution. London, Carrington, 1947.

Kuh, Katharine. Break-up; the core of modern art. Greenwich, NYGS, 1965.

Lenning, Henry F. Art nouveau. The Hague, Nijhoff, 1951.

Madsen, Stephen T. Sources of art nouveau. Trans. by R. Christopherson. N.Y., Wittenborn, 1956.

Meier-Graefe, Julius. Entwicklungsgeschichte der modernen kunst. 2v. Munich, Piper, 1966. 3 ed.

_____Modern art; being a contribution to a new system of aesthetics. Trans. by F. Simmonds and G. W. Chrystal. 2v. N.Y., Putnam, 1908.

*****Moholy-Nagy, László.** The new vision. Trans. by D. M. Hoffman. N.Y., Wittenborn, 1964.

_____Vision in motion. Chicago, Theobald, 1947.

Pach, Walter. The masters of modern art. N.Y., Viking, 1925.

Pauli, Gustav. Die kunst des klassizismus und der romantik. Berlin, Propyläen, 1925.

Read, Herbert E. Art now; an introduction to the theory of modern painting and sculpture. N.Y., Pitman, 1960. 2 ed.

*****Rosenberg, H.** The tradition of the new. N.Y., McGraw, 1965.

*****Rosenblum, Robert.** Cubism and twentieth century art. N.Y., Abrams, 1961.

Rothschild, Edward F. The meaning of unintelligibility in modern art. Chicago, Univ. of Chicago, 1934.

Schmutzler, Robert. Art nouveau. N.Y., Abrams, 1964.

Selz, Peter. Art nouveau; art and design at the turn of the century. N.Y., Doubleday, 1960.

——Seven decades, 1895–1965; cross currents in modern art. Greenwich, NYGS, 1966.

Soby, James T. Modern art and the new past. Norman, Univ. of Oklahoma, 1957.

*Sypher, Wylie. Rococo to cubism in art and literature. N.Y., Random, 1960.

Waldmann, Emil. Die kunst des realismus und des impressionismus im 19 jahrhundert. Berlin, Propyläen, 1927.

Wilenski, Reginald H. The modern movement in art. London, Faber, 1946.

Zeitler, Rudolf. Die kunst des 19 jahrhunderts. Berlin, Propyläen, 1966.

Zervos, Christian. Histoire de l'art contemporain. Paris, Cahiers d'Art, 1938.

History — Canada

Colgate, William G. Canadian art, its origin and development. Toronto, Ryerson, 1943.

McInnes, Graham. A short history of Canadian art. Toronto, Macmillan, 1950.

MacTavish, Newton. The fine arts in Canada. Toronto, Macmillan, 1925.

History — France

Aubert, Marcel. L'art français a l'époque romane, architecture et sculpture. 4v. Paris, Morancé, 1929–1951.

Blunt, Anthony. Art and architecture in France, 1500–1700. London, Penguin, 1954.

Bréhier, Louis. L'art en France dès invasions barbares à l'époque romane. Paris, Renaissance du Livre, 1930.

Brownell, William C. French art; classic and contemporary painting and sculpture. N.Y., Scribner, 1920.

Du Columbier, Pierre. L'art renaissance en France. Paris, Le Prat, 1946.

Du Peloux de Saint Romain, Charles. Répertoire general des ouvrages modernes relatifs au dix-huitième siècle français (1715–1789). 2v. Paris, Grund, 1926–1927.

Enlart, Camille. Manuel d'archéologie française depuis les temps Mérovingiens jusqu'à la renaissance. 5v. Paris, Picard, 1927–1932.

Evans, Joan. Art in medieval France, 987–1498. London, Oxford, 1948.

_____Cluniac art of the Romanesque period. Cambridge, Cambridge Univ., 1950.

Fontainas, André. Les doctrines d'art en France de Poussin à Diderot. Paris, Laurens, 1909

Fontainas, André and others. Histoire générale de l'art français de la révolution à nos jours. 3v. Paris, Libr. de France, 1922.

Gischia, Léon. Les arts primitifs français. Paris, Arts et Métiers, 1939.

Hildebrandt, Edmund. Malerei und plastik des 18 jahrhunderts in Frankreich. Berlin, Athenaion, 1924.

Inventaire Génerale des Richesses d'Art de la France. 22v. Paris, Plon, 1876–1913.

Lantier, Raymond. Les origines de l'art français. Paris, Le Prat, 1947.

Lefrançois, Louise P. L'art roman en France; architecture, sculpture, peinture, arts mineurs. Paris, Le Prat, 1943.

Lemonnier, Henry. L'art français au temps de Louis XIV (1661–1690). Paris, Hachette, 1911.

_____L'art français au temps de Richelieu et de Mazarin. Paris, Hachette, 1913. 2 ed.

Markham, Violet R. Romanesque France; studies in the archaeology and history of the twelfth century. London, Murray, 1929.

Mauricheau-Beaupré, Charles. L'art au XVII siècle en France. 2v. Paris, Le Prat, 1946–1947.

Réau, Louis. L'art gothique en France. Paris, Le Prat, 1945.

Rocheblave, Samuel. L'art et le goût en France de 1600 à 1900. Paris, Colin, 1930. 2 ed.

Roy, Maurice. Artistes et monuments de la renaissance en France; récherches nouvelles et documents inédits. 2v. Paris, Champion, 1929–1934.

History – Germany, Austria, Switzerland

Beenken, Hermann T. Das neunzehnte jahrhundert in der deutschen kunst. Munich, Bruckmann, 1944.

Benz, Richard E. Die kunst der deutschen romantik. Munich, Piper, 1939.

Christoffel, Ulrich. Die deutsche kunst als form und ausdruck. Augsburg, Filser, 1928.

Clemen, Paul. Die deutsche kunst und die denkmalpflege. Berlin, Deutscher Kunstverlag, 1933.

Dehio, Georg G. Geschichte der deutschen kunst. 3v. Berlin, deGruyter, 1923-1934. 3 ed.

──── Handbuch der deutschen denkmaler. v.1- . Berlin, Akademie-verlag, 1966- .

Doering, Oskar. Deutschlands mittelalterliche kunstdenkmäler als geschichts-quelle. Leipzig, Hiersemann, 1910.

Gantner, Joseph. Kunstgeschichte der Schweiz von den anfangen bis zum beginn des 20 jahrhunderts. 3v. Leipzig, Huber, 1936-1956.

Hagen, Oskar F. L. Deutsches sehen; gestaltungsfragen der deutschen kunst. Munich, Piper, 1923. 2 ed.

Hempel, Eberhard. Baroque art and architecture in central Europe; Germany, Austria, Switzerland, Hungary, Czechoslovakia, Poland. London, Penguin, 1965.

Knackfuss, Hermann. Deutsche kunstgeschichte. 2v. Bielefeld, Velhagen, 1888.

Merin, Peter. Modern German art. London, Penguin, 1938.

Picton, Harold W. Early German art and its origins from the beginnings to about 1050. London, Batsford, 1939.

Schmitt, Otto. Reallexikon zur deutschen kunstgeschichte. v.1- . Stuttgart, Metzler, 1933- .

Sitwell, Sacheverell, German baroque art. N.Y. Doran, 1928.

Weigert, Hans. Geschichte der deutschen kunst von der vorzeit bis zur gegen-wart. Berlin, Propyläen, 1942.

Witte, Fritz. Tausend jahre deutscher kunst am Rhein. v.1- . Berlin, Verlag f. Kunstwissenschaft, 1932- .

History — Great Britain

Boase, Thomas S. R. English art, 1100-1216. N.Y., Oxford, 1953.

Boase, Thomas S. R., ed. The Oxford history of English art. v.1- . Oxford, Clarendon, 1949- .

Brown, Gerard B. The arts in early England. 6v. London, Murray, 1903-1937.

Evans, Joan. English art, 1307-1461. Oxford, Clarendon, 1949.

Henry, Françoise. Irish art during the Viking invasions (A.D. 800-1200). Ithaca, Cornell Univ., 1967.

Henry (cont.)

———Irish art in the early Christian period (to 800 A.D.). Ithaca, Cornell Univ., 1966.

Irwin, David. English neoclassical art; studies in inspiration and taste. Greenwich, NYGS, 1966.

Kendrick, Thomas D. Anglo-Saxon art to A.D. 900. London, Methuen, 1938.

———Late Saxon and Viking art. London, Methuen, 1949.

*Pevsner, Nikolaus. The Englishness of English art. London, Penguin, 1964.

Rothenstein, John. British art since 1900. N.Y., Phaidon, 1962.

Saunders, O. Elfrida. A history of English art in the middle ages. Oxford, Clarendon, 1932.

Saxl, Fritz and Wittkower, Rudolf. British art and the Mediterranean. London, Oxford, 1948.

Thomas, Stanley. Pre-Roman Britain. Greenwich, NYGS, 1965.

Waagen, Gustav F. Galleries and cabinets of art in Great Britain. London, Murray, 1857.

———Treasures of art in Great Britain. 3v. London, Murray, 1854.

———Summary and index to Waagen by Algernon Graves. London, Graves, 1912.

Whinney, Margaret D. The inter-relations of the fine arts in England in the early middle ages. London, Benn, 1930.

History — Italy

Ancona, Paola d'. L'arte italiana. 3v. Florence, Bemporad, 1937–1947.

———Umanesimo e rinascimento. Turin, Ed. Torinese, 1948. 3 ed.

*Blunt, Anthony. Artistic theory in Italy, 1450–1600. Oxford, Clarendon, 1957. 2 ed.

Bode, Wilhelm von. Die kunst der frührenaissance in Italien. Berlin, Propyläen, 1923. 3 ed.

*Burckhardt, Jacob C. Civilization of the renaissance in Italy. Trans. by S. G. C. Middlemore. N.Y., Phaidon, 1960. 3 ed.

Castelfranchi Vegas, Liana. International Gothic art in Italy. Trans. by B. D. Philipps and T. Rice. Leipzig, Edit. Leipzig, 1966.

Chastel, André. Italian art. Trans. by P. and L. Murray. N.Y., Yoseloff, 1963.

Collison-Morley, Lacy. Italy after the renaissance; decadence and display in the seventeenth century. London, Routledge, 1930.

Costantini, Vincenzo. Storia dell'arte italiana. 4v. Milan, Ceschina, 1945–1949.

Decker, Hans. Romanesque art in Italy. N.Y., Abrams, 1959.

Dvořák, Max. Geschichte der italienischen kunst im zeitalter der renaissance. 2v. Munich, Piper, 1927–1928.

Golzio, Vincenzo. Il seicento e il settecento. 2v. Turin, Edit. Torinese, 1960. 2 ed.

*Klein, Robert and Zerner, H. Italian art, 1500–1600. N.Y., Prentice-Hall, 1966.

Lavagnino, Emilio. L'arte moderna dai neoclassici ai contemporanei. 2v. Turin, Edit. Torinese, 1956.

_____ Storia dell'arte medioevale italiana. Turin, Edit. Torinese, 1936.

Martin, Camille. L'art roman en Italie; l'architecture et la décoration. 2v. Paris, Eggiman, 1912–1924.

Milanesi, Gaetano. Documenti per la storia dell'arte senese. 3v. Siena, Porri, 1854–1856.

Muñoz, Antonio. Roma barocca. Milan, Bestetti, 1928.

Schubring, Paul. Die kunst der hochrenaissance in Italien. Berlin, Propyläen, 1926. 2 ed.

Sitwell, Sacheverell. Southern baroque art; a study of painting, architecture and music in Italy and Spain of the 17th and 18th centuries. London, Duckworth, 1931. 3 ed.

*Symonds, John A. The renaissance in Italy. 3v. Magnolia, P. Smith. Reprint.

Toesca, Pietro. Storia dell'arte italiana. 3v. Turin, Edit. Torinese, 1927–1951.

Venturi, Adolfo. Storia dell'arte italiana. 11v. Milan, Hoepli, 1901–1940. N.Y., Kraus, 1967. Reprint.

White, John. Art and architecture in Italy, 1250–1400. London, Penguin, 1966.

Wittkower, Rudolf. Art and architecture in Italy, 1600–1750. London, Penguin, 1965. 2 ed.

*Wölfflin, Heinrich. The art of the Italian renaissance. Trans. by W. Armstrong. N.Y., Schocken, 1963.

_____Classic art; an introduction to the Italian renaissance. Trans. by P. and L. Murray. N.Y., Phaidon, 1953. 2 ed.

*Young, George F. The Medici. London, Murray, 1928. 2v.

History — Low Countries

Bredius, Abraham. Kunstler-inventaire; urkunden zur geschichte der Holland-ischen kunst des XVI und XVIII jahrhunderts. 6v. The Hague, Nijhoff, 1915–1922.

Clemen, Paul. Belgische kunstdenkmäler. 2v. Munich, Bruckmann, 1923.

Fierens, Paul. L'art en Belgique du moyen âge à nos jours. Brussels, Renaissance du Livre, 1947.

_____L'art flamand. Paris, Larousse, 1945.

Gerson, Horst and Kuile, E. H. ter. Art and architecture in Belgium 1600–1800. Trans. by Olive Renier. London, Penguin, 1960.

Hymans, Henri S. Belgische kunst des 19 jahrhunderts. Leipzig, Seemann, 1906.

Leurs, Stan. Geschiedenis van de vlaamsche kunst. 2v. Antwerp, deSikkel, 1936–1940.

Puyvelde, Leo van. The genius of Flemish art. London, Phaidon, 1949.

Rosenberg, Jakob and Slive, Seymour. Dutch art and architecture, 1600–1800. London, Penguin, 1966.

Valentiner, Wilhelm R. The art of the Low Countries. N.Y., Doubleday, 1924.

Ysendyck, Jules J. Documents classés de l'art dans les Pays-Bas du X au XVIII siècle. 5v. Antwerp, Maes, 1880–1889.

History — Mexico, Latin America

Angulo Iñiguez, Diego. Historia del arte Hispano-Americano. v.1– . Barcelona, Salvat, 1941– .

Bardi, Pietro M. The arts in Brazil. Milan, Milione, 1956.

Covarrubias, Miguel. The eagle, the jaguar, and the serpent; Indian art of the Americas. N.Y., Knopf, 1954.

Dockstader, Frederick J. Indian art in middle America. Greenwich, NYGS, 1964.

_____Indian art in South America; pre-Columbian and contemporary arts and crafts. Greenwich, NYGS, 1967.

Fernández, Justino. El arte moderno en Mexico. Mexico City, Porrua, 1937.

Joyce, Thomas A. Central American and West Indian archaeology. London, Warner, 1916.

_____Maya and Mexican art. London, Studio, 1927.

Joyce (cont.)

____Mexican archaeology; an introduction to the archaeology of the Mexican and Mayan civilizations of pre-Spanish America. London, Warner, 1920.

____South American archaeology; an introduction to the archaeology of the South American continent with special reference to the early history of Peru. N.Y., Putnam, 1912.

*Kelemen, Pál. Baroque and rococo in Latin America. N.Y., Macmillan, 1951.

Lehmann, Walter and Ubbelohde-Doering, Heinrich. The art of old Peru. London, Benn, 1957. 2 ed.

Lothrop, Samuel K. Essays in pre-Columbian art and archaeology. Cambridge, Harvard Univ., 1961.

Marshall, John H. Taxila. 3v. Cambridge, Harvard Univ., 1951.

Medioni, Gilbert and Pinto, M. Art in ancient Mexico. N.Y., Oxford, 1941.

Morley, Sylvanus G. The ancient Maya. Rev. by G. W. Brainerd. Stanford, Stanford Univ., 1956. 3 ed.

Proskouriakoff, Tatiana A. An album of Maya architecture. Norman, Univ. of Oklahoma, 1963.

____A study of classic Maya sculpture. Washington, Carnegie Inst., 1950.

Schmidt, Max. Kunst und kultur von Peru. Berlin, Propyläen, 1929.

Smith, Robert C. and Wilder, Elizabeth. A guide to the art of Latin America. Washington, Library of Congress, 1948.

Solá, Miguel. Historia del arte Hispano-Americano. Barcelona, Labor, 1935.

Spinden, Herbert J. Ancient civilizations of Mexico and Central America. N.Y., Amer. Mus. of Nat. Hist., 1946. 3 ed.

____Maya art and civilization. Indian Hills, Falcon's Wing, 1957. This is a revision of his Study of Maya art.

Taullard, Alfredo. Plateria sudamericana. Buenos Aires, Peuser, 1941.

Toor, Frances. Mexican popular arts. Mexico, Toor, 1939.

Toscano, Salvador. Arte pre-colombino de México y de la América central. Mexico, Inst. de Invest. Estéticas, 1944.

Totten, George O. Maya architecture. Washington, Maya Press, 1926. 3 ed. N.Y., Franklin, Reprint.

Toussaint, Manuel. Arte colonial en México. Mexico, Universitaria, 1962. 2 ed.

____Arte mudejar en América. Mexico, Porrúa, 1946.

Ubbelohde-Doering, Heinrich. The art of ancient Peru. N.Y., Praeger, 1952.

*Vaillant, George C. Aztecs of Mexico. N.Y., Doubleday, 1962.

History — Russia

Alpatov, Mikhail V. Art treasures of Russia. N.Y., Abrams, 1967
_____ Russian impact on art. Trans. by I. Litvinov. N.Y., Philosophical Lib., 1950.
Alpastov, Mikhail V. and Brunov, Nikolai I. Geschichte der altrussischen kunst. 2v. Augsburg, Filser, 1932.
Bunt, Cyril G. E. A history of Russian art. London, Studio, 1946.
Conway, William M. Art treasures in soviet Russia. London, Arnold, 1925.
Hamilton, George H. Art and architecture of Russia. London, Penguin, 1954.
Hare, Richard. The art and artists of Russia. Greenwich, NYGS, 1966.
Holme, Geoffrey. Art in the USSR; architecture, sculpture, painting, graphic arts, theatre, film, crafts. London, Studio, 1935.
London, Kurt. The seven soviet arts. New Haven, Yale Univ., 1938.
Matthey, Werner von. Russische kunst. Einsiedeln, Benziger, 1948.
Réau, Louis. L'art russe. 2v. Paris, Laurens, 1921–1922.
Rice, David T. Russian art; an introduction. London, Gurney, 1935
*Rice, Tamara. A concise history of Russian art. N.Y., Praeger, 1963.
Rubissow, Helen. The art of Russia. N.Y., Philosophical Lib., 1946.
Strzygowski, Josef. Die altslavische kunst. Augsburg, Filser, 1929.
Voyce, Arthur. The art and architecture of medieval Russia. Norman, Univ. of Oklahoma, 1966.
Wulff, Oskar K. Die neurussische kunst im rahmen der kultur-entwicklung Russlands von Peter dem grossen bis zur revolution. 2v. Augsburg, Filser, 1932.

History — Scandinavia

Adama van Scheltema, Frederick. Die altnordische kunst; grundprobleme vorhistorischer kunstentwicklung. Berlin, Mauritius, 1924
Alfons, Sven and Lindwall, Bo. Svensk konstkrönika under 100 år. Stockholm, Natur och Kultur, 1944.
Cornell, Henrik. Den Svenska konstens historia. 2v. Stockholm, Bonnier, 1966.
Hannover, Emil. Dänische kunst des 19 jahrhunderts. Leipzig, Seemann, 1907.
Holme, Charles. Peasant art in Sweden, Lapland and Iceland. London, Studio, 1910.

Laurin, Carl. Scandinavian art. N.Y., Amer.-Scan. Foundation, 1922.
Lexow, Einar Jacob. Norges kunst. Oslo, Steenske, 1926.
Nordensvan, Georg G. Schwedische kunst des 19 jahrhunderts. Leipzig, Seemann, 1904.
Nørlund, Poul. Danish art through the ages. Copenhagen, Tidsk. Denmark, 1948.
Okkonen, Onni. L'art finlandais aux XIX et XX siècles. Trans. by H. Goldthwaite. Helsinki, Söderström, 1946. 2 ed.
Racz, Istyan. Art treasures of medieval Finland. Trans. by J. Beesley and D. Tullberg. N.Y., Praeger, 1967.
____Early Finnish art from pre-history to the middle ages. Trans. by D. Tullberg. N.Y., Praeger, 1967.
Roosval, Johnny A. E. Swedish art. Princeton, Princeton Univ., 1932.
Tikkanen, Johan J. Modern art in Finland. Helsinki, Govt. Print. Office, 1926.
Wettergren, Erik. The modern decorative arts in Sweden. N.Y., Amer.-Scan. Foundation, 1926.
Wollin, Nils G. A. Modern Swedish arts and crafts in pictures. N.Y., Scribner, 1931.

History — Spain

Azcárate, José M. de. Monumentos españoles; catálogo de los declarados histórico-artisticos. 3v. Madrid, Con. Sup. de Invest. Cient., 1953–1954.
Cirici-Pellicer, Alexandre. The treasures of Spain from Charles V to Goya. Cleveland, World (Skira), 1965.
Gaya Nuño, Juan A. Historia del arte español. Madrid, Plus-ultra, 1946.
Gudiol y Ricart, José. Ars hispaniae; historia universale del arte hispánico. 6v. Madrid, Plus-ultra, 1947.
Hagen, Oskar F. L. Patterns and principles of Spanish art. Madison, Univ. of Wisconsin, 1948. 2 ed.
Jiménez-Placer, Fernando and Cirici-Pellicer, Alexandre. Historia del arte español. 2v. Barcelona, Labor, 1955.
Kubler, George and Soria, Martin S. Art and architecture in Spain and Portugal and their American dominions, 1500–1800. London, Penguin, 1967. 2 ed.
Lozoya, Juan C. Historia del arte hispánico. 5v. Barcelona, Salvat, 1931–1949.

Palol, Pedro. Early medieval art in Spain. N.Y., Abrams, 1967.

Pita-Andrade, José M. Treasures of Spain from Altamira to the Catholic kings. Cleveland, World (Skira), 1967.

Rafols, José F. El arte romantico en España. Barcelona, Juventud, 1954.

Santos, Reynoldo dos. L'art portugais: architecture, sculpture et peinture. Paris, Plon, 1953.

Stirling-Maxwell, William. Annals of the artists of Spain. 4v. London, Nimmo, 1891. 2 ed.

Tatlock, Robert R. and others. Spanish art; an introductory review of architecture, painting, sculpture, textiles, ceramics, woodwork, metalwork. London, Batsford, 1927.

Tormo y Monzó, Elías. Pintura, escultura y arquitectura en España; estudios dispersos. Madrid, Inst. Diego Velázquez, 1949.

Weisbach, Werner. Spanish baroque art. Cambridge, Univ., 1941.

History — United States

Baur, John I. H. Between the fairs; twenty-five years of American art, 1939–1964. N.Y., Praeger, 1964.

_____New art in America. Greenwich, NYGS, 1957.

_____Revolution and tradition in modern American art. N.Y., Praeger, 1967.

Cahill, Holger and Barr, Alfred H. Art in America; a complete survey. N.Y., Halcyon, 1939.

Dockstader, Frederick J. Indian art in America. Greenwich, NYGS, 1966. 3 ed.

Douglas, Frederic H. and Harnoncourt, René d'. Indian art of the United States. N.Y., Museum of Modern Art, 1941.

Dow, George Francis. The arts and crafts in New England, 1704–1775. N.Y., Plenum, 1967. Reprint.

Drepperd, Carl W. American pioneer arts and artists. Springfield, Pond, 1942.

Dunlap, William. A history of the rise and progress of the arts of design in the United States. 3v. N.Y., Blom, 1966. Reprint.

Goodrich, Lloyd. Three centuries of American art. N.Y., Praeger, 1967.

Goodrich, Lloyd and Baur, John I. H. American art of our century. N.Y., Praeger, 1961.

Green, Samuel M. American art; a historical survey. N.Y., Ronald, 1966.

Griffin, James B. Archaeology of the eastern United States. Chicago, Univ. of Chicago, 1952.

Hipkiss, Edwin J. Eighteenth century American arts. Cambridge, Harvard Univ., 1941.

***Inverarity, Robert B.** Art of the northwest coast Indians. Berkeley, Univ. of California, 1967. 2 ed.

Kelby, William. Notes on American artists, 1754–1820, copied from the advertisements appearing in the newspapers of the day. N.Y., N.Y. Hist. Society, 1922. N.Y., Franklin. Reprint.

Kelemen, Pál. Medieval American art. 2v. N.Y., Macmillan, 1943.

Kidder, Alfred V. An introduction to the study of southeastern archaeology, with a preliminary account of the excavations at Pecos. New Haven, Yale Univ., 1924.

Kouwenhoven, John A. Made in America; the arts in modern civilization. N.Y., Doubleday, 1948.

Kubler, George. Art and architecture of ancient America. London, Penguin, 1961.

LaFollette, Suzanne. Art in America. N.Y., Norton, 1939.

Larkin, Oliver W. Art and life in America. N.Y., Holt, 1960. 2 ed.

Mather, Frank J. and others. The American spirit in art. New Haven, Yale, 1927. N.Y., U.S. Publishers. Reprint.

McMahon, Amos P. Preface to an American philosophy of art. Chicago, Univ. of Chicago, 1945.

Mellquist, Jerome. The emergence of an American art. N.Y., Scribner, 1942.

***Mumford, Lewis.** The brown decades; a study of the arts in America, 1865–1895. N.Y., Harcourt, 1955. 2 ed.

Neuhaus, Eugen. The history and ideals of American art. Stanford, Stanford Univ., 1931.

Rourke, Constance. The roots of American culture and other essays. N.Y., Kennikat, 1965.

Tuckerman, Henry T. Book of the artists; American artist life. N.Y., Carr, 1966. Reprint.

Vaillant, George C. Indian arts in North America. N.Y., Harper, 1939.

Whitehill, Walter M. The arts in early American history, needs and opportunities for study; an essay with a bibliography by Wendel D. and Jane N. Garrett. Chapel Hill, Univ. of N.C., 1965.

Wingert, Paul S. American Indian sculpture; a study of the northwest coast. N.Y., Augustin, 1949.

Wissler, Clark. The American Indian; an introduction to the anthropology of the New World. Magnolia, P. Smith, 1950. Reprint.

Wyckoff, Alexander. Art and artists in America, 1735–1835. N.Y., Blom, 1966.

ARCHITECTURE

General

Alexander, William, ed. Masters of world architecture. v.1- . N.Y., Braziller, 1966- .

Allsop, Bruce and others. The great tradition of western architecture. N.Y., Hastings, 1967.

Behrendt, Walter C. Modern building; its nature, problems and forms. N.Y., Harcourt, 1937.

Bell, Edward. The origins of architecture. 4v. London, Bell, 1915–1926.

Benoit, François. L'architecture. 4v. Paris, Laurens, 1911–1934.

*Branner, Robert. Gothic architecture. N.Y., Braziller, 1961.

Briggs, Martin Shaw. Baroque architecture. London, Unwin, 1913. N.Y., DaCapo, 1967. Reprint.

____The homes of the Pilgrim fathers in England and America, 1620–1685. N.Y., Oxford, 1932.

Brownell, Baker. Architecture and modern life. N.Y., Harper, 1937.

Burckhardt, Jacob and Lübke, Wilhelm. Geschichte der neueren baukunst. 10v. Stuttgart, Ebner, 1882–1927.

Clapham, Alfred W. Romanesque architecture in western Europe. Oxford, Clarendon, 1936.

*Clark, Kenneth M. The Gothic revival; an essay in the history of taste. N.Y., Scribner, 1962. 3 ed.

Clasen, K. H. Die gotische baukunst. Berlin, Athenaion, 1930.

Conant, Kenneth J. Benedictine contributions to church architecture. Latrobe, Archabbey, 1949.

____Carolingian and Romanesque architecture, 800–1200. London, Penguin, 1959.

Crowfoot, J. W. Early churches in Palestine. N.Y., Oxford, 1941.

Daly, Cesar. Motifs historiques d'architecture et de sculpture d'ornement. Series 1-2. 4v. Paris, Daly, 1880-1881.

Ebersolt, Jean. Monuments d'architecture byzantine. Paris, Édit. d'Art et d'Hist., 1934.

Fergusson, James. A history of architecture in all countries from the earliest times to the present day. Rev. by R. P. Spiers and R. Kerr. 2v. London, Murray, 1907.

Fletcher, Banister. A history of architecture on the comparative method. N.Y., Scribner, 1961. 17 ed.

Frankl, Paul. Gothic architecture. Trans. by D. Pevsner. London, Penguin, 1962.

Giedion, Siegfried. A decade of new architecture. Zurich, Girsberger, 1951.

_____The eternal present, v.1- . Princeton, Princeton Univ., 1962- .

_____Space time and architecture; the growth of a new tradition. Cambridge, Harvard Univ., 1967. 5 ed.

Grodecki, Louis. L'architecture Ottonienne. Paris, Colin, 1958.

Hamlin, Talbot F. Architecture, an art for all men. N.Y., Columbia Univ., 1947.

_____Architecture through the ages. N.Y., Putnam, 1953.

_____The forms and functions of twentieth century architecture. 4v. N.Y., Columbia Univ., 1952.

Hitchcock, Henry-Russell. Architecture of the nineteenth and the twentieth centuries. London, Penguin, 1963.

_____Modern architecture; romanticism and re-integration. N.Y., Payson, 1929.

_____World architecture; a pictorial history. N.Y., McGraw, 1963.

*__Hitchcock, Henry-Russell and Johnson, Philip C__. The international style; architecture since 1922. N.Y., Norton, 1966. 2 ed.

Hudnut, Joseph. Architecture and the spirit of man. Cambridge, Harvard Univ., 1949.

Jackson, Thomas G. Byzantine and romanesque architecture. 2v. Cambridge, Cambridge Univ., 1920. 2 ed.

_____Gothic architecture in France, England and Italy. 2v. Cambridge, Cambridge Univ., 1915.

_____The renaissance of Roman architecture. 3v. Cambridge, Cambridge Univ., 1921-1925

Johnson, Philip C. Architecture 1949-1965. N.Y., Holt, 1966.

*Kaufmann, Emil. Architecture in the age of reason: baroque and post-baroque in England, Italy and France. Cambridge, Harvard Univ., 1955.

Kimball, S. Fiske and Edgell, George H. A history of architecture. N.Y., Harper, 1946. 2 ed.

Kraeling, Carl H. The synagogue. New Haven, Yale Univ., 1956.

Krautheimer, Richard. Early Christian and Byzantine architecture. London, Penguin, 1965.

*Lowry, Bates. Renaissance architecture. N.Y., Braziller, 1962.

*MacDonald, William L. Early Christian and Byzantine architecture. N.Y., Braziller, 1962.

Mansbridge, John. Graphic history of architecture. N.Y., Viking, 1967.

*Millon, Henry A. Baroque and rococo architecture. N.Y., Braziller, 1961.

____Key monuments of the history of architecture. N.Y., Abrams, 1964.

Moore, Charles H. Character of renaissance architecture. N.Y., Macmillan, 1905.

____Development and character of Gothic architecture. N.Y., Macmillan, 1899. 2 ed.

Newcomb, Rexford. History of modern architecture. Scranton, Internat'l. Text., 1942.

Peter, John. Masters of modern architecture. N.Y., Braziller, 1958.

*Pevsner, Nikolaus. An outline of European architecture. London, Penguin, 1960. 6 ed.

*____Pioneers of modern design from William Morris to Walter Gropius. London, Penguin, 1964.

*Richards, James M. An introduction to modern architecture. London, Penguin, 1947.

*Robertson, Donald. Pre-Columbian architecture. N.Y., Braziller, 1963.

Roth, Alfred. The new architecture. Zurich, Girsberger, 1940.

*Saalman, Howard. Medieval architecture. N.Y., Braziller, 1962.

Sartoris, Alberto. Encyclopédie de l'architecture nouvelle. 3v. Milan, Hoepli, 1948-1957.

*Scully, Vincent. Modern architecture. N.Y., Braziller, 1961.

Sharp, Dennis. Modern architecture and expressionism. N.Y., Braziller, 1966.

*____Sources of modern architecture; a bibliography. N.Y., Wittenborn, 1966.

Simpson, Frederick M. A history of architectural development. v.1- . London, Longmans, 1954- . 2 ed.

Statham, Henry H. A history of architecture. London, Batsford, 1950. 3 ed.

Stewart, Cecil. Early Christian, Byzantine and Romanesque architecture. London, Longmans, 1954. (Simpson, v.2).

_____Gothic architecture. London, Longmans, 1961. (Simpson, v.3).

Sturgis, Russell. A dictionary of architecture and building; biographical, historical and descriptive. 3v. N.Y., Macmillan, 1901. N.Y., Gale, Reprint.

Taut, Bruno. Modern architecture. N.Y., Boni, 1929.

Viollet-le-Duc, Eugène E. Discourses on architecture. Trans. by B. Bucknell. 2v. N.Y., Grove, 1959.

*****Vitruvius Pollio.** On architecture. Trans. by F. Granger. 2v. Cambridge, Harvard Univ., 1945.

Wasmuth, Gunther. Wasmuth's lexikon der baukunst. 5v. Berlin, Wasmuth, 1929–1932.

Whittick, Arnold. European architecture in the twentieth century. 2v. London, Lockwood, 1950–1953.

Zevi, Bruno. Storia dell'architettura moderna. Turin, Einaudi, 1953. 2 ed.

_____Towards an organic architecture. London, Faber, 1950.

Architecture — France

*****Adams, Henry.** Mont-St.-Michel and Chartres. Boston, Houghton, 1963.

Androuet du Cerceau, Jacques. Les plus excellents bâtiments de France. 2v. Paris, Lévy, 1868–1870.

Aubert, Marcel. L'architecture cistercienne en France. 2v. Paris, Édit. d'Art et d'Hist., 1947. 2 ed.

_____L'architecture française à l'époque gothique. Paris, Édit. d'Art et d'Hist., 1943.

Baum, Julius. Romanesque architecture in France. London, Country Life, 1928.

Blomfield, Reginald T. A history of French architecture from the death of Mazarin till the death of Louis XV (1661–1774). 2v. London, Bell, 1921.

_____A history of French architecture from the reign of Charles VIII till the death of Mazarin. 2v. London, Bell, 1911.

_____Three hundred years of French architecture, 1494–1794. N.Y., Macmillan, 1936.

Bony, Jean and Hürlimann, Martin. French cathedrals. London, Thames, 1967.

Colas, René. Le style gothique en France dans l'architecture et la décoration des monuments. Paris, Colas, 1926.

Colas (cont.)

—— Le style roman en France dans l'architecture et la décoration des monuments. Paris, Colas, 1927.

Crosby, Sumner M. L'abbaye royale de Saint-Denis. Paris, Hartmann, 1953.

Deshoulières, François. Au début de l'art roman, les églises de l'onzième siècle en France. Paris, Édit. d'Art et d'Hist., 1943. 2 ed.

Evans, Joan. Monastic architecture in France from the renaissance to the revolution. Cambridge, Cambridge Univ., 1964.

—— The romanesque architecture of the order of Cluny. Cambridge, Cambridge Univ., 1938.

Flipo, Vincent. Mémento pratique d'archéologie française. Paris, Firmin-Didot, 1930.

Gardner, Arthur. An introduction to French church architecture. N.Y., Macmillan, 1938.

Haupt, Albrecht. Baukunst der renaissance in Frankreich und Deutschland. Berlin, Athenaion, 1923.

Hautecoeur, Louis. Histoire de l'architecture classique en France, v.1– . Paris, Picard, 1963– . 2 ed.

Houvet, Étienne. Cathédrale de Chartres. 7v. Chelles, Faucheux, 1919.

Howgrave-Graham, Robert P. The cathedrals of France. London, Batsford, 1959.

Hubert, Jean. L'architecture religieuse du haut moyen âge en France. Paris, Imp. Nat., 1952.

Lasteyrie du Saillant, Robert C. L'architecture religieuse en France à l'époque gothique. 2v. Paris, Picard, 1926–1927.

—— L'architecture réligieuse en France à l'époque romane. Paris, Picard, 1929. 2 ed.

Lavedan, Pierre. L'architecture française. Paris, Larousse, 1944.

Martin, Camille. L'art roman en France—l'architecture et la décoration. 2v. Paris, Eggimann, 1910–1914.

Martin, Camille and Enlart, Camille. L'art gothique en France—l'architecture et la décoration. 2v. Paris, Eggimann, 1913–1925.

Seymour, Charles. Notre-Dame of Noyon in the twelfth century. New Haven, Yale Univ., 1939.

Stoddard, Whitney S. Monastery and cathedral in France. Middletown, Wesleyan, 1966.

Suger, Abbot. On the abbey church of St. Denis and its art treasures. Trans. and comments by Erwin Panofsky, Princeton, Princeton Univ., 1946.

Viollet-le-Duc, Eugène E. Dictionnaire raisonné de l'architecture française du XI au XVI siècle. 10v. Paris, Morel, 1867–1873.

Ward, William H. The architecture of the renaissance in France. 2v. N.Y., Scribner, 1926. 2 ed.

Architecture — Germany, Austria, Switzerland, Low Countries

Brinckmann, Albert E. Stadtbaukunst. Berlin, Athenaion, 1920.

Dehio, Georg G. and Bezold, Gustav. Die kirchliche baukunst des abendlandes. 2v. Stuttgart, Cotta, 1887–1901. Hildesheim, 1966. Reprint. 8v.

Dohme, Robert. Geschichte der deutschen baukunst. Berlin, Grote, 1888.

Godefroy, J. Geschiedenis van de bouwkunst in Nederland. Amsterdam, Kosmos, 1920.

Hempel, Eberhard. Geschichte der deutschen baukunst. Munich, Bruckmann, 1956. 2 ed.

Horst, Carl. Die architecture der deutschen renaissance. Berlin, Propyläen, 1928.

Kasper, Karl. New German architecture. London, Architectural Press, 1956.

Koepf, Hans. Deutsche baukunst von der römerzeit bis zur gegenwart. 2v. Stuttgart, Deutscher Fachzeitschriften-und Fachbuch-Verlag, 1956.

Lehmann, Edgar. Der frühe deutsche kirchenbau. Berlin, Deutscher Verein f. Kunstwissenschaft, 1938.

Oswald, Friedrich and others. Vorromanische kirchenbauten. Katalog der denkmäler bis zum ausgang der Ottonen. v.1– . Munich, Prestel, 1966– .

Pinder, Wilhelm. Deutsche dome des mittelalters. Königstein im Taunus, Langewiesche, 1941.

____Deutscher barock; die grossen baumeister des 18 jahrhunderts. Königstein im Taunus, Langewiesche, 1940.

Platz, Gustav A. Die baukunst der neuestein zeit. Berlin, Propyläen, 1927.

Popp, Hermann. Die architektur der barock und rokokozeit im Deutschland und der Schweiz. Stuttgart, Hoffmann, 1913.

Rittich, Werner. Architektur und bauplastik der gegenwart. Berlin, Rembrandt, 1944. 3 ed.

Sedlmayr, Hans. Österreische barockarchitektur, 1690–1740. Vienna, Filser, 1930.

Smith, George E. K. Switzerland builds; its native and modern architecture. N.Y., Bonnier, 1950.

Stange, Alfred. Die deutsche baukunst der renaissance. Munich, Schmidt, 1926.

Vermeulen, Frans. Handboek tot de geschiedenis der Nederlandsche bouw-kunst. 3v. The Hague, Nijhoff, 1923–1941.

Wackernagel, Martin. Baukunst des 17 und 18 jahrhunderts in den german-ischen ländern. Berlin, Athenaion, 1915.

Weissman, Adriaan W. Geschiedenis der Nederlandsche bouwkunst. Amster-dam, van Looy, 1917.

Architecture – Great Britain

Blomfield, Reginald T. A history of renaissance architecture in England. 2v. London, Bell, 1897.

Bond, Francis. The cathedrals of England and Wales. N.Y., Scribner, 1912.

——Gothic architecture in England. London, Batsford, 1930.

——An introduction to English church architecture from the eleventh to the sixteenth century. 2v. London, Milford, 1913.

Britton, John. Architectural antiquities of Great Britain. 5v. London, Long-mans, 1807–1826.

——Cathedral antiquities. 5v. London, Nattali, 1836.

Clapham, Alfred W. English romanesque architecture. 2v. N.Y., Oxford, 1965.

Cox, John C. The parish churches of England. N.Y., Scribner, 1935.

Dugdale, William. Monasticon anglicanum. 6v. London, Longmans, 1817–1830.

Gardner, Alfred H. Outline of English architecture; an account for the general reader of its development from early times to the present day. London, Batsford, 1946. 2 ed.

Garner, Thomas and Stratton, Arthur. The domestic architecture of England during the Tudor period. 2v. N.Y., Scribner, 1929. 2 ed.

Godfrey, Walter H. The story of architecture in England. 2v. N.Y., Harper, 1931.

Goodhart-Rendel, Harry S. English architecture since the Regency; an inter-pretation. London, Constable, 1953.

Gotch, John A. Architecture of the renaissance in England. 2v. London, Batsford, 1894.

——Early renaissance architecture in England. London, Batsford, 1914. 2 ed.

_____The growth of the English house from early feudal times to the close of the 18th century. London, Batsford, 1928. 2 ed.

Great Britain. Royal Commission on the ancient and historical monuments. Inventory, v.1- . London, HMSO, 1911- .

Harvey, John D. An introduction to Tudor architecture. London, Art and Technics, 1949.

Hitchcock, Henry-Russell. Early Victorian architecture in Britain. 2v. New Haven, Yale Univ., 1954.

Lloyd, Nathaniel. A history of the English house from primitive times to the Victorian period. London, Architectural Press, 1949.

MacGibbon, David and Ross, Thomas. The castellated and domestic architecture of Scotland from the twelfth to the eighteenth century. 5v. Edinburgh, Douglas, 1887–1892.

Moore, Charles H. The medieval church architecture of England. N.Y., Macmillan, 1912.

Nash, Joseph. Mansions of England in the olden time. 4v. London, Heinemann, 1912.

Pilcher, Donald. The Regency style, 1800–1830. London, Batsford, 1947.

Prior, Edward S. A history of Gothic art in England. London, Bell, 1900.

Reilly, Paul. An introduction to Regency architecture. N.Y., Pellegrini, 1948.

Richardson, Albert E. An introduction to Georgian architecture. London, Art and Technics, 1949.

Sitwell, Sacheverell. British architects and craftsmen; a survey of taste, design and style during three centuries, 1600–1840. London, Batsford, 1948. 4 ed.

Stoll, Robert. Architecture and sculpture in early Britain; Celtic, Saxon and Norman. N.Y., Viking, 1967. A translation of Britannica romanica.

Summerson, John N. Architecture in Britain, 1530–1830. London, Penguin, 1963.

_____Georgian London. N.Y., Scribner, 1946.

*_____Heavenly mansions. N.Y., Norton, 1963.

Tallmadge, Thomas E. The story of England's architecture. N.Y., Norton, 1934.

Taylor, Harold M. and Taylor, Joan. Anglo-Saxon architecture. 2v. Cambridge, Cambridge Univ., 1965.

Tipping, Henry A. English homes. 9v. London, Country Life, 1921–1937. Reprint 1955–1958.

Turner, Reginald. Nineteenth century architecture in Britain. London, Batsford, 1950.

Webb, Geoffrey. Architecture in Britain; the middle ages. London, Penguin, 1966. 2 ed.

Architecture – Italy

Anderson, William J. The architecture of the renaissance in Italy. London, Batsford, 1927. 5 ed.

Baum, Julius. Baukunst und dekorative plastik der frührenaissance in Italien. Stuttgart, Hoffmann, 1920.

Brinckmann, Albert E. Die baukunst des 17 und 18 jahrhunderts in den romanischen ländern. 2v. Berlin, Athenaion, 1919–1920.

Cummings, Charles A. A history of architecture in Italy from the time of Constantine to the dawn of the renaissance. 2v. Boston, Houghton, 1927.

Delogu, Giuseppe. Italienische baukunst; eine anthologie vom 11 bis 19 jahrhundert. Zurich, Fretz, 1947.

Frey, Dagobert. Architecture of the renaissance from Brunelleschi to Michelangelo. The Hague, Naeff, 1925.

Gromort, Georges. Italian renaissance architecture. Trans. by G. F. Waters. Paris, Vincent, 1922.

Letarouilly, Paul M. Édifices de Rome moderne. 4v. Paris, Morel, 1868–1874.

Meeks, Carroll V. Italian architecture, 1750–1914. New Haven, Yale Univ., 1967.

Pagani, Carlo. Architettura italiana oggi; Italy's architecture today. N.Y., Heinemann, 1955.

Porter, A. Kingsley. Lombard architecture. 4v. New Haven, Yale Univ., 1915–1917. N.Y., Hacker, 1967. Reprint.

Ricci, Corrado. Architecture and decorative sculpture of the high and late renaissance in Italy. N.Y., Brentano, 1923.

——Baroque architecture and sculpture in Italy. Stuttgart, Hoffmann, 1926.

——Romanesque architecture in Italy. N.Y., Brentano, 1925.

Rivoira, Giovanni, T. Lombardic architecture. Trans. by G. M. Rushforth. 2v. London, Heinemann, 1910.

Schubring, Paul. Die architektur der italienischen frührenaissance. Munich, Schmidt, 1923.

——Die architektur der italienischen hochrenaissance. Munich, Schmidt, 1924.

Stegmann, Carl M. and Geymüller, Heinrich von. Architecture of the renaissance in Tuscany. 2v. N.Y., Architectural Pub. Co., 1924.

Willich, Hans. Die baukunst der renaissance in Italien bis zum tode Michelangelos. 2v. Berlin, Athenaion, 1924–1929.

*Wittkower, Rudolf. Architectural principles in the age of humanism. N.Y., Random, 1965.

Zürcher, Richard. Stilprobleme der italienischen baukunst des cinquecento. Basel, Holbein, 1947.

Architecture – Mexico, Latin America

Baxter, Sylvester. La arquitectura hispano colonial en México. México, D.F., 1934.

Benavides Rodriguez, Alfredo. La arquitectura en el virreinato del Perú y en la capitania general de Chile. Santiago de Chile, Ercilla, 1941.

Buschiazzo, Mario·J. Estudios de arquitectura colonial hispano america. Buenos Aires, Kraft, 1944.

Costa Torres, Raul. A arquitectura dos descobrimentos e o renascimento ibérico. Braga, Cruz, 1943.

Goodwin, Philip L. Brazil builds; architecture old and new, 1652–1942. N.Y., Museum of Modern Art, 1943.

Kubler, George. Mexican architecture of the sixteenth century. 2v. New Haven, Yale Univ., 1948.

Marquina, Ignacio. Arquitectura prehispanica. Mexico City, Inst. Nac. de Antropologia e Historia, 1951.

Mindlin, Henrique E. Modern architecture in Brazil. N.Y., Reinhold, 1956.

Palm, Erwin W. Los monumentos arquitectónicos de la Española. 2v. Trujillo, Univ. de Santo Domingo, 1955.

Sanford, Trent E. The story of architecture in Mexico. N.Y., Norton, 1947.

Toussaint, Manuel. Tres siglos de arquitectura colonial. Mexico City, Porrua, 1933.

Wethey, Harold E. Colonial architecture and sculpture in Peru. Cambridge, Harvard Univ., 1949.

Architecture – Russia

Buxton, David. Russian medieval architecture; with an account of the Transcaucasian styles and their influence in the West. Cambridge, Cambridge Univ., 1934.

Eliasberg, Alexander. Russische baukunst. Munich, Müller, 1922.
Voyce, Arthur. The Moscow Kremlin. Berkeley, Univ. of California, 1954.
_____Russian architecture; trends in nationalism and modernism. N.Y., Philosophical Lib., 1948.

Architecture – Scandinavia

Langberg, Harald. Danmarks bygningskultur, en historisk oversight. 2v.
Copenhagen, Nordisk Forlag, 1955.
Lundberg, Erik. Byggnadskonsten i Sverige. 2v. Stockholm, Nordisk
Rotogravyr, 1940–1948.
Redslob, Edwin. Alt Dänemark. Munich, Delphin, 1922. 3 ed.
Smith, George E. K. Sweden builds; its modern architecture and land policy,
background, development and contribution. N.Y., Bonnier, 1950.

Architecture – Spain, Portugal

Bevan, Bernard. History of Spanish architecture. N.Y., Scribner, 1939.
Byne, Arthur and Byne, Mildred Stapley. Spanish architecture of the sixteenth
century; general view of the plateresque and Herrera styles. London, Putnam, 1917.
Camón Aznar, José. La arquitectura plateresca. 2v. Madrid, Aguirre, 1945.
Gómez-Moreno, Manuel. Iglesias mozárabes; arte español de los siglos IX à XI.
2v. Madrid, Centro de Estud. Hist., 1919.
Haupt, Albrecht. Baukunst der renaissance in Portugal von den zeiten Emmanuel's des glücklichen bis zu dem schlusse der spanischen herrschaft. 2v.
Frankfurt, Heller, 1890–1895.
Lambert, Élie. L'art gothique en Espagne. Paris, Laurens, 1931.
Lampérez y Romea, Vicente. Arquitectura civil española de los siglos I al
XVIII. 2v. Madrid, Saturnino Calleja, 1922–1923.
_____Historia de la arquitectura cristiana española en la edad media según el
estudio de los elementos y los monumentos. 3v. Madrid, Espasa, 1930.
2 ed.
Puig y Cadafalch, José. L'arquitectura romanica a Catalunya. 3v. Barcelona,
Inst. d'Estud. Catalans, 1934. 2 ed.

Reis Santos, Luiz. Monuments of Portugal. Lisbon, Nat. Sec. of Inform., 1940- .

Sarthou Carreres, Carlos. Cathedrales de España. Madrid, Espasa, 1946.

Watson, Walter C. Portuguese architecture. London, Constable, 1908.

Weise, Georg. Studien zur spanischen architektur der spätgotik. Reutlingen, Gryphius, 1933.

Whitehill, Walter M. Spanish romanesque architecture of the eleventh century. London, Oxford, 1941.

Architecture – United States, Canada

*Andrews, Wayne. Architecture, ambition and Americana; a history of American architecture from the beginning to the present. N.Y., Harper, 1955.

Bunting, Bainbridge. Houses of Boston's Back Bay; an architectural history, 1840-1917. Cambridge, Harvard Univ., 1967.

Condit, Carl W. American building art. 2v. N.Y., Oxford, 1960-1961.

Downing, Antoinette F. and Scully, Vincent J. The architectural heritage of Newport, Rhode Island, 1640-1915. N.Y., Potter, 1965. 2 ed.

Eberlein, Harold D. The architecture of colonial America. Boston, Little, 1927.

Edgell, George H. The American architecture of today. N.Y., Scribner, 1928.

Fitch, James M. American building; the forces that shape it. Boston, Houghton, 1948.

Forman, Henry C. The architecture of the old South. N.Y., Russell, 1948.

Gowans, Alan, Building Canada; an architectural history of Canadian life. N.Y., Oxford, 1966.

____Church architecture in New France. Toronto, Univ. of Toronto, 1956.

Hamlin, Talbot F. The American spirit in architecture. New Haven, Yale Univ., 1926.

*____Greek revival architecture in America. London, Oxford, 1944.

Historic American Buildings Survey. Catalogue of the measured drawings and photographs of the survey in the Library of Congress. Washington, Govt. Print. Office, 1941. 2 ed. N.Y., Franklin. Reprint.

Hitchcock, Henry-Russell. American architectural books; a list of books, portfolios and pamphlets on architecture and related subjects. Minneapolis, Univ. of Minnesota, 1946.

Kimball, S. Fiske. American architecture. Indianapolis, Bobbs, 1928.

*____Domestic architecture of the American colonies and of the early republic. N.Y., Scribner, 1927. N.Y., Dover, 1966.

McCallum, Ian R. M. Architecture U.S.A. N.Y., Reinhold, 1959.

Major, Howard. The domestic architecture of the early American republic, the Greek revival. Philadelphia, Lippincott, 1926.

Meeks, Carroll V. The railway station. New Haven, Yale Univ., 1956.

Mock, Elizabeth. Built in U.S.A., 1932–1944. N.Y., Museum of Modern Art, 1944.

Morrison, Hugh. Early American architecture, from the first colonial settlements to the national period. N.Y., Oxford, 1952.

Mumford, Lewis. The roots of contemporary American architecture. N.Y., Reinhold, 1952.

____The South in architecture. N.Y., Harcourt, 1941. N.Y. Plenum. Reprint.

*____Sticks and stones; a study of American architecture and civilization. N.Y., Dover, 1955. 2 ed. Reprint.

Pratt, Richard A. A treasury of early American houses. N.Y., Whittlesey, 1949.

Roos, Frank J. Writings on early American architecture; an annotated list of books and articles on architecture constructed before 1860 in the eastern half of the United States. Columbus, Ohio State, 1943.

Stotz, Charles M. The architectural heritage of early western Pennsylvania. Pittsburgh, Univ. of Pittsburgh, 1966.

Tallmadge, Thomas E. The story of architecture in America. N.Y., Norton, 1936.

Waterman, Thomas T. The dwellings of colonial America. Chapel Hill, Univ. of N.C., 1950.

SCULPTURE

General

Agard, Walter R. The new architectural sculpture. N.Y., Oxford, 1935.

Brinckmann, Albert E. Barock-bozzetti. 4v. Frankfurt am Main, Frankfurter Verlagsanstalt, 1923–1925.

——Barocksculptur. Berlin, Athenaion, 1932. 3 ed.

Busch, Harald and Lohse, Bernd. Baroque sculpture. Trans. by P. Gorge. N.Y., Macmillan, 1965.

——Gothic sculpture. Trans. by P. Gorge. N.Y., Macmillan, 1963.

Casson, Stanley. Some modern sculptors. London, Oxford, 1929.

——XXth century sculptors. N.Y., Books for Librarians, 1967. Reprint.

Chase, George H. and Post, Chandler R. A history of sculpture. N.Y., Harper, 1925.

Giedion-Welcker, Carola. Contemporary sculpture, an evolution in volume and space. N.Y., Wittenborn, 1961. 3 ed.

Hill, George F. Medals of the renaissance. Oxford, Clarendon, 1920.

Kohlbach, Rochus. Steirische bildhauer vom römerstein zum rokoko. Graz, Grazer Domverlag, 1956.

Kowalczyk, Georg. Decorative sculpture. N.Y., Weyhe, 1927.

Kuhn, Alfred. Die neuere plastik von achtzehnhundert bis zur gegenwart. Munich, Delphin, 1922. 2 ed.

Lenormant, François. Monnaies et médailles. Paris, Quantin, 1885.

Licht, Fred S. Sculpture; the nineteenth and twentieth centuries. Greenwich, NYGS, 1967.

Maryon, Herbert. Modern sculpture, its methods and ideals. London, Pitman, 1933.

Maskell, Alfred. Wood sculpture. N.Y., Putnam, 1911.

Miller, Alec. Tradition in sculpture. N.Y., Studio, 1949.

Mills, John W. The technique of sculpture. N.Y., Reinhold, 1965.

Post, Chandler R. A history of European and American sculpture from the early Christian period to the present day. 2v. Cambridge, Harvard Univ., 1921.

*Read, Herbert E. A concise history of modern sculpture. N.Y., Praeger, 1964.

Rich, Jack C. The materials and methods of sculpture. N.Y., Oxford, 1947.

Ritchie, Andrew C. Sculpture of the twentieth century. N.Y., Museum of Modern Art, 1952.

Rothschild, Lincoln. Sculpture through the ages. N.Y., Whittlesey, 1942.

Salvini, Roberto. Medieval sculpture. Greenwich, NYGS, 1967.

Schottmüller, Frida. Bronze statuetten und geräte. Berlin, Schmidt, 1921. 2 ed.

Seuphor, Michel. La sculpture de ce siècle. Neuchâtel, Griffon, 1959.

Seymour, Charles. Tradition and experiment in modern sculpture. Washington, Amer. Univ., 1949.

Sobotka, Georg. Die bildhauerei der barockzeit. Vienna, Schroll, 1927.

Taft, Lorado. Modern tendencies in sculpture. Chicago, Univ. of Chicago, 1921.

Toft, Albert. Modelling and sculpture; a full account of the various methods and processes employed in these arts. N.Y., Macmillan, 1950.

Valentiner, Wilhelm R. The origins of modern sculpture. N.Y., Wittenborn, 1946.

*Wilenski, Reginald H. The meaning of modern sculpture; an essay on some original sculpture of the present day. London, Faber, 1932.

Wilm, Hubert. Die gotische holzfigur, ihr wesen und ihre enstehung. Stuttgart, Metzler, 1944. 2 ed.

Sculpture – France

Aubert, Marcel. Le Bourgogne; la sculpture. 3v. Paris, VanOest, 1930.

──── French sculpture at the beginning of the Gothic period, 1140–1225. N.Y., Harcourt, 1929.

──── La sculpture française au moyen âge. Paris, Flammarion, 1947.

Babelon, Jean. La médaille en France. Paris, Larousse, 1948.

Benoist, Luc. La sculpture française. Paris, Larousse, 1945.

Deschamps, Paul. French sculpture of the romanesque period, eleventh and twelfth centuries. N.Y., Harcourt, 1930.

Deschamps (cont.)
____La sculpture française, époque romane. Paris, Édit. du Chêne, 1947.

Devigne, Marguerite. La sculpture mosane du XII au XVI siècle; contribution à l'étude de l'art dans la région de la Meuse moyenne. Paris, VanOest, 1932.

Gardner, Arthur. French sculpture of the thirteenth century. London, Medici Society, 1915.

____Medieval sculpture in France. Cambridge, Camb. Univ., 1931. N.Y., Russell, 1967. Reprint.

Gonse, Louis. La sculpture française depuis le XIV siècle. Paris, Libr. Imp. Réunies, 1895.

Lefrançois, Louise P. Les sculpteurs français du XII siècle. Paris, Plon, 1931.

____Les sculpteurs français du XIII siècle. Paris, Plon, 1931.

Rousseau, Henry. La sculpture aux XVII et XVIII siècles. Brussels, VanOest, 1911.

Roussel, Jules. La sculpture française. 5v. Paris, Morancé, 1927–1932.

Vitry, Paul. French sculpture during the reign of St. Louis, 1226–1270. N.Y., Harcourt, 1929.

Vitry, Paul and Brière, Gaston. Documents de sculpture française. 3v. Paris, Longuet, 1906–1911.

Sculpture – Germany, Austria, Switzerland, Low Countries

Baier-Fütterer, Ilse. Gotische bildwerke der deutschen Schweiz, 1220–1440. Augsburg, Filser, 1930.

Bange, Ernst F. Deutschen bronzestatuetten des 16 jahrhunderts. Berlin, Deut. Ver. f. Kunstwissenschaft, 1949.

____Die kleinplastik der deutschen renaissance in holz und stein. Leipzig, Schmidt, 1928.

Beenken, Hermann T. Bildhauer des vierzehnten jahrhunderts am Rhein und in Schwaben. Leipzig, Insel, 1927.

____Romanische skulptur in Deutschland (11 und 12 jahrhundert) Leipzig, Klinkhardt, 1924.

Bode, Wilhelm von. Geschichte der deutschen plastik. Berlin, Grote, 1888.

Burger, Willy. Altdeutsche holzplastik. Berlin, Schmidt, 1926.

Decker, Heinrich. Barockplastik in den Alpenländern. Vienna, Andermann, 1943.

Deonna, Waldemar. La sculpture suisse dès origines à la fin du XVI siècle. Basel, Birkhaeuser, 1946.

Feulner, Adolf. Die deutsche plastik des sechzehnten jahrhunderts. Florence, Pantheon, 1926.

_____ Die deutsche plastik des siebzehnten jahrhunderts. Florence, Pantheon, 1926.

_____ Geschichte der deutschen plastik. Munich. Bruckmann, 1953.

_____ Skulptur und malerei des 18 jahrhunderts in Deutschland. Berlin, Athenaion, 1929.

Halm, Philipp M. Studien zur süddeutsche plastik; Altbayern und Schwaben, Tirol und Salzberg. 2v. Augsburg, Filser, 1926–1927.

Jantzen, Hans. Deutsche plastik des 13 jahrhunderts. Munich, Bruckmann, 1944.

Karlinger, Hans. Die romanische steinplastik in Altbayern und Salzburg, 1050–1260. Augsburg, Filser, 1924.

Konrad, Martin. Meisterwerke der skulptur in Flandern und Brabant. Berlin, Imago, 1928.

Kuhn, Charles L. German and Netherlandish sculpture, 1280–1800. Cambridge, Harvard Univ., 1965.

Lüthgen, Eugen. Romanische plastik in Deutschland. Bonn, Schroder, 1923.

Meller, Simon. Die Deutschen bronzestatuetten der renaissance. Florence, Pantheon, 1926.

Müller, Theodor. Deutsche plastik der renaissance bis zum Dreissigjährigen Krieg. Königstein im Taunus, Langewiesche, 1963.

Panofsky, Erwin. Die deutsche plastik des elften bis dreizehnten jahrhunderts. 2v. Munich, Wolff, 1924.

Piltz, Georg. Deutsche bildhauerkunst. Berlin, Neues Leben, 1962.

Pinder, Wilhelm. Deutsche barockplastik. Königstein im Taunus, Langewiesche, 1933.

_____ Die deutsche plastik des fünfzehnten jahrhunderts. Munich, Wolff, 1924.

_____ Die deutsche plastik des vierzehnten jahrhunderts. Munich, Wolff, 1925.

_____ Die deutsche plastik vom ausgehenden mittelalter bis zum ende der renaissance. 2v. Berlin, Athenaion, 1924–1929.

Reitzenstein, Alexander. Deutsche plastik der früh-und hochgotik. Königstein im Taunus, Langewiesche, 1962.

Sauerlandt, Max. Die deutsche plastik des achtzehnten jahrhunderts. Munich, Wolff, 1926.

Schädler, Alfred. Deutsche plastik der spätgotik. Königstein im Taunus, Lange-
wiesche, 1962.
Schönberger, Arno. Deutsche plastik des barock. Königstein im Taunus, Lange-
wiesche, 1963.
Sitwell, Sacheverell. German baroque sculpture. London, Duckworth, 1938.
Wilm, Hubert. Gotische tonplastik in Deutschland. Augsburg, Filser, 1929.

Sculpture – Great Britain

Crossley, Frederick H. English church monuments, A.D. 1150–1550; an intro-
duction to the study of tombs and effigies of the medieval period. Lon-
don, Batsford, 1921.
Esdaille, Katharine A. M. English church monuments, 1510 to 1840. London,
Batsford, 1946.
_____English monumental sculpture since the renaissance. N.Y., Macmillan,
1927.
Gardner, Arthur. English medieval sculpture. Cambridge, Camb. Univ., 1951.
Prior, Edward S. and Gardner, Arthur. An account of medieval figure-
sculpture in England. Cambridge, Camb. Univ., 1912.
Saxl, Fritz. English sculptures of the twelfth century. London, Faber, 1954.
Stone, Lawrence. Sculpture in Britain; the middle ages. London, Penguin,
1955.
Whinney, Margaret D. Sculpture in Britain; 1530–1850. London, Penguin,
1964.
Zarnecki, George. English romanesque sculpture, 1066–1140. London,
Tiranti, 1951.
_____Later English romanesque sculpture, 1140–1210. London, Tiranti, 1953.

Sculpture – Italy

Armand, Alfred. Les médailleurs italiens des quinzième et seizième siècles. 3v.
Paris, Plon, 1883–1887. 2 ed.
Baroni, Costantino. Sculptura gotica lombarda. Milan, Bestetti, 1944.
Biehl, Walther. Toskanische plastik des frühen und hohen mittelalters. Leip-
zig, Seemann, 1926.

Bode, Wilhelm von. Denkmäler der renaissance-sculptur Toscanas. 12v. Munich, Bruckmann, 1892–1905.

——Florentine sculptors of the renaissance. Trans. by F. L. R. Brown, London, Methuen, 1928.

——Italian bronze statuettes of the renaissance. Trans. by William Grétor. 3v. London, Grevel, 1908–1912.

Crawford, David, A. E. L. The evolution of Italian sculpture. London, Murray, 1909.

Crichton, George H. Romanesque sculpture in Italy. London, Routledge, 1954.

Davies, Gerald S. Renascence; the sculptured tombs of the fifteenth century in Rome, with chapters on the previous centuries from 1100. London, Murray, 1900.

Delogu, Giuseppe. Italienische bildhauerei; eine anthologie vom 12 bis 19 jahrhundert. Zurich, Fretz, 1942.

Fabriczy, Cornelius von. Italian medals. Trans. by Mrs. G. W. Hamilton. London, Duckworth, 1904.

Galassi, Giuseppe. La scultura fiorentina del quattrocento. Milan, Hoepli, 1949.

Habich, Georg. Die medaillen der italienischen renaissance. Stuttgart, Deutsche Verlags-Anstalt, 1924.

Haseloff, Arthur E. G. Pre-Romanesque sculpture in Italy. N.Y., Harcourt, 1931.

Hill, George F. A corpus of Italian medals of the renaissance before Cellini. 2v. London, British Museum, 1930.

Jullian, René. L'éveil de la sculpture italienne. 2v. Paris, VanOest, 1945–1950.

Lankheit, Klaus. Florentinische barockplastik; die kunst am hofe der letzten Medici, 1670–1743. Munich, Bruckmann, 1962.

Maclagan, Eric R. D. Italian sculpture of the renaissance. Cambridge, Harvard Univ., 1935.

Mayer, August L. Mittelalterliche plastik in Italien. Munich, Delphin, 1923.

Planiscig, Leo. Piccoli bronzi italiani del rinascimento. Milan, Treves, 1930.

——Venezianische bildhauer der renaissance. Vienna, Schroll, 1921.

Pope-Hennessy, John. Introduction to Italian sculpture. 3v. N.Y., Phaidon, 1955–1962.

Reymond, Marcel. La sculpture florentine. 4v. Florence, Alinari, 1897–1900.

Salmi, Mario. Scultura romanica in Toscana. Florence, Rinascimento del Libro, 1928.

Schubring, Paul. Italienische plastik des quattrocento. Berlin, Athenaion, 1924.

Seymour, Charles. Sculpture in Italy, 1400–1500. London, Penguin, 1967.

Waters, William G. Italian sculptors. London, Methuen, 1926. 2 ed.

Wiles, Bertha H. The fountains of the Florentine sculptors and their followers from Donatello to Bernini. Cambridge, Harvard Univ., 1933.

Sculpture – Spain, Portugal, Latin America

Gaillard, Georges. Les débuts de la sculpture romane espagnole; Leon, Jaca, Compostelle. Paris, Hartmann, 1938.

Gómez-Moreno, Manuel. The golden age of Spanish sculpture. Greenwich, NYGS, 1964.

Mayer, August L. Mittelalterliche plastik in Spanien. Munich, Delphin, 1922.

____Spanische barock-plastik. Munich, Riehn, 1923.

Pillement, Georges. La sculpture baroque espagnole. Paris, Michel, 1945.

Porter, A. Kingsley. Spanish romanesque sculpture. 2v. Florence, Pantheon, 1928.

Proske, Beatrice. Castilian sculpture, Gothic to renaissance. N.Y., Hispanic Society, 1951.

Weise, Georg. Die plastik der renaissance und des frühbarock in nördlichen Spanien; Aragón, Navarra, die Baskischen provinzen und die Rioja. v.1– . Tübingen, Hopfer, 1957– .

____Spanische plastik aus sieben jahrhunderten. 4v. Reutlingen, Gryphus, 1925-1939.

Weismann, Elizabeth W. Mexico in sculpture, 1521–1821. Cambridge, Harvard Univ., 1950.

Sculpture – United States

Gardner, Albert Ten Eyck. American sculpture. Greenwich, NYGS, 1964.

____Yankee stonecutters; the first American school of sculpture, 1800–1850. N.Y., Columbia Univ., 1945.

Ludwig, Allen I. Graven images; New England stone-carving and its symbols, 1650–1815. Middletown, Wesleyan Univ., 1966.

Schnier, Jacques P. Sculpture in modern America. Berkeley, Univ. of California, 1948.

Taft, Lorado. The history of American sculpture. N.Y., Macmillan, 1930.

PAINTING

General

Abbot, Edith R. The great painters in relation to the European tradition. N.Y., Harcourt, 1927.

*Apollinaire, Guillaume. The cubist painters; aesthetic meditations, 1913. Trans. by Lionel Abel. N.Y., Wittenborn, 1949. 2 ed.

Argan, Giulio C. and Lassaigne, Jacques. The fifteenth century; from Van Eyck to Botticelli. Cleveland, World (Skira), 1955.

Barr, Alfred H. Cubism and abstract art. N.Y., Museum of Modern Art, 1936.

____Fantastic art, Dada, surrealism. N.Y., Museum of Modern Art, 1936.

____Masters of modern art. N.Y., Museum of Modern Art, 1954.

*____What is modern painting? N.Y., Museum of Modern Art, 1953.

Bell, Clive. Landmarks in nineteenth century painting. N.Y., Harcourt, 1927.

____Since Cézanne. N.Y., Harcourt, 1928.

Boehn, Max von. Miniaturen und silhouetten, ein kapital aus kulturgeschichte und kunst. Munich, Bruckmann, 1917. 3 ed.

Cheney, Sheldon. Expressionism in art. N.Y., Boni, 1958.

*Clark, Kenneth M. Landscape into art. London, Murray, 1952. Alternate title: Landscape painting.

*Constable, William G. The painter's workshop. London, Oxford, 1954.

Davenport, Cyril J. H. Miniatures, ancient and modern. Chicago, McClurg, 1908.

Diringer, David. The illuminated book; its history and production. N.Y., Praeger, 1967. 2 ed.

Dorival, Bernard. Twentieth century painters. 2v. N.Y., Universe, 1958.

*Duthuit, Georges. The fauvist painters. N.Y., Wittenborn, 1950.

*Friedländer, Max J. Art and connoisseurship. London, Cassirer, 1942.

Friedländer (cont.)

____Genuine and counterfeit. Trans. by C. van Honstett and L. Pelham. N.Y., Boni, 1930.

*____Landscape, portrait, still-life; their origin and development. Trans. by R. F. C. Hull, N.Y., Schocken, 1963.

Gardner, Albert Ten Eyck. A history of watercolor painting in America, v.1- . N.Y., Reinhold, 1966- .

Golding, John. Cubism; a history and an analysis, 1907–1914. London, Faber, 1959.

*Goldwater, Robert J. Primitivism in modern painting. N.Y., Harper, 1938.

Gowans, Alan. The restless art; a history of painters and painting, 1760–1960. Philadelphia, Lippincott, 1966.

Gudiol i Cunill, Josep. Els primitius. 3v. Barcelona, Babra, 1927–1955.

*Haftmann, Werner. Painting in the twentieth century. 2v. N.Y., Praeger, 1965.

Hauser, Arnold. Mannerism; the crisis of the renaissance and the origin of modern art. 2v. N.Y., Knopf, 1965.

Heath, Dudley. Miniatures. N.Y., Putnam, 1905.

Herbert, John A. Illuminated manuscripts. London, Methuen, 1912. N.Y., Franklin. Reprint.

Huyghe, René. Les contemporains. Notices biographiques par Germain Bazin. Paris, Tisné, 1949.

____Histoire de l'art contemporain; la peinture. Paris, Alcan, 1934.

Jakovsky, Anatole. Peintres naïfs; a dictionary of primitive painters. N.Y., Universe, 1967.

Johnston, Edward. Writing, illuminating and lettering. N.Y., Pitman, 1944.

Kahnweiler, Daniel-H. The rise of cubism. Trans. by Henry Aronson, N.Y., Wittenborn, 1949.

Leroquais, Victor. Les breviaires. 6v. Paris, Macon, 1934.

____Les livres d'heures. 3v. Paris, Macon, 1927.

____Les pontificaux manuscrits. 4v. Paris, Macon, 1937.

____Les psautiers. 3v. Paris, Macon, 1940–1941.

____Les sacramentaires et les missels. 4v. Paris, Macon, 1924.

*Levey, Michael. From rococo to revolution; major trends in eighteenth century painting. N.Y., Praeger, 1966.

Leymarie, Jean. Impressionism. Trans. by J. Emmons. 2v. Cleveland, World (Skira), 1955.

Mather, Frank J. Modern painting. N.Y., Doubleday, 1934.

____Western European painting of the renaissance. N.Y., Cooper, 1966.

Motherwell, Robert. The Dada painters and poets. N.Y., Wittenborn, 1951.

Muther, Richard. The history of modern painting to the end of the nineteenth century. 4v. London, Dent, 1907.

Myers, Bernard. Modern art in the making. N.Y., McGraw, 1959. 2 ed.

*Nadeau, Maurice. The history of surrealism. N.Y., Macmillan, 1965.

*Newton, Eric. European painting and sculpture. N.Y., Barnes, 1961.

Ponente, Nello. Modern painting; contemporary trends. Cleveland, World (Skira), 1966.

Pope-Hennessy, John. The portrait in the renaissance. Princeton, Princeton Univ., 1967.

*Rathbun, Mary C. and Hayes, Bartlett H. A layman's guide to modern art; painting for a scientific age. N.Y., McKay, 1954.

Raynal, Maurice. Modern painting. Cleveland, World (Skira), 1956.

_____Nineteenth century painting from Goya to Gauguin. Cleveland, World (Skira), 1952.

*Read, Herbert E. A concise history of modern painting. N.Y., Praeger, 1959.

_____Surrealism. N.Y., Harcourt, 1936.

Réau, Louis. Histoire de la peinture au moyen âge (la miniature) v.1- . Melun, Libr. d'Argences, 1946- .

Reinach, Salomon. Répertoire de peintures du moyen âge et de la renaissance. 6v. Paris, Leroux, 1905–1923.

Rewald, John. The history of impressionism. N.Y., Doubleday, 1961.

_____Post-impressionism from Van Gogh to Gauguin. N.Y., Doubleday, 1958.

*Richter, Hans. Dada; art and anti-art. N.Y., McGraw, 1965.

Robb, David M. The Harper history of painting; the occidental tradition. N.Y., Harper, 1951.

Smyth, Craig H. Mannerism and maniera. Locust Valley, Augustin, 1962.

Soby, James T. After Picasso. N.Y., Dodd, 1935.

_____Contemporary painters. N.Y., Museum of Modern Art, 1948.

Stefănescu, Ioan D. Évolution de la peinture religieuse en Bucovine et en Moldavie dépuis les origines jusqu'au XIX siècle. 2v. Paris, Geuthner, 1928–1929.

Sterling, Charles. Les peintres primitifs. Paris, Nathan, 1949.

Sullivan, Edward. The Book of Kells. London, Studio, 1952. 5 ed.

Swarzenski, Hanns. Vorgotische miniaturen; die ersten jahrhunderts deutscher malerei. Königstein im Taunus, Langewiesche, 1931. 2 ed.

Sweeney, James J. Plastic redirections in twentieth century painting. Chicago, Univ. of Chicago, 1934.

Uhde, Wilhelm. The impressionists. Vienna, Phaidon, 1937.

Venturi, Lionello. Les archives de l'impressionisme. 2v. N.Y., Durand-Ruel, 1939. N.Y., Franklin. Reprint.

____Impressionists and symbolists. Trans. by F. Steegmuller. N.Y., Scribner, 1950.

____Modern painters. N.Y., Scribner, 1947.

*____Painting and painters; how to look at a picture, from Giotto to Chagall. Cleveland, World, 1945.

*Waldberg, Patrick. Surrealism. N.Y., McGraw, 1966.

Weitzmann, Kurt. Illustrations in roll and codex; a study of the origin and method of text illustration. Princeton, Princeton Univ., 1947.

Weitzmann, Kurt and others. A treasury of icons; sixth to seventeenth centuries, from the Sinai Peninsula, Greece, Bulgaria and Yugoslavia. N.Y., Abrams, 1966.

Williamson, George C. The history of portrait miniatures. 2v. London, Bell, 1904.

Zimmermann, Ernst H. Vorkarolingische miniaturen. 5v. Berlin, Deutscher Verein f. Kunstwissenschaft, 1916.

*Zucker, Paul. Styles in painting; a comparative study. N.Y., Viking, 1950.

Painting – Technique and Theory

Berger, Ernst. Beiträge zur entwickelungsgeschichte der maltechnik. 5v. Munich, Callway, 1904–1909.

*Cennini, Cennino. Il libro dell'arte. 2v. (v.2 – The craftsman's handbook. Trans. by D. V. Thompson.) New Haven, Yale, 1932–1933. N.Y., Dover, 1960.

Chevreul, Michel E. The principles of harmony and contrasts of color. N.Y., Reinhold, 1966. Reprint.

Doerner, Max. The materials of the artist and their use in painting, with notes on the techniques of the old masters. Trans. by E. Neuhaus. N.Y., Harcourt, 1949.

*Eastlake, Charles L. Materials for a history of oil painting. 2v. London, Longmans, 1847–1869.

Evans, Ralph M. An introduction to color. N.Y., Wiley, 1948.

*Gettens, Rutherford J. and Stout, George L. Painting materials, a short encyclopedia. N.Y., Van Nostrand, 1942. N.Y., Dover, 1965.

Holmes, Charles J. Notes on the science of picture-making. London, Chatto, 1923.

Hubbard, Eric. Materia pictoria; an encyclopedia of methods in painting and the graphic arts. v.1– . London, Pitman, 1948– . 2 ed.

Johnson, Charles. The language of painting. Cambridge, Cambridge Univ,, 1949.

Laurie, Arthur P. The materials of the painter's craft in Europe and Egypt from earliest times to the end of the XVIIth century. Philadelphia, Lippincott, 1911.

____The painter's methods and materials; the handling of pigments in oil, tempera, water-colour and in mural painting. Philadelphia, Lippincott, 1926.

____The technique of the great painters. London, Carroll, 1949.

Luckiesh, Matthew. Color and its applications. N.Y., Van Nostrand, 1927.

Mayer, Ralph. The artist's handbook of materials and techniques. N.Y., Viking, 1957.

____The painter's craft; an introduction to artists' materials. N.Y., Van Nostrand, 1966. 2 ed.

*****Merrifield, Mary P.** Original treatises, dating from the XIIth to XVIIIth centuries on the arts of painting in oil, miniature, mosaic, and on glass. 2v. London, Murray, 1849.

Munsell, Albert H. A color notation; an illustrated system defining all colors and their relations by measured scales of hue, value and chroma. Baltimore, Munsell, 1946. 10 ed.

Ostwald, Wilhelm. Colour science; a handbook for advanced students in schools, colleges, and the various arts, crafts and industries depending on the use of colour. 2v. London, Winsor, 1931–1933.

Plenderleith, Harold J. The conservation of antiquities and works of art; treatment, repair and restoration. London, Oxford Univ., 1956.

Pope, Arthur. The language of drawing and painting. Cambridge, Harvard Univ., 1949.

Ross, Denman W. On drawing and painting. Boston, Houghton, 1922.

____The painter's palette; a theory of tone relations, an instrument of expression. Boston, Houghton, 1919.

____A theory of pure design; harmony, balance, rhythm. Boston, Houghton, 1907.

Schmid, Frederic. The practice of painting. London, Faber, 1948.

Stout, George L. The care of pictures. N.Y., Columbia Univ., 1948.

*Thompson, Daniel V. The materials of medieval painting. New Haven, Yale
   Univ., 1936.
*____The practice of tempera painting. New Haven, Yale Univ., 1936.
 Toch, Maximilian. The chemistry and technology of paintings. N.Y., Van
   Nostrand, 1925. 3 ed.
____Paint, paintings and restoration. N.Y., Van Nostrand, 1945. 2 ed.
Wild, Angenitus M. de. The scientific examination of pictures; an investiga-
   tion of the pigments used by the Dutch and Flemish masters. Trans. by
   L. C. Jackson. London, Bell, 1929.
Worringer, Wilhelm. Die anfänge der tafelmalerei. Leipzig, Insel, 1924.

Painting – Canada

Buchanan, Donald W. Canadian painters from Paul Kane to the Group of
   Seven. London, Phaidon, 1945.
____The growth of Canadian painting. London, Collins, 1950.
Harper, J. Russell. Painting in Canada; a history. Toronto, Univ. of Toronto,
   1966.
Housser, F. B. A Canadian art movement; the story of the Group of Seven.
   Toronto, Macmillan, 1926.

Painting – France

Barnes, Albert C. and DeMazia, Violette. The French primitives and their
   forms from their origin to the end of the fifteenth century. Merion,
   Barnes Foundation, 1931.
Bell, Clive. An account of French painting. London, Chatto, 1931.
Blum, André and Lauer, Philippe. La miniature française au XV et XVI siècles.
   Paris, VanOest, 1930.
Bouchot, Henri. Les primitifs français, 1292–1500; complément documentaire
   au catalogue officiel de l'exposition. Paris, Libr. d'Art, 1904.
Chatelet, Albert and Thuillier, Jacques. French Painting. v.1– . Cleveland,
   World (Skira), 1963– .
Crespelle, Jean-Paul. The Fauves. Greenwich, NYGS, 1962.
Diderot, Denis. Salons. Ed. by Jean Adhémar and Jean Seznec. 4v. N.Y., Ox-
   ford, 1957–1967.

Dimier, Louis. French painting in the sixteenth century. N.Y., Scribner, 1911.

——Histoire de la peinture de portrait en France au XVI siècle. 3v. Paris, VanOest, 1924–1926.

——Histoire de la peinture française au XIX siècle, 1793–1890; avec un epilogue allant jusqu'à nos jours. Paris, Delagrave, 1926. 2 ed.

——Les peintres français du XVIII siècle; histoire des vies et catalogue des oeuvres. 2v. Paris, VanOest, 1928–1930.

Dimier, Louis and Réau, Louis. Histoire de la peinture française depuis les origines jusqu'à David. 5v. Paris, VanOest, 1925–1927.

Dorival, Bernard. Les étapes de peinture française contemporaine. 3v. Paris, Gallimard, 1943–1946.

——La peinture française. 2v. Paris, Larousse, 1942.

Escholier, Raymond. La peinture française, XIX siècle. 2v. Paris, Floury, 1941–1943.

——La peinture française, XX siècle. Paris, Floury, 1937.

Florisoone, Michel. Le dix-huitième siècle; la peinture française. Paris, Tisné, 1948.

Friedländer, Walter F. From David to Delacroix. Cambridge, Harvard Univ., 1953.

Gauss, Charles E. The aesthetic theories of French artists, 1855 to the present. Baltimore, Johns Hopkins, 1950.

Goncourt, Edmond and Jules de. French eighteenth century painters. Trans. by Robin Ironside. N.Y., Phaidon, 1948.

Guiffrey, Jean and Marcel, Pierre. Le peinture française; les primitifs. 2v. Paris, Eggiman, 1913–1925.

Hunter, Sam. Modern French painting, 1855–1956. N.Y., Dell, 1956.

Jamot, Paul. La peinture en France. Paris, Plon, 1934.

Jewell, Edward A. French impressionists and their contemporaries represented in American collections. N.Y., Hyperion, 1944.

Laver, James. French painting and the nineteenth century. N.Y., Scribner, 1937.

Lemoisne, Paul A. Gothic painting in France, fourteenth and fifteenth centuries. N.Y., Harcourt, 1931.

Leroy, Alfred. Évolution de la peinture française dès origines à nos jours. Paris, Horizons, 1943.

——Histoire de la peinture française (1800–1933) son évolution et ses maîtres. Paris, Michel, 1934.

Leroy (cont.)

———Histoire de la peinture française au moyen âge et à la renaissance, son évolution et ses maitres. Paris, Michel, 1937.

Martin, Henry M. R. La miniature française du XIII au XV siècle. Paris, Van-Oest, 1924. 2 ed.

Meiss, Millard. French painting in the time of Jean de Berry. 2v. N.Y., Phaidon, 1967.

Michel, Paul H. Romanesque wall paintings in France. Paris, Édit. du Chêne, 1949.

Nacenta, Raymond. The School of Paris; the painters and the artistic climate since 1910. Greenwich, NYGS, 1965. 2 ed.

Réau, Louis. French painting in the XIV, XV, and XVI centuries. Trans. by Mary Chamot. London, Hyperion, 1939.

Ring, Grete. A century of French painting, 1400–1500. London, Phaidon, 1949.

Rocheblave, Samuel. French painting in the XVIIIth century. Trans. by G. F. Lees. London, Commodore, 1936.

———French painting of the nineteenth century. Trans. by Douglas Lord. London, Commodore, 1936.

Sloane, Joseph C. French painting between the past and the present; artists, critics and traditions from 1848 to 1870. Princeton, Princeton Univ., 1951.

Sterling, Charles. La peinture française; les peintres du moyen âge. Paris, Tisné, 1942.

Terrasse, Charles. French painting in the XXth century. Trans. by E. B. Shaw. N.Y., Hyperion, 1939.

Thomson, David C. The Barbizon school of painters: Corot, Rousseau, Diaz, Millet, Daubigny, etc. London, Chapman, 1902.

Troescher, Georg. Burgundische malerei; maler und malerwerke um 1400 in Burgund, dem Bery mit der Auvergne und in Savoyen mit ihren quellen und ausstrahlungen. 2v. Berlin, Mann, 1966.

Wilenski, Reginald H. French painting. Boston, Branford, 1949.

*———Modern French painters. N.Y., Harcourt, 1963.

Painting – Germany, Austria

Benesch, Otto. German painting from Dürer to Holbein. Trans. by H. S. B. Harrison. Cleveland, World (Skira), 1966.

Burger, Fritz. Die deutsche malerei vom ausgehenden mittelalter bis zum ende der renaissance. 3v. Berlin, Athenaion, 1913–1922.

Deusch, Werner R. Deutsche malerei des dreizehnten und vierzehnten jahrhunderts; die frühzeit der tafelmalerei. Berlin, Genius, 1940.

_____Deutsche malerei des fünfzehnten jahrhunderts; die malerei der spätgotik. Berlin, Wolff, 1936.

_____Deutsche malerei des sechzehnten jahrhunderts; die malerei der Dürerzeit. Berlin, Wolff, 1935.

_____Malerei der deutschen romantiker und ihrer zeitgenossen. Berlin, Wolff, 1937.

Dickinson, Helena A. S. German masters of art. N.Y., Stokes, 1914.

Drost, Willi. Barockmalerei in den germanischen ländern. Berlin, Athenaion, 1927.

Fischer, Otto. Geschichte der deutsche malerei. Munich, Bruckmann, 1943.

Glaser, Curt. Die altdeutsche malerei. Munich, Bruckmann, 1924.

_____Les peintres primitifs allemands du milieu du XIV siècle à la fin du XV. Paris, VanOest, 1931.

Goering, Max. Deutsche malerei des siebzehnten und achtzehnten jahrhunderts, von dem manieristen bis zum klassizismus. Berlin, Genius, 1940.

Goldschmidt, Adolph. German illumination. 2v. N.Y., Harcourt, 1928.

Hamann, Richard. Die deutsche malerei im 19 jahrhundert. Leipzig, Teubner, 1914.

_____Die deutsche malerei vom rokoko bis zum expressionismus. Leipzig, Teubner, 1925.

Heise, Carl G. Norddeutsche malerei; studien zu ihrer entwicklungsgeschichte im 15 jahrhundert von Köln bis Hamburg. Leipzig, Wolff, 1918.

Kuhn, Charles L. German expressionism and abstract art. Cambridge, Harvard Univ., 1957

*Myers, Bernard. The German Expressionists, a generation in revolt. N.Y., McGraw, 1963.

Pataky, Dénes. Eight centuries of Hungarian drawings and water colors. Greenwich, NYGS, 1965.

Pevsner, Nikolaus. Barockmalerei in den romanische ländern. Berlin, Athenaion, 1928.

Rave, Paul O. Deutsche malerei des 19 jahrhunderts. Berlin, Mann, 1949.

Selz, Peter. German expressionist painting. Berkeley, Univ. of California, 1957.

Stange, Alfred. Deutsche malerei der gotik, v.1– . Berlin, Deutscher Kunstver-
lag, 1934– .
——German painting, XIV–XVI centuries. N.Y., Macmillan, 1950.
Winkler, Friedrich. Altdeutsche tafelmalerei. Munich, Bruckmann, 1941.

Painting – Great Britain

Baker, Charles H. C. British painting. London, Medici Society, 1933.
Baker, Charles H. C. and Constable, William G. Fnglish painting of the six-
teenth and seventeenth centuries. N.Y., Harcourt, 1930.
Binyon, Laurence. English water-colours. N.Y., Barnes, 1962. 2 ed.
Borenius, Tancred. English painting in the XVIII century. Paris, Hyperion,
1938.
Borenius, Tancred and Tristram, Ernest W. English medieval painting. N.Y.,
Harcourt, 1929.
Cundall, Herbert M. A history of British water-colour painting, with a bio-
graphical list of painters. London, Murray, 1908.
Cursiter, Stanley. Scottish art to the close of the nineteenth century. London,
Harrap, 1949.
Fergusson, John D. Modern Scottish painting. Glasgow, MacLellan, 1943.
Fredeman, William E. Pre-Raphaelitism; a bibliocritical study. Cambridge, Har-
vard Univ., 1965.
Fry, Roger E. Reflections on British painting. N.Y., Macmillan, 1934.
Grant, Maurice H. A chronological history of the old English landscape
painters (in oil) from the XVIth century to the XIX century (describing
more than 500 painters). 2v. London, Grant, 1926.
Hardie, Martin. Water-colour painting in Britain. v.1– . N.Y., Barnes, 1966– .
Ironside, Robin. Pre-Raphaelite painters. London, Phaidon, 1948.
Johnson, Charles. English painting from the seventh century to the present
day. London, Bell, 1932.
Long, Basil S. British miniaturists, 1520–1860. N.Y., Saifer, reprint.
Masai, François. Essai sur les origines de la miniature dite irlandaise. Brussels,
Erasmus, 1947.
Micheli, Géneviève. L'enluminure du haut moyen âge et les influences
irlandaises. Brussels, Connaissance, 1939.
Millar, Eric G. English illuminated manuscripts from the Xth to the XIIIth
century. Paris, VanOest, 1926.

Millar (cont.)

_____English illuminated manuscripts of the XIVth and XVth centuries. Paris, VanOest, 1928.

Oakeshott, Walter F. The sequence of English medieval art, illustrated chiefly from illuminated manuscripts, 650–1450. London, Faber, 1950.

Redgrave, Richard. A century of British painters. London, Phaidon, 1947.

Reynolds, Graham. Victorian painting. N.Y., Macmillan, 1966.

Rickert, Margaret. Painting in Britain; the middle ages. London, Pelican, 1965. 2 ed.

Ritchie, Andrew C. Masters of British painting. N.Y., Doubleday, 1958.

Rothenstein, John. An introduction to English painting. N.Y., Norton, 1967.

Saunders, O. Elfrida. English illumination. 2v. Florence, Pantheon, 1928.

Smith, Bernard. Australian painting, 1788–1960. London, Oxford, 1962.

Tristram, Ernest W. English medieval wall painting. 3v. London, Oxford, 1944–1950.

_____English wall painting of the fourteenth century. London, Routledge, ·1955.

Walpole, Horace. Ancedotes of painting in England, with some account of the principal artists; and incidental notes on other arts, collected by the late George Vertue. 5v. Strawberry Hill, Farmer, 1762–1771.

_____Anecdotes of painting in England, 1760–1795, with some account of the principal artists, published from his original manuscripts by Frederick W. Hilles and Philip B. Daglian. New Haven, Yale Univ., 1937.

Waterhouse, Ellis K. Painting in Britain, 1530–1790. London, Pelican, 1953.

Whitley, William T. Art in England, 1800–1820. Cambridge, Cambridge Univ., 1928.

_____Art in England, 1821–1837. Cambridge, Cambridge Univ., 1930.

_____Artists and their friends in England, 1700–1799. 2v. London, Medici Society, 1928.

Wilenski, Reginald H. English painting. London, Faber, 1943.

Painting – Italy

Ancona, Paola d'. La miniatura fiorentina (secoli XI–XVI). 2v. Florence, Olschki, 1914.

_____La miniature italienne du X au XVI siècle. Trans. by P. Poirier. Paris, VanOest, 1925.

Ancona (cont.)

____Les primitifs italiens du XI au XIII siècle. Paris, Éditions d'Art et d'Hist., 1935.

Antal, Frederick. Florentine painting and its social background; the bourgeois republic before Cosimo de' Medici's advent to power: XIV and early XV centuries. London, Kegan Paul, 1948.

Ballo, Guido. Modern Italian painting from futurism to the present day. N.Y., Praeger, 1958.

Bercken, Erich von der. Malerei der renaissance in Italien. Berlin, Athenaion, 1927.

*__Berenson, Bernard__. The Italian painters of the renaissance. N.Y., Phaidon, 1957.

____Italian pictures of the renaissance; a list of the principal artists and their works. Oxford, Clarendon, 1932.

____Italian pictures of the renaissance; the Florentine school. 2v. N.Y., Phaidon, 1963.

____Italian pictures of the renaissance; the Venetian school. 2v. London, Phaidon, 1957.

*____The study and criticism of Italian art. 3v. London, Bell, 1914–1930. N.Y., Schocken, 1962. 2v.

      v.1 – The sense of quality.

      v.2 – Rudiments of connoisseurship.

____Three essays in method. Oxford, Clarendon, 1927.

Borenius, Tancred. Florentine frescoes. London, Jack, 1930.

Borsook, Eve. The mural painters of Tuscany. N.Y., Phaidon, 1960.

Brandi, Cesare. Quattrocentisti senesi. Milan, Hoepli, 1949.

Carli, Enzo. Italian primitives. N.Y., Abrams, 1965.

____Sienese painting. Greenwich, NYGS, 1957.

Cecchi, Emilio. The Sienese painters of the trecento. Trans. by Leonard Penlock. London, Warne, 1931.

Crowe, Joseph A. and Cavalcaselle, Giovanni B. A history of painting in Italy, Umbria, Florence and Siena from the second to the sixteenth century. 6v. London, Murray, 1903–1914. 2 ed.

____A history of painting in north Italy, Venice, Padua, Vicenza, Verona, Ferrara, Milan, Friuli, Brescia, from the fourteenth to the sixteenth century. 3v. London, Murray, 1912. 2 ed.

Delogu, Giuseppe. Antologia della pittura italiana dal XIII al XIX secolo. Bergamo, Ist. Ital. d'Arti Grafiche, 1947. 2 ed.

Dewald, Ernest T. Italian painting, 1200–1600. N.Y., Holt, 1961.

Edgell, George H. A history of Sienese painting. N.Y., Dial, 1932.

Escher, Konrad. Malerei der renaissance in Italien. Berlin, Athenaion, 1922.

Fiocco, Giuseppe. Venetian painting of the seicento and the settecento. N.Y., Harcourt, 1929.

Freedberg, Sydney J. Painting of the high renaissance in Rome and Florence. 2v. Cambridge, Harvard Univ., 1961.

*****Friedländer, Walter F.** Mannerism and anti-mannerism in Italian painting. N.Y., Schocken, 1965.

Garrison, Edward B. Italian Romanesque panel painting; an illustrated index. Florence, Olschki, 1949.

Gnoli, Umberto. Pittori e miniatori nell'Umbria. Spoleto, Argentieri, 1925–26.

Goering, Max. Italian painting of the sixteenth century. London, Zwemmer, 1936.

Gould, Cecil. An introduction to Italian renaissance painting. N.Y., Phaidon, 1957.

Levey, Michael. Painting in eighteenth century Venice. N.Y., Phaidon, 1959.

Longhi, Roberto. Proporzioni; studi di storia dell'arte, v.1– . Florence, Sansoni, 1943– .

McComb, Arthur K. The baroque painters of Italy; an introductory historical survey. Cambridge, Harvard, 1934.

Marle, Raimond van. The development of the Italian schools of painting. 19v. The Hague, Nijhoff, 1923–1938.

Mather, Frank J. A history of Italian painting. N.Y., Holt, 1927.

_____Venetian painters. N.Y., Holt, 1936.

*****Meiss, Millard.** Painting in Florence and Siena after the Black Death. N.Y., Harper, 1964.

Offner, Richard. A critical and historical corpus of Florentine painting, v.1– . N.Y., NYU College of Fine Arts, 1930– .

Ojetti, Ugo. La pittura italiana del seicento e del settecento alla mostra di Palazzo Pitti. Milan, Bestetti, 1924.

_____La pittura italiana dell'ottocento. Milan, Ed. d'Arte, 1929.

Pallucchini, Rodolfo. La pittura veneziana del cinquecento. 2v. Novara, Ist. Geog. de Agostini, 1944.

_____La pittura veneziana del trecento. Venice, Ist. per la Collab. Culturale, 1964.

Pope-Hennessy, John. Sienese quattrocento painting. London, Phaidon, 1947.

Ricci, Corrado. North Italian painting of the cinquecento: Piedmont, Liguria, Lombardy, Emilia. N.Y., Harcourt, 1929.

Rinaldis, Aldo de. Neapolitan painting of the seicento. N.Y., Harcourt, 1929.

Schubring, Paul. Cassoni; truhen und truhenbilder der italienischen frührenaissance. 2v. Leipzig, Hiersemann, 1915. Supplement, 1923.

Toesca, Pietro. Florentine painting of the trecento. N.Y., Harcourt, 1929.

____La pittura e la miniatura nella Lombardia, dai più antichi monumenti alla metà del quattrocento. Milan, Hoepli, 1912.

Turner, Richard A. The vision of landscape in renaissance Italy. Princeton, Princeton Univ., 1966.

Vavalà, Evelyn S. Uffizi studies; the development of the Florentine school of painting. Florence, Olschki, 1948.

Venturi, Adolfo. North Italian painting of the quattrocento: Emilia. N.Y., Harcourt, 1931.

____North Italian painting of the quattrocento: Lombardy, Piedmont, Liguria. N.Y., Harcourt, 1931.

Venturi, Lionello. Italian painting. 3v. N.Y., Skira, 1950–1951.

Voss, Hermann G. A. Die malerei des barock in Rom. Berlin, Propyläen, 1924.

____Die malerei der spätrenaissance in Rom und Florenz. 2v. Berlin, Grote, 1920.

Waterhouse, Ellis K. Baroque painting in Rome, the seventeenth century. London, Macmillan, 1937.

____Italian baroque painting. N.Y., Phaidon, 1963.

Weigelt, Curt H. Sienese painting of the trecento. N.Y., Harcourt, 1930.

Painting – Low Countries

Baker, Charles H. C. Dutch painting of the seventeenth century. London, 1926.

Bernt, Walther. Niederländischen maler des 17 jahrhunderts. 4v. Munich, Münchner Verlag, 1960–1962. 2 ed.

Bode, Wilhelm von. Great masters of Dutch and Flemish painting. Trans. by M. L. Clarke. N.Y., Scribner, 1909. Freeport, Books for Libraries, 1967. Reprint.

Burger, Willy. Die malerei in den Niederlanden, 1400–1500. Munich, Günther, 1925.

Cornette, Arthur J. J. The art of painting in the Low Countries. Amsterdam, Veen, 1947.

Crowe, Joseph A. and Cavalcaselle, Giovanni B. Lives of the early Flemish painters; notices of their lives and works. London, Murray, 1879. 3 ed.

Dülberg, Franz. Niederländische malerei der spätgotik und renaissance. Berlin, Athenaion, 1929.

Durrieu, Paul. La miniature flamande au temps de la cour de Bourgogne, 1415–1530. Paris, VanOest, 1921.

Elst, Joseph J. The last flowering of the middle ages. N.Y., Doubleday, 1944.

Fierens, Paul. La peinture flamande de Bruegel au XVIII siècle. Paris, Éditions d'Art et d'Hist., 1942.

——La peinture flamande dès origines à Quentin Metsys. Paris, Éditions d'Art et d'Hist., 1938.

Fierens-Gevaert, Hippolyte. Histoire de la peinture flamande dès origines à la fin du XV siècle. 3v. Paris, VanOest, 1927–1929.

——Les primitifs flamands. 4v. Paris, VanOest, 1908–1912.

Fokker, Theodore H. Werke niederländischer meister in den kirchen italiens. The Hague, Nijhoff, 1931.

Friedländer, Max J. Die altniederländische malerei. 14v. Berlin, Cassirer, 1924–1937.

——Early Netherlandish painting. Trans. by H. Norden. v.1– . N.Y., Praeger, 1967– .

——From Van Eyck to Bruegel; early Netherlandish painting. N.Y., Phaidon, 1965. 2 ed.

——Die niederländische maler des 17 jahrhunderts. Berlin, Propyläen, 1923.

Fromentin, Eugène. The masters of past time; Dutch and Flemish painting from Van Eyck to Rembrandt. Trans. by Andrew Boyle. London, Phaidon, 1948.

Hofstede de Groot, Cornelis. Beschreibendes und kritisches verzeichnis der werke der hervorragendsten holländischen maler des XVII jahrhunderts. 10v. Esslingen, Neff, 1907–1928.

Hoogewerf, Godefridus J. De Noord-nederlandsche schilderkunst. 5v. The Hague, Nijhoff, 1936–1947.

Lambotte, Paul. Flemish painting before the eighteenth century. Trans. by H. B. Grimsditch. London, Studio, 1927.

Lassaigne, Jacques and Delevoy, Robert L. Flemish painting. 2v. N.Y., Skira, 1958.

Lemonnier, Camille. L'école belge de peinture, 1830–1905. Brussels, VanOest, 1906.

Leymarie, Jean. Dutch painting. Cleveland, World (Skira), 1956.

Mander, Carel van. Dutch and Flemish painters. Trans. by Constant Van de Wall. N.Y., McFarlane, 1936.

____Schilderboek. Amsterdam, Wereldbibliotheek, 1936. 3 ed.

Panofsky, Erwin. Early Netherlandish painting, its origins and character. 2v. Cambridge, Harvard Univ., 1954.

Les Primitifs Flamands. v.1- . Antwerp, deSikkel, 1951- .

Puyvelde, Leo van. La peinture flamande à Rome. Brussels, Encyclopédique, 1950.

____La peinture flamande au siècle de Bosch et Breughel. Paris, Elsevier, 1966.

Roh, Franz. Holländische malerei. Jena, Diederichs, 1921.

Rooses, Max. Dutch painters of the nineteenth century. Trans. by F. Knowles. 4v. London, Low, 1898-1901.

Stechow, Wolfgang. Dutch landscape painting of the seventeenth century. N.Y., Phaidon, 1966.

Tovell, Ruth M. Flemish artists of the Valois courts; a survey of the fourteenth and early fifteenth century development of book illumination and panel painting at the courts of the princes of the House of Valois. Toronto, Univ. of Toronto, 1950.

Voll, Karl. Die altniederländische malerei von Jan van Eyck bis Memling. Leipzig, Insel, 1923.

Warner, Ralph. Dutch and Flemish flower and fruit painters of the XVIIth and XVIIIth centuries. London, Mills, 1928.

Wilenski, Reginald H. Dutch painting. London, Faber, 1955.

____Flemish painters, 1430-1830. 2v. N.Y., Viking, 1960.

Winkler, Friedrich. Die altniederländische malerei; die malerei in Belgien und Holland von 1400-1600. Berlin, Propyläen, 1924.

____Die flämische buchmalerei des XV und XVI jahrhunderts; künstler und werke von den brüdern van Eyck bis zu Simon Bening. Leipzig, Seemann, 1925.

Painting — Mexico, Latin America

Gómez Sicre, José. Cuban painting of today. Trans. by H. T. Tiddle. Havana, Mena, 1944.

Helm, MacKinley. Modern Mexican painters. N.Y., Harper, 1941.

Myers, Bernard. Mexican painting in our time. N.Y., Oxford, 1956.
Reis, José Maria dos. História de pintura no Brazil. São Paolo, LEIA, 1944.
Romero Brest, Jorge. La pintura brasileña contemporánea. Buenos Aires, Poseidon, 1945.
Schmeckebier, Laurence E. Modern Mexican art. Minneapolis, Univ. of Minnesota, 1939.
Soria, Martin S. La pintura del siglo XVI en Sud America. Buenos Aires, Univ., of Buenos Aires, 1956.
Velazquez Chavez, Austin. Tres siglas de pintura colonial Mexicana. Mexico City, Pollis, 1939.

Painting — Russia

Benois, Aleksandr N. The Russian school of painting. N.Y., Knopf, 1916.
Farbman, Michael S. Masterpieces of Russian painting; reproductions of Russian icons and frescoes from the XI to the XVIII centuries. London, Europa, 1930.
Grabar, Igor. Early Russian icons. Greenwich, NYGS, 1958.
Kondakov, Nikodim P. The Russian icon. Trans. by E. H. Minns. Oxford, Clarendon, 1927.
Lukomskii, Georgii K. The history of modern Russian painting (1840–1940). London, Hutchinson, 1945.
Muratov, Pavel P. L'ancienne peinture russe. Trans. by A. Caffi. Rome, Stock, 1925.
___Les icones russes. Paris, Schriffrin, 1927.
Ouspensky, L. and Lossky, Vladimir. The meaning of icons. Boston, Boston Book and Art, 1955.
Schweinfurth, Philipp. Geschichte der russischen malerei im mittelalter. The Hague, Nijhoff, 1930.

Painting — Scandinavia

Lindblom, Andreas A. F. La peinture gothique en Suède et en Norvège; étude sur les relations entre l'Europe occidentale et les pays scandinaves. Stockholm, Wahlström, 1916.
Østby, Leif. Modern Norwegian painting. Trans. by Christopher Norman. Oslo, Mittet, 1949.

Painting — Spain, Portugal

Beruete y Moret, Aureliano de. Historia de la pintura española en el siglo XIX; elementos nacionales y extranjeros que han influido en ella. Madrid, Ruiz, 1926.

Costa, Felix da. The antiquity of the art of painting. Trans. by George Kubler. New Haven, Yale Univ., 1967.

Domínguez Bordona, Jesús. Spanish illumination. 2v. N.Y., Harcourt, 1930.

Harris, Enriqueta. Spanish painting. N.Y., French and European, 1937.

Kuhn, Charles L. The Romanesque mural painting of Catalonia. Cambridge, Harvard Univ., 1930.

Lafuente Ferrari, Enrique. Breve historia de la pintura española. Madrid, Dossat, 1946. 3 ed.

Lassaigne, Jacques. Spanish painting. 2v. Cleveland, World (Skira), 1952.

Mayer, August L. Historia de la pintura española. Madrid, Espasa, 1942.

Post, Chandler R. A history of Spanish painting. 14v. Cambridge, Harvard Univ., 1930–1966. (v.13–14 edited by Harold E. Wethey).

Sanpere y Miquel, Salvador. Los cuatrocentistas catalanes; historia de la pintura en Cataluña en el siglo XV. 2v. Barcelona, L'Avenc, 1906.

Sanpere y Miquel, Salvador and Gudiol i Cunill, Josep. Els trecentistes. 2v. Barcelona, Babra, 1924.

Sentenach y Cabreras, Narciso. Los grandes retratistas en España. Madrid, Hauser, 1914.

Painting — Switzerland

Bovy, Adrien. La peinture suisse de 1600 à 1900. Basel, Birkhaeuser, 1948.

Ganz, Paul. La peinture suisse avant la renaissance. Trans. by Paul Budry. Paris, Budry, 1925.

Gradmann, Erwin. Schweizer malerei und zeichnung im 17 und 18 jahrhundert. Basel, Holbein, 1944.

Jedlicka, Gotthard. Zur schweizerischen malerei der gegenwart. Zurich, Rentsch, 1947.

Neuweiler, Arnold. La peinture à Génève de 1700–1900. Geneva, Jullien, 1945.

Nicolas, Raoul. Die schöne alte Schweiz; die kunst der schweizer kleinmeister. Stuttgart, Montana, 1926.

Schmidt, George. Schweizer malerei und zeichnung im 15 und 16 jahrhundert. Basel, Holbein, 1940.

Wescher, Paul R. Die romantik in der schweizer malerei. Frauenfeld, Huber, 1947.

Painting — United States

Barker, Virgil. American painting, history and interpretation. N.Y., Macmillan, 1950.

Baur, John I. H. American painting in the nineteenth century. N.Y., Praeger, 1953.

Bolton, Theodore. Early American portrait painters in miniature. N.Y., Sherman, 1921.

Born, Wolfgang. American landscape painting; an interpretation. New Haven, Yale Univ., 1948.

____Still-life painting in America. N.Y., Oxford, 1947.

Brown, Milton W. American painting from the Armory Show to the depression. Princeton, Princeton Univ., 1955.

Burroughs, Alan. Limners and likenesses; three centuries of American painting. N.Y., Russell, 1936. Reprint.

Flexner, James T. American painting. 2v. Boston, Houghton, 1947–1954.
(v.1 — First flowers of our wilderness. v.2 — The light of distant skies).

*____America's old masters; first artists of the new world. N.Y., Dover, 1967.

Gardner, Albert Ten Eyck and Feld, Stuart P. American paintings; painters born by 1815. Greenwich, NYGS, 1965.

Geldzahler, Henry. American painting in the twentieth century. Greenwich, NYGS, 1965.

Hagen, Oskar F. L. The birth of the American tradition in art. N.Y., Kennikat. Reprint.

***Hunter, Sam.** Modern American painting and sculpture. N.Y., Dell, 1959.

Isham, Samuel. The history of American painting. Suppl. chapters by R. Cortissoz. N.Y., Macmillan, 1936.

Janis, Sidney. They taught themselves; American primitive painters of the 20th century. N.Y., Kennikat, 1965. Reprint.

Lipman, Jean H. American primitive painting. London, Oxford Univ., 1942.

Lipman, Jean H. and Winchester, Alice. Primitive painters in America, 1750–1950; an anthology. N.Y., Dodd, 1950.

Richardson, Edgar P. American romantic painting. N.Y., Weyhe, 1944.
____Painting in America; the story of 450 years. N.Y., Crowell, 1965.
Sears, Clara E. Some American primitives. N.Y., Kennikat. Reprint.
Soby, James T. and Miller, Dorothy C. Romantic painting in America. N.Y., Museum of Modern Art, 1943.
Sweet, Frederick A. The Hudson River school and the early American landscape tradition. N.Y., Whitney Museum, 1945.
Walker, John and James, Macgill. Great American paintings from Smibert to Bellows, 1729–1924. N.Y., Oxford, 1945.
Wehle, Harry B. American miniatures, 1730–1850. N.Y., Metropolitan Museum, 1927.
Wight, Frederick S. Milestones of American painting in our century. N.Y., Chanticleer, 1949.

GRAPHIC ARTS

General

Adhémar, Jean. Graphic art of the eighteenth century. N.Y., McGraw, 1964.

Bartsch, Adam von. Le peintre graveur. 21v. Würzburg, Verlagsdruckerei, 1920.

Baudi di Vesme, Alessandro. Le peintre-graveur italien; ouvrage faisant suite au peintre-graveur de Bartsch. Milan, Hoepli, 1906.

Baudicour, Prosper de. Le peintre-graveur français continué, ou, catalogue raisonné des estampes gravées par les peintres et les dessinateurs de l'école française nés dans le XVIII siècle, ouvrage faisant suite au peintre-graveur français de M. Robert-Dumesnil. 2v. Paris, Bouchard, 1859–1861.

Ivins, William M. Prints and books; informal papers. Cambridge, Harvard Univ., 1926.

____Prints and visual communication. Cambridge, Harvard Univ., 1953.

Lugt, Frits. Les marques de collections de dessins et d'estampes; marques estampillées et écrites de collections particulières et publiques. 2v. Amsterdam, Vereenigde Druk., 1921–1956.

Passavant, Johann D. Le peintre-graveur; contenant l'histoire de la gravure sur bois, sur métal et au burin jusque vers la fin du XVI siècle. 6v. Leipzig, Weigel, 1860–1864. N.Y., Franklin, 1964. Reprint.

Robert-Dumesnil, A. P. F. Le peintre-graveur français; ou, catalogue raisonné des estampes gravées par les peintres et les dessinateurs de l'école française. 11v. Paris, Warée, 1835–1871.

Roger-Marx, Claude. Graphic art of the nineteenth century. Trans. by E. M. Gwyer. N.Y., McGraw, 1963.

Sachs, Paul J. Modern prints and drawings; a guide to a better understanding of modern draughtsmanship. N.Y., Knopf, 1954.

Salaman, Malcolm C. The great painter-etchers from Rembrandt to Whistler. N.Y., Studio, 1914.

Stubbe, Wolf. Graphic arts in the twentieth century. N.Y., Praeger, 1963.

Updike, Daniel B. Printing types, their history, forms and uses; a study in survivals. 2v. Cambridge, Harvard Univ., 1951. 3 ed.

Graphic Arts — Drawings

Becker, Felix. Handzeichnungen alter meister in privatsammlungen. Leipzig, Tauchnitz, 1922.

Behne, Adolf B. Alte deutsche zeichner; meisterwerke deutscher graphik von den Karolingern bis zum Barock. Berlin, Deutsche Buch-Gemeinschaft, 1943.

Benesch, Otto. Österreichische handzeichnungen des XV und XVI jahrhunderts. Freiburg im Breisgau, Urban, 1936.

——Venetian drawings of the eighteenth century in America. N.Y., Bittner, 1947.

Berenson, Bernard. The drawings of the Florentine painters. 3v. Chicago, Univ. of Chicago, 1938.

Berger, Klaus. French master drawings of the nineteenth century. Trans. by R. Allen. N.Y., Harper, 1950.

Bernt, Walther. Niederländischen zeichner des 17 jahrhunderts. 3v. Munich, Bruckmann, 1957–1958.

Blake, Vernon. The art and craft of drawing. London, Oxford Univ., 1927.

Blunt, Anthony. The French drawings in the collection of His Majesty the King at Windsor castle. London, Phaidon, 1945.

Blunt, Anthony and Cooke, Hereward L. The Roman drawings of the XVII and XVIII centuries in the collection of Her Majesty the Queen at Windsor castle. N.Y., Phaidon, 1960.

Bock, Elfried. Die deutsche graphik. Munich, Hanfstängl, 1922.

——Geschichte der graphischen kunst von ihren anfängen bis zur gegenwart. Berlin, Propyläen, 1930.

Cogniat, Raymond. Le dessin français au XVIII siècle. Monaco, Documents d'Art, 1943.

Degenhart, Bernhard. Europäische handzeichnungen aus fünf jahrhunderten. Berlin, Atlantis, 1943.

Delacre, Maurice and Lavallée, Pierre. Dessins de maîtres anciens. Paris, Van-Oest, 1927.

Delen, Adrien J. J. Flemish master drawings of the seventeenth century. Trans. by R. Allen. N.Y., Harper, 1950.

Delogu, Giuseppe. Venezianische zeichnungen aus dem 18 jahrhundert. Zurich, Fretz, 1947.

Dimier, Louis. Dessins français du XVI siècle. Paris, Alpina, 1937.

Dörries, Bernhard. Deutsche ziechnungen des 18 jahrhunderts. Munich, Bruckmann, 1943.

Friedländer, Max J. and Bock, Elfried. Handzeichnungen deutscher meister des 15 und 16 jahrhunderts. Berlin, Propyläen, 1921.

Ganz, Paul. Handzeichnungen schweizerischer meister des XV–XVIII jahrhunderts. 3v. Basel, Helbing, 1904–1908.

Garzarolli-Thurnlackh, Karl. Die barocke handzeichnung in Österreich. Zurich, Amalthea, 1928.

Geiger, Benno. Handzeichnungen alter meister. Zurich, Amalthea, 1948.

Gelder, Jan G. van. Dutch drawings and prints. N.Y., Abrams, 1958.

George, Waldemar. Le dessin français de David à Cézanne et l'esprit de la tradition baroque. Paris, Chronique du Jour, 1929.

Gradmann, Erwin. Dessins de maîtres espagnols. Trans. by S. Stelling-Michaud. Basel, Holbein, 1944.

———French master drawings of the eighteenth century. Trans. by R. Allen. N.Y., Harper, 1949.

Hadeln, Detlev von. Venezianische zeichnungen der hochrenaissance. Berlin, Cassirer, 1925.

———Venezianische zeichnungen der spätrenaissance. Berlin, Cassirer, 1926.

———Venezianische zeichnungen des quattrocento. Berlin, Cassirer, 1925.

Hagen, Oskar F. L. Deutsche zeichner von der gotik bis zum rokoko. Munich, Piper, 1921.

Henkel, Max D. Le dessin hollandais dès origines au XVII siècle. Paris, VanOest, 1931.

Hubbard, Eric H. Some Victorian draughtsmen. Cambridge, Cambridge Univ., 1944.

Hugelshofer, Walter. Dessins et aquarelles de maîtres français du XIX siècle. Trans. by S. Stelling-Michaud. Basel, Holbein, 1947.

———Schweizer handzeichnungen des XV und XVI jahrhunderts. Freiburg im Breisgau, Urban, 1928.

Huyghe, René. French drawings of the 19th century. N.Y., Vanguard, 1966.

Lavallée, Pierre. Le dessin français. Paris, Larousse, 1948.

———Le dessin français du XIII au XVI siècle. Paris, VanOest, 1950.

Leporini, Heinrich. Die stilentwicklung der handzeichnung, XIV bis XVIII jahrhunderts. Vienna, Manz, 1925.

Mayer, August L. Dibujos originales de maestros españoles. 2v. N.Y., Hispanic Society, 1928.

Meder, Joseph. Die handzeichnung; ihre technik und entwicklung. Vienna, Schroll, 1923. 2 ed.

Mellaart, J. H. J. Dutch drawings of the seventeenth century. N.Y., McBride, 1926.

Mongan, Agnes. One hundred master drawings. Cambridge, Harvard Univ., 1949.

Mongan, Agnes and Sachs, Paul J. Drawings in the Fogg Museum of Art. 2v. Cambridge, Harvard Univ., 1946. 2 ed.

Muchall-Viebrook, Thomas W. Deutsche barockzeichnungen. Munich, Delphin, 1925.

———Flemish drawings of the seventeenth century. N.Y., McBride, 1926.

Oppé, Adolf P. English drawings, Stuart and Georgian periods, in the collection of His Majesty the King at Windsor castle. London, Phaidon, 1950.

Parker, Karl T. Drawings of the early German schools. N.Y., McBride, 1926.

———Elsässiche handzeichnungen des XV und XVI jahrhunderts. Freiburg im Breisgau, Urban, 1928.

———North Italian drawings of the quattrocento. London, Benn, 1927.

Popham, Arthur E. Drawings of the early Flemish school. N.Y., McBride, 1926.

———A handbook to the drawings and watercolours in the department of prints and drawings, British Museum. London, British Museum, 1939.

———The Italian drawings of the XV and XVI centuries in the collection of His Majesty the King at Windsor castle. London, Phaidon, 1949.

———Italian drawings in the department of prints and drawings in the British Museum, the fourteenth and fifteenth centuries. 2v. London, British Museum, 1950.

Puyvelde, Leo van. The Dutch drawings in the collection of His Majesty the King at Windsor castle. London, Phaidon, 1944.

———The Flemish drawings in the collection of His Majesty the King at Windsor castle. London, Phaidon, 1944.

Ratouis de Limay, Paul. Le pastel en France au XVIII siècle. Paris, Baudinière, 1946.

Regteren-Altena, Johan Q. van. Holländische meisterzeichnungen des siebzehnten jahrhunderts. Basel, Holbein, 1949.

Reitlinger, Henry S. Old master drawings; a handbook for amateurs and collectors. N.Y., Moffat, 1923.

Reynolds, Graham. Nineteenth century drawings, 1850–1900. London, Pleiades, 1949.

___Twentieth century drawings. London, Pleiades, 1946.

*****Sachs, Paul J.** The pocket book of great drawings. N.Y., Washington Square, 1961.

Schendel, Arthur F. E. van. Le dessin en Lombardie jusqu'à la fin du XV siècle. Brussels, Connaissance, 1938.

Schilling, Edmund. Altdeutsche meisterzeichnungen. Frankfurt am Main, Prestel, 1934.

___Deutsche romantiker-zeichnungen. Frankfurt am Main, Prestel, 1935.

___Nürnberger handzeichnungen des XV und XVI jahrhunderts. Freiburg im Breisgau, Urban, 1929.

Schoolman, Regina L. and Slatkin, Charles E. Six centuries of French master drawings in America. N.Y., Oxford Univ., 1950.

Serullaz, Maurice and Vantoura, André. French drawings from Prud'hon to Daumier. Greenwich, NYGS, 1966.

Slatkin, Charles E. and Schoolman, Regina L. A treasury of American drawings. N.Y., Oxford Univ., 1947.

Stix, Alfred. Meisterwerke der graphik im XVIII jahrhundert. Vienna, Wolff, 1920–1921.

Sutton, Denys. French drawings of the eighteenth century. London, Pleiades, 1949.

Swarzenski, Georg and Schilling, Edmund. Handzeichnungen alter meister aus deutschen privatbesitz. Frankfurt am Main, Frankfurter Verlags, 1924.

Tietze, Hans. European master drawings in the United States. N.Y., Augustin, 1947.

Tietze, Hans and Tietze-Conrat, Erika. The drawings of the Venetian painters in the 15th and 16th centuries. N.Y., Augustin, 1944.

Tolnay, Charles de. History and technique of old master drawings; a handbook. N.Y., Bittner, 1943.

Vasari Society. Reproductions of drawings by old masters. N.Y., Oxford Univ., 1905–1935. Ser. I (10 parts). Ser. II (16 parts).

Voss, Hermann G. A. Zeichnungen der italienischen spätrenaissance. Munich, Delphin, 1928.

*Watrous, James. The craft of old master drawings. Madison, Univ. of Wisconsin, 1957

Weinberger, Martin. Deutsche rokokozeichnungen. Munich, Delphin, 1923.

Winkler, Friedrich. Mittel-niederrheinische und westfälische handzeichnungen des XV und XVI jahrhunderts. Freiburg im Breisgau, Urban, 1932.

Winzinger, Franz. Deutsche meisterzeichnungen der gotik. Munich, Prestel, 1949.

Graphic Arts — Engravings

Bliss, Douglas P. A history of wood engraving. N.Y., Dutton, 1928.

Blum, André. La gravure en Angleterre au XVIII siècle. Paris, VanOest, 1930.

——The origins of printing and engraving. Trans. by H. M. Lydenberg. N.Y., Scribner, 1940.

Calabi, Augusto. L'incisione italiana. Milan, Treves, 1931.

Carrington, Fitz Roy. Prints and their makers; essays on engravers and etchers old and modern. N.Y., Century, 1912.

Colin, Paul. La gravure et les graveurs. 2v. Brussels, VanOest, 1916–1918.

Courboin, François. Histoire illustré de la gravure en France. 4v. Paris, Le Garrec, 1923–1928.

Courboin, François and Roux, Marcel. La gravure française; essai de bibliographie. 3v. Paris, Le Garrec, 1927–1928.

Cundall, Joseph. A brief history of wood-engraving from its invention. London, Low, 1895.

Dacier, Émile. La gravure française. Paris, Larousse, 1945.

Davenport, Cyril J. H. Mezzotints. N.Y., Putnam, 1903.

Delen, Adrien J. J. Histoire de la gravure dans les anciens Pays-Bas et dans les provinces belges dès origines jusqu'à la fin du XVIII siècle. 3v. Paris, VanOest, 1924–1935.

Delteil, Loÿs. Manuel de l'amateur d'estampes des XIX et XX siècles (1801–1924). 4v. Paris, Dorbon, 1925.

——Manuel de l'amateur d'estampes du XVIII siècle. Paris, Dorbon, 1910.

——Le peintre-graveur illustré (XIX et XX siècles). 31v. Paris, Chez l'Auteur, 1906–1930. Reprint 1967.

Dilke, Emilia F. S. French engravers and draughtsmen of the XVIII century. London, Bell, 1902.

Donati, Lamberto. Incisioni fiorentine del quattrocento. Bergamo, Ist. Ital. d'Arti Grafiche, 1944.

Dussler, Luitpold. Italienische meisterzeichnungen. Frankfurt am Main, Prestel, 1938.

Ede, Harold S. Florentine drawings of the quattrocento. N.Y., McBride, 1926.

Fielding, Mantle. American engravers upon copper and steel. Philadelphia, Fielding, 1917.

Fischel, Oskar. Die zeichnungen der Umbrer. Berlin, Grote, 1917.

Friedländer, Max J. Der holzschnitt. Berlin, deGruyter, 1926. 3 ed.

Furst, Herbert. The modern woodcut; a study of the evolution of the craft. N.Y., Dodd, 1924.

_____Original engraving and etching, an appreciation. London, Nelson, 1931.

Geisberg, Max. Bilder-katalog zu der deutsche einblatt-holzschnitt in der ersten hälfte des XVI jahrhunderts. Ed. by Hugo Schmidt. Munich, Schmidt, 1930.

_____Geschichte der deutschen graphik vor Dürer. Berlin, Deutscher Verein f. Kunstwissenschaft, 1939.

Glaser, Curt. Gotische holzschnitte. Berlin, Propyläen, 1923.

_____Die graphik der neuzeit vom anfang des XIX jahrhunderts bis zur gegenwart. Berlin, Cassirer, 1922.

Gray, Basil. The English print. London, Black, 1937.

Hamerton, Philip G. Etching and etchers. Boston, Little, Brown, 1916.

*__**Hayden, Arthur.** Chats on old prints. London, Unwin, 1913. 2 ed.

Hind, Arthur M. Early Italian engravings; a critical catalogue with complete reproduction of all the prints described. 7v. London, Quaritch, 1938–1948.

_____Engraving in England in the sixteenth and seventeenth centuries; a descriptive catalogue with introductions. v.1– . Cambridge, Cambridge Univ., 1957– .

_____A guide to the processes and schools of engraving represented in the exhibition of select prints. London, British Museum, 1933.

*_____A history of engraving and etching from the 15th century to the year 1914. London, Constable, 1927. 3 ed.

*_____An introduction to a history of woodcut, with a detailed survey of work done in the fifteenth century. 2v. London, Constable, 1935.

Hollstein, F. W. H. Dutch and Flemish etchings, engravings and woodcuts, ca. 1450–1700. v.1– . Amsterdam, Hertzberger, 1949– .

_____German engravings, etchings and woodcuts, ca. 1400–1700. v.1– . Amsterdam, Hertzberger, 1954– .

Holme, Charles. Old English mezzotints. London, Studio, 1910.

Holme, Geoffrey. Modern woodcuts and lithographs by British and French artists. London, Studio, 1919.

Kristeller, Paul. Early Florentine woodcuts. London, Kegan, 1897.

_____Kupferstich und holzschnitt in vier jahrhunderten. Berlin, Cassirer, 1922. 4 ed.

Laver, James. A history of British and American etching. London, Benn, 1929.

Lehrs, Max. Geschichte und kritischer katalog des deutschen, niederländischen und französischen kupferstichs im XV jahrhundert. 9v. Vienna, Gesell. f. Vervielfältigende Kunst, 1908–1934.

Leipnik, F. L. A history of French etching from the sixteenth century to the present day. London, Lane, 1924.

Leporini, Heinrich. Die künstlerzeichnung; ein handbuch für liebhaber und sammler. Berlin, Schmidt, 1928.

_____Der kupferstichsammler; ein hand- und nachschlagebuch samt künstlerverzeichnis für den sammler druckgraphischer kunst. Berlin, Schmidt, 1924.

Lippmann, Friedrich. Engraving and etching; a handbook for the use of students and print collectors. London, Grevel, 1906. 3 ed.

Nijhoff, Wouter and Henkel, Max D. Nederlandsche houtschneden, 1500–1550. 4v. The Hague, Nijhoff, 1931–1939.

Osborn, Max. Der holzschnitt. Bielefeld, Velhagen, 1905.

Pennell, Elizabeth R. Lithography and lithographers. N.Y., Macmillan, 1915.

Portalis, Roger and Beraldi, Henri. Graveurs du XIX siècle. 3v. Paris, Morgand, 1880–1882. N.Y., Franklin, 1964. Reprint.

Prideaux, Sarah T. Aquatint engraving. London, Duckworth, 1909.

Roger-Marx, Camille. French original engravings. London, Hyperion, 1939.

Rosenthal, Léon. La gravure. Rev. by J. Adhémar. Paris, Laurens, 1939. 2 ed.

Salaman, Malcolm C. The new woodcut. London, Studio, 1930.

_____Old English colour prints. N.Y., Studio, 1909.

_____Old English mezzotints. London, Studio, 1910.

Schreiber, William L. Handbuch der holz-und metallschnitte des XV jahrhunderts. 8v. Leipzig, Harrassowitz, 1926–1930. 2 ed. N.Y., Franklin, reprint.

Slater, John H. Engravings and their value; a complete guide to the collection and prices of all classes of prints. Rev. by F. W. Maxwell-Barbour. N.Y., Scribner, 1929. 6 ed.

Soares, Ernesto. História da gravura artística em Portugal os artistas e as suas obras. 2v. Lisbon, Santelmo, 1940–1941.

Stauffer, David M. American engravers upon copper and steel. 2v. N.Y., Grolier, 1907. N.Y., Franklin, 1964. Reprint.

Weber, Wilhelm. A history of lithography. N.Y., McGraw, 1966.

Wedmore, Frederick. Etchings. London, Methuen, 1912. 2 ed.

_____Fine prints. Edinburgh, Grant, 1905.

Weitenkampf, Frank. American graphic art. N.Y., Macmillan, 1924.

_____How to appreciate prints. N.Y., Scribner, 1942. 4 ed.

Whitman, Alfred. Print collector's handbook. London, Bell, 1912. 6 ed.

Zigrosser, Carl. The book of fine prints; an anthology of printed pictures and introduction to the study of graphic art in the west and the east. N.Y., Crown, 1948. (Original title: Six centuries of fine prints.).

Graphic Arts — Techniques

Arms, John T. Handbook of print making and print makers. 2v. N.Y., Macmillan, 1934.

Bersier, Jean E. La gravure; les procédés, l'histoire. Paris, Table Ronde, 1948.

Brown, Bolton. Lithography for artists; a complete account of how to grind, draw upon, etch and print from the stone. Chicago, Univ. of Chicago, 1930.

Cumming, David. A handbook of lithography; a practical treatise for all who are interested in the process. London, Black, 1933. 3 ed.

Hayter, Stanley W. New ways of gravure. N.Y., Pantheon, 1966. 2 ed.

Holman, Louis A. The graphic processes: intaglio, relief and planographic. Boston, Goodspeed, 1929.

Hubbard, Eric. On making and collecting etchings; a handbook for etchers, students and collectors. London, Ringwood, 1920.

Ivins, William M. How prints look; photographs with a commentary. N.Y., Metropolitan Museum, 1943. Boston, Beacon. Reprint.

Lavallée, Pierre. Les techniques du dessin, leur évolution dans les différents écoles de l'Europe. Paris, VanOest, 1943.

Lumsden, Ernest S. The art of etching; a complete and fully illustrated description of etching, drypoint, soft-ground etching, aquatint, and their allied arts. Philadelphia, Lippincott, 1925.

Peterdi, Gabor. Print making: methods old and new. N.Y., Macmillan, 1959.

Plenderleith, Harold J. The conservation of prints, drawings and manuscripts. London, Oxford Univ., 1937.

Poortenaar, Jan. The technique of prints and art reproduction processes. London, Lane, 1933.

Silsby, Wilson. Etching methods and materials; a new and simplified technique. N.Y., Dodd, 1943.

Singer, Hans W. Handbuch für kupferstichsammler; technische erklärungen ratschläge für das sammeln und das aufbewahren. Leipzig, Hiersemann, 1922. 2 ed.

Singer, Hans W. and Strang, William. Etching, engraving and the other methods of printing pictures. London, Paul, 1897.

Sternberg, Harry. Modern methods and materials of etching. N.Y., McGraw, 1949.

MINOR ARTS

General

Alexandre, Arsène. Histoire de l'art décoratif du XVI siècle à nos jours. Paris, Laurens, 1892.

Baltrusaitis, Jurgis. La stylistique ornementale. Paris, Leroux, 1931.

Berlin, Staatliche Kunstbibliothek. Katalog der ornamentstichsammlung. Berlin, Verlag f. Kunstwissenschaft, 1936–1939. 2 ed. N.Y., Franklin, 1958. Reprint.

Berliner, Rudolf. Ornamentale verlage-blätter des 15 bis 18 jahrhunderts. 3v. Leipzig, Klinkhardt, 1925–1926.

Bossert, Helmuth T. An encyclopedia of colour decoration from the earliest times to the middle of the XIX century. N.Y., Weyhe, 1928.

_____Folk art of Europe. Trans. by S. Moholy-Nagy. N.Y., Praeger, 1964.

_____Geschichte des kunstgewerbes aller zeiten und völker, in verbindung mit zahlreichen in fachgelehrten. 6v. Berlin, Wasmuth, 1928–1935.

_____Ornament in applied art. N.Y., Weyhe, 1924.

Britten, Frederick J. Old clocks and watches and their makers. London, Spon, 1956. 7 ed.

Christensen, Erwin O. The Index of American design. N.Y., Macmillan, 1950.

Christie, Archibald. Traditional methods of pattern designing; an introduction to the study of formal ornament. Oxford, Clarendon, 1929. 2 ed.

Debes, Dietmar. Das ornament, wesen und geschichte; eine schriftenverzeichnis. Leipzig, Seemann, 1956.

Evans, Joan. Pattern, a study of ornament in western Europe from 1180 to 1900. 2v. Oxford, Clarendon, 1931.

_____Style in ornament. London, Oxford Univ., 1950.

Glazier, Richard. Manual of historic ornament. N.Y., Scribner, 1948. 6 ed.

Hamlin, Alfred D. F. A history of ornament, renaissance and modern. 2v. N.Y., Century, 1916–1923.

Jones, Owen. The grammar of ornament. London, Quaritch, 1910.

*Meyer, Franz. A handbook of ornament. Chicago, Wilcox, 1945. N.Y., Dover. Reprint.

Molinier, Émile. Histoire générale des arts appliqués à l'industrie du V à la fin du XVIII siècle. 6v. Paris, Lévy, 1896–1910.

Ostwald, Wilhelm. Die welt der formen. 4v. Leipzig, Unesma, 1922–1925.

Racinet, Auguste. L'ornement polychrome. 2v. Paris, Firmin-Didot, 1888.

Scott, Robert G. Design fundamentals. N.Y., McGraw, 1951.

*Speltz, Alexander. Styles of ornament, exhibited in designs, and arranged in historical order, with descriptive text. N.Y., Grosset, 1936. Reprint.

Minor Arts — Costume

Boehn, Max von. Modes and manners. Trans. by J. Joshua. 4v London, Harrap, 1932–1936.

_____Modes and manners of the nineteenth century as represented in the pictures and engravings of the time. Trans. by M. Edwardes. 4v. London, Dent, 1927.

Brooke, Iris. A history of English costume. London, Methuen, 1949. 3 ed.

Bruhn, Wolfgang. Das kostümwerk; eine geschichte des kostüms aller zeiten und völker vom altertum bis zur neuzeit einschliesslich der volkstrachten Europas und der trachten der susseuropaïschen länder. Berlin, Wasmuth, 1941.

Colas, René. Bibliographie générale du costume et de la mode. 2v. Paris, Colas, 1933.

Davenport, Millia. The book of costume. N.Y., Crown, 1948.

Earle, Alice M. Two centuries of costume in America, MDCXX–MDCCCXX. 2v. N.Y., Macmillan, 1903.

Houston, Mary G. Ancient Egyptian, Mesopotamian and Persian costume and decoration. N.Y., Barnes, 1954. 2 ed.

_____Ancient Greek, Roman and Byzantine costume and decoration. N.Y., Barnes, 1959. 2 ed.

_____Medieval costume in England and France; the 13th, 14th and 15th centuries. N.Y., Barnes, 1950. 2 ed.

Kelly, Francis M. and Schwabe, Randolph. Historic costume, a chronicle of fashion in western Europe, 1450–1790. N.Y., Blom, 1966. 2 ed.

Laver, James. Costume of the western world, v.1– . London, Harrap, 1950– .

Leloir, Maurice. Dictionnaire du costume et de ses accessoires, des armes et des étoffes, dès origines à nos jours. Paris, Gründ, 1951.

_____Histoire du costume de l'antiquité à 1914. v.1– . Paris, Ernst, 1933– . 2 ed.

Lipperheide, Franz J. von. Katalog der freiherrlich von Lipperheideschen Kostümbibliothek. 2v. Berlin, Lipperheide, 1896–1905.

McClellan, Elisabeth. History of American costume, 1607–1870; with an introductory chapter on dress in the Spanish and French settlements in Florida and Louisiana. N.Y., Tudor, 1937.

Monro, Isabel S. and Cook, Dorothy E. The costume index; a subject index to plates and to illustrated texts. 2v. N.Y., Wilson, 1937–1957.

Pisetzky, Rosita L. Storia del costume in Italia. Milan, Ist. Edit. Italiano, 1964.

Planché, James R. A cyclopedia of costume or dictionary of dress, including notices of contemporaneous fashions on the continent; a general chronlogical history of the costumes of the principal countries of Europe, from the commencement of the Christian era to the accession of George the third. 2v. London, Chatto, 1876–1879.

Racinet, Auguste. Le costume historique. 6v. Paris, Firmin-Didot, 1888.

Minor Arts – Enamels

Chamot, Mary. English medieval enamels. London, Benn, 1930.

Cunynghame, Henry H. European enamels. London, Methuen, 1906.

Marquet de Vasselot, Jean J. Les émaux limousins de la fin du XV siècle et de la première partie du XVI; étude sur Nardon Pénicaud et ses contemporains. 2v. Paris, Picard, 1921.

Minor Arts – Furniture

Aronson, Joseph. The encyclopedia of furniture. N.Y., Crown, 1967. 3 ed.

Baker, Hollis S. Furniture in the ancient world; origins and evolution, 3100–475 B.C. N.Y., Macmillan, 1966.

Bode, Wilhelm von. Italian renaissance furniture. Trans. by M. E. Herrick. N.Y., Helburn, 1921.

Brackett, Oliver. English furniture illustrated; a pictorial review of English furniture from Chaucer to Queen Victoria. Rev. by H. C. Smith. N.Y., Macmillan, 1950.

Burr, Grace H. Hispanic furniture, with examples in the collection of the Hispanic Society of America. N.Y., Archive, 1964. 2 ed.

Byne, Arthur and Byne, Mildred Stapley. Spanish interiors and furniture. 4v. N.Y., Helburn, 1921-1922.

Cescinsky, Herbert. English furniture from Gothic to Sheraton; a concise account of the development of English furniture and woodwork from the Gothic of the fifteenth century to the classic revival of the early nineteenth. London, Routledge, 1929.

———English furniture of the eighteenth century. 3v. London, Routledge, 1909-1911.

Cescinsky, Herbert and Gribble, E. R. Early English furniture and woodwork. 2v. London, Routledge, 1922.

Cescinsky, Herbert and Hunter, George L. English and American furniture; a pictorial handbook of furniture made in Great Britain and in the American colonies, some in the sixteenth century but principally in the seventeenth, eighteenth and early nineteenth centuries. London, Routledge, 1929.

Cornelius, Charles O. Early American furniture. N.Y., Century, 1926.

Dilke, Emilia F. S. French furniture and decoration in the XVIIIth century. London, Bell, 1901.

Dreyfus, Carle. French furniture. 2v. N.Y., Brentano, 1921.

Eberlein, Harold D. and McClure, Abbot. The practical book of period furniture, treating of furniture of the English, American colonial and post-colonial and principal French periods. Philadelphia, Lippincott, 1914.

Eberlein, Harold D. and Ramsdell, Roger W. The practical book of Italian, Spanish and Portuguese furniture. Philadelphia, Lippincott, 1927.

Falke, Otto von. Deutsche möbel des mittelalters und der renaissance. Stuttgart, Hoffmann, 1924.

Félice, Roger de. French furniture in the middle ages and under Louis XIII. Trans. by F. M. Atkinson. London, Heinemann, 1920.

———French furniture under Louis XIV. Trans. by F. M. Atkinson. London, Heinemann, 1920.

Felice (cont.)

_____French furniture under Louis XV. Trans. by Florence Simmonds. London, Heinemann, 1927.

_____French furniture under Louis XVI and the empire. Trans. by F. M. Atkinson. London, Heinemann, 1920.

Feulner, Adolf. Kunstgeschichte des möbels seit dem altertum. Berlin, Propyläen, 1927. 3 ed.

Havard, Henry. Dictionnaire de l'ameublement et de la décoration depuis le XIII siècle jusqu'à nos jours. 4v. Paris, Quantin, 1894.

Holloway, Edward S. American furniture and decoration, colonial and federal. Philadelphia, Lippincott, 1928.

Hunter, George L. Italian furniture and interiors. 2v. N.Y., Helburn, 1918.

Jourdain, Margaret. English decoration and furniture of the early renaissance, 1500–1650, an account of its development and characteristic forms. London, Batsford, 1924.

_____English decoration and furniture of the later XVIII century, 1760–1820; an account of its development and characteristic forms. London, Batsford, 1922.

Kettell, Russell H. The pine furniture of early New England. N.Y., Doubleday, 1929. N.Y., Dover. Reprint.

Lenygon, Francis. Decoration in England from 1640 to 1760. London, Batsford, 1927. 2 ed.

_____Furniture in England from 1660 to 1760. London, Batsford, 1914.

Litchfield, Frederick. Illustrated history of furniture from the earliest to the present time. London, Truslove, 1922. 7 ed.

Lockwood, Luke V. Colonial furniture in America. 2v. N.Y., Scribner, 1926. 3 ed.

Luthmer, Ferdinand. Deutsche möbel der vergangenheit. Leipzig, Klinkhardt, 1924.

Macquoid, Percy. A history of English furniture. 4v. London, Lawrence, 1926.

Macquoid, Percy and Edwards, Ralph. The dictionary of English furniture, from the middle ages to the late Georgian period. 3v. N.Y., Scribner, 1924–1927.

Nagel, Charles. American furniture, 1650–1850; a brief background and illustrated history. N.Y., Chanticleer, 1949.

Neal, Ambrose. The London furniture makers, from the Restoration to the Victorian era, 1660–1840. London, Batsford, 1953.

*****Nutting, Wallace.** Furniture of the Pilgrim century (of American origin), 1620–1720, including colonial untensils and hardware. Boston, Jones, 1921. Magnolia, P. Smith. Reprint.

Nutting (cont.)

_____Furniture treasury, mostly of American origin; all periods of American furniture with some foreign examples in America, also American hardware and household utensils. 2v. N.Y., Macmillan, 1948.

Odom, William M. A history of Italian furniture from the fourteenth to the early ninteenth centuries. 2v. N.Y., Archive, 1966. Reprint.

Olmer, Pierre. Le mobilier français d'aujourd'hui, 1910–1925. Paris, VanOest, 1926.

_____La renaissance du mobilier français, 1890–1910. Paris, VanOest, 1927.

Rogers, Meyric R. American interior design; the traditions and development of domestic design from the colonial times to the present. N.Y., Norton, 1947.

Saglio, André. French furniture. London, Batsford, 1913.

Salverte, François de. Les ébénistes du XVIII siècle, leurs oeuvres et leurs marques. Paris, VanOest, 1934. 3 ed.

Schmitz, Hermann. The encyclopedia of furniture. N.Y., Praeger, 1957.

Schottmüller, Frida. Furniture and interior decoration of the Italian renaissance. N.Y., Westermann, 1928. 2 ed.

Singleton, Esther. Dutch and Flemish furniture. N.Y., McClure, 1907.

Strange, Thomas A. English furniture, decoration, woodwork and allied arts during the last half of the 17th century, the whole of the 18th century and the earlier part of the 19th. London, Simpkin, 1903.

_____An historical guide to French interiors, furniture, decoration, woodwork and allied arts during the last half of the 17th century, the whole of the 18th century and the early part of the 19th. London, McCorquodale, 1907.

Taullard, Alfredo. El meuble colonial sudamericano. Buenos Aires, Peuser, 1944.

Theunissen, André. Meubles et sièges du XVIII siècle. Paris, Le Document, 1934.

Viollet-le-Duc, Eugène E. Dictionnaire raisonné du mobilier français de l'époque carlovingiènne à la renaissance. 6v. Paris, Gründ, 1914.

Minor Arts – Glass

Arnold, Hugh and Saint, Lawrence B. Stained glass of the middle ages in England and France. N.Y., Barnes, 1956.

Aubert, Marcel. Le vitrail en France. Paris, Larousse, 1946.

Buckley, Wilfred. European glass; a brief outline of the history of glass making. Boston, Houghton, 1926.

Connick, Charles J. Adventures in light and color; an introduction to the stained glass craft. N.Y., Random, 1937.

Corpus Vitrearum Medii Aevi. v.1– . Paris, Union Acad. Internationale, 1956– .

Day, Lewis F. Windows; a book about stained and painted glass. London, Batsford, 1909. 3 ed.

Dillon, Edward. Glass. N.Y., Putnam, 1907.

Drake, Maurice. A history of English glass-painting, with some remarks upon the Swiss glass miniatures of the sixteenth and seventeenth centuries. London, Laurie, 1912.

Drake, Wilfred. A dictionary of glass-painters and "glasyers" of the tenth to the eighteenth centuries. N.Y., Metropolitan Museum, 1955.

Eisen, Gustav. Glass, its origin, history, chronology, technic and classification to the sixteenth century. 2v. N.Y., Rudge, 1927.

Fischer, Josef L. Handbuch der glasmalerei für forscher sammler und kunstfreunde, wie für künstler, architekten und glasmaler. Leipzig, Hiersemann, 1914.

Garnier, Édouard. Histoire de la verrerie et de l'émaillerie. Tours, Mame, 1886.

Grodecki, Louis. The stained glass of French churches. Paris, duChêne, 1947.

Honey, William B. Glass; a handbook for the study of glass vessels of all periods and countries and a guide to the museum collection. London, Victoria and Albert Museum, 1946.

Janneau, Guillaume. Modern glass. London, Studio, 1931.

Kampfer, Fritz and Beyer, Klaus G. Glass; a world history. Trans. by E. Launert. Greenwich, NYGS, 1966.

Knittle, Rhea M. Early American glass. N.Y., Century, 1927.

McKearin, Helen and George S. American glass. N.Y., Crown, 1948.

_____Two hundred years of American blown glass. N.Y., Doubleday, 1950.

Moore, Hannah H. Old glass, European and American. N.Y., Tudor, 1935. Reprint.

Pazaurek, Gustav E. Glaser der empire und Biedermeierzeit. Leipzig, Klinkhardt, 1923.

_____Kunstgläser der gegenwart. Leipzig, Klinkhardt, 1925.

_____Moderne gläser. Leipzig, Seemann, 1910.

Read, Herbert E. English stained glass. N.Y., Putnam, 1926.

Rogers, Frances and Beard, Alice. 5000 years of glass. Philadelphia, Lippincott, 1948.

Schmidt, Robert. Das glas. Berlin deGruyter, 1922. 2 ed.
Thorpe, William A. English glass. London, Black, 1950. 2 ed.
_____A history of English and Irish glass. 2v. London, Medici Society, 1929.
Watkins, Lura. American glass and glassmaking. N.Y., Chanticleer, 1950.
Westlake, Nat H. J. A history of design in painted glass. 4v. London, Parker,
    1881-1894.
Woodforde, Christopher. The Norwich school of glass-painting in the fifteenth
    century. London, Oxford Univ., 1950.
_____Stained glass in Somerset, 1250-1830. London, Oxford Univ., 1946.

Minor Arts — Ivory

Cust, Anna M. E. The ivory workers of the middle ages. London, Bell, 1906.
Goldschmidt, Adolph. Die elfenbeinskulpturen. 4v. Berlin, Cassirer, 1914-
    1926.
Goldschmidt, Adolph and Weitzmann, Kurt. Die byzantinischen elfenbein-
    skulpturen des X-XIII jahrhunderts. 2v. Berlin, Cassirer, 1930-1934.
Grodecki, Louis. Ivoires français. Paris, Larousse, 1947.
Koechlin, Raymond. Les ivoires gothiques français. 3v. Paris, Picard, 1924.
Longhurst, Margaret H. Catalogue of carvings in ivory. 2v. London, Victoria
    and Albert Museum, 1927-1929.
_____English ivories. London, Putnam, 1926.
Maskell, Alfred. Ivories. Rutland, Tuttle, 1966. Reprint.
Natanson, Joseph. Early Christian ivories. London, Tiranti, 1953.
_____Gothic ivories of the 13th and 14th centuries. London, Tiranti, 1953.
Pelka, Otto. Elfenbein. Berlin, Schmidt, 1923. 2 ed.
Philippowich, Eugen von. Elfenbein. Brunswick, Klinkhardt, 1961.

Minor Arts — Metals

Anderson, Lawrence L. The art of the silversmith in Mexico, 1519-1936. 2v.
    N.Y., Oxford Univ., 1941.
Avery, Clara L. Early American silver. N.Y., Century, 1930.
Babelon, Jean. Orfèvrerie française. Paris, Larousse, 1946.
Bell, Malcolm. Old pewter. London, Batsford, 1913.

Bigelow, Francis H. Historic silver of the colonies and its makers. N.Y., Macmillan, 1941.

Blanc, Louis. Le fer forgé en France aux XVI et XVII siècles; oeuvres gravées des anciens maîtres, serruriers, architectes, dessinateurs et graveurs. Paris, Van Oest, 1928.

_____Le fer forgé en France; la régence, aurore, apogée, déclin. Paris, VanOest, 1930.

Braun, Joseph. Meisterwerke der deutschen goldschmiedekunst der vorgotischen zeit. 2v. Munich, Riehn, 1922.

Byne, Arthur and Byne, Mildred Stapley. Spanish ironwork. N.Y., Hispanic Society, 1915.

Carré, Louis. A guide to old French plate. London, Chapman, 1931.

_____Les poinçons de l'orfèvrerie française du quatorzième siècle jusq'au début du dix-neuvième siècle. Paris, Carré, 1928. N.Y., Franklin, reprint.

Chaffers, William. Handbook to hall marks on gold and silver plate. Ed. by C. Bunt. London, Reeves, 1922. 10 ed. Los Angeles, Borden. Reprint.

Churchill, Sidney J. A. The goldsmiths of Italy; some account of their guilds, statues and work. London, Hopkinson, 1926.

Clouzot, Henri. Les arts du métal; métaux précieux, le bronze et le cuivre, le fer, les armes, la parure. Paris, Laurens, 1934.

Cotterell, Howard H. Old pewter, its makers and marks in England, Scotland and Ireland; an account of the old pewterer and his craft. Rutland, Tuttle, 1963. Reprint.

Cripps, Wilfred J. Old English plate, ecclesiastical, decorative and domestic; its makers and marks. London, Murray, 1914. 10 ed.

_____Old French plate, its makers and marks. London, Murray, 1920. 3 ed.

Dawson, Nelson. Goldsmiths' and silversmiths' work. N.Y., Putnam, 1907.

Ensko, Stephen G. C. American silversmiths and their marks. N.Y., Ensko, 1948.

_____English silver, 1675-1825. N.Y., Ensko, 1937.

Evans, Joan. A history of jewellery, 1100-1870. London, Faber, 1953.

Ferrari, Giulio. Il ferro nell'arte italiana. Milan, Hoepli, 1910.

Ffoulkes, Constance J. Decorative ironwork from the eleventh to the eighteenth century. London, Methuen, 1913.

Frank, Edgar B. Old French ironwork; the craftsman and his art. Cambridge, Harvard Univ., 1950.

Frederiks, Johann W. Dutch silver. v.1- . The Hague, Nijhoff, 1952- .

French, Hollis. Silver collector's glossary: a list of early American silversmiths and their marks. N.Y., Plenum, 1917.

Gardner, John S. English ironwork of the XVIIth and XVIIIth centuries; an historical and analytical account of the development of exterior smithcraft. London, Batsford, 1911.

———Ironwork. 2v. London, HMSO, 1927–1930. 4 ed.

Havard, Henry. Histoire de l'orfèvrerie française. Paris, May, 1896.

Höver, Otto. An encyclopedia of ironwork; examples of hand wrought ironwork from the middle ages to the end of the eighteenth century. N.Y., Weyhe, 1927.

Jackson, Charles J. English goldsmiths and their marks; a history of the goldsmiths and plate workers of England, Scotland and Ireland. London, Macmillan, 1921. 2 ed. N.Y., Dover, reprint.

———An illustrated history of English plate, ecclesiastical and secular. 2v. London, Country Life, 1911.

Johnson, Ada M. Hispanic silverwork. N.Y., Hispanic Society, 1944.

Jones, Edward A. Old silver of Europe and America from early times to the nineteenth century. Philadelphia, Lippincott, 1928.

Kerfoot, John B. American pewter. N.Y., Crown, 1942.

Laughlin, Ledlie I. Pewter in America, its makers and their marks. 2v. Boston, Houghton, 1940.

Marquet de Vasselot, Jean J. Bibliographie de l'orfèvrerie et de l'émaillerie françaises. Paris, Picard, 1925.

Neal, Ambrose. The London goldsmiths, 1200–1800. Cambridge, Cambridge, Univ., 1935.

Nocq, Henry. Le poinçon de Paris, répertoire des maîtres-orfèvres de la juridiction de Paris depuis le moyen-âge jusqu'à la fin du XVIII siècle. 5v. Paris, Floury, 1926–1931.

Phillips, John M. American silver. N.Y., Chanticleer, 1949.

Pollen, John H. Gold and silversmiths' work. London, Chapman, 1879.

Rosenberg, Marc. Geschichte der goldschmiedekunst auf technischer grundlage, v.1– . Frankfurt am Main, Keller, 1910– .

———Der goldschmiede merkzeichen. 4v. Frankfurt am Main, Frankfurter Verlagsanstalt, 1922–1928. 3 ed. 1955 reprint.

Scheffler, Wolfgang. Goldschmiede Niedersachsens. 2v. Berlin, deGruyter, 1965.

Smith, Harold C. Jewellery. London, Methuen, 1908.

Sonn, Albert H. Early American wrought iron. 3v. N.Y., Scribner, 1928.

Steingräber, Erich. Antique jewelry. London, Thames, 1957.
Thorn, C. Jordan. Handbook of Ameican silver and pewter marks. N.Y., Tudor, 1949.
Wenham, Edward. Domestic silver of Great Britain and Ireland. N.Y., Oxford Univ., 1935.
_____Practical book of American silver. Philadelphia, Lippincott, 1949.
Wyler, Seymour B. The book of old silver; English, American, foreign, with all available hallmarks including Sheffield plate marks. N.Y., Crown, 1937.

Minor Arts − Mosaics

Anthony, Edgar W. A history of mosaics. Boston, Sargent, 1935.
Babelon, Jean. Mosaïques chrétiennes. Paris, Alpina, 1942.
Berchem, Marguerite van and Clouzot, Étienne. Mosaïques chrétiennes du IV a X siècle. Geneva, Journal de Genève, 1924.   .
Demus, Otto. Byzantine mosaic decoration. London, Kegan, 1948.
_____The mosaics of Norman Sicily. London, Routledge, 1950.
Diez, Ernst and Demus, Otto. Byzantine mosaics in Greece: Hosios Lucas and Daphni. Cambridge, Amer. School of Classical Studies at Athens, 1931.
Galassi, Giuseppe. Roma o Bizanzio. 2v. Rome, Libreria della Stato, 1930–1953.
Levi, Doro. Antioch mosaic pavements. 2v. Princeton, Princeton Univ., 1947.
Morey, Charles R. The mosaics of Antioch. London, Longmans, 1938.
Salvini, Roberto. Mosaici medievali in Sicilia. Florence, Sansoni, 1949.
Volbach, Wolfgang F. Early Christian mosaics, from the fourth to the seventh centuries, Rome, Naples, Milan, Ravenna. N.Y., Oxford Univ., 1946.
Wilpert, Josef. Die römischen mosaiken und malereien der kirchlichen bauten vom IV bis XIII jahrhundert. 4v. Freiburg im Breisgau, Herder, 1917. 2 ed.

Minor Arts − Photography

Boni, Albert. Photographic literature. N.Y., Morgan, 1962.
Braive, Michel F. The era of the photograph; a social history. Trans. by D. Britt. N.Y., McGraw, 1966.
Freund, Gisèle. La photographie en France au dix-huitième siècle. Paris, Monnier, 1936.

Gernsheim, Helmut. The history of photography from the earliest use of the camera obscura in the eleventh century up to 1914. London, Oxford Univ., 1955.

Newhall, Beaumont. The history of photography, 1839–1965. N.Y., Doubleday, 1966.

——On photography: history in facsimile. Watkins Glen, Century House, 1956.

Pollock, Peter. The picture history of photography. N.Y., Abrams, 1958.

*****Taft, Robert.** Photography and the American scene. N.Y., Macmillan, 1942. Magnolia, P. Smith. Reprint.

Minor Arts — Pottery and Porcelain

Barber, Edwin A. Marks of American potters, with facsimiles of 1000 marks, and illustrations of rare examples of American wares. Philadelphia, Patterson, 1904.

——The pottery and porcelain of the United States; an historical review of American ceramic art from the earliest times to the present day. N.Y., Putnam, 1909. 3 ed.

Burton, William. A general history of porcelain. 2v. London, Cassell, 1921.

Burton, William and Hobson, Robert L. Handbook of marks on pottery and porcelain. London, Macmillan, 1929.

Bushnell, Geoffrey H. S. and Digby, Adrian. Ancient American pottery. N.Y., Pitman, 1955.

Chaffers, William. Collector's handbook of marks and monograms on pottery and porcelain of the renaissance and modern periods. London, Reeves, 1957. 3 ed.

——Marks and monograms on European and Oriental pottery and porcelain. Los Angeles, Borden, 1946. 14 ed.

——The new keramic gallery. 2v. London, Reeves, 1926. 3 ed.

Charleston, R. J. English porcelain, 1745–1850. London, Benn, 1965.

Chavagnac, Xavier R. M. and Grolier, Gaston A. Histoire des manufactures françaises de porcelaine. Paris, Picard, 1906.

Cox, Warren E. The book of pottery and porcelain. N.Y., Crown, 1944.

Cushion, J. P. and Honey, William B. Handbook of pottery and porcelain marks. London, Faber, 1956.

Danckert, Ludwig. Handbuch des europäischen porzellans. Munich, Prestel, 1954.

Dillon, Edward. Porcelain. London, Putnam, 1904.

Eberlein, Harold D. and Ramsdell, Roger W. The practical book of chinaware. Philadelphia, Lippincott, 1948.

Fontaine, Georges. La céramique française. Paris, Larousse, 1947.

Hannover, Emil. Pottery and porcelain; a handbook for collectors. Ed. by B. Rackham. 3v. N.Y., Scribner, 1951. 5 ed.

Hofmann, Friedrich H. Das porzellan de europäischen manufakturen im XVIII jahrhundert; eine kunst- und kulturgeschichte. Berlin, Propyläen, 1932.

Honey, William B. The art of the potter; a book for the collector and connoisseur. N.Y., Whittlesey, 1950.

_____Dresden china; an introduction to the study of Meissen porcelain. London, Faber, 1954.

_____English pottery and porcelain. N.Y., Barnes, 1964. 5 ed.

_____European ceramic art, from the end of the middle ages to about 1815. 2v. London, Faber, 1949–1952.

_____Old English porcelain; a handbook for collectors. N.Y., McGraw, 1949.

Kenny, John B. Ceramic sculpture. N.Y., Chilton, 1953.

_____The complete book of pottery making. N.Y., Chilton, 1959.

Lane, Arthur. French faïence. London, Faber, 1948.

_____Style in pottery. London, Oxford Univ., 1948.

Leach, Bernard. A potter's book. N.Y., Transatlantic, 1948.

Litchfield, Frederick. Pottery and porcelain; a guide to collectors. N.Y., Barrowes, 1963. 6 ed.

Mankowitz, Wolf and Haggar, Reginald C. The concise encyclopedia of English pottery and porcelain. N.Y., Hawthorn, 1957.

March, Benjamin. Standards of pottery description. Ann Arbor, Univ. of Michigan, 1934.

Minghetti, Aurelio. Ceramisti. Milan, Tosi, 1939.

Norton, Frederick H. Ceramics for the artist potter. Reading, Addison, 1956.

Penkala, Maria. European pottery; 5000 marks on maiolica, faïence and stoneware. Hengelo, Smit, 1951.

Phillips, John G. China-trade porcelain; an account of the historical background, manufacture and decoration. Greenwich, NYGS. 1956.

Ramsay, John. American potters and pottery. Boston, Hale, 1939.

Rhodes, Daniel. Clay and glazes for the potter. N.Y., Chilton, 1959.

*Savage, George. Porcelain through the ages; a survey of the main porcelain factories of Europe and Asia. N.Y., Barnes, 1961.

Solon, Louis M. E. Ceramic literature; an analytical index to the works published in all languages on the history and the technology of the ceramic art. London, Griffin, 1910.

———A history and description of Italian majolica. N.Y., Cassell, 1907.

Spargo, John. Early American pottery and china. N.Y., Century, 1926.

Thorn, C. Jordan. Handbook of old pottery and porcelain marks. N.Y., Tudor, 1947.

Watkins, Lura. Early New England potters and their wares. Cambridge, Harvard Univ., 1950.

Minor Arts — Tapestry and Textiles

Ackerman, Phyllis. Tapestry, the mirror of civilization. N.Y., Oxford Univ., 1933.

Albers, Anni. On weaving. Middletown, Wesleyan, 1965.

Algoud, Henri. La soie, art et histoire. Paris, Payot, 1928.

Baschet, Jacques. Tapisseries de France. Paris, Nouv. Editions Françaises, 1947.

Christie, Grace. Embroidery and tapestry weaving. N.Y., Macmillan, 1906.

———English medieval embroidery; a brief survey of English embroidery dating from the beginning of the tenth century until the end of the fourteenth. Oxford, Clarendon, 1938.

Clouzot, Henri. Painted and printed fabrics; a history of the manufactory at Jouy and other ateliers in France, 1760–1815. New Haven, Yale Univ., 1927.

Demotte, Georg J. La tapisserie gothique. N.Y., Demotte, 1924.

Dilley, Arthur U. Oriental rugs and carpets; a comprehensive study. Philadelphia, Lippincott, 1959.

Falke, Otto von. Decorative silks. N.Y., Helburn, 1922.

Faraday, Cornelia B. European and American carpets and rugs. Grand Rapids, Dean-Hicks, 1929.

Fenaille, Maurice. État géneral des tapisseries de la manufacture des Gobelins depuis son origine jusqu'à nos jours, 1600–1900. 5v. Paris, Hachette, 1903–1925.

Glazier, Richard. Historic textile fabrics; a short history of the tradition and development of pattern in woven and printed stuffs. London, Batsford, 1923.

Göbel, Heinrich. Wandteppiche. 6v. Leipzig, Klinkhardt, 1923–1924.

Guiffrey, Jules. Histoire générale de la tapisseries. 3v. Paris, Société Anonyme de Publ. Périodiques, 1875–1885.

———Les manufactures nationales de tapisseries: les Gobelins et Beauvais. Paris, Laurens, 1907.

———La tapisserie. Paris, Picard, 1904.

Hawley, Walter A. Oriental rugs, antique and modern. N.Y., Tudor, 1937.

Holt, Rosa B. Oriental and occidental rugs, antique and modern. Garden City, Garden City Pub. Co., 1937. 2 ed.(original title: Rugs, oriental and occidental.)

Hulst, Roger A. d'. Tapisseries flamandes du XIV au XVIII siècle. Brussels, Arcade, 1960.

Hunter, George L. The practical book of tapestries. Philadelphia, Lippincott, 1925.

———Tapestries, their origin, history and renaissance. N.Y., Lane, 1913.

Jaques, Renate and Flemming, Ernst R. An encyclopedia of textiles from the earliest times to the beginning of the 19th century. N.Y., Praeger, 1958.

Kendrick, Albert F. Catalogue of tapestries. London, Victoria and Albert Museum, 1924.

———English decorative fabrics of the sixteenth to eighteenth centuries. Benfleet, Lewis, 1934.

Kendrick, Albert F. and Tattersall, Creasy E. C. Handwoven carpets, Oriental and European. 2v. London, Benn, 1922.

Kurth, Betty. Die deutschen bildteppiche des mittelalters. 3v. Vienna, Schroll, 1926.

———Gotische bildteppiche aus Frankreich und Flandern. Munich, Riehn, 1923.

Lehnert, Georg H. Illustrierte geschichte des kunstgewerbes. 2v. Berlin, Oldenbourg, 1907–1909.

Lejard, André. French tapestry. London, Elek, 1946.

———La tapisserie de Bayeux. Paris, du Chêne, 1946.

Lewis, George C. The practical book of Oriental rugs. Philadelphia, Lippincott, 1920. 5 ed.

Little, Frances. Early American textiles. N.Y., Century, 1931.

Lotz, Arthur. Bibliographie der modelbücher; beschreibendes verzeichnis der stich- und spitzenmusterbücher des 16 und 17 jahrhunderts. Leipzig, Hiersemann, 1933.

Lurçat, Jean. Tapisserie française. Paris, Bordas, 1947.

Marquet de Vasselot, Jean J. Bibliographie de la tapisserie, des tapis et de la broderie en France. Paris, Colin, 1925.

Martin, Fredrik R. A history of Oriental carpets before 1800. Vienna, I. & R. State and Court Ptg. Office, 1908.

Migeon, Gaston. Les arts du tissu. Paris, Laurens, 1909.

Moore, Hannah H. The lace book. N.Y., Tudor, 1937.

Morris, Frances and Hague, Marian. Antique laces of American collectors. 5v. N.Y., Helburn, 1920–1926.

Müntz, Eugène. A short history of tapestry; from the earliest times to the end of the eighteenth century. Trans. by L. J. Davis. London, Cassell, 1885.

____La tapisserie. Paris, Picard, 1903. 5 ed.

Mumford, John K. Oriental rugs. N.Y., Scribner, 1923.

Neugebauer, Rudolf. Handbuch der orientalischen teppichkunde. Leipzig, Hiersemann, 1930.

Oelsner, G. H. A handbook of weaves. Rev. by S. S. Dale. N.Y., Dover, 1915. Reprint.

Palliser, Fanny M. A history of lace. N.Y., Scribner, 1902. 4 ed.

Percival, MacIver. The chintz book. London, Heinemann, 1923.

Pethebridge, Jeanette E. A manual of lace. London, Cassell, 1947.

Podreider, Fanny. Storia del tessuti d'arte in Italia, secolo XII–XVIII. Bergamo, Ist. Ital. d'Arti Grafiche, 1928.

Priest, Alan and Simmons, Pauline. Chinese textiles; an introduction to the study of their history, sources, techniques, symbolism, and use occasioned by the exhibition of Chinese court robes and accessories. N.Y., Metropolitan Museum, 1931.

Reath, Nancy A. The weaves of handloom fabrics; a classification with historical notes. Philadelphia, Pennsylvania Museum, 1927.

Reath, Nancy A. and Sachs, Eleanor B. Persian textiles and their technique from the sixth to the eighteenth centuries, including a system for general textile classification. New Haven, Yale Univ., 1937.

Ricci, Elisa. Old Italian lace. 2v. Philadelphia, Lippincott, 1913.

Sangiorgi, Giorgio. Contributi allo studio dell'arte tessile. Milan, Bestetti, 1919.

Schmitz, Hermann. Bildteppiche, geschichte der Gobelinwirkerei, Berlin. Verlag f. Kunstwissenschaft, 1920.

Schuette, Marie. Gestickte bildteppiche und decken des mittelalters. 2v. Leipzig, Hiersemann, 1927–1930.

Tattersall, Creasy E. C. A history of British carpets from the introduction of the craft until the present day. N.Y., Textile Book, 1934.

Thomson, William G. A history of tapestry from the earliest times until the present day. N.Y., Putnam, 1931.

Verlet, Pierre and others. Great tapestries. The web of history from the 12th to the 20th century. Paris, Lausanne, 1965.

Vienna. Österreichisches Museum für Kunst und Industrie. Ancient Oriental carpets. Leipzig, Hiersemann, 1908.

____Old Oriental carpets. 2v. Vienna, Schroll, 1926–1929.

____Oriental carpets. 3v. London, Cousins, 1892–1896.

Volbach, Wolfgang F. and Kühnel, Ernst. Late antique Coptic and Islamic textiles of Egypt. N.Y., Weyhe, 1926.

Weibel, Adèle G. Two thousand years of textiles. N.Y., Pantheon, 1952.

Whiting, Gertrude. A lace guide for makers and collectors, with bibliography and five-language nomenclature. N.Y., Dutton, 1920.

Monographs on Artists

AALTO, ALVAR, 1898–
*Gutheim, Frederick. Alvar Aalto. N.Y., Braziller, 1960.

ABBEY, EDWIN AUSTIN, 1852–1911
Lucas, Edward V. Edwin Austin Abbey, royal academician; the record of his life and work. 2v. London, Methuen, 1921.

ADAM, ROBERT, 1728–1792
Bolton, Arthur T. The architecture of Robert and James Adam (1758–1794). 2v. London, Country Life, 1922.
Fleming, John. Robert Adam and his circle in Edinburgh and Rome. Cambridge, Harvard Univ., 1962.
Lees-Milne, James. The age of Adam. London, Batsford, 1947.
Swarbrick, John. Works in architecture of Robert and James Adam. N.Y., Transatlantic, 1959.

AERTSEN, PIETER, 1507–1573
Sievers, Johannes. Pieter Aertsen; ein beitrag zur geschichte der niederländischen kunst im XVI jahrhunderts. Leipzig, Hiersemann, 1908.

ALBERTI, LEONE BATTISTA, 1404–1472
*Alberti, Leone Battista. On painting. Trans. by J. R. Spencer. New Haven, Yale Univ. 1966.
_____Ten books on architecture. Edit. by J. Rykwert. N.Y., Translantic, 1955.
Mancini, Girolamo. Vita di Leone Battista Alberti. Florence, Carnescchi, 1911. 2 ed.

ALLSTON, WASHINGTON, 1779–1843
Allston, Washington. Lectures on art and poems. Gainesville, Scholars' Facsimiles, 1967.

ALLSTON, WASHINGTON (continued)

Richardson, Edgar P. Washington Allston, a study of the romantic artist in America. Chicago, Univ. of Chicago, 1948.

ALTDORFER, ALBRECHT, 1480–1538

Baldass, Ludwig von. Albrecht Altdorfer. Zurich, Scientia, 1941.

Becker, Hanna L. Die handzeichnungen Albrecht Altdorfers. Munich, Filser, 1938.

Benesch, Otto. Der maler Albrecht Altdorfer. Vienna, Schroll, 1939.

Friedländer, Max J. Albrecht Altdorfer. Berlin, Cassirer, 1923.

Ruhmer, Eberhard. Albrecht Altdorfer. Munich, Bruckmann, 1965.

Tietze, Hans. Albrecht Altdorfer. Leipzig, Insel. 1923

Voss, Hermann G. A. Albrecht Altdorfer und Wolf Huber. Leipzig, Klinkhardt, 1910.

Winzinger, Franz. Albrecht Altdorfer; graphik, holzschnitte, kupferstiche, radierungen. Munich, Piper, 1963.

ALTICHIERI, ALTICHIERO, 1320–1385

Bronstein, Léo. Altichieri, l'artiste et son oeuvre. Paris, Vrin, 1932.

Schubring, Paul. Altichiero und seine schule. Leipzig, Hiersemann, 1898.

AMADEO, GIOVANNI ANTONIO, 1447–1522

Malaguzzi-Valeri, Francesco. Gio. Antonio Amadeo, scultore e architetto lombardo (1447–1522). Bergamo, Ist. Ital. d'Arti Grafiche, 1904.

ANGELICO, FRA (Giovanni da Fiesole) 1387–1455

Argan, Giulio C. Fra Angelico; biographical and critical study. Trans. by James Emmons. Cleveland, World (Skira), 1955.

Douglas, Robert Langton. Fra Angelico. London, Bell, 1902. 2 ed.

Hausenstein, Wilhelm. Fra Angelico. Trans. by Agnes Blake. London, Methuen, 1928.

Orlandi, Stefano. Beato Angelico; monografia storica della vita e delle opere. Florence, Olschki, 1964.

Pope-Hennessy, John. The paintings of Fra Angelico. N.Y., Phaidon, 1952.

Schottmüller, Frida. Fra Angelico da Fiesole. Stuttgart, Deutsche Verlagsanstalt, 1924. 2 ed.

Williamson, George C. Fra Angelico. London, Bell, 1901.

ANTELAMI, BENEDETTO (Benedetto di Parma) fl.1177–1233

Francovich, Géza de. Benedetto Antelami, architetto e scultore, e l'arte del suo tempo. 2v. Milan, Electa, 1952.

ANTONELLO DA MESSINA, 1430–1479
Bottari, Stefano. Antonello da Messina. Greenwich, NYGS, 1956.
Lauts, Jan. Antonello da Messina. Vienna, Schroll, 1940.

ARCHIPENKO, ALEXANDER, 1887–
Archipenko, Alexander. Fifty creative years, 1908–1958. N.Y., Heineman, 1960.
Raynal, Maurice. A. Archipenko. Rome, Valori Plastici, 1923.

ARNOLFO DI CAMBIO, 13th cent.
Mariani, Valerio. Arnolfo di Cambio. Rome, Tumminelli, 1943.

ARP, HANS, 1887–1966
*Arp, Hans. On my way; poetry and essays, 1912–1947. N.Y., Wittenborn, 1948.
Giedion-Welcker, Carola. Hans Arp. Stuttgart, Hatje, 1957.
Soby, James T. Arp. N.Y., Doubleday, 1958.

BALDOVINETTI, ALESSO, 1425–1499
Kennedy, Ruth W. Alesso Baldovinetti, a critical and historical study. New Haven, Yale Univ., 1938.
Londi, Emilio. Alesso Baldovinetti, pittore fiorentino. Florence, Alfani, 1907.

BALDUNG, HANS, 1480–1545
Curjel, Hans. Hans Baldung Grien. Munich, Recht, 1923.
Escherich, Mela. Hans Baldung-Grien; bibliographie 1509–1915. Strassburg, Heitz, 1916.
Koch, Carl. Die zeichnungen Hans Baldung Griens. Berlin, Deutscher Ver. f. Kunstwissenschaft, 1941.
Martin, Kurt. Skizzenbuch des Hans Baldung Grien; "Karlsruher skizzenbuch." 2v. Basel, Holbein, 1950.

BARBARI, JACOPO DE', 1440–1515
Hevesy, André de. Jacopo de Barbari, le maître au caducée. Paris, VanOest, 1925.
Servolini, Luigi. Jacopo de' Barbari. Padua, Tre Venezie, 1944.

BARI, NICCOLÒ DA, 1414–1495
Gnudi, Cesare. Niccolò dell'Arca. Turin, Einaudi, 1942

BARLACH, ERNST, 1870–1938

Barlach, Ernst. Ernst Barlach; ein selbsterzähltes leben. Munich, Piper, 1948.

Flemming, Willi. Ernst Barlach; wesen und werk. Bern, Francke, 1958.

Stubbe, Wolf. Ernst Barlach; plastik. Munich, Piper, 1959.

——Ernst Barlach; zeichnungen. Munich, Piper, 1961.

Werner, Alfred. Ernst Barlach, his life and work. N.Y., McGraw, 1966.

BAROCCI, FEDERIGO, 1528–1612

Krommes, Rudolf H. Studien zu Federigo Barocci. Leipzig, Seemann, 1912.

Olsen, Harald. Federico Barocci. Copenhagen, Munksgaard, 1962. 2 ed.

BARRY, CHARLES, 1795–1860

Barry, Alfred. The life and works of Sir Charles Barry. London, Murray, 1867.

BARTOLOMMEO, FRA, 1472–1517

Gabelentz, Hans von der. Fra Bartolommeo und die Florentiner renaissance. 2v. Leipzig, Hiersemann, 1922.

Knapp, Fritz. Fra Bartolommeo della Porta und die schule von San Marco. Halle, Knapp, 1903.

Rouchès, Gabriel. Fra Bartolommeo, 1472–1517; quatorze dessins. Paris, Musées Nationaux, 1942.

BARYE, ANTOINE LOUIS, 1796–1875

Alexandre, Arsène. A. L. Barye. Paris, Libr. de l'Art, 1889.

Zieseniss, Charles U. Les aquarelles de Barye; étude critique et catalogue raisonné. Paris, Massin, 1955.

BASSANO, JACOPO, 1510–1592

Arslan, Wart. I Bassano. 2v. Milan, Ceschina, 1960.

Bettini, Sergio. L'arte di Jacopo Bassano. Bologna, Apollo, 1933.

Zampetti, Pietro. Jacopo Bassano. Rome, Ist. Poligrafico, 1958.

BAYER, HERBERT, 1900–

*****Dorner, Alexander.** The way beyond "art;" the work of Herbert Bayer. N.Y., New York Univ., 1958.

BEARDSLEY, AUBREY, 1872–1898

Beardsley, Aubrey. Letters; edit. by R. A. Walker. London, First Edit., 1937.

——The early and later work. 2v. N.Y., Da Capo, 1967.

Gallatin, Albert E. Aubrey Beardsley; catalogue of drawings and bibliography. N.Y., Grolier, 1945.

Macfall, Haldane. Aubrey Beardsley, the man and his work. London, Lane, 1928.

Weintraub, Stanley. Beardsley, a biography. N.Y., Braziller, 1967.

BEAUX, CECILIA, 1863–1942

Beaux, Cecilia. Background with figures; autobiography. Boston, Houghton, 1930.

BECKMANN, MAX, 1884–1950

Buchheim, Lothar G. Max Beckmann. Feldafing, Buchheim, 1959.

Busch, Günter. Max Beckmann; eine einführung. Munich, Piper, 1960.

Reifenberg, Benno and Hausenstein, Wilhelm. Max Beckmann. Munich, Piper, 1949.

BELLINI, GENTILE, 1429–1507
        GIOVANNI, 1430–1516
        JACOPO, 1400–1470

Dussler, Luitpold. Giovanni Bellini. Vienna, Schroll, 1949.

Gamba, Carlo. Giovanni Bellini. Milan, Hoepli, 1937.

Gronau, Georg. Giovanni Bellini. Stuttgart, Deutsche Verlagsanstalt, 1930.

———Die künstlerfamilie Bellini. Bielefeld, Velhagen, 1909.

Heinemann, Fritz. Giovanni Bellini e i belliniani. 2v. Venice, Pozza, 1962.

Hendy, Philip and Goldscheider, Ludwig. Giovanni Bellini. N.Y., Phaidon, 1945.

Moschini, Vittorio. Disegni di Jacopo Bellini. Bergamo, Ist. Ital. d'Arti Grafiche, 1943.

———Giambellino. Bergamo, Ist. Ital. d'Arti Grafiche, 1943.

Pallucchini, Rodolfo. Giovanni Bellini. N.Y., Humanities, 1962.

Ricci, Corrado. Jacopo Bellini e i suoi libri di disegni. 2v. Florence, Alinari, 1908.

BELLOTTO, BERNARDO, 1720–1780

Fritsche, Hellmuth A. Bernardo Bellotto, genannt Canaletto. Burg b.M., Hopfer, 1936.

Lippold, Gertrude. Bernardo Bellotto, genannt Canaletto. Leipzig, Seemann, 1963.

BELLOWS, GEORGE WESLEY, 1882–1925

Bellows, George W. George W. Bellows; his lithographs. N.Y., Knopf, 1928.
_____ The paintings of George W. Bellows. N.Y., Knopf, 1929.
Eggers, George W. George Bellows. N.Y., Macmillan, 1931.
Morgan, Charles H. George Bellows, painter of America. N.Y., Reynal, 1965.

BENEDETTO DA MAIANO, 1442–1497

Cendali, Lorenzo. Giuliano e Benedetto da Majano, Fiesole. Florence, Società Ed. Toscana, 1926.
Dussler, Luitpold. Benedetto da Majano, ein Florentiner bildhauer des späten quattrocento. Munich, Schmidt, 1924.

BENTON, THOMAS HART, 1889–

Benton, Thomas H. An artist in America. Kansas City, Univ. of Kansas City, 1951.

BERNARD, JOSEPH, 1866–1931

Cantinelli, Richard. Joseph Bernard; catalogue de l'oeuvre sculpté. Paris, VanOest, 1928.

BERNINI, GIOVANNI LORENZO, 1598–1680

Baldinucci, Filippo. The life of Bernini. Trans. by C. Engass. University Park, Penn. State, 1965.
Boehn, Max von. Lorenzo Bernini; seine zeit, sein leben, sein werk. Bielefeld, Velhagen, 1927. 2 ed.
Brauer, Heinrich and Wittkower, Rudolf. Die zeichnungen des Gianlorenzo Bernini. 2v. Berlin, Keller, 1931.
Chantelou, Paul F. Journal du voyage en France du cavalier Bernini. Edit. by G. Charensol. Paris, Ateliers, 1930.
Grassi, Luigi. Disegni del Bernini. Bergamo, Ist. Ital. d'Arti Grafiche, 1944.
_____ Gianlorenzo Bernini. Rome, Ateneo, 1962.
Hibbard, Benjamin H. Bernini. London, Penguin, 1966.
Wittkower, Rudolf. The sculpture of Bernini. London, Phaidon, 1966. 2 ed.

BERRUGUETE, PEDRO, 1483–1503

Lainez Alcala, Rafel. Pedro Berruguete, pintor de Castilla. Madrid, Espasa, 1943.

BERTOLDO, GIOVANNI DI, 1410–1491

Bode, Wilhelm von. Bertoldo und Lorenzo dei Medici. Freiburg im Breisgau, Pontos, 1925.

BIDDLE, GEORGE, 1885–
Biddle, George. An American artist's story. Boston, Little, Brown, 1939.
____The yes and no of contemporary art; an artist's evaluation. Cambridge, Harvard Univ., 1957.

BINGHAM, GEORGE CALEB, 1811–1879
McDermott, John F. George Caleb Bingham, river portraitist. Norman, Univ. of Oklahoma, 1959.

BLAKE, WILLIAM, 1757–1827
Binyon, Laurence. The drawings and engravings of William Blake. London, Studio, 1922.
Blunt, Anthony. The art of William Blake. N.Y., Columbia Univ., 1959.
Damon, S. Foster. A Blake dictionary; the ideas and symbols of William Blake. Providence, Brown Univ., 1965.
Figgis, Darrell. The paintings of William Blake. London, Benn, 1925.
Keynes, Geoffrey L. A bibliography of William Blake. N.Y., Grolier, 1921.
____Engravings by William Blake. Dublin, Walker, 1956.
Symons, Arthur. William Blake. London, Constable, 1907.

BOCCIONI, UMBERTO, 1882–1916
Ballo, Guido. Umberto Boccioni; la vita e l'opere. Milan, Saggiatore, 1964.

BOILLY, LOUIS LÉOPOLD, 1761–1845
Harrisse, Henry. L. L. Boilly, peintre, dessinateur et lithographe; sa vie et son oeuvre. Paris, Société des Livres d'Art, 1888.
Marmottan, Paul. Le peintre Louis Boilly. Paris, Gateau, 1913.

BONFIGLI, BENEDETTO, 1420–1496
Bombe, Walter. Benedetto Bonfigli; eine kunsthistorische studie. Berlin, Ockler, 1904.

BONHEUR, ROSA, 1822–1899
Klumpke, Anna. Rosa Bonheur; sa vie, son oeuvre. Paris, Flammarion, 1908.

BONINGTON, RICHARD PARKES, 1801–1828
Curtis, Atherton. Catalogue de l'oeuvre lithographié et gravé de R. P. Bonington. Paris, Prouté, 1939.
Dubuisson, A. Richard Parkes Bonington; his life and work. London, Lane, 1924.
Shirley, Andrew. Bonington. London, Kegan, 1940.

BONNARD, PIERRE, 1867–1947
  Dauberville, Jean and Dauberville, Henry. Bonnard; catalogue raisonné de
    l'oeuvre peint. v.1– . Paris, Bernheim, 1966– .
  Rewald, John. Pierre Bonnard. N.Y., Museum of Modern Art, 1948.
  Terrasse, Antoine. Bonnard; biographical and critical study. Trans. by S.
    Gilbert. Cleveland, World (Skira), 1964.
  Vaillant, Annette. Pierre Bonnard, ou le bonheur de voir. Neuchâtel, Ides,
    1966.

BORROMINI, FRANCESCO, 1599–1667
  Hempel, Eberhard. Francesco Borromini. Vienna, Schroll, 1924.
  Muñoz, Antonio. Francesco Borromini. Rome, Società Ed. d'Arte Illus.,
    1921.
  Portoghesi, Paolo. Borromini nella cultura europa. Rome, Officini Ediz.,
    1964.
  Thelen, Heinrich. Francesco Borromini; die handzeichnungen. v.1– . Graz,
    Akad. Druck und Verlagsanstalt, 1967– .

BOS, CORNELIS, 1506–1556
  Schéle, Sune. Cornelis Bos; a study of the origins of the Netherlands
    grotesque. Stockholm, Almquist, 1965.

BOSCH, HIERONYMUS VAN AKEN, 1450–1516
  Baldass, Ludwig von. Hieronymus Bosch. N.Y., Abrams, 1960.
  Combe, Jacques. Jérôme Bosch. N.Y., Universe, 1957.
  Fraenger, Wilhelm. The milennium of Hieronymus Bosch. Trans. by E. Wil-
    kins and E. Kaiser. Chicago, Univ. of Chicago, 1951.
  Lafond, Paul. Hieronymous Bosch — son art, son influence, ses disciples.
    Paris, VanOest, 1914.
  Leymarie, Jean. Jérôme Bosch. Paris, Somogy, 1949.
  Tolnay, Charles de. Hieronymus Bosch. Trans. by M. Bullock and H. Minns.
    N.Y., Reynal, 1966.

BOTTICELLI, SANDRO, 1447–1510
  Argan, Giulio C. Botticelli. Cleveland, World (Skira), 1957.
  Binyon, Laurence. The art of Botticelli; an essay in pictorial criticism. Lon-
    don, Macmillan, 1913.
  Bode, Wilhelm von. Botticelli; des meisters werke. Stuttgart, Deutsche
    Verlaganstalt, 1926.
  Gamba, Carlo. Botticelli. Trans. by Jean Chuzeville. Paris, Gallimard, 1937.

Horne, Herbert P. Alessandro Filipepi, commonly called Sandro Botticelli, painter of Florence. London, Bell, 1908.

Venturi, Lionello. Botticelli. N.Y., Phaidon, 1961.

Yashiro, Yukio. Sandro Botticelli and the Florentine renaissance. London, Medici Society, 1929. 2 ed.

BOUCHER, FRANÇOIS, 1703–1770

Ananoff, Alexandre. L'oeuvre dessiné de François Boucher (1703–1770), catalogue raisonné. v.1– . Paris, deNobèle, 1966– .

Kahn, Gustave. Boucher; biographie critique. Paris, Laurens, 1904.

Lavallée, Pierre. François Boucher, 1703–1770; quatorze dessins. Paris, Musées Nationaux, 1942.

Michel, André. F. Boucher. Paris, Piazza, 1906.

Nolhac, Pierre de. François Boucher, premier peintre du roi, 1703–1770. Paris, Goupil, 1907.

BOUDIN, EUGÈNE, 1824–1898

Cahen, Gustave. Eugène Boudin, sa vie et son oeuvre. Paris, Floury, 1900.

BOURDELLE, ÉMILE ANTOINE, 1861–1929

Lorenz, Paul. Bourdelle, sculptures et dessins. Paris, Rombaldi, 1947.

Varenne, Gaston. Bourdelle par lui-même; sa pensée et son art. Paris, Fasquelle, 1937.

BOUTS, DIERCK, 1420–1475

Schöne, Wolfgang. Dieric Bouts und seine schule. Berlin, Verlag f. Kunstwissenschaft, 1938.

BRAMANTE, DONATO, 1444–1514

Baroni, Costantino. Bramante. Bergamo, Ist. Ital. d'Arti Grafiche, 1944.

Foerster, Otto H. Bramante. Vienna, Schroll, 1956.

Suida, Wilhelm. Bramante pittore e il Bramantino. Milan, Ceschina, 1953.

BRANCUSI, CONSTANTIN, 1876–1957

Geist, Sidney. Brancusi. N.Y., Grossman, 1967.

Giedion-Welcker, Carola. Constantin Brancusi. Basel, Schwabe, 1958.

BRANGWYN, FRANK, 1867–1956

Sparrow, Walter S. Frank Brangwyn and his work. London, Kegan, 1914.

BRAQUE, GEORGES, 1881–1963

Einstein, Carl. Georges Braque. N.Y., Weyhe, 1934.

BRAQUE, GEORGES (continued)
Gieure, Maurice. G. Braque. Paris, Tisné, 1956.
Richardson, John. Braque. Greenwich, NYGS, 1961.
Russell, John. G. Braque. London, Phaidon, 1959.

BREUER, MARCEL, 1902–
Breuer, Marcel. Sun and shadow; the philosophy of an architect. N.Y., Dodd, 1955.

BRILL, MATTHÄUS, 1550–1584
           PAUL, 1554–1626
Mayer, Anton. Das leben und die werke der brüder Matthäus und Paul Brill. Leipzig, Hiersemann, 1910.

BRONZINO, AGNOLO, 1503–1572
Emiliani, Andrea. Il Bronzino. Milan, Bramante, 1960.
McComb, Arthur K. Agnolo Bronzino; his life and works. Cambridge, Harvard Univ., 1928.

BROSSE, SALOMON DE, 1571–1626
Pannier, Jacques. Un architecte français au commencement du XVII siècle: Salomon de Brosse. Paris, Libr. d'Art et d'Arch., 1911.

BROUWER, ADRIAEN, 1606–1638
Bode, Wilhelm von. Adriaen Brouwer, sein leben und seine werke. Berlin, Euphorion, 1924.
Knuttel, Gerhardus. Adriaen Brouwer; the master and his work. Trans. by J. G. Talma-Schilthuis and R. Wheaton. The Hague, Boucher, 1962.
Schmidt-Degener, Frederik. Adriaen Brouwer et son évolution artistique. Brussels, VanOest, 1908.

BROWN, FORD MADOX, 1821–1893
Hueffer, Ford Madox. Ford Madox Brown; a record of his life and work. London, Longmans, 1896.

BRUEGHEL, JAN, 1568–1625
              PIETER (the elder) 1525–1569
Bastelaer, René van. Peter Bruegel l'ancien, son oeuvre et son temps. 2v. Brussels, VanOest, 1907.
Bruhns, Leo. Das Bruegel buch. Vienna, Schroll, 1941.
Denucé, Jean. Brieven en documenten betreffend Jan Breugel I en II. Antwerp, DeSikkel, 1934.

Dvořák, Max. Pierre Brueghel l'ancien. Vienna, Oest. Staatsdruckerei, 1930.

Friedländer, Max J. Pieter Bruegel. Berlin, Propyläen, 1921.

Glück, Gustav. Pieter Brueghel, the elder. Trans. by E. B. Shaw. London, Commodore, 1936.

Grossman, Fritz. The paintings of Breughel. N.Y., Phaidon, 1966. 2 ed.

Jedlicka, Gotthard. Pieter Bruegel der maler in seiner zeit. Erlenbach, Rentsch, 1938.

Münz, Ludwig. Bruegel; drawings. N.Y., Phaidon, 1961.

Tolnay, Charles de. Pierre Bruegel l'ancien. 2v. Brussels, Nouv. Soc. d'Edit., 1935.

BRUNELLESCHI, FILIPPO, 1377-1446

Argan, Giulio C. Brunelleschi. Milan, Mondadori, 1955.

Folnesics, Hans. Brunelleschi; ein beitrag zur entwicklungsgeschichte der frührenaissance architektur. Vienna, Schroll, 1915.

Luporini, Eugenio. Brunelleschi; forma e ragione. Milan, Ediz. di Comunita, 1964.

Sanpaolesi, Piero. Brunelleschi. Milan, Club del Libro, 1962.

BULFINCH, CHARLES, 1763-1844

Bulfinch, Charles. The life and letters of Charles Bulfinch, architect, with other family papers. Edit. by Ellen S. Bulfinch. Boston, Houghton, 1896.

Place, Charles A. Charles Bulfinch, architect and citizen. Boston, Houghton, 1925.

BURCHFIELD, CHARLES, 1893-

Baur, John I. H. Charles Burchfield. N.Y., Macmillan, 1956.

BURGKMAIR, HANS, 1473-1531

Burkhard, Arthur. Hans Burgkmair d.ä. Leipzig, Insel, 1934.

BURNE-JONES, EDWARD, 1833-1898

Bell, Malcolm. Sir Edward Burne-Jones; a record and review. London, Bell, 1903. 4 ed.

Burne-Jones, Georgiana M. Memorials of Edward Burne-Jones. 2v. London, Macmillan, 1909. 2 ed.

Grossman, Fritz. Burne-Jones; paintings. London, Phaidon, 1956.

Wood, T. Martin. Drawings of Sir Edward Burne-Jones. N.Y., Scribner, 1907.

BURNHAM, DANIEL HUDSON, 1846–1912

Moore, Charles H. Daniel H. Burnham, architect and planner of cities. 2v. Boston, Houghton, 1921.

CALDER, ALEXANDER, 1898–

Arnason, H. Harvard and Guerrero, P. E. Alexander Calder. N.Y., VanNostrand, 1966.

Sweeney, James J. Alexander Calder. N.Y., Museum of Modern Art, 1951.

CALLOT, JACQUES, 1592–1635

Bouchot, Henri. Jacques Callot, sa vie, son oeuvre et ses continuateurs. Paris, Hachette, 1889.

Bouchot-Soupique, Jacqueline. Jacques Callot, 1592–1635; quatorze dessins. Paris, Musées Nationaux, 1942.

Lieure, J. Jacques Callot. 3v. Paris, Gazette des Beaux-arts, 1924–1926.

Ternois, Daniel. L'art de Jacques Callot. Paris, deNobèle, 1962.

CANALE, ANTONIO, 1697–1768

Constable, William G. Canaletto, Giovanni Antonio Canal, 1697–1768. 2v. N.Y., Oxford Univ., 1962.

Hadeln, Detlev von. The drawings of Antonio Canal, called Canaletto. Trans. by C. Dodgson. London, Duckworth, 1929.

Parker, Karl T. The drawings of Antonio Canaletto in the collection of His Majesty the King at Windsor Castle. London, Phaidon, 1948.

Uzanne, L. G. Les Canaletto: l'oncle et le neveu, le maître et le disciple; Antonio da Canal, 1697–1768; Bernardo Bellotto, 1723–1780. Paris, Nilsson, 1925.

CANOVA, ANTONIO, 1757–1822

Bassi, Elena. Canova. Bergamo, Ist. Ital. d'Arti Grafiche, 1943.

Foratti, Aldo. Antonio Canova, 1757–1822. Milan, Caddeo, 1922.

Muñoz, Antonio. Antonio Canova; le opere. Rome, Palombi, 1957.

CARAVAGGIO, MICHELANGELO, 1565–1610

Benkard, Ernst. Caravaggio-studien. Berlin, Keller, 1928.

Berenson, Bernard. Caravaggio, his incongruity and his fame. London, Chapman, 1953.

Friedländer, Walter F. Caravaggio studies. Princeton, Princeton Univ., 1955.

Hinks, Roger P. Michelangelo Merisi da Caravaggio, his life, his legend. London, Faber, 1953.

Moir, Alfred K. The Italian followers of Caravaggio. 2v. Cambridge, Harvard Univ., 1967.

Schneider, Arthur von. Caravaggio und die niederländers. Amsterdam, Israel, 1967.

Schudt, Ludwig. Caravaggio. Vienna, Schroll, 1942.

Venturi, Lionello. Il Caravaggio. Rome, Società Edit. d'Arte Illus., 1925. 2 ed.

CARPACCIO, VITTORE, 1455–1525

Fiocco, Giuseppe. Carpaccio. Trans. by Jean Chuzeville. Paris, Crès, 1931.

Hausenstein, Wilhelm. Das werk des Vittore Carpaccio. Stuttgart, Deutsche Verlags-anstalt, 1925.

Lauts, Jan. Carpaccio; paintings and drawings. N.Y., Phaidon, 1962.

Molmenti, Pompeo G. The life and works of Vittore Carpaccio. Trans. by R. H. H. Cust. London, Murray, 1907.

CARPEAUX, JEAN-BAPTISTE, 1827–1875

Clément-Carpeaux, Louise. La vérité sur l'oeuvre et la vie de J.-B. Carpeaux (1827–1875). 2v. Paris, Dousset, 1934–1935.

Laran, Jean and LeBas, Georges. Carpeaux. Paris, Libr. Centrale des Beaux-arts, 1912.

Lecomte, Georges C. La vie héroïque et glorieuse de Carpeaux. Paris, Plon, 1928.

CARRA, CARLO, 1881–

Pacchioni, Guglielmo. Carlo Carra, pittore. Milan, Milione, 1959. 2 ed.

CARRACCI, AGOSTINO, 1557–1602
    ANNIBALE, 1560–1609
    LUDOVICO, 1555–1619

Bodmer, Heinrich. Lodovico Carracci. Burg, Hopfer, 1939.

Foratti, Aldo. I Carracci nella teoria e nella practica. Castello, Lapi, 1913.

Rouchès, Gabriel. Le peinture Bolonaise à la fin du XVI siècle (1575–1619): les Carrache. Paris, Alcan, 1913.

Wittkower, Rudolf. The drawings of the Carracci in the collection of Her Majesty the Queen at Windsor Castle. London, Phaidon, 1952.

CARRIÈRE, EUGÈNE, 1849–1906

Dubray, Jean P. Eugène Carrière; essai critique. Paris, Seheur, 1931.

Faure, Élie. Eugène Carrière, peintre et lithographe. Paris, Floury, 1908.

CARRIÈRE, EUGÈNE (continued)

Séailles, Gabriel. Eugène Carrière; essai de biographie psychologique. Paris, Colin, 1917. 2 ed.

CASSATT, MARY, 1845–1926

Breeskin, Adelyn D. The graphic work of Mary Cassatt; a catalogue raisonné. N.Y., Bittner, 1948.

Carson, Julia M. Mary Cassatt. N.Y., McKay, 1966.

Sweet, Frederick A. Miss Mary Cassatt, impressionist from Pennsylvania. Norman, Univ. of Oklahoma, 1966.

Watson, Forbes. Mary Cassatt. N.Y., Macmillan, 1932.

CASTAGNO, ANDREA DEL, 1423–1457

Richter, George M. Andrea del Castagno. Chicago, Univ. of Chicago, 1943.

CAVALLINI, PIETRO, 1250–1330

Lavagnino, Emilio. Pietro Cavallini. Rome, Palombi, 1953.

CELLINI, BENVENUTO, 1500–1571

Cellini, Benvenuto. Autobiography. Edit. by John Pope-Hennessy. N.Y., Phaidon, 1960.

Cust, Robert H. H. Life of Benvenuto Cellini. London, Methuen, 1912.

Plon, Eugène. Benvenuto Cellini, orfèvre, médailleur, sculpteur; recherches sur sa vie, sur son oeuvre et sur les pièces qui lui sont attribuées. 2v. Paris, Plon, 1883–1884.

Supino, Igino B. L'art di Benvenuto Cellini, con nuovi documenti sull'oreficeria fiorentina del secolo XVI. Florence, Alinari, 1901.

CÉZANNE, PAUL, 1839–1906

Badt, Kurt. The art of Cézanne. Trans. by S. A. Ogilvie. Berkeley, Univ. of California, 1965.

Brion-Guerry, Liliane. Cézanne et l'expression de l'espace. Paris, Michel, 1966.

Cézanne, Paul. Letters. Edit. by John Rewald. London, Cassirer, 1941.

Dorival, Bernard. Cézanne. Paris, Tisné, 1948.

*****Fry, Roger E.** Cézanne, a study of his development. N.Y., Farrar, 1958.

Loran, Erle. Cézanne's composition; analysis of his form with diagrams and photographs of his motifs. Berkeley, Univ. of California, 1963. 3 ed.

Mack, Gerstle. Paul Cézanne. N.Y., Knopf, 1938.

Meier-Graefe, Julius. Cézanne. Trans. by J. Holroyd-Reece. London, Benn, 1927.

Neumeyer, Alfred. Cézanne drawings. N.Y., Yoseloff, 1958.
Novotny, Fritz. Cézanne. N.Y., Phaidon, 1961.
*Rewald, John. Paul Cézanne, a biography. N.Y., Schocken, 1967.
Schapiro, Meyer. Paul Cézanne. N.Y., Abrams, 1952.
Vollard, Ambroise. Paul Cézanne; his life and art. Trans. by H. L. Van Doren. N.Y., Brown, 1923.

CHAGALL, MARC, 1887–
*Cassou, Jean. Chagall. Trans. by A. Jaffa. N.Y., Praeger, 1965.
Chagall, Marc. My life. Trans. by E. Abbott. N.Y., Grossman, 1960.
Erben, Walter. Marc Chagall. N.Y., Praeger, 1966.
Meyer, Franz. Marc Chagall; life and work. N.Y., Abrams, 1961.

CHAMPAIGNE, JEAN BAPTISTE DE, 1631–1681
PHILIPPE DE, 1602–1674
Gazier, A. L. Philippe et Jean Baptiste de Champaigne. Paris, Libr. de l'Art, 1923.

CHARDIN, JEAN-BAPTISTE SIMÉON, 1699–1779
Dayot, Armand P. M. J.-B. Siméon Chardin, avec un catalogue complet de l'oeuvre du maître par Jean Guiffrey. Paris, Piazza, 1907.
Leclère, Tristan. Chardin. Paris, Nilsson, 1924.
Ridder, André de. J.-B. S. Chardin. Paris, Floury, 1932.
Schéfer, Gaston. Chardin, biographie critique. Paris, Laurens, 1907.
Wildenstein, Georges. Chardin. Zurich, Manesse, 1963.

CHASE, WILLIAM MERRITT, 1849–1916
Roof, K. M. The life and times of William Merritt Chase. N.Y., Scribner, 1917.

CHASSÉRIAU, THÉODORE, 1819–1856
Bénedite, Léonce. Théodore Chassériau, sa vie et son oeuvre. 2v. Paris, Braun, 1932.

CHIPPENDALE, THOMAS, 1718–1779
Brackett, Oliver. Thomas Chippendale; a study of his life, work and influence. Boston, Houghton, 1925.
Chippendale, Thomas. The gentleman and cabinet-makers' director. N.Y., Dover, 1966 (reprint of 1762 ed.).

CHIRICO, GIORGIO DE, 1888–
Chirico, Giorgio de. Memorie della mia vita. Rome, Astrolabio, 1945.
Soby, James T. The early Chirico. N.Y., Dodd, 1941
——Giorgio de Chirico. N.Y., Museum of Modern Art, 1955.

CHURCH, FREDERIC EDWIN, 1826–1900
Huntington, David C. The landscape of Frederic Edwin Church; vision of an American era. N.Y., Braziller, 1966.

CIMA DA CONEGLIANO, GIOVANNI BATTISTA, 1460–1517
Burckhardt, Rudolf F. Cima da Conegliano; ein venezianischer maler des ubergangs vom quottrocento zum cinquecento. Leipzig, Hiersemann, 1905.
Coletti, Luigi. Cima da Conegliano. Venice, Pozza, 1959.

CIMABUE, GIOVANNI, 1240–1302
Battista, Eugenio. Cimabue. University Park, Penn State Univ., 1966.
Nicholson, Alfred. Cimabue; a critical study. Princeton, Princeton Univ., 1932.
Salvini, Roberto. Cimabue. Rome, Tuminelli, 1946.

CLAUDE LORRAIN, 1600–1682
Claude Lorrain. Liber veritatis; or, a collection of prints, after the original designs of Claude de Lorrain, in the collection of His Grace, the Duke of Devonshire. 3v. London, Boydell, 1777–1819.
Courthion, Pierre. Claude Gellée, dit Le Lorrain. Paris, Floury, 1932.
Friedländer, Walter F. Claude Lorrain. Berlin, Cassirer, 1921.
Roethlisberger, Marcel. Claude Lorrain; the paintings. 2v. New Haven, Yale Univ., 1961.

CLOUET, FRANÇOIS, 1505–1572
         JEAN, 1475–1541
Germain, Alphonse. Les Clouet; biographie critique. Paris, Laurens, 1907.
Moreau-Nélaton, Étienne. Les Clouet et leurs émules. 3v. Paris, Laurens, 1924.

COECKE, PIETER, 1502–1550
Marlier, Georges. Pierre Coeck d'Alost, 1502–1550; la renaissance flamande. Brussels, Finck, 1966.

COLOMBE, MICHEL, 1430–1512
Pradel, Pierre. Michel Colombe, le dernier imagier gothique. Paris, Plon, 1953.

Vitry, Paul. Michel Colombe et la sculpture française de son temps. Paris, Libr. Centrale des Beaux-arts, 1901.

CONSTABLE, JOHN, 1776–1837

Constable, John. Correspondence, edited by R. B. Beckett. v.1– . London, HMSO, 1962.

Holmes, Charles J. Constable and his influence on landscape painting. Westminster, Constable, 1902.

Leslie, Charles R. Memoirs of the life of John Constable, composed chiefly of his letters. London, Lehmann, 1952.

Peacock, Carlos. John Constable; the man and his work. Greenwich, NYGS, 1965.

Reynolds, Graham. Constable, the natural painter. N.Y., McGraw, 1965.

Shirley, Andrew. John Constable. London, Medici Society, 1948.

COPLEY, JOHN SINGLETON, 1737–1815

Bayley, Frank W. The life and works of John Singleton Copley, founded on the work of Augustus Thorndike Perkins. Boston, Taylor, 1915.

Copley, John S. Letters and papers of John Singleton Copley and Henry Pelham, 1739–1776. Boston, Mass. Hist. Society, 1914.

Flexner, James T. John Singleton Copley. Boston, Houghton, 1948.

Parker, Barbara N. and Wheeler, Anne B. John Singleton Copley; American portraits in oil, pastel and miniature. Boston, Museum of Fine Arts, 1938.

Prown, Jules. John Singleton Copley. 2v. Cambridge, Harvard Univ., 1966.

COROT, JEAN-BAPTISTE CAMILLE, 1796–1875

Baud-Bovy, Daniel. Corot. Geneva, Jullien, 1957.

Bazin, Germain. Corot. Paris, Tisné, 1942.

Corot, Jean-B. C. Corot, raconté par lui-même et par ses amis. 2v. Geneva, Cailler, 1946.

Leymarie, Jean. Corot. Trans. by S. Gilbert. A biographical and critical study. Cleveland, World (Skira), 1966.

Moreau-Nélaton, Étienne. Corot, raconté par lui-même. 2v. Paris, Laurens, 1924.

Robaut, Alfred and Moreau-Nélaton, Étienne. L'oeuvre de Corot. 5v. Paris, Floury, 1905. Reprint 1965–1966.

Schoeller, André and Dieterle, Jean. Corot; premier supplement à l'oeuvre de Corot par A. Robaut et Moreau-Nélaton. Paris, Arts et Métiers Graphiques, 1948.

CORREGGIO, ANTONIO ALLEGRI, 1494–1534

Bodmer, Heinrich. Correggio und die malerei der Emilia. Vienna, Deuticke, 1942.

Gronau, Georg. Correggio; des meisters gemälde. Stuttgart, Deutsche Verlagsanstalt, 1907.

Popham, Arthur E. Correggio's drawings. N.Y., Oxford Univ., 1957.

Ricci, Corrado. Correggio. London, Warne, 1930.

Vito Battaglia, Silvia de. Correggio; bibliografia. Rome, Palombi, 1934.

COTMAN, JOHN SELL, 1782–1842

Kitson, Sydney D. The life of John Sell Cotman. London, Faber, 1937.

Smith, Solomon C. K. Cotman. N.Y., Stokes, 1926.

COURBET, GUSTAVE, 1819–1877

Bénedite, Léonce. Gustave Courbet, with notes by J. Laran and Ph. Baston-Dreyfus. Philadelphia, Lippincott, 1913.

Boas, George. Courbet and the naturalistic movement. N.Y., Russell, 1938.

Courbet, Gustave. Courbet, raconté par lui-même et par ses amis; sa vie et ses oeuvres. v.1– . Geneva, Cailler, 1948– .

Courthion, Pierre. Courbet. Paris, Floury, 1931.

Duret, Théodore. Courbet. Paris, Bernheim, 1918.

Léger, Charles. Courbet. Paris, Crès, 1929.

Mack, Gerstle. Gustave Courbet. N.Y., Knopf, 1951.

COZENS, ALEXANDER, 1717–1786
        JOHN ROBERT, 1752–1797

Oppé, Adolf P. Alexander and John Robert Cozens. London, Black, 1952.

CRAM, RALPH ADAMS, 1863–1942

Cram, Ralph A. My life in architecture. Boston, Little, Brown, 1936.

CRANACH, LUCAS, 1472–1553

Friedländer, Max J. and Rosenberg, Jakob. Die gemälde von Lucas Cranach. Berlin, Deutscher Ver. f. Kunstwissenschaft, 1932.

Glaser, Curt. Lukas Cranach. Leipzig, Insel, 1923.

Lilienfein, Heinrich. Lukas Cranach und seine zeit. Bielefeld, Velhagen, 1942.

Ludecke, Heinz. Lucas Cranach der ältere; der künstler und seine zeit. Berlin, Henschel, 1953.

Posse, Hans. Lucas Cranach. Vienna, Schroll, 1942.

CRIVELLI, CARLO, 1430–1493
Drey, Franz. Carlo Crivelli und seine schule. Munich, Bruckmann, 1927.
Rushforth, Gordon M. Carlo Crivelli. London, Bell, 1900.
Zampetti, Pietro. Carlo Crivelli. Milan, Martello, 1962.

CROME, JOHN, 1768–1821
Baker, Charles H. C. Crome. London, Methuen, 1921.
Mottram, Ralph H. John Crome of Norwich. London, Lane, 1931.
Smith, Solomon C. K. Crome; with a note on the Norwich school. London, Allen, 1923.

CURRY, JOHN STEUART, 1897–1946
Schmeckebier, Laurence E. John Steuart Curry's pageant of America. N.Y., American Artists Group, 1948.

DADDI, BERNARDO, 1280–1350
Vitzhum von Eckstädt, George. Bernardo Daddi. Leipzig, Hiersemann, 1903.

DALI, SALVADOR, 1904–
Dali, Salvador. Diary of a genius. Trans. by R. Howard. N.Y., Doubleday, 1965.
Soby, James T. Paintings, drawings, prints: Salvador Dali. N.Y., Museum of Modern Art, 1941.

DALOU, AIMÉ JULES, 1838–1902
Caillaux, Henriette. Aimé-Jules Dalou (1838–1902) Paris, Delagrave, 1935.
Dreyfous, Maurice. Dalou, sa vie et son oeuvre. Paris, Laurens, 1903.

DAUBIGNY, CHARLES-FRANÇOIS, 1817–1878
Moreau-Nélaton, Étienne. Daubigny, raconté par lui-même. Paris, Laurens, 1925.

DAUMIER, HONORÉ, 1808–1879
Adhémar, Jean. Honoré Daumier. Paris, Tisné, 1954.
Bouvy, Eugène. Daumier; l'oeuvre gravé du maître. 2v. Paris, Le Garrec, 1933.
Courthion, Pierre. Daumier, raconté par lui-même et par ses amis. Geneva, Cailler, 1945.
Fuchs, Eduard. Honoré Daumier; holzschnitte, 1833–1870. Munich, Langen, 1918.
_____Honoré Daumier; lithographien. 3v. Munich, Langen, 1920–1922.
_____Der maler Daumier; nachtrag. Munich, Langen, 1930.

DAUMIER, HONORÉ (continued)

Hausenstein, Wilhelm. Daumier, zeichnungen. Munich, Piper, 1918.

Larkin, Oliver W. Daumier, a man of his time. N.Y., McGraw, 1966.

Maison, Karl E. Honoré Daumier; catalogue raisonné of the paintings, water-colours and drawings. 2v. Greenwich, NYGS, 1967.

Rey, Robert. Honoré Daumier. Trans. by N. Guterman. N.Y., Abrams, 1966.

DAVID, JACQUES-LOUIS, 1748–1825

Cantinelli, Richard. Jacques-Louis David, 1748–1825. Paris, VanOest, 1930.

Dowd, David. Pageant master of the republic: J.-L. David and the French revolution. Lincoln, Univ. of Nebraska, 1948.

Maret, Jacques. David. Monaco, Documents d'Art, 1943.

Maurois, André. J.-L. David. Paris, Dimanche, 1948.

Serullaz, Maurice. J.-L. David, 1748–1825; quatorze dessins. Paris, Musées Nationaux, 1939.

Valentiner, Wilhelm R. Jacques Louis David and the French revolution. N.Y., Sherman, 1929.

DAVID D'ANGERS, PIERRE JEAN, 1788–1856

Jouin, Henri A. David d'Angers; sa vie, son oeuvre, ses écrits et ses contemporains. 2v. Paris, Plon, 1878.

Valotaire, Marcel. David d'Angers; étude critique. Paris, Renouard, 1932.

DAVIES, ARTHUR BOWEN, 1862–1928

Cortissoz, Royal. Arthur B. Davies. N.Y., Macmillan, 1931.

Price, Frederic N. The etchings and lithographs of Arthur B. Davies. N.Y., Kennerley, 1929.

DAVIS, STUART, 1894–

Sweeney, James J. Stuart Davis. N.Y., Museum of Modern Art, 1945.

DEGAS, HILAIRE GERMAIN EDGAR, 1834–1917

Boggs, Jean S. Drawings by Degas. N.Y., Abrams, 1967.

_____Portraits by Degas. Berkeley, Univ. of California, 1962.

Degas, H. G. E. Letters. Ed. by Marcel Guérin. Oxford, Cassirer, 1947.

Jamot, Paul. Degas. Paris, Gazette des Beaux-arts, 1931.

Lafond, Paul. Degas. 2v. Paris, Floury, 1918–1919.

Lemoisne, Paul A. Degas et son oeuvre. 4v. Paris, Brame, 1947.

Meier-Graefe, Julius. Degas. Trans. by J. Holroyd-Reece. London, Benn, 1923.

Rewald, John. Degas, works in sculpture. N.Y., Pantheon, 1944.
*Rich, Daniel C. Degas. N.Y., Abrams, 1951.
Rivière, Henri. Les dessins de Degas. Ser. I–II Paris, Demotte, 1922–1923.
Vollard, Ambroise. Degas, an intimate portrait. Trans. by R. T. Weaver.
    N.Y., Greenberg, 1927.

DELACROIX, EUGÈNE, 1798–1863
Badt, Kurt. Eugène Delacroix drawings. Oxford, Cassirer, 1946.
Baudelaire, Charles. Eugène Delacroix, his life and work. Trans. by J. M.
    Bernstein. N.Y., Lear, 1947.
Cassou, Jean. Delacroix. Paris, Dimanche, 1947.
Courthion, Pierre. La vie de Delacroix. Paris, Gallimard, 1927. 6 ed.
Delacroix, Eugène. Correspondence générale d'Eugène Delacroix, publiée
    par André Joubin. 5v. Paris, Plon, 1936–1938.
_____Journal de Eugène Delacroix, avec notes par André Joubin. 3v. Paris,
    Plon, 1932.
_____Journal. Trans. by Lucy Norton. London, Phaidon, 1952.
*_____Journal. Trans. by W. Pach. N.Y., Grove, 1961.
Escholier, Raymond. Delacroix, peintre, graveur, écrivain. 3v. Paris, Floury,
    1926–1929.
Lavallée, Pierre. Eugène Delacroix; quatorze dessins. Paris, Musées Na-
    tionaux, 1938.
Moreau-Nélaton, Étienne. Delacroix, raconté par lui-même; étude biograph-
    ique d'après ses lettres, son journal. 2v. Paris, Laurens, 1916.
Mras, George P. Eugène Delacroix's theory of art. Princeton, Princeton Univ.,
    1966.
Robaut, Alfred. L'oeuvre complet de Eugène Delacroix, peintures, dessins,
    gravures, lithographies. Paris, Charavay, 1885.
Rudrauf, Lucien. Eugène Delacroix et le problème du romantisme artistique.
    Paris, Laurens. 1942.
Signac, Paul. D'Eugène Delacroix au néo-impressionisme. Paris, Floury,
    1939. 4 ed.

DEMUTH, CHARLES HENRY, 1883–1935
Murrell, William. Charles Demuth. N.Y., Macmillan, 1931.
Ritchie, Andrew C. Charles Demuth. N.Y., Museum of Modern Art, 1950.

DERAIN, ANDRÉ, 1880–1954
Faure, Élie. A. Derain. Paris, Crès, 1926.

DERAIN, ANDRÉ (continued)
Vaughan, Malcolm. Derain. N.Y., Hyperion, 1941.

DESIDERIO DA SETTIGNANO, 1428–1464
Planiscig, Leo. Desiderio da Settignano. Vienna, Schroll, 1942.

DOMENICHINO, 1581–1641
Pope-Hennessy, John. The drawings of Domenichino in the collection of His Majesty the King at Windsor Castle. London, Phaidon, 1948.
Serra, Luigi. Domenico Zampieri, detto il Domenichino. Rome, Calzone, 1909.

DONATELLO, 1386–1466
Cecchi, Emilio. Donatello. Rome, Tumminelli, 1942.
Crawford, David A. E. L. (Lord Balcarres). Donatello. N.Y., Scribner, 1903.
Goldscheider, Ludwig. Donatello. London, Phaidon, 1944.
Janson, Horst W. The sculpture of Donatello. Princeton, Princeton Univ., 1963. 2 ed.
Planiscig, Leo. Donatello. Vienna, Schroll, 1939.
Schubring, Paul. Donatello; des meisters werke. Stuttgart, Deutsche Verlagsanstalt, 1922. 2 ed.

DOSSI, DOSSO, 1479–1542
Mendelsohn, Henriette. Das werk der Dossi. Munich, Muller, 1914.
Zwanziger, W. C. Dosso Dossi. Leipzig, Klinkhardt, 1911.

DOU, GERARD, 1613–1675
Martin, Wilhelm. Gerard Dou. Stuttgart, Deutsche Verlagsanstalt, 1913.

DUBUFFET, JEAN, 1901–
Loreau, Max. Dubuffet; catalogue des travaux. v.1– . Paris, Pauvert, 1964– .
Selz, Peter. The work of Jean Dubuffet. N.Y., Doubleday, 1962.

DUCCIO DI BUONINSEGNA, 1255–1319
Carli, Enzo. Duccio di Buoninsegna. Milan, Electa, 1959.
Weigelt, Curt H. Duccio di Buoninsegna; studien zur geschichte der frühsienesischen tafelmalerei. Leipzig, Hiersemann, 1911.

DUCHAMP, MARCEL, 1887–
Lebel, Robert. Sur Marcel Duchamp. Paris, Trianon, 1967. Reprint.

DURER, ALBRECHT, 1471–1528
Conway, William M. The literary remains of Albrecht Dürer. Cambridge, Cambridge Univ., 1889.
Dodgson, Campbell. Albrecht Dürer. N.Y., Plenum (reprint of 1926).
Dürer, Albrecht. Writings. Trans. by W. M. Conway. Ed. by Alfred Werner. N.Y., Philosoph. Lib., 1958.
Flechsig, Eduard. Albrecht Dürer; sein leben und seine künstlerische entwickelung. 2v. Berlin, Grote, 1928–1931.
Friedländer, Max J. Albrecht Dürer. Leipzig, Insel, 1921.
Knappe, Karl Adolf. Dürer; complete engravings, etchings and woodcuts. N.Y., Abrams, 1965.
Koehler, Sylvester R. A chronological catalogue of the engravings, drypoints and etchings of Albert Dürer. N.Y., Grolier, 1897.
*****Kurth, Willi.** The complete woodcuts of Albrecht Dürer. Trans. by S. M. Welsh. Magnolia, Peter Smith, 1963. Reprint.
Lippmann, Friedrich. Drawings by Albrecht Dürer. 7v. Berlin, Grote, 1883–1929.
Meder, Joseph. Dürer katalog; ein handbuch über Albrecht Dürers stiche, radierungen, holzschnitte, deren zustände, ausgaben und wasserzeichen. Vienna, Gilhofer, 1932.
Panofsky, Erwin. Albrecht Dürer. Princeton, Princeton Univ., 1948. 3 ed. (The later ed. of 1955 has complete text and illus. but lacks the critical catalogue.)
Scherer, Valentin. Dürer; des meisters gemälde, kupferstiche und holzschnitte. Stuttgart, Deutsche Verlagsanstalt, 1928. 4 ed.
Singer, Hans W. Versuch einer Dürer bibliographie. Strassburg, Heitz, 1928. 2 ed.
Tietze, Hans and Tietze-Conrat, Erika. Kritische verzeichnis der werke Albrecht Dürers. v.1– . Augsburg, Filser, 1928– .
Waetzoldt, Wilhelm. Dürer and his times. Trans. by R. H. Boothroyd. London, Phaidon, 1950.
Winkler, Friedrich. Die zeichnungen Albrecht Dürers. 4v. Berlin, Deutscher Ver. f. Kunstwissenschaft, 1936–1939.
Wölfflin, Heinrich. Die kunst Albrecht Dürers. Munich, Bruckmann, 1926. 5 ed.

DUFY, RAOUL, 1877–1953
  Courthion, Pierre. Raoul Dufy. Geneva, Cailler, 1951.
  Zervos, Christian. Raoul Dufy. Paris, Cahiers d'Art, 1928.

DYCK, ANTHONY VAN, 1599–1641
  Cust, Lionel H. Anthony van Dyck, an historical study of his life and works. London, Bell, 1900.
  Delacre, Maurice. Le dessin dans l'oeuvre de van Dyck. Brussels, Hayez, 1934.
  Dyck, Anthony van. Italienisches skizzenbuch. Ed. by Gert Adriani. Vienna, Schroll, 1940.
  Glück, Gustav. Van Dyck; des meisters gemälde. Stuttgart, Deutsche Verlags-anstalt, 1931. 2 ed.
  Knackfuss, Hermann. Van Dyck. Trans. by Campbell Dodgson. Bielefeld, Velhagen, 1899.
  Puyvelde, Leo van. Van Dyck. Brussels, Elsevier, 1950.

EAKINS, THOMAS, 1844–1916
  Goodrich, Lloyd. Thomas Eakins, his life and work. N.Y., Macmillan, 1933.
  McKinney, Roland J. Thomas Eakins. N.Y., Crown, 1942.

EARL, RALPH, 1751–1801
  Goodrich, Laurence B. Ralph Earl, recorder for an era. Albany, State Univ. of N.Y., 1967.

ELSHEIMER, ADAM, 1578–1620
  Bode, Wilhelm von. Adam Elsheimer, der römische maler deutscher nation. Munich, Schmidt, 1920.
  Drost, Willi. Adam Elsheimer und sein kreis. Berlin, Athenaion, 1933.
  Weizsäcker, Heinrich. Adam Elsheimer, der maler von Frankfurt. v.1– . Berlin, Deutscher Ver. f. Kunstwissenschaft, 1936– .

ENSOR, JAMES, 1860–1949
  Damase, Jacques. L'oeuvre gravé de James Ensor. Geneva, Motte, 1966.
  Ensor, James. Écrits. Ed. by H. Vandeputte. Brussels, Lumiere, 1944.
  Haesaerts, Paul. James Ensor. N.Y., Abrams, 1958.
  Leroy, Gregoire. James Ensor. Brussels, VanOest, 1922.

EPSTEIN, JACOB, 1880–1959
  Epstein, Jacob. An autobiography. N.Y., Dutton, 1963.

ERNST, MAX, 1891–
*Ernst, Max. Beyond painting, and other writings by the artist and his friends. N.Y., Wittenborn, 1948.
Russell, John. Max Ernst, life and work. N.Y., Abrams, 1967.

EYCK, HUBERT VAN, 1366–1426
       JAN VAN, 1390–1440
Baldass, Ludwig. Jan van Eyck. N.Y., Phaidon, 1952.
Beenken, Hermann T. Hubert und Jan van Eyck. Munich, Bruckmann, 1941.
Conway, William M. The Van Eycks and their followers. London, Murray, 1921.
Renders, Émile. Hubert van Eyck, personnage de légende. Paris, VanOest, 1933.
Schmarsow, August. Hubert und Jan van Eyck. Leipzig, Hiersemann, 1924.
Tolnay, Charles de. Le Maitre de Flémalle et les frères Van Eyck. Brussels, Connaisance, 1939.
Weale, William H. J. and Brockwell, Maurice W. The Van Eycks and their art. N.Y., Lane, 1912.

FALCONET, ÉTIENNE MAURICE, 1716–1791
Réau, Louis. Étienne Maurice Falconet. 2v. Paris, Demotte, 1922.

FANTIN-LATOUR, IGNACE HENRI JEAN THÉODORE, 1836–1904
Bénédite, Léonce. L'oeuvre lithographique de Fantin-Latour. Paris, Delteil, 1907.
Fantin-Latour, Victoria D. Catalogue de l'oeuvre complète (1849–1904) de Fantin-Latour. Paris, Floury, 1911.
Jullien, Adolphe. Fantin-Latour, sa vie et ses amitiés; lettres inédites et souvenirs personnels. Paris, Laveur, 1909.
Kahn, Gustave. Fantin-Latour. Paris, Rieder, 1927.

FEININGER, LYONEL, 1871–1956
Hess, Hans. Lyonel Feininger. N.Y., Abrams, 1961.

FEKE, ROBERT, 1705–1750
Foote, Henry W. Robert Feke, colonial portrait painter. Cambridge, Harvard Univ., 1930.

FERRARI, GAUDENZIO, 1480–1546
Weber, Siegfried. Gaudenzio Ferrari und seine schule. Strassburg, Heitz,
1927.

FEUERBACH, ANSELM, 1829–1880
Uhde-Bernays, Hermann. Feuerbach; des meisters gemälde. Stuttgart,
Deutsche Verlagsanstalt, 1913.
_____Feuerbach; beschreibender katalog seiner sämtlichen gemälde. Munich,
Bruckmann, 1929.

FILARETE, 1400–1469
Filarete. Treatise on architecture. Trans. by J. R. Spencer. 2v. New Haven,
Yale Univ., 1965.
Tigler, Peter. Die architektur theorie des Filarete. Berlin, deGruyter, 1963.

FINIGUERRA, TOMMASO, 1426–1464
Finiguerra, Tommaso. A Florentine picture-chronicle; critical and descriptive text by Sidney Colvin. London, Quaritch, 1898.

FIORENZO DI LORENZO, 1445–1525
Graham, J. C. The problem of Fiorenzo di Lorenzo of Perugia; a critical and
historical study. Perugia, Terese, 1903.
Weber, Siegfried. Fiorenzo di Lorenzo; eine kunsthistorische studie. Strassburg, Heitz, 1904.

FISCHER VON ERLACH, JOHANN BERNHARD, 1656–1723
Kunoth, George. Die historische architektur Fischers von Erlach. Dusseldorf,
Schwann, 1956.
Sedlmayr, Hans. Johann Bernhard Fischer von Erlach. Vienna, Herold,
1956.

FLAXMAN, JOHN, 1755–1826
Constable, William G. John Flaxman, 1755–1826. London, Univ. of London, 1927.

FOPPA, VINCENZO, 1428–1516
Ffoulkes, Constance J. and Maiocchi, Rodolfo. Vincenzo Foppa of Brescia,
founder of the Lombard school, his life and work. N.Y., Lane, 1909.
Wittgens, Fernanda. Vincenzo Foppa. Milan, Pizzi, 1949.

FORTUNY, MARIANO, 1838–1874
  Maseras, Alfonso and Fages de Climent, Carlos. Fortuny, la mitad de una vida. Madrid, Espasa, 1932.
  Yriarte, C. E. Fortuny. Paris, Libr. de l'Art, 1886.

FOUQUET, JEAN, 1415–1480
  Cox, Trenchard. Jehan Foucquet, native of Tours. London, Faber, 1931.
  Gruyer, Francis A. Les quarante Fouquets à Chantilly. Paris, Plon, 1910.
  Lafenestre, G. E. Jehan Fouquet. Paris, Libr. de l'Art Ancien et Moderne, 1905.
  Perls, Klaus G. Jean Fouquet. London, Hyperion, 1940.
  Wescher, Paul R. Jean Fouquet and his time. Trans. by E. Winkworth. London, Pleiades, 1947.

FRAGONARD, JEAN-HONORÉ, 1732–1806
  Algoud, Henri. Fragonard. Monaco, Documents d'Art, 1941.
  Ananoff, Alexandre. L'oeuvre dessiné de Jean-Honoré Fragonard. v.1– . Paris, deNobèle, 1961– .
  Grappe, Georges. Fragonard, la vie et l'oeuvre. Monaco, Documents d'Art, 1946.
  Lavallée, Pierre. J.-H. Fragonard, quatorze dessins. Paris, Musées Nationaux, 1938.
  Mauclair, Camille. Fragonard; biographie critique. Paris, Laurens, 1904.
  Nolhac, Pierre de. Fragonard, 1732–1806. Paris, Goupil, 1918.
  Portalis, Roger. Honoré Fragonard, sa vie et son oeuvre. 2v. Paris, Rothschild, 1889.
  Wildenstein, Georges. Paintings of Fragonard. Trans. by C. W. Chilton and Mrs. A. L. Kitson. N.Y., Phaidon, 1960.

FRANCESCHI, PIETRO DI BENEDETTO DEI, 1416–1492
  Bianconi, Piero. Piero della Francesca. Trans. by P. Colacicchi. N.Y., Hawthorn, 1962.
  Clark, Kenneth M. Piero della Francesca. London, Phaidon, 1951.
  Fasola, Giustina N. De prospectiva pingendi. Florence, Sansoni, 1942.
  Longhi, Roberto. Piero della Francesca. Florence, Sansoni, 1963. 3 ed.
  Salmi, Mario. Piero della Francesca e il Palazzo ducale di Urbino. Florence, Le Monnier, 1945.
  Waters, William G. Piero della Francesca. London, Bell, 1908.

FRANCESCO DI GIORGIO MARTINI, 1439–1502

Brinton, Selwyn J. C. Francesco di Giorgio Martini of Siena; painter, sculptor, engineer, civil and military architect (1439–1502). 2v. London, Besant, 1934–1935.

Papini, Roberto. Francesco di Giorgio, architetto. 3v. Florence, Electa, 1946.

Weller, Allen S. Francesco di Giorgio, Siena 1439–1475. Chicago, Univ. of Chicago, 1942.

FRANCIA, 1450–1517

Williamson, George C. Francesco Raibolini, called Francia. London, Bell, 1901.

FRENCH, DANIEL CHESTER, 1850–1931

Adams, Adeline V. P. Daniel Chester French, sculptor. Boston, Houghton, 1932.

Cresson, Margaret F. Journey into fame; the life of Daniel Chester French. Cambridge, Harvard Univ., 1947.

French, Mary F. Memories of a sculptor's wife. Boston, Houghton, 1928.

FRIEDRICH, CASPAR DAVID, 1774–1840

Einem, Herbert von. Caspar David Friedrick. Berlin, Rembrandt, 1938.

FUSELI, HENRY, 1741–1825

Antal, Frederick. Fuseli studies. London, Routledge, 1956.

Mason, Eudo C. The mind of Henry Fuseli; selections from his writings. London, Routledge, 1951.

GABO, NAUM, 1890–

Gabo, Naum. Constructions, sculpture, paintings, drawings, engravings. Cambridge, Harvard Univ., 1957.

Olson, Ruth and Chanin, Abraham. Naum Gabo and Antoine Pevsner. N.Y., Museum of Modern Art, 1948.

GABRIEL, JACQUES ANGE, 1699–1782

Gromort, Georges. Jacques-Ange Gabriel, sa vie, son oeuvre. Paris, Fréal, 1933.

GAINSBOROUGH, THOMAS, 1727–1788

Armstrong, Walter. Gainsborough and his place in English art. London, Heinemann, 1898.

Gainsborough, Thomas. Letters. Ed. by Mary Woodall. Greenwich, NYGS, 1963.

Waterhouse, Ellis K. Gainsborough. London, Hulton, 1958.

Whitley, William T. Thomas Gainsborough. London, Murray, 1915.

Woodall, Mary. Gainsborough's landscape drawings. London, Faber, 1939.

____Thomas Gainsborough, his life and work. London, Phoenix, 1949.

GAUDI, ANTONIO, 1852–1926

*Collins, George R. Antonio Gaudi. N.Y., Braziller, 1960.

Sert, José L. and Sweeney, James J. Antonio Gaudi. N.Y., Praeger, 1961.

GAUGUIN, PAUL, 1848–1903

Cogniat, Raymond. Gauguin. Paris, Tisné, 1947.

*Gauguin, Paul. The intimate journals of Paul Gauguin. Trans. by Van Wyck Brooks. Bloomington, Univ. of Indiana, 1958.

____Letters to his wife and friends. Ed. by M. Malingue. Cleveland, World, 1949.

Goldwater, Robert. Gauguin. N.Y., Abrams, 1957.

Guérin, Marcel. L'oeuvre gravé de Gauguin. 2v. Paris, Floury, 1927.

Malingue, Maurice. Gauguin, le peintre et son oeuvre; avant-propos de Pola Gauguin. Paris, Presses de la Cité, 1948.

Rewald, John. Gauguin. Paris, Hyperion, 1938.

Rotonchamp, Jean de. Paul Gauguin, 1848–1903. Paris, Crès, 1925.

GAULLI, GIOVANNI BATTISTA, 1639–1709

Enggass, Robert. The painting of Baciccio (Giovanni Battista Gaulli, 1639–1709) University Park, Penn State, 1964.

GEERTGEN TOT SINT JANS, 1465–1495

Kessler, J. H. H. Geertgen tot Sint Jans; zijn herkomst en invloed in Holland. Utrecht, Oosthoek, 1930.

GELDER, ARENT DE, 1645–1727

Lilienfeld, Karl. Arent de Gelder; sein leben und seine kunst. The Hague, Nijhoff, 1914.

GENTILE DA FABRIANO, 1370–1427

Colasanti, Arduino. Gentile da Fabriano. Bergamo, Ist. Ital. d'Arti Grafiche, 1909.

GÉRICAULT, JEAN-LOUIS ANDRÉ THÉODORE, 1791–1824
Berger, Klaus. Géricault; drawings and watercolors. N.Y., Bittner, 1946.
___Géricault and his work. Trans. by W. Ames. Lawrence, Univ. of Kansas, 1955.
Clément, Charles. Géricault; étude biographique et critique. Paris, Didier, 1879. 3 ed.

GÉRÔME, JEAN-LÉON, 1824–1904
Moreau-Vauthier, Charles. Gérôme, peintre et sculpteur, l'homme et l'artiste. Paris, Hachette, 1906.

GHIBERTI, LORENZO, 1378–1455
Goldscheider, Ludwig. Ghiberti. London, Phaidon, 1949.
Krautheimer, Richard. Lorenzo Ghiberti. Princeton, Princeton Univ., 1956.
Planiscig, Leo. Lorenzo Ghiberti. Vienna, Schroll, 1940.
Schlosser, Julius. Leben und meinungen des florentinischen bildners Lorenzo Ghiberti. Basel, Holbein, 1941.

GHIRLANDAIO, DOMENICO, 1449–1494
Bargellini, Piero. Il Ghirlandaio del bel mondo fiorentino. Florence, Arnaud, 1945.
Davies, Gerald S. Ghirlandaio. London, Methuen, 1908.
Lauts, Jan. Domenico Ghirlandajo. Vienna, Schroll, 1943.
Steinmann, Ernst. Ghirlandajo. Bielefeld, Velhagen, 1897.

GILL, ERIC, 1882–1940
Gill, Eric. Autobiography. London, Cape, 1940.
___Letters. Ed. by Walter Shewring. N.Y., Devin, 1948.

GIORDANO, LUCA, 1635–1705
Ferrari, Oreste and Scavizzi, Giuseppe. Luca Giordano. 3v. Naples, Ediz. Scient. Ital., 1966.

GIORGIONE DA CASTELFRANCO, 1477–1510
Baldass, Ludwig von. Giorgione. Trans. by J. M. Brownjohn. N.Y., Abrams, 1965.
Boehn, Max von. Giorgione und Palma Vecchio. Bielefeld, Velhagen, 1908.
Conway, William M. Giorgione, a new study of his art as a landscape painter. London, Benn, 1929.

Cook, Herbert F. Giorgione, London, Bell, 1904. 2 ed.

Fiocco, Giuseppe. Giorgione. Bergamo, Ist. Ital d'Arti Grafiche, 1948. 2 ed.

Hourticq, Louis. Le problème de Giorgione; sa légende, son oeuvre, ses élèves. Paris, Hachette, 1930.

Justi, Ludwig. Giorgione. 2v. Berlin, Reimer, 1936. 3 ed.

Richter, George M. Giorgio da Castelfranco, called Giorgione. Chicago, Univ. of Chicago, 1937.

Venturi, Lionello. Giorgione e il Giorgionismo. Milan, Hoepli, 1913.

GIOTTO DI BONDONE, 1266–1337

Battisti, Eugenio. Giotto, biographical and critical study. Trans. by J. Emmons. Cleveland, World (Skira), 1966.

Carli, Enzo. Giotto. Milan, Mondadori, 1951.

Cecchi, Emilio. Giotto. Milan, Hoepli, 1937.

Hausenstein, Wilhelm. Giotto. Berlin, Propyläen, 1923.

Marle, Raimond van. Récherches sur l'iconographie de Giotto et de Duccio. Strassburg, Heitz, 1920.

Salvini, Roberto. Giotto bibliografia. Rome, Palombi, 1938.

Sirén, Osvald. Giotto and some of his followers. Trans. by Frederick Schenck. 2v. Cambridge; Harvard Univ., 1917. N.Y., Russell. Reprint.

Supino, Igino B. Giotto. 2v. Florence, Ist. di Ediz. Artistiche, 1920.

Weigelt, Curt H. Giotto; des meisters gemälde. Stuttgart, Deutsche Verlagsanstalt, 1925.

GIOVANNI DA BOLOGNA, 1529–1608

Desjardins, Abel. La vie et l'oeuvre de Jean Bologne. Paris, Quantin, 1883.

GIOVANNI DA MILANO, 1300–1370

Marabottini, Alessandro. Giovanni da Milano. Florence, Sansoni, 1950.

GIOVANNI DI PAOLO, 1403–1483

Brandi, Cesare. Giovanni di Paolo. Florence, Le Monnier, 1947.

Pope-Hennessy, John. Giovanni di Paolo, 1403–1483. London, Chatto, 1937.

GIRARDON, FRANÇOIS, 1628–1715

Francastel, Pierre. Girardon; biographie et catalogue critiques; l'oeuvre complète de l'artiste. Paris, Beaux-arts, 1928.

GIRTIN, THOMAS, 1775–1802
  Binyon, Laurence. Thomas Girtin. London, Seeley, 1900.
  Davies, Randall. Thomas Girtin's water-colours. London, Studio, 1924.
  Mayne, Jonathan. Thomas Girtin. Leigh-on-sea, Lewis, 1949.

GISLEBERTUS, fl. 1125–1135
  Grivot, Denis and Zarnecki, George. Gislebertus, sculptor of Autun. N.Y., Grossman, 1961.

GIULIO ROMANO, 1499–1546
  Hartt, Frederick. Giulio Romano. New Haven, Yale Univ., 1958.

GLEYRE, MARC CHARLES GABRIEL, 1806–1874
  Clément, Charles. Gleyre; étude biographique et critique. Paris, Perrin, 1886. 2 ed.

GOES, HUGO VAN DER, 1435–1482
  Destrée, Joseph. Hugo van der Goes. Brussels, VanOest, 1914.
  Rey, Robert. Hugo van der Goes. Brussels, Cercle d'Art, 1945.
  Winkler, Friedrich. Das werk des Hugo van der Goes. Berlin, deGruyter, 1964.

GOGH, VINCENT VAN, 1853–1890
  Brooks, Charles M. Vincent van Gogh, a bibliography comprising a catalogue of the literature published from 1890 through 1940. N.Y., Museum of Modern Art, 1942.
  Duret, Théodore. Van Gogh, Vincent. Paris, Bernheim, 1919.
  Gogh, Vincent van. Complete letters. Trans. by Mrs. J. van Gogh-Bonger and C. de Dood. 3v. Greenwich, NYGS, 1959. 2 ed.
  Goldscheider, Ludwig. Vincent van Gogh. London, Phaidon, 1947.
  Hautecoeur, Louis. Van Gogh. Monaco, Documents d'Art, 1946.
  La Faille, J. Bernard de. Les faux Van Gogh. Paris, VanOest, 1930.
  ____L'oeuvre de Vincent van Gogh; catalogue raisonné. 4v. Paris, VanOest, 1928.
  Meier-Graefe, Julius. Vincent van Gogh; a biographical study. Trans. by J. Holroyd-Reece, 2v. N.Y., Harcourt, 1933.
  ____Vincent van Gogh, der zeichner. Berlin, Wacker, 1928.
  Schapiro, Meyer. Vincent van Gogh. N.Y., Abrams, 1950.
  Uhde, Wilhelm. Vincent van Gogh. London, Phaidon, 1936. 2 ed.

GORKY, ARSHILE, 1904–1948
Schwabacher, E. Arshile Gorky. N.Y., Macmillan, 1957.

GOSSAERT, JAN, 1470–1532
Segard, Achille. Jean Gossaert, dit Mabuse. Brussels, VanOest, 1923.

GOUJON, JEAN, 1510–1565
Du Colombier, Pierre. Jean Goujon. Paris, Michel, 1949.
Vitry, Paul. Jean Goujon; biographie critique. Paris, Laurens, 1908.

GOYA Y LUCIENTES, FRANCISCO JOSÉ DE, 1746–1828
Adhémar, Jean. Goya. Paris, Tisné, 1941.
Beruete y Moret, Aureliano de. Goya as a portrait painter. Trans. by Selwyn Brinton. London, Constable, 1922. 2 ed.
Desparmet Fitz-Gerald, Xavière. L'oeuvre peint de Goya; catalogue raisonné. 2v. Paris, deNobèle, 1928–1950.
Estrada, Genaro. Bibliografía de Goya. Mexico, Casa de España, 1940.
Gassier, Pierre. Goya. Cleveland, World (Skira), 1955.
Huxley, Aldous L. The complete etchings of Goya. N.Y., Crown, 1943.
Malraux, André. Dessins de Goya au Musée du Prado. Paris, Skira, 1947.
Mayer, August L. Francisco de Goya. Trans. by Robert West. London, Dent, 1924.
Rothe, Hans. Francisco Goya; handzeichnungen. Munich, Piper, 1943.
Ruiz Cabriada, Agustín. Aportación a una bibliografía de Goya. Madrid, Junta Técnica de Archivos, 1946.
Sanchez-Canton, Francisco J. Goya. Trans. by G. Pillement. N.Y., Reynal, 1964.

GOYEN, JAN VAN, 1596–1656
Volhard, Hans. Die grundtypen der landschaftsbilder Jan van Goyens und ihre entwicklung. Frankfurt, Hemp, 1927.

GOZZOLI, BENOZZO, 1420–1497
Bargellini, Piero. La fiaba pittorica di Benozzo Gozzoli. Florence, Arnaud, 1946.
Stokes, Hugh. Benozzo Gozzoli. London, Newnes, 1912.

GRECO, EL, 1541–1614
Babelon, Jean. El Greco. Paris, Tisné, 1946.
Bronstein, Léo. El Greco (Domenicos Theotocopoulos). N.Y., Abrams, 1950.

GRECO, EL (continued)
  Camón Aznar, José. Dominico Greco. 2v. Madrid, Espasa, 1950.
  Cossío, Manuel B. El Greco (Domenico Theotopuli). 2v. Madrid, Suarez, 1908.
  Goldscheider, Ludwig. El Greco. N.Y., Phaidon, 1938.
  Mayer, August L. El Greco. Berlin, Klinkhardt, 1931.
  *****Trapier, Elizabeth du Gué.** El Greco; early years at Toledo. N.Y., Hispanic Society, 1958.
  Wethey, Harold E. El Greco and his school. 2v. Princeton, Princeton Univ., 1962.
  Zervos, Christian. Les oeuvres du Greco en Espagne. Paris, Cahiers d'Art, 1939.

GREUZE, JEAN-BAPTISTE, 1725–1805
  Bouchot-Saupique, Jacqueline. J.-B. Greuze, 1725–1805; quatorze dessins. Paris, Musées Nationaux, 1939.
  Mauclair, Camille. Jean-Baptiste Greuze. Paris, Piazza, 1905.

GRIS, JUAN, 1887–1927
  Kahnweiler, Daniel H. Juan Gris, his life and work. Trans. by Douglas Cooper. N.Y., Valentin, 1947.
  Soby, James T. Juan Gris. N.Y., Museum of Modern Art, 1958.

GROPIUS, WALTER, 1883–
  *****Fitch, James M.** Walter Gropius. N.Y., Braziller, 1960.
  *****Gropius, Walter.** The new architecture and the Bauhaus. Boston, M.I.T., 1955.
  *____The scope of total architecture. N.Y., Collier, 1955.

GROS, ANTOINE-JEAN, 1771–1835
  Escholier, Raymond. Gros, ses amis et ses élèves. Paris, Floury, 1936.
  Lemonnier, Henry. Gros; biographie critique. Paris, Laurens, 1905.

GROSZ, GEORGE, 1893–1959
  Grosz, George. Drawings. N.Y., Bittner, 1944.
  ____A little yes and a big no; autogiography. N.Y., Dial, 1946.

GRÜNEWALD, MATTHIAS, 1470–1528
  Burkhard, Arthur. Matthias Grünewald; personality and accomplishment. Cambridge, Harvard Univ., 1936.
  Escherich, Mela. Grünewald-bibliographie (1489–juni 1914). Strassburg, Heitz, 1914.

Hagen, Oskar F. L. Matthias Grünewald. Munich, Piper, 1923. 4 ed.

Hürlimann, Martin. Grünewald, das werk des meisters Mathis Gothardt Neithardt. Berlin, Atlantis, 1939.

Pevsner, Nikolaus and Meier, Michael. Grünewald. N.Y., Abrams, 1958.

Schoenberger, Guido. The drawings of Mathis Gothart Nithart, called Grünewald. N.Y., Bittner, 1948.

GUARDI,. FRANCESCO, 1712–1793

Fiocco, Giuseppe. Francesco Guardi. Florence, Battistelli, 1923.

Goering, Max. Francesco Guardi. Vienna, Schroll, 1944.

Moschini, Vittorio. Francesco Guardi. Milan, Electa, 1956.

Pallucchini, Rodolfo. I disegni del Guardi al Museo Correr di Venezia. Venice, Guaranti, 1943.

Shaw, James B. The drawings of Francesco Guardi. London, Faber, 1955.

GUARINI, GUARINO, 1624–1683

Guarini, Guarino. Architettura civile. 2v. Turin, 1737. Ridgewood, Gregg, 1964. Reprint.

Passanti, Mario. Nel mondo magico di Guarino Guarini. Turin, Toso, 1963.

GUERCINO, IL, 1591–1666

Bottari, Stefano. Guercino; disegni. Florence, Nuova Italia, 1966.

Russell, Archibald G. B. Drawings by Guercino. London, Arnold, 1923.

GUIDO DA SIENA, 13th cent.

Stubblebine, James H. Guido da Siena. Princeton, Princeton Univ., 1964.

HALS, FRANS, 1584–1666

Bode, Wilhelm von and Binder, M. J. Frans Hals, his life and work. Trans. by W. W. Brockwell. 2v. Berlin, Photo. Gesellschaft, 1914.

Davies, Gerald S. Frans Hals. London, Bell, 1902.

Moes, Ernst W. Frans Hals, sa vie et son oeuvre. Trans. by Jean de Bosschère. Brussels, VanOest, 1909.

Trivas, Numa S. The paintings of Frans Hals. London, Phaidon, 1949. 2 ed.

Valentiner, Wilhelm R. Frans Hals; des meisters gemälde. Berlin, Deutsche Verlagsanstalt, 1923. 2 ed.

HARNETT, WILLIAM, 1848–1892

Frankenstein, Alfred V. After the hunt; William Harnett and other American still-life painters. Berkeley, Univ. of California, 1953.

HARRISON, PETER, 1716–1775
  Bridenbaugh, Carl. Peter Harrison, the first American architect. Chapel Hill, Univ. of North Carolina, 1949.

HARTLEY, MARSDEN, 1877–1943
  McCausland, Elizabeth. Marsden Hartley. Minneapolis, Univ. of Minn., 1952.

HASSAM, CHILDE, 1859–1935
  Adams, Adeline V. P. Childe Hassam. N.Y., Amer. Acad. of Arts and Letters, 1938.
  Cortissoz, Royal. Catalogue of the etchings and dry-points of Childe Hassam. N.Y., Scribner, 1925.

HEEMSKERK, MARTIN VAN, 1498–1574
  Huelsen, Christian and Egger, Hermann. Die römischen skizzenbücher von Marten van Heemskerk, im Königlichen kupferstichkabinett zu Berlin. 2v. Berlin, Bard, 1913–1916.

HENRI, ROBERT, 1865–1929
  *****Henri, Robert.** The art spirit. Comp. by Margery Ryerson. Philadelphia, Lippincott, 1951.
  Read, Helen A. Robert Henri. N.Y., Macmillan, 1931.

HILDEBRANDT, JOHANN LUCAS VON, 1668–1745
  Grimschitz, Bruno. Johann Lucas von Hildebrandt. Vienna, Herold, 1959.

HILER, HILAIRE, 1898–
  *****George, Waldemar.** Hilaire Hiler and structuralism; new concept of form-color. N.Y., Wittenborn, 1958.
  Hiler, Hilaire. Why abstract? N.Y., Laughlin, 1945.

HOBBEMA, MEINDERT, 1638–1709
  Broulhiet, Georges. Meindert Hobbema (1638–1709) Paris, Firmin-Didot, 1938.
  Michel, Émile. Hobbema et les paysagistes de son temps en Hollande. Paris, Libr. de l'Art, 1890.

HODLER, FERDINAND, 1853–1918
  Loosli, Carl A. Ferdinand Hodler; leben, werk und nachlass. 4v. Bern, Sluter, 1921–1924.

HOFFMAN, MALVINA CORNELL, 1887–1966

Alexandre, Arsène. Malvina Hoffman. Paris, Pouterman, 1930.

Hoffman, Malvina C. Sculpture inside and out. N.Y., Norton, 1939.

_____Yesterday is tomorrow; a personal history. N.Y., Crown, 1965.

HOGARTH, WILLIAM, 1697–1764

Antal, Frederick. Hogarth and his place in European art. N.Y., Basic Books, 1962.

Ayrton, Michael. Hogarth's drawings. London, Avalon, 1948.

Beckett, Ronald B. Hogarth. London, Routledge, 1949.

Brown, Gerard B. William Hogarth. N.Y., Scribner, 1905.

Dobson, Austin. William Hogarth. London, Heinemann, 1907.

Hind, Arthur M. William Hogarth; his original engravings and etchings. N.Y., Stokes, 1912.

Hogarth, William. Analysis of beauty. Ed. by Joseph Burke. Oxford, Clarendon, 1955.

Ireland, John. Hogarth illustrated from his own manuscripts. 3v. London, Boydell, 1812.

Moore, Robert E. Hogarth's literary relationships. Minneapolis, Univ. of Minn., 1948.

Oppé, Adolf P. The drawings of William Hogarth. N.Y., Phaidon, 1948.

Paulson, Ronald. Hogarth's graphic works. 2v. New Haven, Yale Univ., 1964.

Wheatley, Henry B. Hogarth's London; pictures of the manners of the eighteenth century. N.Y., Dutton, 1909.

HOLBEIN, HANS (the elder), 1460–1524
HANS (the younger), 1497–1543

Chamberlain, Arthur B. Hans Holbein the younger. 2v. London, Allen, 1913.

Ganz, Paul. Les dessins de Hans Holbein le jeune. 9v. Geneva, Boissonnas, 1939.

_____Die handzeichnungen Hans Holbein, d. j.; kritischer katalog. Berlin, Bard, 1937.

_____Hans Holbein, d. j.; des meisters gemälde. Stuttgart, Deutsche Verlagsanstalt, 1912.

_____The paintings of Hans Holbein the younger. Trans. by R. H. Boothroyd, London, Phaidon, 1950.

Glaser, Curt. Hans Holbein d. j. N.Y., Weyhe, 1924.

_____Hans Holbein der ältere. Leipzig, Hiersemann, 1908.

Holbein, Hans. The dance of death. Notes by James M. Clark. London, Phaidon, 1947.

HOLBEIN, HANS (the elder) (continued)
           HANS (the younger)
  Koegler, Hans. Hans Holbein d. j.; die bilder zum gebetbuch Hortulus animae.
    2v. Basel, Schwabe, 1943.
  Leroy, Alfred. Hans Holbein et son temps. Paris, Michel, 1943.
  Parker, Karl T. The drawings of Hans Holbein in the collection of His
    Majesty the King at Windsor Castle. London, Phaidon, 1945.
  Schilling, Edmund. Zeichnungen der künstlerfamilie Holbein. Frankfurt am
    Main, Prestel, 1937.
  Schmid, Heinrich A. Hans Holbein der jüngere, sein aufstieg zur meisterschaft
    und sein senglischer stil. v.1- . Basel, Holbein, 1948- .
  Waetzoldt, Wilhelm. Hans Holbein der jüngere; werk und welt. Berlin, Grote,
    1938.
  Woltmann, Alfred F. G. A. Holbein und seine zeit. 2v. Leipzig, Seemann,
    1874–1876. 2 ed.

HOMER, WINSLOW, 1836–1910
  Beam, Philip C. Winslow Homer at Prout's Neck. Boston, Little, Brown,
    1966.
  Downes, William H. The life and works of Winslow Homer. Boston, Hough-
    ton, 1911.
  Goodrich, Lloyd. American watercolor and Winslow Homer. Minneapolis,
    Walker Art Center, 1945.
  ____Winslow Homer. N.Y., Braziller, 1959.

HONTHORST, GERRIT VAN, 1590–1656
  Judson, Jay R. Gerrit van Honthorst; a discussion of his position in Dutch
    art. The Hague, Nijhoff, 1959.

HOOCH, PIETER DE, 1629–1684
  Rudder, Arthur de. Pieter de Hooch et son oeuvre. Brussels, VanOest, 1914.
  Valentiner, Wilhelm R. Des meisters gemälde; mit einem anhang über die
    genremaler um Pieter de Hooch und die kunst Hendrik van der Burch.
    Stuttgart, Deutsche Verlagsanstalt, 1929.

HOPPER, EDWARD, 1882–
  Du Bois, Guy P. Edward Hopper. N.Y., Macmillan, 1931.
  Goodrich, Lloyd. Edward Hopper. London, Penguin, 1949.

HOPPNER, JOHN, 1758–1810

McKay, William and Roberts, William. John Hoppner. London, Colnaghi, 1909.

HOUDON, JEAN-ANTOINE, 1741–1828

Giacometti, Georges. La vie et l'oeuvre de Houdon. 2v. Paris, Camoin, 1921.

Maillard, Elisa. Houdon. Paris, Rieder, 1931.

Réau, Louis. Houdon; sa vie et son oeuvre, suivi d'un catalogue systématique. 2v. Paris, de Nobèle, 1964.

HUGUET, JAIME, 1448–1487

Gudiol y Ricart, José. Huguet. Barcelona, Inst. Amatller, 1948.

Rowland, Benjamin. Jaume Huguet; a study of late Gothic painting in Catalonia, Cambridge, Harvard Univ., 1932.

HUNT, WILLIAM HOLMAN, 1827–1910

Gissing, Alfred C. William Holman Hunt, a biography. London, Duckworth, 1936.

Hunt, William H. Pre-Raphaelitism and the pre-Raphaelite brotherhood. 2v. N.Y., Dutton, 1914. 2 ed.

Schleinitz, Otto J. W. von. William Holman Hunt. Bielefeld, Velhagen, 1907.

Williamson, George C. Holman Hunt. London, Bell, 1902.

INGRES, JEAN-AUGUSTE DOMINIQUE, 1780–1867

Alazard, Jean. Ingres et l'ingrisme. Paris, Michel, 1950.

____**J. D.** Ingres, 1780–1867; quatorze dessins. Paris, Musées Nationaux, 1942.

Cassou, Jean. Ingres. Brussels, Connaissance, 1947.

Courthion, Pierre. Ingres, raconté par lui-même et par ses amis; pensées et écrits du peintre. 2v. Geneva, Cailler, 1947–1948.

Fröhlich-Bum, Lili. Ingres, his life and art. Trans. by M. V. White. London, Heinemann, 1926.

Lapauze, Henry. Les dessins de J.-A. D. Ingres du Musée de Montauban. Paris, Bulloz, 1901.

____Ingres, sa vie et son oeuvre (1780–1867) d'après des documents inédits. Paris, Petit, 1911.

Malingue, Maurice. Ingres. Monaco, Documents d'Art, 1943.

Mongan, Agnes and Naef, Hans. Ingres centennial; drawings, watercolors and oil sketches from American collections. Greenwich, NYGS, 1967.

INGRES, JEAN-AUGUSTE DOMINIQUE (continued)
Pach, Walter. Ingres. N.Y., Harper, 1939.
Wildenstein, Georges. Ingres. London, Phaidon, 1954.

INNESS, GEORGE, 1825–1894
Inness, George, Jr. Life, art and letters of George Inness. N.Y., Century, 1917.
McCausland, Elizabeth. George Inness, an American landscape painter, 1825–1894. N.Y., Amer. Artists Group, 1946.

ISRAELS, JOZEF, 1824–1911
Eisler, Max. Josef Israels. London, Studio. 1924.
Phythian, J. E. Josef Israels. London, Allen, 1912.

JEFFERSON, THOMAS, 1745–1826
Frary, Ihna T. Thomas Jefferson, architect and builder. Richmond, Garrett, 1931.
Kimball, S. Fiske. Thomas Jefferson, architect; original designs in the collection of Thomas Jefferson Coolidge, junior. Boston, Riverside, 1916.

JOHN, AUGUSTUS, 1878–1961
John, Augustus. Chiarascuro; fragments of autobiography. London, Cape, 1952.

JONES, INIGO, 1576–1652
Gotch, John A. Inigo Jones. London, Methuen, 1928.
*Summerson, John N. Inigo Jones. N.Y., Penguin, 1967.

JONGKIND, JOHAN BARTHOLD, 1819–1891
Moreau-Nélaton, Étienne. Jongkind raconté par lui-même. Paris, Laurens, 1918.
Roger-Marx, Claude. Jongkind. Paris, Crès, 1932.

JORDAENS, JAKOB, 1593–1678
Fierens-Gevaert, Hippolyte. Jordaens; biographie critique. Paris, Laurens, 1905.
Rooses, Max. Jacob Jordaens, his life and work. Trans. by E. C. Broers. N.Y., Dutton, 1908.

KANDINSKY, WASSILY, 1866–1944
Grohmann, Will. Kandinsky. Paris, Cahiers d'Art, 1930.

_____Wassily Kandinsky, life and work. Trans. by N. Guterman. N.Y., Abrams, 1958.

*Kandinsky, Wassily. Concerning the spiritual in art, and painting in particular. Trans. by Michael Sadleir. N.Y., Wittenborn, 1964.

Korn, Rudolf. Kandinsky und die theorie der abstrakten malerei. Berlin, Henschel, 1960.

KIRCHNER, ERNST LUDWIG, 1880–1938

Dube-Heynig, Annemarie. Kirchner; his graphic art. Greenwich, NYGS, 1966.

Grohmann, Will. E. L. Kirchner. Stuttgart, Kohlhammer, 1958.

Schiefler, Gustav. Die graphik Ernst Ludwig Kirchners bis 1924. v.1- . Berlin, Euphorion, 1924- .

KLEE, PAUL, 1879–1940

Grohmann, Will. Paul Klee. N.Y., Abrams, 1965.

Klee, Paul. On modern art. Trans. by Paul Findlay. London, Faber, 1948.

*_____Pedagogical sketchbook. Trans. by Sibyl Peech. N.Y., Praeger, 1953.

Miller, Margaret. Paul Klee. N.Y., Museum of Modern Art, 1945.

Nierendorf, Karl. Paul Klee; paintings, watercolors, 1913 to 1939. N.Y., Oxford Univ., 1941.

Soby, James T. The prints of Paul Klee. N.Y., Valentin, 1945. 2 ed.

KLINGER, MAX, 1857–1920

Kühn, Paul. Max Klinger. Leipzig, Breitkopf, 1907.

Pastor, Willy. Max Klinger. Berlin, Amsler, 1919. 2 ed.

Servaes, Franz. Max Klinger. Berlin, Bard, 1904.

KNELLER, GODFREY, 1646–1723

Killanin, Michael M. Sir Godfrey Kneller and his times, 1646–1723, being a review of English portraiture of the period. London, Batsford, 1948.

KOKOSCHKA, OSKAR, 1886–

Hodin, J. P. Kokoschka; the artist and his time. Greenwich, NYGS, 1966.

Hoffmann, Edith. Kokoschka, his life and work. London, Faber, 1947.

Plaut, James S. Oskar Kokoschka. N.Y., Chanticleer, 1948.

KOLBE, GEORG, 1877–1947

Justi, Ludwig. Georg Kolbe. Berlin, Klinkhardt, 1931.

Valentiner, Wilhelm R. Georg Kolbe, plastik und zeichnung. Munich, Wolff, 1922.

KOLLWITZ, KÄTHE SCHMIDT, 1867–1945

Bittner, Herbert. Käthe Kollwitz drawings. N.Y., Yoseloff, 1959.

Klipstein, August. Käthe Kollwitz; verzeichnis des graphischen werkes. Bern, Klipstein, 1955.

Kollwitz, Käthe. Diary and letters. Trans. by R. and C. Winston. Chicago, Regnery, 1956.

Zigrosser, Carl. Kaethe Kollwitz. N.Y., Bittner, 1946.

KONINCK, PHILIPS, 1619–1688

Gerson, Horst. Philips Koninck; ein beitrag zur erforschung der holländischen malerei des XVII jahrhunderts. Berlin, Mann, 1936.

KOONING, WILLEM DE, 1904–

Hess, Thomas B. Willem de Kooning. N.Y., Braziller, 1959.

KUHN, WALT, 1877–1949

Bird, Paul. Fifty paintings by Walt Kuhn. N.Y., Studio, 1940.

Kuhn, Walt. The story of the Armory Show. N.Y., 1938.

KULMBACH, HANS SUESS VON, 1480–1522

Winkler, Friedrich. Die zeichnungen Hans Süss von Kulmbachs und Hans Leonhard Schäufeleins. Berlin, Deutscher Ver. f. Kunstwissenschaft, 1942.

LACHAISE, GASTON, 1882–1935

Kramer, Hilton. The sculpture of Gaston Lachaise. N.Y., Eakins, 1967.

LA FARGE, JOHN, 1835–1910

Cortissoz, Royal. John La Farge, a memoir and a study. Boston, Houghton, 1911.

La Farge, John. Considerations on painting. N.Y., Macmillan, 1901.

Waern, Cecilia. John La Farge, artist and writer. N.Y., Macmillan, 1896.

LANCRET, NICOLAS, 1690–1743

Wildenstein, Georges. Lancret; biographie et catalogue critique. Paris, Servant, 1924.

LANE, FITZ HUGH, 1804–1865

Wilmerding, John. Fitz Hugh Lane, 1804–1865, American marine painter. Magnolia, P. Smith, 1967.

LARGILLIÈRE, NICOLAS DE, 1656–1746

Pascal, Georges. Largillière. Paris, Beaux-arts, 1928.

LA TOUR, GEORGES DUMÉSNIL DE, 1593–1652
Erhard, Hermann. La Tour, der pastellmaler Ludwigs XV. Munich, Piper, 1920. 4 ed.

Furness, S. M. M. Georges de La Tour, of Lorraine, 1593–1652. London, Routledge, 1949.

Jamot, Paul. Georges de La Tour. Paris, Floury, 1942.

Pariset, François G. Georges de La Tour. Paris, Laurens, 1948.

Tourneux, Maurice. La Tour; biographie critique. Paris, Laurens, 1909.

LA TOUR, MAURICE-QUENTIN DE, 1704–1788
Besnard, Albert and Wildenstein, Georges. La Tour; la vie et l'oeuvre de l'artiste. Paris, Beaux-arts, 1928.

Lapauze, Henry. Les pastels de Maurice-Quentin de La Tour du Musée Lécuyer à Saint-Quentin. Paris, Renaissance, 1919.

_____La Tour et son oeuvre au Musée de Saint-Quentin. 2v. Paris, Manzi, 1905.

LATROBE, BENJAMIN, 1764–1820
Hamlin, Talbot F. Benjamin Henry Latrobe. N.Y., Oxford, 1955.

LAURANA, FRANCESCO, 1425–1502
Burger, Fritz. Francesco Laurana, eine studie zur italienischen quattrocento-skulptur. Strassburg, Heitz, 1907.

Rolfs, Wilhelm. Franz Laurana. 2v. Berlin, Bong, 1907.

LAWRENCE, THOMAS, 1769–1830
Armstrong, Walter. Lawrence. N.Y., Scribner, 1913.

Garlick, Kenneth. Sir Thomas Lawrence. London, Routledge, 1954.

Gower, Ronald C. S. Sir Thomas Lawrence. London, Goupil, 1900.

LE BRUN, CHARLES, 1619–1690
Jouin, Henri A. Charles LeBrun et les arts sous Louis XIV, le premier peintre, sa vie, son oeuvre, ses écrits, ses contemporains, son influence, d'après le manuscrit de Nivelon et de nombreuses pièces inédits. Paris, Imp. Nat., 1889.

Marcel, Pierre. Charles LeBrun. Paris, Plon, 1927.

LE BRUN, MARIE LOUISE ÉLISABETH (VIGÉE) 1755–1842
Hautecoeur, Louis. Madame Vigée-Le Brun; étude critique. Paris, Laurens, 1917.

LE BRUN, MARIE LOUISE ÉLISABETH (VIGÉE) (continued)
Le Brun, Marie L. E. V. The memoirs of Mme. Élisabeth Louise Vigée-Le Brun, 1755–1789. Trans. by Gerard Shelley. N.Y., Doran, 1927.
Nolhac, Pierre de. Madame Vigée-Le Brun, peintre de la reine Marie Antoinette, 1755–1842. Paris, Goupil, 1908.

LE CORBUSIER, 1887–1965
*Choay, Françoise. Le Corbusier. N.Y., Braziller, 1960.
Le Corbusier. Creation is a patient search. N.Y., Praeger, 1966.
———Towards a new architecture. N.Y., Praeger, 1959.
Le Corbusier and Jeanneret, Pierre. Oeuvre complète. v.1– . N.Y., Wittenborn, 1910– .
Papadaki, Stamo. Le Corbusier, architect, painter, writer. N.Y., Macmillan, 1948.

LEDOUX, CHARLES NICHOLAS, 1736–1806
Raval, Marcel. Claude Nicholas Ledoux, 1736–1806. Paris, Arts et Métiers, 1946.

LÉGER, FERNAND, 1881–1955
Cooper, Douglas. Fernand Léger et le nouvel espace. London, Lund, 1949.
Kuh, Katharine. Léger. Urbana, Univ. of Illinois, 1953.
Tériade, E. Fernand Léger. Paris, Cahiers d'Art, 1928.

LEHMBRUCK, WILHELM, 1881–1919
Hoff, August. Wilhelm Lehmbruck; seine sendung und sein werk. Berlin, Rembrandt, 1936.
Westheim, Paul. Wilhelm Lehmbruck. Berlin, Kiepenheuer, 1922. 2 ed.

LELY, PETER, 1618–1680
Baker, Charles H. C. Lely and the Stuart portrait painters; a study of English portraiture before and after Van Dyck. 2v. London, Warner, 1912.
Beckett, Ronald B. Lely. London, Routledge, 1951.

LE NAIN, ANTOINE, 1588–1648
        LOUIS, 1593–1648
        MATHIEU, 1607–1677
Fierens, Paul. Les Le Nain. Paris, Floury, 1933.
Jamot, Paul. Les Le Nain; biographie critique. Paris, Laurens, 1929.

LE NÔTRE, ANDRÉ, 1613–1700
Ganay, Ernest de. André LeNôtre, 1613–1700. Paris, Freal, 1962.
Guiffrey, Jules. André LeNostre. Paris, Laurens, 1912.

LEONARDO DA VINCI, 1452–1519

Bodmer, Heinrich. Disegni di Leonardo. Florence, Sansoni, 1943. 2 ed.

——Leonardo; des meisters gemälde und zeichnungen. Stuttgart, Deutsche Verlagsanstalt, 1931.

Clark, Kenneth M. A catalogue of the drawings of Leonardo da Vinci in the collection of His Majesty the King at Windsor Castle. 2v. Cambridge, Cambridge,Univ., 1935.

*——Leonardo da Vinci; an account of his development as an artist. N.Y., Macmillan, 1952. 2 ed.

Douglas, Robert Langton. Leonardo da Vinci; his life and his pictures. Chicago, Univ. of Chicago, 1944.

Goldscheider, Ludwig. Leonardo da Vinci; paintings and drawings. N.Y., Phaidon, 1944. 2 ed.

Heydenreich, Leonard H. Leonardo da Vinci. N.Y,, Macmillan, 1954.

Leonardo da Vinci. Treatise on painting. Trans. by A. P. McMahon. 2v. Princeton, Princeton Univ., 1956.

Mabbott, Maureen C. A check list of the editions of Leonardo da Vinci's works in college and public libraries in the United States. N.Y., N.Y. Public Library, 1935.

McCurdy, Edward. The notebooks of Leonardo da Vinci. N.Y., Braziller, 1955.

Panofsky, Erwin. The Codex Huygens and Leonardo da Vinci's art theory. London, Warburg Inst., 1940. N.Y., Kraus. Reprint.

Philipson, Morris. Leonardo da Vinci; aspects of the renaissance genius. N.Y., Braziller, 1966.

Popham, Arthur E. The drawings of Leonardo da Vinci. N.Y., Reynal, 1945.

Richter, Jean P. The literary works of Leonardo da Vinci. Comp. and edited from the original manuscripts. 2v. London, Oxford Univ., 1939. 2 ed.

Sirén, Osvald. Leonardo da Vinci. 3v. Paris, VanOest, 1928.

Suida, Wilhelm. Leonardo und sein kreis. Munich, Bruckmann, 1929.

Verga, Ettore. Bibliographie vinciana, 1493–1930. 2v. Bologna, Zanichelli, 1931. N.Y., Franklin. Reprint.

LESCAZE, WILLIAM, 1896–

Lescaze, William H. On being an architect. N.Y., Putnam, 1942.

LE SUEUR, EUSTACHE, 1617–1655

Rouchès, Gabriel. Eustache Le Sueur. Paris, Alcan, 1923.

LIEBERMANN, MAX, 1847–1935
  Elias, Julius. Max Liebermann; eine biographie. Berlin, Cassirer, 1917.
  Friedländer, Max J. Max Liebermanns graphische kunst. Dresden, Arnold, 1922.
  Hancke, Erich. Max Liebermann; sein leben und seine werke. Berlin, Cassirer, 1923.
  Pauli, Gustav. Max Liebermann. Stuttgart, Deutsche Verlagsanstalt, 1911.

LIPPI, FILIPPINO, 1457–1504
  Neilson, Katharine B. Filippino Lippi; a critical study. Cambridge, Harvard Univ., 1938.
  Scharf, Alfred. Filippino Lippi. Vienna, Schroll, 1950.

LIPPI, FILIPPO, 1406–1469
  Oertel, Robert. Fra Filippo Lippi. Vienna, Schroll, 1942.
  Pittaluga, Mary. Filippo Lippi. Florence, Del Turco, 1949.
  Supino, Igino B. Les deux Lippi. Trans. by J. de Crozals. Florence, Alinari, 1904.

LOCHNER, STEFAN, 1410–1451.
  Schrade, Hubert. Stephan Lochner. Munich, Recht, 1923.

LONGHI, PIETRO, 1702–1785
  Moschini, Vittorio. Pietro Longhi. Milan, Martelli, 1956.

LORENZETTI, AMBROGIO, 1323?–1348
              PIETRO, 1280–1348
  Cecchi, Emilio. Pietro Lorenzetti. Milan, Treves, 1930.
  Dewald, Ernest T. Pietro Lorenzetti. Cambridge, Harvard Univ., 1930.
  Rowley, George. Ambrogio Lorenzetti. 2v. Princeton, Princeton Univ., 1958.
  Sinibaldi, Giulia. I Lorenzetti. Siena, Ist. Com. d'Arte e di Storia, 1933.

LORENZO DI CREDI, 1456–1537
  Dalli Regoli, Gigetta. Lorenzo di Credi. Milan, Ediz. di Comunita, 1966.

LORENZO MONACO, 1370–1425
  Sirén, Osvald. Don Lorenzo Monaco. Strassburg, Heitz, 1905.

LOTTO, LORENZO, 1480–1556
  Banti, Anna and Boschetto, Antonio. Lorenzo Lotto. Florence, Sansoni, 1953.

Berenson, Bernard. Lorenzo Lotto; an essay in constructive art criticism. N.Y., Phaidon, 1956.

Biagi, Luigi. Lorenzo Lotto. Rome, Tumminelli, 1943. 2 ed.

Bianconi, Piero. Lorenzo Lotto. Trans. by P. Colacicchi. 2v. N.Y., Hawthorn, 1963.

Zampetti, Pietro. Lorenzo Lotto nelle Marche. Urbino, Ist. Statale d'Arte, 1953.

LUCAS VAN LEYDEN, 1494–1533

Baldass, Ludwig von. Die gemälde des Lucas van Leyden. Vienna, Hölzel, 1923.

Beets, Nicholas. Lucas de Leyde. Brussels, VanOest, 1913.

Friedländer, Max J. Lucas van Leyden. Edit. by F. Winkler. Berlin, deGruyter, 1963.

____Lucas van Leyden. Leipzig, Klinkhardt, 1925.

Lavalleye, Jacques. Lucas van Leyden, Peter Bruegel l'ancien. Gravures. Oeuvre complète. Paris, Arts et Métiers Graphiques, 1966.

LUINI, BERNARDINO, 1475–1533

Della Chiesa, Angela Ottino. Bernardino Luini. Novara, Ist. Geog. de Agostini, 1956.

Williamson, George C. Bernardino Luini. London, Bell, 1907.

MACINTIRE, SAMUEL, 1757–1811

Kimball, S. Fiske. Mr. Samuel McIntire, carver, the architect of Salem. Magnolia, P. Smith, 1966.

MCKIM, CHARLES FOLLEN, 1847–1909

Moore, Charles H. The life and times of Charles Follen McKim. Boston, Houghton, 1929.

MACKINTOSH, CHARLES RENNIE, 1868–1928

Howarth, Thomas. Charles Rennie MacIntosh and the modern movement. N.Y., Wittenborn, 1953.

MADERNO, CARLO, 1556–1629

Caflisch, Nina. Carlo Maderno; ein beitrag zur geschichte der römischen barockarchitektur. Munich, Bruckmann, 1934.

Donati, Ugo. Carlo Maderno, architetto Ticinese à Roma. Lugano, Banco di Roma, 1957.

Muñoz, Antonio. Carlo Maderno. Rome, Società Edit. d'Arte Illus., 1922.

MAES, NICOLAES, 1632–1693
  Valentiner, Wilhelm R. Nicolaes Maes. Stuttgart, Deutsche Verlagsanstalt, 1924.

MAGNASCO, ALESSANDRO, 1667–1749
  Geiger, Benno. I disegni del Magnasco. Padua, Tre Venezia, 1945.
  ———Magnasco. Bergamo, Ist. Ital d'Arti Grafiche, 1949.
  Pospisil, Maria. Magnasco. Florence, Alinari, 1944.

MAGRITTE, RENÉ, 1898–
  ***Soby, James T.** René Magritte. N.Y., Doubleday, 1965.
  Waldberg, Patrick. René Magritte. Trans. by A. Wainhouse. Brussels, de Roche, 1965.

MAILLOL, ARISTIDE JOSEPH BONAVENTURE, 1861–1944
  Denis, Maurice. A. Maillol. Paris, Crès, 1923.
  ———Maillol; dessins et pastels. Paris, Carré, 1942.
  George, Waldemar. Maillol. Greenwich, NYGS, 1965.
  Guérin, Marcel. Catalogue raisonné de l'oeuvre gravé et lithografié de Aristide Maillol. v.1– . Geneva, Cailler, 1965– .
  Rewald, John. Maillol. N.Y., Hyperion, 1939.
  ———The woodcuts of Aristide Maillol. N.Y., Pantheon, 1943.

MANET, ÉDOUARD, 1832–1883
  Duret, Théodore. Manet and the French impressionists: Pissaro, Claude Monet, Sisley, Renoir, Berthe Morisot, Cézanne, Guillaumin. Philadelphia, Lippincott, 1910.
  Florisoone, Michel. Manet. Monaco, Documents d'Art, 1947.
  Guérin, Marcel and Wildenstein, Georges. L'oeuvre gravé de Manet. Paris, Floury, 1944.
  Hamilton, George H. Manet and his critics. New Haven, Yale Univ., 1954.
  Jamot, Paul. Manet. 2v. Paris, Beaux-arts, 1932.
  Mathey, Jacques. Graphisme de Manet. v.1– . Paris, Quatre-chemins, 1961– .
  Moreau-Nélaton, Étienne. Manet, raconté par lui-même. 2v. Paris, Laurens, 1926.
  Rewald, John. Édouard Manet pastels. Oxford, Cassirer, 1947.
  Tabarant, Adolphe. Manet et ses oeuvres. Paris, Gallimard, 1947.

MANSART, FRANÇOIS, 1598–1666
  Blunt, Anthony. François Mansart and the origins of French classical architecture. London, Warburg Inst., 1941.

MANSART, JULES HARDOUIN, 1646–1708
  Bourget, Pierre and Cattani, George. Jules Hardouin-Mansart. Paris, Vincent, 1960.

MANSHIP, PAUL, 1885–1966
  Murtha, Edwin. Paul Manship. N.Y., Macmillan, 1957.
  Vitry, Paul. Paul Manship, sculpteur américain. Paris, Gazette des Beaux-arts, 1917.

MANTEGNA, ANDREA, 1431–1506
  Beyen, Hendrik G. Andrea Mantegna en de verovering der ruinote on der schilderkunst. The Hague, Nijhoff, 1931.
  Blum, André. Mantegna; biographie critique. Paris, Laurens, 1912.
  Cruttwell, Maud. Andrea Mantegna. London, Bell, 1908.
  Fiocco, Giuseppe. L'arte di Andrea Mantegna. Venice, Pozza, 1959.
  Hind, Arthur M. Andrea Mantegna and the Italian pre-Raphaelite engravers. N.Y., Stokes, 1911.
  Knapp, Fritz. Andrea Mantegna; des meisters gemälde und kupferstiche. Stuttgart, Deutsche Verlagsanstalt, 1919. 2 ed.
  Kristeller, Paul. Andrea Mantegna. N.Y., Longmans, 1901.
  Meiss, Millard. Andrea Mantegna as illuminator. N.Y., Columbia Univ., 1957.
  Tietze-Conrat, Erica. Mantegna. London, Phaidon, 1955.

MANZÙ, GIACOMO, 1908–
  Rewald, John. Giacomo Manzù. Greenwich, NYGS, 1967.

MARC, FRANZ, 1880–1916
  Schardt, Alois J. Franz Marc. Berlin, Rembrandt, 1936.

MARIN, JOHN, 1870–1953
  Helm, MacKinley. John Marin. Boston, Pellegrini, 1948.
  Marin, John. Letters. Edit. by H. J. Seligmann. N.Y., An American Place, 1931.
  _____ Selected writings. N.Y., Pellegrini, 1949.

MARIS, MATTHEW, 1835–1917
        WILLEM, 1844–1910
  Thomson, David C. The brothers Maris. London, Studio, 1907.

MARTIN, HOMER DODGE, 1836–1897
  Mather, Frank J. Homer Martin, poet in landscape. N.Y., Mather, 1924.

MARTINI, SIMONE, 1285-1344

Marle, Raimond van. Simone Martini et les peintres de son école. Strassburg, Heitz, 1920.

Paccagnini, Giovanni. Simone Martini. Milan, Martello, 1955.

Rinaldis, Aldo de. Simone Martini. Rome, Palombi, 1936.

MASACCIO, 1401-1428

Berti, Luciano. Masaccio. University Park, Penn State Univ., 1966.

Hendy, Philip. Masaccio; frescoes in Florence. Greenwich, NYGS, 1956.

Mesnil, Jacques. Masaccio et les débuts de la renaissance. The Hague, Nijhoff, 1927.

Pittaluga, Mary. Masaccio. Florence LeMonnier, 1935.

Procacci, Ugo. Masaccio. 2v. N.Y., Hawthorn, 1966.

Salmi, Mario. Masaccio. Rome, Valori plastici, 1932.

Schmarsow, August H. Masaccio, der begründer des klassischen stils der italienischen malerei. Kassel, Fischer, 1909.

Steinbart, Kurt. Masaccio. Vienna, Schroll, 1948.

MASOLINO DA PANICALE, 1383-1440

Toesca, Pietro. Masolino da Panicale. Bergamo, Ist. Ital d'Arti Grafiche, 1908.

MASSYS, QUENTIN, 1466-1530

Bosschère, Jean de. Quinten Metsys. Brussels, VanOest, 1907.

MATISSE, HENRI, 1869-1954

Barr, Alfred H. Matisse; his art and his public. N.Y., Museum of Modern Art, 1951.

Diehl, Gaston. Henri Matisse. Paris, Tisné, 1954.

Faure, Élie. Henri Matisse. Paris, Crès, 1923.

Fry, Roger E. Henri Matisse. Paris, Chroniques du Jour, 1935.

Testori, Gianni. Henri Matisse; 25 disegni. Milan, Görlich, 1943. 2 ed.

Zervos, Christian. Henri Matisse. N.Y., Weyhe, 1931.

MATTEO DI GIOVANNI, 1435-1495

Hartlaub, Gustav F. Matteo da Siena und seine zeit. Strassburg, Heitz, 1910.

MEISSONIER, JEAN LOUIS ERNEST, 1815-1891

Bénédite, Léonce. Meissonier. Paris, Laurens, 1910.

MELOZZO DA FORLÌ, 1438-1494

Buscaroli, Rezio. Melozzo da Forlì, nei documenti delle testimonianze dei contemporanei e nella bibliografia. Rome, Reale Acad. d'Italia, 1938.

_____Melozzo e il Melozzismo. Bologna, Athena, 1955.

Ricci, Corrado. Melozzo da Forlì. Rome, Anderson, 1911.

Schmarsow, August H. Melozzo da Forlì; ein beitrag zur kunst-und kultur-geschichte italiens im XV jahrhundert. Berlin, Spemann, 1886.

MEMLING, HANS, 1433-1494

Baldass, Ludwig von. Hans Memling. Vienna, Schroll, 1942.

Bazin, Germain. Memling. Paris, Tisné, 1939.

Voll, Karl. Memling. Stuttgart, Deutsche Verlagsanstalt, 1909.

MENDELSOHN, ERICH, 1887-1953

Mendelsohn, Erich. Three lectures on architecture: Architecture in a world crisis; Architecture today; Architecture in a rebuilt world. Berkeley, Univ. of California, 1944.

Whittick, Arnold. Eric Mendelsohn. London, Faber, 1940.

MEŠTROVIĆ, IVAN, 1883-1962

Ćurchin, Milan. Ivan Meštrović, a monograph. London, Williams, 1919.

Rice, Norman L. Sculpture of Ivan Meštrović. Syracuse, Syracuse Univ., 1948.

Schmeckebier, Lawrence. Ivan Meštrović, sculptor and patriot. Syracuse, Syracuse Univ., 1959.

MEUNIER, CONSTANTIN, 1831-1905

Lemonnier, Camille. Constantin Meunier, sculpteur et peintre. Paris, Floury, 1904.

Thiery, A. Catalogue complet des oeuvres dessinées, peintes et sculptées de Constantin Meunier. Louvain, Nova, 1909.

MICHELANGELO BUONARROTI, 1475-1564

Ackerman, James S. The architecture of Michelangelo. 2v. N.Y., Viking, 1966. 2 ed.

Carli, Enzo. Michelangelo. Bergamo, Ist. Ital.d'Arti Grafiche, 1946.

Delacre, Maurice. Le dessin de Michel-Ange. Brussels, Palais des Académies, 1938.

Delogu, Giuseppe. Michelangelo, plastik, gemälde und handzeichnungen. Zurich, Fretz, 1939.

Frey, Carl. Die handzeichnungen Michelagniolos Buonarroti. 3v. Nachtrag hrsg. von Fritz Knapp. Berlin, Bard, 1925.

Frey, Dagobert. Michelangelo-studien. Vienna, Schroll, 1920.

MICHELANGELO BUONARROTI (continued)

Goldscheider, Ludwig. The drawings of Michelangelo. N.Y., Phaidon, 1951.

———Michelangelo; paintings, sculptures, architecture. N.Y., Phaidon, 1962. 4 ed.

Hartt, Frederick. Michelangelo; paintings. N.Y., Abrams, 1965.

Knackfuss, Hermann. Michelangelo. Bielefeld, Velhagen, 1903. 7 ed.

Knapp, Fritz. Michelangelo. Stuttgart, Deutsche Verlagsanstalt, 1906.

Kriegbaum, Friedrich. Michelangelo Buonarroti, die bildwerke. Berlin, Rembrandt, 1940.

Michelangelo. Letters. Trans. by E. H. Ramsden. 2v. Stanford, Stanford Univ., 1963.

Schiavo, Armando. Michelangelo architetto. Rome, Libr. dello Stato, 1949.

Steinmann, Ernst and Wittkower, Rudolf. Michelangelo bibliographie 1510–1926. Leipzig, Klinkhardt, 1927.

*****Symonds, John A**. The life of Michelangelo Buonarroti, based on studies in the archives of the Buonarroti family at Florence. 2v. N.Y., Scribner, 1925. 3 ed.

Thode, Henry. Michelangelo und das ende der renaissance. 3v. Berlin, Grote, 1902–1912.

Tolnay, Charles de. The art and thought of Michelangelo. Trans. by N. Buranelli. N.Y., Pantheon, 1964.

———Michelangelo. 5v. Princeton, Princeton Univ., 1943–1960.

Weinberger, Martin. Michelangelo the sculptor. 2v. N.Y., Columbia Univ., 1967.

Zevi, Bruno. Michelangelo architetto. Turin, ETAS, 1964.

MILLAIS, JOHN EVERETT, 1829–1896

Baldry, Alfred L. Sir John Everett Millais, his art and influence. London, Bell, 1899.

Millais, John G. The life and letters of Sir John Everett Millais. 2v. London, Methuen, 1902.

MILLER, KENNETH HAYES, 1876–1952

Burroughs, Alan. Kenneth Hayes Miller. N.Y., Macmillan, 1931.

Goodrich, Lloyd. Kenneth Hayes Miller. N.Y., The Arts, 1930.

MILLES, CARL, 1875–1955

Rogers, Meyric R. Carl Milles; an interpretation of his work. New Haven, Yale Univ., 1940.

Verneuil, Maurice P. Carl Milles, sculpteur suédois; suivi de deux études. 2v. Paris, VanOest, 1929.

MILLET, JEAN-FRANÇOIS, 1814–1875

Bénédite, Léonce. The drawings of Jean-François Millet. Philadelphia, Lippincott, 1906.

Cartwright, Julia. Jean François Millet. N.Y., Macmillan, 1910.

Moreau-Nélaton, Étienne. Millet; raconté par lui-même. 3v. Paris, Laurens, 1921.

Sensier, Alfred. Jean-François Millet, peasant and painter. Trans. by Helena de Kay. Boston, Osgood, 1881.

MINO DA FIESOLE, 1429–1484

Angeli, Diego. Mino da Fiesole. Florence, Alinari, 1905.

MIRÓ, JOÁN, 1893–

Bonnefoy, Yves. Miró. N.Y., Viking, 1967.

Greenberg, Clement. Joán Miró. N.Y., Quadrangle, 1948.

Soby, James T. Joán Miró. N.Y., Doubleday, 1959.

MODIGLIANI, AMADEO, 1884–1920

Ceroni, Ambrogio. Amadeo Modigliani, dessins et sculptures. Milan, Milione, 1965.

____Amadeo Modigliani, peintre. Milan, Milione, 1958.

Pfannstil, Arthur. Modigliani. Paris, Seheur, 1929.

Sichel, Pierre. Modigliani; a biography. N.Y., Dutton, 1967.

Soby, James T. Modigliani; paintings, drawings, sculpture. N.Y., Museum of Modern Art, 1951.

Werner, Alfred. Amadeo Modigliani. N.Y., Abrams, 1966.

MONDRIAAN, PIETER CORNELIS, 1872–1944

Mondriaan, Pieter C. Plastic art and pure plastic art, 1937; and other essays, 1941–1943. N.Y., Wittenborn, 1945.

Seuphor, Michel. Piet Mondriaan, life and work. N.Y., Abrams, 1956.

MONET, CLAUDE, 1840–1926

Alexandre, Arsène. Claude Monet. Paris, Bernheim, 1921.

Fels, Marthe de. La vie de Claude Monet. Paris, Gallimard, 1929.

Geffroy, Gustave. Claude Monet, sa vie, son oeuvre. 2v. Paris, Crès, 1924.

Malingue, Maurice. Claude Monet. Monaco, Documents d'Art, 1943.

Mauclair, Camille. Claude Monet. Trans. by J. L. May. N.Y., Dodd, 1924.

Seitz, William. Claude Monet. N.Y., Abrams, 1960.

MOORE, HENRY SPENCER, 1898–
 Hall, Donald. Henry Moore, the life and work of a great sculptor. N.Y., Harper, 1966.
 Moore, Henry S. On sculpture. Ed. by Philip James. N.Y., Viking, 1967.
 *Read, Herbert E. Henry Moore; a study of his life and work. N.Y., Praeger, 1965.
 ____Henry Moore, sculptures and drawings. v.1– . London, Lund, 1949– .
 Sweeney, James J. Henry Moore. N.Y., Museum of Modern Art, 1947.
 Sylvester, David. Henry Moore; sculpture and drawings. v.1– . London, Lund, 1957– .

MORALES, LUIS DE, 1509?–1586
 Berjano Escobar, Daniel. El pintor Luis de Morales (el Divino). Madrid, Matev, 1921.

MOREAU, JEAN MICHEL, 1741–1815
        LOUIS GABRIEL, 1740–1805
 Moreau, Adrien. Les Moreau. Paris, Libr. de l'Art, 1893.
 Schéfer, Gaston. Moreau le jeune, 1741–1814. Paris, Goupil, 1915.
 Wildenstein, Georges. Un peintre de paysage au XVIII siècle: Louis Moreau. Paris, Beaux-arts, 1923.

MORETTO, IL, 1498–1554
 Gombosi, György. Moretto da Brescia. Basel, Holbein, 1943.
 Molmenti, Pompeo. Il Moretto da Brescia. Florence, Bemporad, 1898.

MORISOT, BERTHE, 1841–1895
 Fourreau, Armand. Berthe Morisot. Paris, Rieder, 1925.
 Morisot, Berthe. Correspondance de Berthe Morisot avec sa famille et ses amis: Manet, Puvis de Chavannes, Degas, Monet, Renoir et Mallarmé. Ed. by Denis Rouart. Paris, Quatre Chemins, 1950.

MORO, ANTONIO, 1519–1576
 Hymans, Henri S. Antonio Moro, son oeuvre et son temps. Brussels, VanOest, 1910.
 Marlier, Georges. Antonio Moro. Brussels, VanOest, 1939.

MORRIS, WILLIAM, 1834–1896
 Cary, Elisabeth L. William Morris, poet, craftsman, socialist. N.Y., Putnam, 1902.
 Mackail, John W. The life of William Morris. London, Oxford Univ., 1950.

Morris, William. The letters of William Morris to his family and friends. Ed. by Philip Henderson. N.Y., Longmans, 1950.

____On art and socialism. London, Lehmann, 1947.

MORSE, SAMUEL FINLEY BREESE, 1791–1872

Larkin, Oliver W. Samuel F. B. Morse and American democratic art. Boston, Little, Brown, 1954.

Mabee, Carleton. The American Leonardo, a life of Samuel F. B. Morse. N.Y., Octagon, 1967.

Wehle, Harry B. Samuel F. B. Morse, American painter. N.Y., Southworth, 1932.

MOUNT, WILLIAM SIDNEY, 1807–1868

Cowdrey, Bartlett and Williams, Hermann W. William Sidney Mount, 1807–1868, an American painter. N.Y., Columbia Univ., 1944.

MUNCH, EDVARD, 1863–1944

Deknatel, Frederick B. Edvard Munch. Boston, Inst. of Contemp. Art, 1950.

Glaser, Curt. Edvard Munch. Berlin, Cassirer, 1922. 3 ed.

Sarvig, Ole. Edvard Munch; graphik. Zurich, Flamberg, 1965. 2 ed.

Schiefler, Gustav. Edvard Munch; das graphische werk, 1906–1926. Berlin, Euphorion, 1928.

MURILLO, BARTOLOMÉ ESTEBAN, 1617–1682

Calvert, Albert F. Murillo, a biography and appreciation. N.Y., Lane, 1907.

Lafond, Paul. Murillo; biographie critique. Paris, Laurens, 1908.

Mayer, August L. Murillo. Stuttgart, Deutsche Verlagsanstalt, 1923.

Muñoz, Antonio. Murillo. Novara, Ist. Geog. de Agostini, 1942.

NANNI DI BANCO, 1373–1421

Vaccarino, Paolo. Nanni di Banco. Florence, Sansoni, 1950.

NASH, JOHN, 1752–1835

Summerson, John N. John Nash, architect to King George IV. London, Allen, 1949. 2 ed.

NASH, PAUL, 1889–1946

Nash, Paul. Outline, an autobiography and other writings. London, Faber, 1949.

Read, Herbert E. Paul Nash. London, Penguin, 1944. 2 ed.

NATTIER, JEAN-MARC, 1685-1766
  Nolhac, Pierre de. Nattier, peintre de la cour de Louis XV. Paris, Floury,
  1925.

NERVI, PIER LUIGI, 1891-
  ***Huxtable, Ada L.** Pier Luigi Nervi. N.Y., Braziller, 1960.
  Nervi, Pier L. Buildings, projects, structures, 1953-63. N.Y., Praeger, 1963.
  ———Structures. N.Y., McGraw, 1956.

NEUTRA, RICHARD J., 1892-
  Neutra, Richard J. Buildings and projects. 2v. N.Y., Praeger, 1951-1959.
  ———Survival through design. N.Y., Oxford Univ., 1954.

NICCOLO DA FOLIGNO, 1430-1502
  Passavant, Johann D. Niccolo Alunno da Foligno. Rome, Barbera, 1872.

NIEMEYER, OSCAR, 1907-
  ***Papadaki, Stamo.** Oscar Niemeyer. N.Y., Braziller, 1960.

NOLDE, EMIL, 1867-1956
  Schiefler, Gustav. Emil Nolde: das graphische werk. Neu bearb. von Christel
  Mosel. 2v. Cologne, DuMont-Schauberg, 1966-67.

NUZI, ALLEGRETTO, 1346-1373
  Romagnoli, Fernanda. Allegretti Nuzi, littore fabrianese. Fabriano, Gentile,
  1927.

O'KEEFFE, GEORGIA, 1887-
  Rich, Daniel C. Georgia O'Keeffe. Chicago, Art Inst., 1943.

ORCAGNA, ANDREA, 1308-1368
  Steinweg, Klara. Andrea Orcagna; quellengeschichtliche und stilkritische
  untersuchung. Strassburg, Heitz, 1929.

ORLEY, BERNAERT VAN, 1485-1542
  Wauters, Alphonse J. Bernard van Orley. Paris, Libr. de l'Art, 1893.

ORME, PHILIBERT DE L', 1515-1576
  Blunt, Anthony. Philibert de l'Orme. London, Zwemmer, 1958.

OROZCO, JOSÉ CLEMENTE, 1883–1949
Fernández, Justino. José Clemente Orozco; forme e idea. Mexico, Porrua, 1944.
Helm, MacKinley. Man of fire: J. C. Orozco. Boston, Inst. of Contemp. Art, 1953.
Orozco, José C. Autobiography. Trans. by R. C. Stephenson. Austin, Univ. of Texas, 1962.

ORPEN, WILLIAM, 1878–1931
Konody, Paul G. and Dark, Sidney. Sir William Orpen, artist and man. London, Seeley, 1932.

OSTADE, ADRIEN VAN, 1610–1685
        ISAAC VAN, 1621–1649
Godefroy, Louis. L'oeuvre gravé de Adriaen van Ostade. Paris, Godefroy, 1930.
Rosenberg, Adolf. Adriaen und Isack van Ostade. Bielefeld, Velhagen, 1900.
Wiele, Marguerite van de. Les frères van Ostade. Paris, Libr. de l'Art, 1893.

OUDRY, JEAN-BAPTISTE, 1686–1755
Lavallée, Pierre. J.-B. Oudry, 1686–1755; quatorze dessins. Paris, Musées Nationaux, 1938.
Locquin, Jean. Catalogue raisonné de l'oeuvre de J. B. Oudry, peintre du roi, 1686–1755. Paris, Schémit, 1912.

PACHER, MICHAEL, 1435–1498
Allesch, Gustav J. von. Michael Pacher. Leipzig, Insel, 1931.
Hempel, Eberhard. Das werk Michael Pachers. Vienna, Schroll, 1940. 4 ed.

PALLADIO, ANDREA, 1508–1580
*****Ackerman, James S.** Palladio. London, Penguin, 1967.
Burger, Fritz. Die villen des Andrea Palladio; ein beitrag zur entwicklungsgeschichte der renaissance-architektur. Leipzig, Klinkhardt, 1909.
Pane, Roberto. Andrea Palladio. Turin, Einaudi, 1961.
Reynolds, James. Andrea Palladio and the winged device. N.Y., Creative Age, 1948.
Spielmann, Heinz. Andrea Palladio und die antike. Munich, Deutscher Kunstverlag, 1966.

PALLADIO, ANDREA (continued)
  Zorzi, Giangiorgio. Le opere pubbliche e i palazzi privati di Andrea Palladio. Venice, Pozza, 1965.

PALMA, GIACOMO, 1480–1528
  Gombosi, György. Palma Vecchio, des meisters gemälde und zeichnungen. Stuttgart, Deutsche Verlagsanstalt, 1937.
  Spahn, Annemarie. Palma Vecchio. Leipzig, Hiersemann, 1932.

PARMIGIANINO, IL, 1503–1540
  Freedberg, Sydney J. Parmigianino; his works in painting. Cambridge, Harvard Univ., 1950.
  Frölich-Bum, Lili. Parmigianino und der manierismus. Vienna, Schroll, 1921.
  Quintavale, Armando O. Il Parmigianino. Milan, Ist. Edit. Italiano, 1948.

PATER, JEAN-BAPTISTE-JOSEPH, 1695–1736
  Ingersoll-Smouse, Florence. Pater; biographie et catalogue critiques, l'oeuvre complète de l'artiste. Paris, Beaux-arts, 1928.

PEALE, CHARLES WILLSON, 1741–1827
  Sellers, Charles C. Charles Willson Peale. 2v. Philadelphia, Amer. Philos. Society, 1947.

PERRAULT, CLAUDE, 1613–1688
  Hallays, André. Les Perrault. Paris, Perrin, 1926.

PERUGINO, 1446–1524
  Bombe, Walter. Perugino, des meisters gemälde. Stuttgart, Deutsche Verlagsanstalt, 1914.
  Canuti, Fiorenzo. Il Perugino. 2v. Siena, La Diana, 1931.
  Gnoli, Umberto. Pietro Perugino. Spoleto, Argentieri, 1923.
  Knapp, Fritz. Perugino. Bielefeld, Velhagen, 1907.
  Williamson, George C. Pietro Vannucci, called Perugino. London, Bell, 1903.

PERUZZI, BALDASSARE, 1481–1536
  Kent, William W. The life and works of Baldassare Peruzzi of Siena. N.Y., Architectural Book, 1925.

PESELLINO, 1422–1457
  Weisbach, Werner. Francesco Pesellino und die romantik der renaissance. Berlin, Cassirer, 1901.

PEVSNER, ANTOINE, 1886–1962
Giedion-Welcker, Carola. Antoine Pevsner's spatial imagination. Neuchâtel, Griffon, 1961.

PIAZZETTA, GIOVANNI BATTISTA, 1683–1754
Pallucchini, Rodolfo. L'arte di Giovanni Battista Piazzetta. Bologna, Maylender, 1934.
____Piazzetta. Milan, Martello, 1956.

PICASSO, PABLO, 1881–
Barr, Alfred H. Picasso; fifty years of his art. N.Y., Museum of Modern Art, 1946.
Boeck, Wilhelm and Sabartes, Jaime. Picasso. N.Y., Abrams, 1955.
Daix, Pierre. Picasso. N.Y., Praeger, 1965.
Daix, Pierre and Boudaille, Georges. Picasso: the blue and rose periods; a catalogue raisonné of the paintings, 1900–1906. Trans. by P. Pool. Greenwich, NYGS, 1967.
Geiser, Bernhard. Pablo Picasso; lithographs, 1945–1948. N.Y., Valentin, 1948.
____Picasso, peintre-graveur catalogue illustré de l'oeuvre gravé et lithographie, 1899–1931. v.1– . Bern, Geiser, 1933– .
Kahnweiler, Daniel H. Les sculptures de Picasso. Paris, duChêne, 1948.
*****Penrose, Roland.** The sculpture of Picasso. N.Y., Museum of Modern Art, 1967.
*****Stein, Gertrude.** Picasso. Magnolia, P. Smith, 1938.
Zervos, Christian. Pablo Picasso. v.1– . Paris, Cahiers d'Art, 1932– .
____Picasso; oeuvres. v.1– . Paris, Cahiers d'Art, 1951– .

PIERO DI COSIMO, 1462–1521
Bacci, Mina. Piero di Cosimo. Milan, Bramante, 1966.
Douglas, Robert Langton. Piero di Cosimo. Chicago, Univ. of Chicago, 1946.
Knapp, Fritz. Piero di Cosimo; ein übergangsmeister vom Florentiner quattrocento zum cinquecento. Halle, W. Knapp, 1899.

PIETRO DA CORTONA, 1596–1669
Briganti, Giuliano. Pietro da Cortona, o della pittura barocca. Florence, Sansoni, 1962.

PIGALLE, JEAN-BAPTISTE, 1714–1785
Réau, Louis. J.-B. Pigalle. Paris, Tisné, 1950.

PIGALLE, JEAN-BAPTISTE (continued)
Rocheblave, Samuel. Jean-Baptiste Pigalle. Paris, Lévy, 1919.

PILON, GERMAIN, 1536-1590
Babelon, Jean. Germain Pilon; biographie et catalogue critiques, l'oeuvre complète de l'artiste. Paris, Beaux-arts, 1927.
Terrasse, Charles. Germain Pilon. Paris, Laurens, 1930.

PINTURICCHIO, 1454-1513
Goffin, Arnold. Pinturicchio, biographie critique. Paris, Laurens, 1908.
Phillipps, Evelyn M. Pintoricchio. London, Bell, 1901.
Ricci, Corrado. Pintoricchio (Bernardino di Betto of Perugia) his life, work and time. Trans. by Florence Simmonds. Philadelphia, Lippincott, 1902.
Steinmann, Ernst. Pinturicchio. Bielefeld, Velhagen, 1898.

PIOMBO, SEBASTIANO LUCIANI, 1485-1547
Dussler, Luitpold. Sebastiano del Piombo. Basel, Holbein, 1942.
Pallucchini, Rodolfo. Sebastian Viniziano (fra Sebastiano del Piombo). Milan, Mondadori, 1944.

PIRANESI, GIOVANNI BATTISTA, 1720-1778
Focillon, Henri. Giovanni Battista Piranesi. Paris, Renouard, 1963. Reprint.
Giesecke, Albert. Studien über Giov. Batt. Piranesi (1720-1778). Leipzig, Hedrick, 1911.
Hermanin, Federico. Giambattista Piranesi. Rome, Sansaini, 1922.
Hind, Arthur M. Giovanni Battista Piranesi; a critical study, with a list of his published works and detailed catalogues of the prisons and views of Rome. Philadelphia, Saifer, 1922. Reprint.
Keller, Luzius. Piranèse et les romantiques français. Paris, Corti, 1966.
Mayor, A. Hyatt. Giovanni Battista Piranesi. N.Y., Bittner, 1952.

PISANELLO, 1395-1455
Degenhart, Bernhard. Pisanello. Vienna, Schroll, 1940.
Fossi Todorow, Maria. I disegni del Pisanello e della sua cerchia. Florence, Olschki, 1966.
*****Hill, George F.** Dessins de Pisanello. Paris, VanOest, 1929.
____Pisanello. N.Y., Scribner, 1905.
Venturi, Adolfo. Pisanello. Rome, Palombi, 1939.

PISANO, ANDREA, 1270-1348
Toesca, Ilaria. Andrea e Nino Pisano. Florence, Sansoni, 1950.

PISANO, GIOVANNI, 1240–1320
Keller, Harald. Giovanni Pisano. Vienna, Schroll, 1942.
Venturi, Adolfo. Giovanni Pisano; sein leben und sein werk. 2v. Florence, Pantheon, 1935.

PISANO, NICOLA, 1206–1280
Fasola, Giustina N. Nicola Pisano; orientamenti sulle formazione del gusto italiano. Rome, Palombi, 1941.
Swarzenski, Georg. Nicolo Pisano. Frankfurt am Main, Iris, 1926.

PISSARRO, CAMILLE JACOB, 1830–1903
Pissarro, Camille J. Letters to his son Lucien. Ed. by John Rewald. Trans. by Lionel Abel. N.Y., Pantheon, 1943. 2 ed.
Pissarro, Ludovic R. Camille Pissarro, son art, son oeuvre. 2v. Paris, Rosenberg, 1939.
Tabarant, Adolphe. Pissarro. Paris, Rieder, 1924.

POLLAIUOLO, ANTONIO, 1429–1498
Colacicchi, Giovanni. Antonio del Pollaiuolo. Florence, Chessa, 1945.
Cruttwell, Maud. Antonio Pollaiuolo. London, Duckworth, 1911.
Ortolani, Sergio. Il Pollaiuolo. Milan, Hoepli, 1948.
Sabatini, Attilio. Antonio e Piero del Pollaiuolo. Florence, Sansoni, 1944.

POLLOCK, JACKSON, 1912–1956
O'Hara, Frank. Jackson Pollock. N.Y., Praeger, 1959.

PONTORMO, JACOPO DA, 1494–1557
Becherucci, Luisa. Disegni del Pontormo. Bergamo, Ist. Ital. d'Arti Grafiche, 1943.
Clapp, Frederick M. Les dessins de Pontormo; catalogue raisonné. Paris, Champion, 1914.
_____Jacopo Carucci da Pontormo, his life and work. New Haven, Yale Univ., 1916.
Rearich, Janet C. The drawings of Pontormo. 2v. Cambridge, Harvard Univ., 1964.
Toesca, Elena. Il Pontormo. Rome, Tumminelli, 1943.

PORDENONE, GIOVANNI ANTONIO, 1484–1539
Fiocco, Giuseppe. Giovanni Antonio Pordenone. Padua, Tre Venezia, 1943. 2 ed.

POUSSIN, NICOLAS, 1594–1665
  Blunt, Anthony. Nicolas Poussin. 2v. Princeton, Princeton Univ., 1966.
  ____Nicolas Poussin; a critical catalogue of his paintings. N.Y., Phaidon, 1966.
  Courthion, Pierre. Nicolas Poussin. Paris, Plon, 1929.
  Félibien, André. Entretiens sur la vie et les ouvrages de Nicolas Poussin. Geneva, Cailler, 1947.
  Friedländer, Walter F. The drawings of Nicolas Poussin; catalogue raisonné. v.1– . London, Warburg Inst., 1939– .
  ____Nicolas Poussin; die entwicklung seiner kunst. Munich, Piper, 1914.
  Grautoff, Otto. Nicolas Poussin. 2v. Munich, Müller, 1914.
  Jamot, Paul. Connaissance de Poussin. Paris, Floury, 1948.
  Magne, Émile. Nicolas Poussin, premier peintre du roi, 1594–1665 (documents inédits) suivi d'un catalogue raisonné. Paris, VanOest, 1914.
  Poussin, Nicolas. Letters. Intro. by Pierre du Colombier. Paris, Cité des Livres, 1929.
  Rouchès, Gabriel. Nicolas Poussin; quatorze dessins. Paris, Musées Nationaux, 1938.

PRENDERGAST, MAURICE BRAZIL, 1859–1924
  Breuning, Margaret. Maurice Prendergast. N.Y., Macmillan, 1931.

PRIMATICCIO, FRANCESCO, 1504–1570
  Dimier, Louis. Le Primatice. Paris, Michel, 1928.

PRUD'HON, PIERRE-PAUL, 1758–1823
  Goncourt, Edmond de. Catalogue raisonné de l'oeuvre peint, dessiné et gravé de P. P. Prud'hon. Paris, Rapilly, 1876.
  Guiffrey, Jean. L'oeuvre de P. P. Prud'hon. Paris, Colin, 1924.
  Régamey, Raymond. Prud'hon. Paris, Rieder, 1928.

PUGET, PIERRE, 1620–1694
  Alibert, François P. Pierre Puget. Paris, Rieder, 1930.
  Auquier, Phillippe. Pierre Puget. Paris, Laurens, 1903.

PUVIS DE CHAVANNES, PIERRE, 1824–1898
  Laran, Jean and Michel, André. Puvis de Chavannes, with a biographical and critical study by André Michel. Philadelphia, Lippincott, 1912.
  Mauclair, Camille. Puvis de Chavannes. Paris, Plon, 1928.
  Werth, Léon. Puvis de Chavannes. Paris, Crès, 1926.

QUERCIA, JACOPO DELLA, 1372–1438

Bacci, Pèleo. Jacopo della Quercia; nuovi documenti e commenti. Siena, Libr. Ediz. Senese, 1929.

Biagi, Luigi. Jacopo della Quercia. Florence, Arnaud, 1946.

Gielly, Louis J. Jacopo della Quercia. Paris, Michel, 1930.

RAEBURN, HENRY, 1756–1823

Armstrong, Walter. Sir Henry Raeburn. London, Heinemann, 1901.

Greig, James. Sir Henry Raeburn, R. A.; his life and work. London, Connoisseur, 1911.

RAPHAEL, 1483–1520

Crowe, Joseph A. and Cavalcaselle, Giovanni B. Raphael, his life and works. 2v. London, Murray, 1885.

Dussler, Luitpold. Raphael; kritisches verzeichnis der gemälde, wandbilder und bildteppiche. Munich, Bruckmann, 1966.

Fischel, Oskar. Raphael. Trans. by Bernard Rackham. 2v. London, Kegan, 1948.

———Raphael Sanzio. Zeichnungen. abt. 1– . Berlin, Grote, 1913– .

Hofmann, Theobald. Raffael in seiner bedeutung als architekt. 4v. Zittau, Menzel, 1900–1911.

Holmes, Charles J. Raphael and the modern use of the classical tradition. London, Christophers, 1933.

McCurdy, Edward. Raphael Santi. London, Hodder, 1917.

Middeldorf, Ulrich A. Raphael's drawings. N.Y., Bittner, 1945.

Müntz, Eugène. Raphael. London, Chapman, 1896.

Passavant, Johann D. Raphael of Urbino and his father Giovanni Santi. London, Macmillan, 1872.

Pope-Hennessy, John. The complete paintings of Raphael. Cleveland, World (Skira), 1967.

Rosenberg, Adolf. Raphael, des meisters gemälde. Stuttgart, Deutsche Verlagsanstalt, 1923. 5 ed.

Rouchès, Gabriel. Raphael; quatorze dessins. Paris, Musées Nationaux, 1938.

Serra, Luigi. Raffaello. Turin, Unione Tip. Edit. Torinese, 1945.

Suida, Wilhelm. Raphael. London, Phaidon, 1948. 2 ed.

REDON, ODILON, 1840–1916

Bacou, Roseline. Odilon Redon. 2v. Geneva, Cailler, 1956.

REDON, ODILON (continued)

Berger, Klaus. Odilon Redon; fantasy and colour. Trans. by Michael Bullock. N.Y., McGraw, 1965.

Destrée, Jules. L'oeuvre lithographique de Odilon Redon. Brussels, Deman, 1891.

Mellerio, André. Odilon Redon, peintre, dessinateur et graveur. Paris, Floury, 1923. N.Y, Plenum. Reprint.

Redon, Odilon. A soi-même, journal (1867–1915); notes sur la vie, l'art et les artistes. Paris, Floury, 1922.

_____Lettres; 1878–1916. Paris, VanOest, 1923.

REGNAULT, HENRI, 1843–1871

Cazalis, Henry. Henry Regnault; sa vie et son oeuvre. Paris, Lemerre, 1872.

Regnault, Henri. Correspondance. Recueillé et annotée par Arthur Duparc. Paris, Charpentier, 1873.

Roger-Marx, Claude. Henri Regnault, 1843–1871. Paris, Rouam, 1886.

REMBRANDT HERMANSZOON VAN RIJN, 1606–1669

Bauch, Kurt. Rembrandt; gemälde. Berlin, deGruyter, 1966.

Benesch, Otto. The drawings of Rembrandt. 6v. London, Phaidon, 1954–1957.

Blanc, Charles. L'oeuvre complet de Rembrandt. Paris. Guérin, 1870.

Bode, Wilhelm. The complete work of Rembrandt. 8v. Paris, Sedelmeyer, 1897–1906.

Borenius, Tancred. Rembrandt; selected paintings. London, Phaidon, 1942.

Bredius, Abraham. The paintings of Rembrandt. Vienna, Phaidon, 1936.

*****Clark, Kenneth M.** Rembrandt and the Italian renaissance. London, Murray, 1966.

Focillon, Henri and Goldscheider, Ludwig. Rembrandt; paintings, drawings, and etchings. N.Y., Phaidon, 1960.

Hamann, Richard. Rembrandt. Berlin, Stichnote, 1948.

Hind, Arthur M. Rembrandt. Cambridge, Harvard Univ., 1932.

_____Rembrandt's etchings; an essay and a catalogue. 2v. London, Methuen, 1912.

Hofstede de Groot, Cornelis. Die handzeichnungen Rembrandts. Haarlem, Bohn, 1906.

Laurie, Arthur P. The brush-work of Rembrandt and his school. London, Oxford Univ., 1932.

Michel, Émile. Rembrandt, his life, his work and his time. Trans. by
　Florence Simmonds. 2v. London, Heinemann, 1903.
Münz, Ludwig. The etchings of Rembrandt. 2v. London, Phaidon, 1952.
Rosenberg, Adolf. Rembrandt, des meisters gemälde. Stuttgart, Deutsche
　Verlagsanstalt, 1908. 3 ed.
Rosenberg, Jakob. Rembrandt, life and work. N.Y., Phaidon, 1964. 2 ed.
Rovinskii, D. A. L'oeuvre gravé de Rembrandt. 4v. St. Petersburg, Acad.
　Imp. des Sciences, 1890.
Singer, Hans W. Rembrandt, des meisters radierungen. Stuttgart, Deutsches
　Verlagsanstalt, 1910. 2 ed.
*Slive, Seymour. Drawings of Rembrandt, with a selection of drawings by his
　pupils and followers. N.Y., Dover, 1965.
＿＿＿Rembrandt and his critics, 1630-1730. The Hague, Nijhoff, 1953.
Valentiner, Wilhelm R. Rembrandt; handzeichnungen. 2v. Stuttgart,
　Deutsche Verlagsanstalt, 1925-1934.
＿＿＿Rembrandt; wiedergefundene gemälde (1910-1922). Stuttgart,
　Deutsche Verlagsanstalt, 1923.

RENI, GUIDO, 1575-1642
Boehn, Max von. Guido Reni. Bielefeld, Velhagen, 1910.
Malaguzzi-Valeri, Francesco. Guido Reni. Florence, LeMonnier, 1929.

RENOIR, PIERRE AUGUSTE, 1841-1919
Coquiot, Gustave. Renoir. Paris, Michel, 1925.
Drucker, Michel. Renoir. Paris, Tisné, 1944.
Duret, Théodore. Renoir. Trans. by Madelaine Boyd. N.Y., Crown, 1937.
Meier-Graefe, Julius. Renoir. Leipzig, Klinkhardt, 1929.
Pach, Walter. Pierre Auguste Renoir. N.Y., Abrams, 1950.
＿＿＿Renoir. London, Idehurt, 1957.
Rewald, John. Renoir; drawings. N.Y., Bittner, 1946.
Rivière, Georges. Renoir et ses amis. Paris, Floury, 1921.
Vollard, Ambroise. Renoir, an intimate record. Trans. by H. L. Van Doren
　and R. T. Weaver. N.Y., Knopf, 1934.

RETHEL, ALFRED, 1816-1859
Ponten, Josef. Alfred Rethel. Stuttgart, Deutsche Verlagsanstalt, 1911.
Schmid, Max. Rethel. Bielefeld, Velhagen, 1898.

REYNOLDS, JOSHUA, 1723-1792
Armstrong, Walter. Sir Joshua Reynolds. London, Heinemann, 1900.

REYNOLDS, JOSHUA (continued)

Graves, Algernon and Cronin, William V. A history of the works of Sir Joshua Reynolds. 4v. London, Graves, 1899–1901.

Reynolds, Joshua. Discourses on art. Ed. by Robert Wark. San Marino, Huntington Libr., 1959.

——Letters. Collected and edited by Frederick Whiley Hilles. Cambridge, Cambridge Univ., 1929.

Steegman, John. Sir Joshua Reynolds. London, Duckworth, 1933.

Waterhouse, Ellis K. Reynolds. London, Kegan, 1939.

RIBERA, JUSEPE, 1591–1652

Lafond, Paul. Ribera et Zurbarán. Paris, Laurens, 1909.

Mayer, August L. Jusepe de Ribera (lo Spagnoletto). Leipzig, Hiersemann, 1923.

Pillement, Georges. Ribera. Paris, Rieder, 1929.

Trapier, Elizabeth du Gué. Ribera. N.Y., Hispanic Society, 1952.

RICHARDSON, HENRY HOBSON, 1838–1886

Giedion, Siegfried. The architecture of H. H. Richardson and his times. N.Y., Museum of Modern Art, 1936.

*****Hitchcock, Henry-Russell.** The architecture of H. H. Richardson and his times. Cambridge, M. I. T., 1961. 2 ed.

RIEMENSCHNEIDER, TILMAN, 1460–1531

Bier, Justus. Tilman Riemenschneider. Vienna, Schroll, 1948. 6 ed.

Gerstenberg, Kurt. Tilman Riemenschneider. Vienna, Schroll, 1943. 2 ed.

Schrade, Hubert. Tilman Riemenschneider. 2v. Heidelberg, Hain, 1927.

RIGAUD, HYACINTHE, 1659–1743

Roman, Joseph. Le livre de raison du peintre Hyacinthe Rigaud. Paris, Laurens, 1919.

RIVERA, DIEGO, 1886–1957

Secker, Hans F. Diego Rivera. Dresden, Verlag der Kunst, 1957.

Wolfe, Bertram D. Diego Rivera; his life and times. London, Hale, 1939.

ROBBIA, ANDREA DELLA, 1435–1525
   GIOVANNI DELLA, 1469–1529
   LUCA DELLA, 1400–1482

Cruttwell, Maud. Luca and Andrea della Robbia and their successors. N.Y., Dutton, 1902.

Marquand, Allan. Andrea della Robbia and his atélier. 2v. Princeton, Princeton Univ., 1922.

_____The brothers of Giovanni della Robbia; Fra Mattia, Luca, Girolamo, Fra Ambrogio. Princeton, Princeton Univ., 1928.

_____Giovanni della Robbia. Princeton, Princeton Univ., 1920.

_____Luca della Robbia. Princeton, Princeton Univ., 1914.

_____Robbia heraldry. Princeton, Princeton Univ., 1919.

Planiscig, Leo. Luca della Robbia. Vienna, Schroll, 1940.

Reymond, Marcel. Les della Robbia. Florence, Alinari, 1897.

ROBERT, HUBERT, 1733–1808

Leclère, Tristan. Hubert Robert et les paysagistes français de XVIII siècle. Paris, Laurens, 1913.

Nolhac, Pierre de. Hubert Robert, 1733–1808. Paris, Goupil, 1910.

RODIN, AUGUSTE, 1840–1917

Cladel, Judith. Rodin; the man and his art. Trans. by S. K. Star. N.Y., Century, 1917.

Descharnes, Robert and Chabrun, Jean F. August Rodin. Trans. by H. Chevalier. N.Y., Viking, 1967.

Grappe, Georges. Le Musée Rodin. Paris, Taupin, 1947.

Rodin, Auguste. Art. Trans. by Mrs. Romilly Fedden. N.Y., Dodd, 1928.

Story, Sommerville. Rodin. N.Y., Phaidon, 1964.

Sutton, Denys. Triumphant satyr; the world of August Rodin. N.Y., Hawthorn, 1966.

Waldman, Emil. Auguste Rodin. Vienna, Schroll, 1945.

ROGERS, JOHN, 1829–1904

Smith, Chetwood. Rogers groups, throught and wrought. Boston, Goodspeed, 1934.

Wallace, David H. John Rogers, the peoples' sculptor; catalogue raisonné. Middletown, Wesleyan, 1967.

ROHE, LUDWIG MIES VAN DER, 1886–

*Drexler, Arthur. Ludwig Mies van der Rohe. N.Y., Braziller, 1960.

Johnson, Philip C. Mies van der Rohe. N.Y., Museum of Modern Art, 1953. 2 ed.

ROMANINO, GIROLAMO, 1485–1566

Nicodemi, Giorgio di. Gerolamo Romanino. Brescia, Poligraphica, 1925.

186 MONOGRAPHS ON ARTISTS

ROMNEY, GEORGE, 1754-1802
Chamberlain, Arthur B. George Romney. N.Y., Scribner, 1910.
Davies, Randall. Romney. London, Black, 1914.
Gower, Ronald C. S. George Romney. London, Duckworth, 1904.
Maxwell, Herbert E. George Romney. N.Y., Scribner, 1902.
Ward, Thomas H. and Roberts, William. Romney; a biographical and critical essay, with a catalogue raisonné of his work. 2v. N.Y., Scribner, 1904.

ROOT, JOHN WELLBORN, 1850-1891
Monroe, Harriet. John Wellborn Root, architect; a study of his life and work. Park Forest, Prairie School, 1966. Reprint.

ROSA, SALVATORE, 1615-1675
Cattaneo, Irene. Salvatore Rosa. Milan, Alpes, 1929.
Ozzola, Leandro. Vita e opere di Salvator Rosa, pittore, poeta, incisore. Strassburg, Heitz, 1908.
Salerno, Luigi. Salvator Rosa. Florence, Barbera, 1963.

ROSSELLINO, BERNARDO, 1409-1464
ANTONIO, 1427-1479
Planiscig, Leo. Bernardo und Antonio Rossellino. Vienna, Schroll, 1942.

ROSSETTI, DANTE GABRIEL, 1828-1882
Beerbohm, Max. Rossetti and his circle. London, Heinemann, 1922.
Cary, Elisabeth L. The Rossettis; Dante Gabriel and Christina. N.Y., Putnam, 1900.
Fleming, Gordon H. Rossetti and the Pre-Raphaelite Brotherhood. London, Hart-Davis, 1967.
Marillier, Henry C. Dante Gabriel Rossetti. London, Bell, 1904. 3 ed.
Rossetti, Dante G. Letters. Ed. by O. Doughty and J. B. Wahl. 2v. N.Y., Oxford Univ., 1965.
Rossetti, William M. Preraphaelite diaries and letters (Some early correspondence of Dante Gabriel Rossetti, 1835-54; Madox Brown's diary, 1844-56; the P. R. B. journal kept by W. M. Rossetti, 1849-53). London, Hurt, 1900.
Waugh, Evelyn. Rossetti, his life and works. London, Duckworth, 1928.

ROSSI, GIOVANNI ANTONIO, 1616-1695
Spagnesi, Gianfranco. Giovanni Antonio de Rossi, architetto romano. Rome, Off. Ediz., 1964.

ROSSO, IL, 1494–1541
Barocchi, Paola. Il Rosso Fiorentino. Rome, Gismondi, 1950.
Kusenberg, Kurt. Le Rosso. Paris, Michel, 1931.

ROUAULT, GEORGES, 1871–1958
Jewell, Edward A. Georges Rouault. Paris, Hyperion, 1947.
Soby, James T. Georges Rouault; paintings and prints. N.Y., Doubleday, 1958. 3 ed.
Venturi, Lionello. Rouault; biographical and critical study. Cleveland, World (Skira) 1959.
Wheeler, Monroe. The prints of Georges Rouault. N.Y., Museum of Modern Art, 1938.

ROUBILLIAC, LOUIS-FRANÇOIS, 1695–1762
Esdaile, Katharine A. M. The life and works of Louis François Roubilliac. London, Oxford Univ., 1928.

ROUSSEAU, HENRI JULIEN FÉLIX, 1844–1910
Bouret, Jean. Henri Rousseau. Trans. by M. Leake. Greenwich, NYGS, 1961.
Courthion, Pierre. Henri Rousseau, le douanier. Geneva, Skira, 1944.
Grey, Roch. Henri Rousseau. Paris, Tel, 1943.
Rich, Daniel C. Henri Rousseau. N.Y., Museum of Modern Art, 1946. 2 ed.

ROUSSEAU, PIERRE ÉTIENNE THÉODORE, 1812–1867.
Dorbec, Prosper. Théodore Rousseau. Paris, Laurens, 1910.

ROWLANDSON, THOMAS, 1756–1827
Falk, Bernard. Thomas Rowlandson; his life and art. London, Hutchinson, 1949.

RUBENS, PETER PAUL, 1577–1640
Arents, Prosper. Rubens-bibliographie, geschriften van en aan Rubens. Brussels, De Lage Landen, 1943.
Burchard, Ludwig and Hulst, R. A. d'. Rubens drawings. 2v. Brussels, Arcade, 1963.
Burckhardt, Jacob C. Recollections of Rubens. N.Y., Phaidon, 1950.
Evers, Hans G. Peter Paul Rubens. Munich, Bruckmann, 1942.
——Rubens und sein werk; neue forschungen. Brussels, De Lage Landen, 1944.
Glück, Gustav. Rubens, Van Dyck und ihr kreis. Vienna, Schroll, 1933.
Goris, Jan A. and Held, Julius. Rubens in America. N.Y., Pantheon, 1947.

RUBENS, PETER PAUL (continued)

Held, Julius S. Rubens; selected drawings. 2v. N.Y., Phaidon, 1959.

Michel, Émile. Rubens; his life, his work and his times. Trans. by H. Lee. 2v. London, Heinemann, 1899.

Oldenbourg, Rudolf. P. P. Rubens; des meisters gemälde. Stuttgart, Deutsche Verlagsanstalt, 1921. 4 ed.

Puyvelde, Leo van. Les esquisses de Rubens. Basel, Holbein, 1940.

_____Rubens. Paris, Elsevier, 1952.

Rooses, Max. Rubens. Trans. by Harold Child. 2v. London, Duckworth, 1904.

Rosenberg, Adolf. P. P. Rubens. Stuttgart, Deutsche Verlagsanstalt, 1910. 4 ed.

Rubens, Peter P. Letters. Ed. by Ruth Magurn. Cambridge, Harvard Univ., 1955.

Stevenson, Robert A. M. Rubens, paintings and drawings. London, Phaidon, 1939.

RUDE, FRANÇOIS, 1784–1855

Calmette, Joseph L. A. François Rude. Paris, Floury, 1920.

Fourcaud, Louis de. François Rude, sculpteur; ses oeuvres et son temps, 1784–1855. Paris, Libr. de l'Art, 1904.

RUSH, WILLIAM, 1756–1833

Marceau, Henri. William Rush, 1756–1833, the first native American sculptor. Philadelphia, Penn. Museum of Art, 1937.

RUYSDAEL, JACOB ISAACSZOON VAN 1628–1682

Michel, Émile. Jacob van Ruysdael et les paysagistes de l'école de Harlem. Paris, Libr. de l'Art, 1890.

Riat, Georges. Ruysdael. Paris, Laurens, 1907.

Rosenberg, Jakob. Jacob van Ruisdael. Berlin, Cassirer, 1928.

RUYSDAEL, SALOMON VAN, 1600–1670

Stechow, Wolfgang. Salomon van Ruysdael; eine einführung in seine kunst. Berlin, Mann, 1938.

RYDER, ALBERT PINKHAM, 1847–1917

Price, Frederic N. Ryder (1847–1917); a study of appreciation. N.Y., Rudge, 1932.

Sherman, Frederic F. Albert Pinkham Ryder. N.Y., Sherman, 1920.

SAARINEN, ELIEL, 1873–1950
Christ-Janer, Albert. Eliel Saarinen. Chicago, Univ. of Chicago, 1948.
***Saarinen, Eliel.** The city, its growth, its decay, its future. Cambridge, M.I.T.,
1943.
____The search for form; a fundamental approach to art. N.Y., Reinhold,
1948.

SAINT-AUBIN, GABRIEL JACQUES DE, 1724–1780
Dacier, Èmile. Gabriel de Saint-Aubin, peintre, dessinateur et graveur (1724–
1780). 2v. Paris, VanOest, 1929–1931.

SAINT-GAUDENS, AUGUSTUS, 1848–1907
Cortissoz, Royal. Augustus Saint-Gaudens. Boston, Houghton, 1907.
Hind, Charles L. Augustus Saint-Gaudens. London, Lane, 1908.
Saint-Gaudens, Augustus. Reminiscences. Ed. by Homer Saint-Gaudens. 2v.
N.Y., Century, 1913.

SANGALLO, ANTONIO DA, 1445–1516
ANTONIO DA, 1455–1534
GIULIANO DA,1483–1546
Clausse, Gustave. Les San Gallo, architectes, peintres, sculpteurs, médailleurs,
XV et XVI siècles. 3v. Paris, Leroux, 1900–1902.
Giovannoni, Gustavo. Antonio da Sangallo il giovane. 2v. Rome, Univ. di
Rome, 1959.
Marchini, Giuseppe. Giuliano da Sangallo. Florence, Sansoni, 1942.

SANO DI PIETRO, 1406–1481
Gaillard, Émile. Un peintre siennois aux XV siècle, Sano di Pietro, 1406–
1481. Chambéry, Dardel, 1923.
Trübner, Jörg. Die stilistische entwickelung der tafelbilder des Sano di Pietro,
1405–1481. Strassburg, Heitz, 1925.

SANSOVINO, ANDREA, 1460–1529
Huntley, George H. Andrea Sansovino, sculptor and architect of the Italian
renaissance. Cambridge, Harvard Univ., 1935.

SANSOVINO, JACOPO, 1486–1570
Sapori, Francesco. Jacopo Tatti, detto il Sansovino. Rome, Libr. dello Stato,
1928.

SANZIO, GIOVANNI, 1435–1494
Schmarsow, August. Giovanni Santi, der vater Raphaels. Berlin, Haack, 1887.

SARGENT, JOHN SINGER, 1856–1925
Charteris, Evan E. John Sargent. N.Y., Scribner, 1927.
Downes, William H. John S. Sargent, his life and work. Boston, Little, Brown, 1925.
Meynell, Alice C. The work of John S. Sargent, R. A. 3v. London, Heinemann, 1903.

SARTO, ANDREA DEL, 1486–1531
Fraenckel, Ingeborg. Andrea del Sarto; gemälde und zeichnungen. Strassburg, Heitz, 1935.
Freedberg, Sydney J. Andrea del Sarto; catalogue raisonné. 2v. Cambridge, Harvard Univ., 1963.
Knapp, Fritz. Andrea del Sarto. Bielefeld, Velhagen, 1907.
Monti, Raffaele. Andrea del Sarto. Milan, Ediz. di Comunità, 1965.
Rouchès, Gabriel. Andrea del Sarto, 1486–1531; quatorze dessins. Paris, Musées Nationaux, 1939.
Shearman, John. Andrea del Sarto. 2v. N.Y., Oxford, 1965.

SASSETTA, 1392–1450
Berenson, Bernard. A Sienese painter of the Franciscan legend. London, Dent, 1910.
Pope-Hennessy, John. Sassetta. London. Chatto, 1939.

SAVOLDO, GIOVANNI GIROLAMO, 1480–1548
Boschetto, Antonio. Giovanni Girolamo Savoldo. Milan, Bramante, 1963.

SCHIELE, EGON, 1890–1918
Kallir, Otto. Egon Schiele; oeuvre catalogue. N.Y., Crown, 1966.

SCHLÜTER, ANDREAS, 1664–1714
Benkard, Ernst. Andreas Schlüter. Frankfurt am Main, Iris, 1925.
Ladendorf, Heinz. Andreas Schlüter. Berlin, Rembrandt, 1937.

SCHONGAUER, MARTIN, 1450–1491
Baum, Julius. Martin Schongauer. Vienna, Schroll, 1948.
Buchner, Ernst. Martin Schongauer als maler. Berlin, Deut. Ver. f. Kunstwissenschaft, 1941.
Champion, Claude. Schongauer. Paris, Alcan, 1925.
Rosenberg, Jakob. Martin Schongauer; handzeichnungen. Munich, Piper, 1923.

SCHWIND, MORITZ VON, 1804–1871
  Elster, Hanns M. Moritz von Schwind; sein leben und schaffen. Berlin, Flemming, 1924.
  Haack, Friedrich. Moritz von Schwind. Bielefeld, Velhagen, 1898.
  Weigmann, Otto A. Schwind. Stuttgart, Deutsche Verlagsanstalt, 1906.

SCHWITTERS, KURT, 1887–1948
  Schmalenbach, Werner. Kurt Schwitters; leben und werk. Cologne, DuMont-Schauberg, 1967.
  Steinitz, Kate T. Kurt Schwitters. Erinnerungen aus den jahren 1918–1930. Zurich, Arche, 1963.

SCOREL, JAN VAN, 1495–1562
  Hoogewerf, Godefridus J. Jan van Scorel, peintre de la renaissance hollandaise. The Hague, Nijhoff, 1923.

SEGHERS, HERCULES PIETERSZ, 1590–1640
  Springer, Jaro. Die radierungen des Hercules Seghers. Berlin, Cassirer, 1910–1912.

SERT, JOSÉ LUIS, 1902–
  Sert, José Luis. Architecture, city planning, urban design. Ed. by Kurt Bastlund. N.Y., Praeger, 1966.

SEURAT, GEORGES PIERRE, 1859–1891
  Blunt, Anthony. Seurat, with an essay by Roger Fry. N.Y., Phaidon, 1965.
  Kahn, Gustave. Les dessins de Georges Seurat, 1859–1891. 2v. Paris, Bernheim, 1928.
  Laprade, Jacques de. Georges Seurat. Monaco, Taupin, 1945.
  Rewald, John. Georges Seurat. N.Y., Wittenborn, 1946. 2 ed.
  Rewald, John and Dorra, Henri. Seurat. Paris, Wildenstein, 1960.
  Rich, Daniel C. Seurat and the evolution of "La Grande Jatte." Chicago. Univ. of Chicago, 1935.
  *__Russell, John.__ Seurat. N.Y., Praeger, 1965.
  Seligman, Germain. The drawings of Georges Seurat. N.Y., Valentin, 1947.

SHAHN, BEN, 1898–
  Rodman, Selden. Portrait of the artist as an American: Ben Shahn. N.Y., Harper, 1951.
  *__Shahn, Ben.__ The shape of content. Cambridge, Harvard Univ., 1957.

SHEELER, CHARLES, 1883–1965
Rourke, Constance M. Charles Sheeler, artist in the American tradition. N.Y., Harcourt, 1938.
Williams, William C. Charles Sheeler; paintings, drawings, photographs. N.Y., Museum of Modern Art, 1939.

SICKERT, WALTER RICHARD, 1860–1942
Emmons, Robert. The life and opinions of Walter Richard Sickert. London, Faber, 1941.
Sickert, Walter R. A free house; or the artist as craftsman. London, Macmillan, 1947.

SIGNAC, PAUL, 1863–1935
Besson, George. Signac, dessins. Paris, Braun, 1950.

SIGNORELLI, LUCA, 1441–1523
Cruttwell, Maud. Luca Signorelli. London, Bell, 1907.
Dussler, Luitpold. Signorelli, des meisters gemälde. Stuttgart, Deutsche Verlagsanstalt, 1927.
Venturi, Adolfo. Luca Signorelli. Florence, Alinari, 1922.

SIQUEIROS, DAVID ALFARO, 1898–
Tibol, Raquel. Siqueros, introductor de realidades. Mexico, Univ. Press, 1961.

SISLEY, ALFRED, 1839–1899
Daulte, François. Alfred Sisley; catalogue raisonné de l'oeuvre peint. Lausanne, Durand-Ruel, 1959.

SLOAN, JOHN, 1871–1951
Brooks, Van Wyck. John Sloan; a painter's life. N.Y., Dutton, 1955.
Du Bois, Guy P. John Sloan. N.Y., Macmillan, 1931.
Goodrich, Lloyd. John Sloan. N.Y., Macmillan, 1952.
Sloan, John. The gist of art; principles and practice expounded in the classroom and studio. N.Y., Amer. Artists Group, 1939.

SLUTER, CLAUS, 1340–1406
David, Henri. Claus Sluter. Paris, Tisné, 1951.
Kleinclausz, Arthur J. Claus Sluter et la sculpture bourguignonne au XV siècle. Paris, Libr. de l'Art, 1905.
Liebreich, Aenne. Claus Sluter. Brussels, Dietrich, 1936.

SMIBERT, JOHN, 1688–1751
  Foote, Henry W. John Smibert, painter. Cambridge, Harvard Univ., 1950.

SMYTHSON, ROBERT, 16th cent.
  Girouard, Mark. Robert Smythson and the architecture of the Elizabethan era, N.Y., Barnes, 1967.

SOANE, JOHN, 1753–1837
  Bolton, Arthur T. The portrait of John Soane (1753–1837) set forth in letters from his friends (1775–1837). London, Butler, 1927.
  Stroud, Dorothy. The architecture of Sir John Soane. London, Studio, 1961.
  Summerson, John N. Sir John Soane, 1753–1837. London, Art and Technics, 1952.

SODOMA, IL, 1477–1549
  Cust, Robert H. H. Giovanni Antonio Bazzi, hitherto usually styled "Sodoma," the man and the painter, 1477–1549; a study. N.Y., Dutton, 1906.
  Hauvette, Henri. Le Sodoma, biographie critique. Paris, Laurens, 1911.
  Jacobsen, Emil. Sodoma und das cinquecento in Siena. Strassburg, Heitz, 1910.
  Marciano-Agostinelli Tozzi, M. T. Il Sodoma. Messina, d'Amico, 1951.
  Segard, Achille. Giov.-Antonio Bazzi detto Sodoma et la fin de l'école de Sienne aux XVI siècle. Paris, Floury, 1910.

SOLARIO, ANDREA, 1465–1515
  Badt, Kurt. Andrea Solario, sein leben und seine werke; ein beitrag zur kunstgeschichte der Lombarden. Leipzig, Klinkhardt, 1914.

SOROLLA Y BASTIDA, JOAQUIN, 1863–1923
  Domenech Gallissa, Rafael. Sorolla, sa vie et son oeuvre. Madrid, Miguel, 1910.
  Hispanic Society of America. Eight essays on Joaquin Sorolla y Bastida. 2v. N.Y., Hispanic Society, 1909.
  Lopez Jiminez, José. Sorolla; estudio biografico y critica. Madrid, Comp. Bibliog. Espanola, 1963.

SOUTINE, CHAIM, 1894–1943
  Szittya, Emil. Soutine et son temps. Paris, Bibl. des Arts, 1955.

SPINELLO ARETINO, 1346–1410

Gombosi, György. Spinello Aretino; eine stilgeschichtliche studie über die florentinische malerei des ausgehenden XIV jahrhunderts. Budapest, Selbstverlag des Ferfassers, 1926.

STAËL, NICOLAS, 1914–1955

Cooper, Douglas. Nicolas de Stael. N.Y., Norton, 1962.

STEEN, JAN HAVICKSZ, 1626–1679

Martin, Wilhelm. Jan Steen. Amsterdam, Meulenhoff, 1954.

Schmidt-Degener, Frederik. Jan Steen. London, Lane, 1927.

STEVENS, ALFRED, 1828–1906

Boucher, François. Alfred Stevens. Paris, Rieder, 1931.

Lemonnier, Camille. Alfred Stevens et son oeuvre, suivi des impressions sur la peinture par Alfred Stevens. Brussels, VanOest, 1906.

Vanzype, Gustave. Les frères Stevens. Brussels, Nouvelle Société d'Éditions, 1936.

STEVENS, ALFRED GEORGE, 1817–1875

Armstrong, Walter. Alfred Stevens; a biographical study. Paris, Libr. de l'Art, 1881.

Stevens, Alfred G. Drawings of Alfred Stevens. N.Y., Scribner, 1908.

Towndrow, Kenneth R. The works of Alfred Stevens, sculptor, painter, designer in the Tate Gallery. London, Tate, 1950.

STOSS, VEIT, 1438–1533

Daun, Berthold. Veit Stoss und seine schule in Deutschland, Polen, Ungarn und Siebenbürgen. Leipzig, Hiersemann, 1916. 2 ed.

Lutze, Eberhard. Veit Stoss. Berlin, Deutscher Kunstverlag, 1938.

STRICKLAND, WILLIAM, 1788–1854

Gilchrist, Agnes E. A. William Strickland, architect and engineer, 1788–1854. Philadelphia, Univ. of Penn., 1950.

STROZZI, BERNARDO, 1581–1644

Mortari, Luisa. Bernardo Strozzi. Rome, de Luca, 1966.

STUART, GILBERT, 1755–1828

Morgan, John H. Gilbert Stuart and his pupils. N.Y., N.Y. Hist. Society, 1939.

Park, Lawrence and others. Gilbert Stuart; an illustrated descriptive list of his works. 4v. N.Y., Rudge, 1926.
Whitley, William T. Gilbert Stuart. Cambridge, Harvard Univ., 1932.

SULLIVAN, LOUIS HENRY, 1856–1924
*Morrison, Hugh. Louis Sullivan, prophet of modern architecture. Magnolia, P. Smith, 1958.
*Sullivan, Louis H. The autobiography of an idea. Magnolia, P. Smith, 1949.
*____Kindergarten chats (revised 1918) and other writings. Ed. by Isabella Athey. N.Y., Wittenborn, 1947.

SULLY, THOMAS, 1783–1872
Biddle, Edward and Fielding, Mantle. The life and works of Thomas Sully (1783–1872). Philadelphia, Priv. Pr., 1921.
Hart, Charles H. A register of portraits painted by Thomas Sully, 1801–1871. Philadelphia, Priv. Pr., 1909.
Sully, Thomas. Hints to young painters; a historic treatise on the color expression and painting techniques of American artists of the colonial and federal periods. Intro. by Faber Birren. N.Y., Reinhold, 1965. Reprint.

SUTTERMANS, JUSTUS, 1597–1681
Bautier, Pierre. Juste Suttermans, peintre des Medicis. Brussels, VanOest, 1912.

TADDEO DI BARTOLO, 1362–1422
Symeonides, Sibilla. Taddeo di Bartolo. Siena, Accad. Senese, 1965.

TAFT, LORADO, 1860–1936
Taft, Ada B. Lorado Taft, sculptor and citizen. Greensboro, Smith, 1946.

TENIERS, DAVID, 1610–1690
Peyre, Roger R. David Teniers, biographie critique. Paris, Laurens, 1910.
Rosenberg, Adolf. Teniers der jüngere. Bielefeld, Velhagen, 1901. 2 ed.

TERBORCH, GERARD, 1617–1681
Gudlaugsson, Sturla J. Geraert ter Borch. 2v. The Hague, Nijhoff, 1959–1963.
Hellens, Franz. Gerard Terborch. Brussels, VanOest, 1911.
Michel, Émile. Gérard Terburg (Ter Borch) et sa famille. Paris, Rouam, 1887.

TERBORCH, GERARD (continued)

Plietzsch, Eduard. Gerard ter Borch. Vienna, Schroll, 1944.

Rosenberg, Adolf. Terborch und Jan Steen. Bielefeld, Velhagen, 1897.

TERBRUGGHEN, HENDRIK, 1588–1629

Nicolson, Benedict. Hendrick Terbrugghen. London, Humphries, 1958.

THOMA, HANS, 1839–1924

Ostini, Fritz von. Thoma. Bielefeld, Velhagen, 1925.

Thode, Henry. Thoma. Stuttgart, Deutsche Verlagsanstalt, 1909.

THORVALDSEN, BERTEL, 1770–1844

Rave, Paul O. Thorvaldsen. Berlin, Rembrandt, 1947.

Rosenberg, Adolf. Thorwaldsen. Bielefeld, Velhagen, 1896.

TIEPOLO, GIOVANNI BATTISTA, 1696–1770

Hadeln, Detlev von. The drawings of Tiepolo. Florence, Pantheon, 1929.

Hegemann, Hans W. Giovanni Battista Tiepolo. Berlin, Rembrandt, 1940.

Meissner, Franz H. Tiepolo. Bielefeld, Velhagen, 1897.

Molmenti, Pompeo G. G. B. Tiepolo, la sua vita e le sue opere. Milan, Hoepli, 1909.

Morassi, Antonio. G. B. Tiepolo, his life and work. 2v. N.Y., Phaidon, 1962.

_____Tiepolo. Bergamo, Ist. Ital. d'Arti Grafiche, 1943.

Sack, Eduard. Giambattista und Domenico Tiepolo, ihr leben und ihre werke. Hamburg, Clarmann, 1910.

TINO DI CAMAINO, 1280–1337

Carli, Enzo. Tino di Camaino, scultore. Florence, Le Monnier, 1934.

Valentiner, Wilhelm R. Tino di Camaino, a Sienese sculptor of the fourteenth century. Paris, Pegasus, 1935.

TINTORETTO, IL, 1518–1594

Bercken, Erich von der. Die gemälde des Jacopo Tintoretto. Munich, Piper, 1942.

Coletti, Luigi. Il Tintoretto. Bergamo, Ist. Ital. d'Arti Grafiche, 1944. 2 ed.

Hadeln, Detlev von. Zeichnungen des Giacomo Tintoretto. Berlin, Cassirer, 1922.

Osmaston, Francis P. B. The art and genius of Tintoret. 2v. London, Bell, 1915.

Pittaluga, Mary. Il Tintoretto. Bologna, Zanichelli, 1925.

Tietze, Hans. Tintoretto; the paintings and drawings. London, Phaidon, 1948.

TITIAN, 1477–1576

Babelon, Jean. Titien. Paris, Plon, 1950.

Crowe, Joseph A. and Cavalcaselle, G. B. Titian; his life and times. 2v. London, Murray, 1877.

Fischel, Oskar. Tizian. Stuttgart, Deutsche Verlagsanstalt, 1925. 5 ed.

Hadeln, Detlev von. Titian's drawings. London, Macmillan, 1927.

Knackfuss, Hermann. Tizian. Bielefeld, Velhagen, 1900.

Morassi, Antonio. Titian. Greenwich, NYGS, 1965.

Suida, Wilhelm. Tizian. Zurich, Füssli, 1934.

Tietze, Hans. Titian; paintings and drawings. London, Phaidon, 1950. 2 ed.

Waldmann, Emil. Tizian. Berlin, Propyläen, 1922.

TOULOUSE-LAUTREC, HENRI, 1864–1901

Adhémar, Jean. Toulouse-Lautrec; his complete lithographs and drypoints. N.Y., Abrams, 1965.

Cooper, Douglas. Toulouse-Lautrec. N.Y., Abrams, 1956.

Coquiot, Gustave. Lautrec; ou, Quinze ans de moeurs parisiennes, 1885–1900. Paris, Ollendorf, 1921.

Duret, Théodore. Lautrec. Paris, Bernheim, 1920.

Jedlicka, Gotthard. Henri de Toulouse-Lautrec. Zurich, Rentsch, 1943.

Joyant, Maurice. Henri de Toulouse-Lautrec, 1864–1901. 2v. Paris, Floury, 1926–1927.

Mack, Gerstle. Toulouse-Lautrec. N.Y., Knopf, 1938.

TROYON, CONSTANT, 1810–1865

Dumesnil, Henri. Troyon; souvenirs intimes. Paris, Laurens, 1888.

Hustin, Arthur. Constant Troyon. Paris, Libr. de l'Art, 1895.

TRUMBULL, JOHN, 1756–1843

Sizer, Theodore. The works of Colonel John Trumbull. New Haven, Yale Univ., 1967.

Trumbull, John. The autobiography of Colonel John Trumbull, patriot artist, 1756–1843. Ed. by Theodore Sizer. New Haven, Yale Univ., 1953.

TURA, COSIMO, 1430–1495

Ruhmer, Eberhard. Tura; paintings and drawings. N.Y., Phaidon, 1958.

Salmi, Mario. Cosmè Tura. Milan, Electa, 1957.

TURNER, JOSEPH MALLARD WILLIAM, 1775–1851

Armstrong, Walter. Turner. 2v. N.Y., Scribner, 1902.

TURNER, JOSEPH MALLARD WILLIAM (continued)

Finberg, Alexander J. The history of Turner's Liber Studiorum, with a new catalogue raisonné. London, Benn, 1924.

____The life of J. M. W. Turner. Rev. by H. F. Finberg. Oxford, Clarendon, 1961. 2 ed.

*____Turner's sketches and drawings. N.Y., Schocken, 1967. Reprint.

Lindsay, Jack. J. M. W. Turner; a critical biography. Greenwich, NYGS, 1966.

Mauclair, Camille. Turner. Trans. by E. B. Shaw. London, Heinemann, 1939.

Rawlinson, William G. The engraved work of J. M. W. Turner. 2v. London, Macmillan, 1908–1913.

Thornbury, George W. The life of J. M. W. Turner, founded on letters and papers furnished by his friends and fellow Academicians. 2v. London, Chatto, 1877.

UBERTINI, FRANCESCO, 1494–1557

Nikolenko, Lada. Francesco Ubertini, called Bacchiacca. N.Y., Augustin, 1966.

UCCELLO, PAOLO, 1397–1475

Boeck, Wilhelm. Paolo Uccello, der Florentiner meister und sein werk. Berlin, Grote, 1939.

Pittaluga, Mary. Paolo Uccello. Rome, Tumminelli, 1946.

Pope-Hennessy, John. Paolo Uccello. N.Y., Phaidon, 1950.

Salmi, Mario. Paolo Uccello, Andrea del Castagno, Domenico Veneziano. Milan, Hoepli, 1938.

UHDE, FRITZ VON, 1848–1911

Ostini, Fritz von. Uhde. Bielefeld, Velhagen, 1902.

Rosenhagen, Hans. Uhde. Stuttgart, Deutsches Verlagsanstalt, 1908.

UPJOHN, RICHARD, 1802–1878

Upjohn, Everard M. Richard Upjohn, architect and churchman. N.Y., Columbia Univ., 1939.

UTRILLO, MAURICE, 1883–1955

Gros, Gabriel J. Maurice Utrillo. Paris, Crès, 1927.

Pétrides, Paul. L'oeuvre complet de Maurice Utrillo. v.1– . Paris, Pétrides, 1959– .

Tabarant, Adolphe. Utrillo. Paris, Bernheim, 1926.

VALDÉS LEAL, JUAN DE, 1622–1690

Beruete y Moret, Aureliano de. Valdés Leal, estudio critico. Madrid, Suarez, 1911.

Gestoso y Perez, José. Biografia del pintor sevillano, Juan de Valdés Leal. Seville, Girones, 1916.

Lafond, Paul. Juan de Valdés Leal; essai sur sa vie et son oeuvre. Paris, Sansot, 1914.

VANBRUGH, JOHN, 1664–1726

Whistler, Laurence. Sir John Vanbrugh, architect and dramatist, 1664–1726. N.Y., Macmillan, 1939.

VASARI, GIORGIO, 1511–1574

Vasari, Giorgio. Lives of seventy of the most eminent painters, sculptors and architects. Ed. by E. H. and E. W. Blashfield. 4v. N.Y., Scribner, 1913.

____Lives of the painters, sculptors and architects. Ed. by W. Gaunt. N.Y., Dutton, 1963. 4v.

*____On technique. Trans. by L. S. Maclehose. N.Y., Dover, 1960. Reprint.

VELÁZQUEZ, DIEGO RODRÍGUEZ DE SILVA Y, 1599–1660

Allende-Salazar, Juan. Velázquez; des meisters gemälde. Stuttgart, Deutsche Verlagsanstalt, 1925. 4 ed.

Angulo Iñiguez, Diego. Velázquez; cómo compuso sus principales cuadros. Seville, Univ. de Seville, 1947.

Camón Aznar, José. Velázquez. 2v. Madrid, Espasa, 1964.

Gaya Nuño, Juan Antonio. Bibliografia critica y antologia de Velázquez. Madrid, Fund. Lazaro Galdiano, 1963.

Knackfuss, Hermann. Velázquez. Bielefeld, Velhagen, 1898. 3 ed.

Lafuente Ferrari, Enrique. Velázquez. London, Phaidon, 1943.

Lopez Rey, José. Velázquez; a catalogue raisonné of his oeuvre. London, Faber, 1963.

Mayer, August L. Velázquez. Paris, Tisné, 1940.

Muñoz, Antonio. Velázquez. Leipzig, Goldmann, 1941.

Trapier, Elizabeth du Gué. Velázquez. N.Y., Hispanic Society, 1948.

VELDE, JAN VAN DE, 1593–1642

Gelder, Jan G. van. Jan van de Velde. The Hague, Nijhoff, 1934.

VERMEER, JAN, 1632–1675

Bodkin, Thomas. The paintings of Jan Vermeer. N.Y., Phaidon, 1940.

VERMEER, JAN (continued)
  Goldscheider, Ludwig. Jan Vermeer; the paintings. N.Y., Phaidon, 1958.
  Hale, Philip L. Vermeer. Ed. by W. Coburn and R. T. Hale. Boston, Hale, 1937.
  Swillens, P. T. A. Johannes Vermeer, painter of Delft, 1632–1675. Trans. by C. M. Breuning-Williamson. Utrecht, Spectrum, 1950.
  Vries, Ary B. de. Jan Vermeer van Delft. Trans. by Robert Allen. London, Batsford, 1948.

VERNET, CARLE, 1758–1836
        HORACE, 1789–1863
        JOSEPH, 1712–1789
  Blanc, Charles. Une famille d'artistes, les trois Vernet: Joseph, Carle, Horace. Paris, Rénouard, 1898.
  Dayot, Armand P. M. Carle Vernet; étude sur l'artiste, suivie d'un catalogue de l'oeuvre gravé et lithographie et du catalogue de l'exposition rétrospective de 1925. Paris, Goupy, 1925.
  Ingersoll-Smouse, Florence. Joseph Vernet, peintre de marine, 1714–1789. 2v. Paris, Bignou, 1926.

VERONESE, PAOLO, 1528–1588
  Fiocco, Giuseppe. Paolo Veronese, 1528–1588. Bologna, Apollo, 1928.
  Lukomskii, Georgii K. Les fresques de Paul Véronese et de ses disciples. Paris, Seheur, 1928.
  Meissner, Franz H. Veronese. Bielefeld, Velhagen, 1897.
  Pallucchini, Rodolfo. Veronese. Bergamo, Ist. Ital. d'Arti Grafiche, 1943. 2 ed.
  Venturi, Adolfo. Paolo Veronese (per il IV centenario dalla nascita). Milan, Hoepli, 1928.

VERROCCHIO, ANDREA DEL, 1435–1488
  Cruttwell, Maud. Verrocchio. London, Duckworth, 1911.
  Planiscig, Leo. Andrea del Verrocchio. Vienna, Schroll, 1941.
  Reymond, Marcel. Verrocchio. Paris, Libr. de l'Art, 1906.

VIGNOLA, 1507–1573
  Lotz, Wolfgang. Vignola-studien. Wurzburg, Triltsch, 1939.
  Lukomskii, Georgii K. Vignole (Jacopo Barozzi da Vignola). Paris, Vincent, 1927.
  Vignola. The five orders of architecture. Trans. by A. L. Tuckermann. N.Y., Comstock, 1891.

Walcher-Cassotti, Maria. Il Vignola. 2v. Trieste, Ist. di Storia dell'Arte, 1960.
Willich, Hans. Giacomo Barozzi da Vignola. Strassburg, Heitz, 1906.

VILLARD DE HONNECOURT, 13th cent.
Hahnloser, Hans. R. Villard de Honnecourt. Vienna, Schroll, 1935.
Villard de Honnecourt. Sketchbook. Ed. by Theodore Bowie. Bloomington, Univ. of Indiana, 1959.

VISCHER, PETER, 1460–1529
           PETER, 1487–1528
Daun, Berthold. P. Vischer und A. Krafft. Bielefeld, Velhagen, 1905.
Meller, Simon. Peter Vischer der ältere und seine werkstatt. Leipzig, Insel, 1925.
Réau, Louis. Peter Vischer et la sculpture franconienne du XIV au XVI siècle. Paris, Plon, 1909.
Seeger, Georg. Peter Vischer der jüngere. Leipzig, Seemann, 1897.

VIVARINI, ALVISE, 1445–1505
             ANTONIO, 1415–1484
             BARTOLOMMEO, 1415–1484
Pallucchini, Rodolfo. I Vivarini: Antonio, Bartolommeo, Alvise. Venice, Pozza, 1962.

VLAMINCK, MAURICE DE, 1876–1958
Kahnweiler, Daniel-H. Maurice de Vlaminck. Leipzig, Klinkhardt, 1920.
Perls, Klaus G. Vlaminck. N.Y., Harper, 1941.
Sauvage, Marcel. Vlaminck, sa vie et son message. Geneva, Cailler, 1956.
Selz, Jean. Vlaminck. Paris, Flammarion, 1962.

WATTEAU, JEAN-ANTOINE, 1684–1721
Adhémar, Hélène. Watteau, sa vie, son oeuvre. Paris, Tisné, 1950.
Brinckmann, Albert E. J. A. Watteau. Vienna, Schroll, 1943.
Dacier, Émile. Jean de Jullienne et les graveurs de Watteau au XVIII siècle. 3v. Paris, Societé pour l'Etude de la Grav. Fran., 1921–1929.
Gillet, Louis, Watteau, un grand maître du XVIII siècle. Paris, Plon, 1943. 4 ed.
Goncourt, Edmond de. Catalogue raisonné de l'oeuvre peint, dessiné et gravé d'Antoine Watteau. Paris, Rapilly, 1875.

WATTEAU, JEAN-ANTOINE (continued)
 Lavallée, Pierre. Antoine Watteau, 1684–1721; quatorze dessins. Paris, Musées Nationaux, 1939.
 Parker, Karl T. The drawings of Antoine Watteau. London, Batsford, 1931.
 Rosenberg, Adolf. Antoine Watteau. Bielefeld, Velhagen, 1896.
 Zimmermann, Ernst H. Watteau. Stuttgart, Deutsche Verlagsanstalt, 1912.

WATTS, GEORGE FREDERICK, 1817–1904
 Chesterton, Gilbert K. G. F. Watts. London, Dutton, 1909.
 Schleinitz, Otto J. W. George Frederick Watts. Bielefeld, Velhagen, 1904.
 Watts, Mary S. George Frederick Watts. 3v. London, Macmillan, 1912.

WEBER, MAX, 1881–1961
 Cahill, Holger. Max Weber. N.Y., Downtown Gallery, 1930.
 Goodrich, Lloyd. Max Weber. N.Y., Macmillan, 1949.

WENGENROTH, STOW, 1906–
 Wengenroth, Stow. Making a lithograph. N.Y., Studio, 1936.

WEYDEN, ROGER VAN DER, 1400–1464
 Burger, Willy. Roger van der Weyden. Leipzig, Hiersemann, 1923.
 Destrée, Jules. Roger de la Pasture van der Weyden. 2v. Paris, VanOest, 1930.
 Lafond, Paul. Roger van der Weyden. Brussels, VanOest, 1912.
 Renders, Émile. La solution du problème Van der Weyden — Flémalle — Campin. Bruges, Beyaert, 1931.
 Winkler, Friedrich. Der meister von Flémalle und Rogier van der Weyden. Strassburg, Heitz, 1913.

WHISTLER, JAMES ABBOT McNEILL, 1834–1903
 Cary, Elisabeth L. The works of James McNeill Whistler. N.Y., Moffat, 1913.
 Duret, Théodore. Whistler. Trans. by Frank Rutter. Philadelphia, Lippincott, 1917.
 Kennedy, Edward G. The etched work of Whistler. 4v. N.Y., Grolier, 1910.
 Laver, James. Whistler. London, Faber, 1930.
 Pearson, Hesketh. The man Whistler. London, Methuen, 1952.
 Pennell, Elizabeth R. The life of James McNeill Whistler. Philadelphia, Lippincott, 1919. 6 ed.
 ____The Whistler journal. Philadelphia, Lippincott, 1921.
 ____Whistler the friend. Philadelphia, Lippincott, 1930.

Salaman, Malcolm. James McNeill Whistler. 2v. London, Studio, 1927–1932.

Sutton, Denys. James McNeill Whistler; paintings, etchings, pastels and watercolors. Greenwich, NYGS, 1966.

Wedmore, Frederick. Whistler's etchings; a study and a catalogue. London, Colnaghi, 1899. 2 ed.

*****Whistler, James A. M.** The gentle art of making enemies, as pleasantly exemplified in many instances. London, Heinemann, 1916.

WILIGELMUS, fl. 1099–1110

Salvini, Roberto. Wiligelmo e le origini della scultura romanica. Milan, Martelli, 1956.

WILKIE, DAVID, 1785–1841

Gower, Ronald C. S. Sir David Wilkie. London, Bell, 1902.

WILSON, RICHARD, 1714–1782

Bury, Adrian. Richard Wilson, the grand classic. Leigh-on-Sea, Lewis, 1947.

Constable, William G. Richard Wilson, Cambridge, Harvard Univ., 1953.

Ford, Brinsley, The drawings of Richard Wilson. London, Faber, 1950.

WITTEL, GASPAR VAN, 1653–1736

Briganti, Giuliano. Caspar van Wittel e l'origine della veduta settecentesca. Rome, Bozzi, 1966.

WITZ, KONRAD, 1400–1446

Escherich, Mela. Konrad Witz. Strassburg, Heitz, 1916.

Gantner, Joseph. Konrad Witz. Vienna, Schroll, 1943. 2 ed.

Ganz, Paul L. Meister Konrad Witz von Rottweil. Bern, Urs Graf, 1947.

Meng-Koehler, Mathilde. Die bilder des Konrad Witz und ihre quellen: Legenda aurea, Speculum humanae salvationis, Bibel. Basel, Holbein, 1947.

WOOD, GRANT, 1892–1942

Garwood, Darrell. Artist in Iowa; a life of Grant Wood. N.Y., Norton, 1944.

WREN, CHRISTOPHER, 1632–1723

Dirks, Rudolf. Sir Christopher Wren, A.D. 1632–1723; bicentenary memorial volume published under the auspices of the Royal Institute of British Architects. London, Hodder, 1923.

Fürst, Viktor. The architecture of Sir Christopher Wren. London, Humphries, 1956.

WREN, CHRISTOPHER (continued)

Sekler, Edward F. Wren and his place in European architecture. N.Y., Macmillan, 1956.

Webb, Geoffrey. Wren. London, Duckworth, 1937.

Whitaker-Wilson, Cecil. Sir Christopher Wren, his life and times. London, Methuen, 1932.

Wren, Christopher. Life and works of Sir Christopher Wren; from the Parentalia, or memoirs by his son, Christopher. Campden, Essex House, 1903.

WRIGHT, FRANK LLOYD, 1869–1959

Hitchcock, Henry-Russell. In the nature of materials, 1887–1941; the buildings of Frank Lloyd Wright. N.Y., Duell, 1942.

*****Scully, Vincent**. Frank Lloyd Wright. N.Y., Braziller, 1960.

Wright, Frank Lloyd. An American architecture. Ed. by Edgar Kaufman. N.Y., Horizon, 1955.

_____An autobiography. N.Y., Duell, 1943.

_____Drawings for a living architecture. N.Y., Horizon, 1962.

*_____On architecture; selected writings, 1894–1940. Ed. by Frederick Gutheim. N.Y., Duell, 1941.

Wright, Olgivanna Lloyd. Frank Lloyd Wright, his life, his work, his words. N.Y., Horizon, 1966.

WYETH, ANDREW, 1911–

Mongan, Agnes. Andrew Wyeth; dry brush and pencil drawings. Greenwich, NYGS, 1966.

ZORACH, WILLIAM, 1887–

Wingert, Paul S. The sculpture of William Zorach. N.Y., Pitman, 1938.

Zorach, William. Art is my life. Cleveland, World, 1967.

_____Zorach explains sculpture; what it means and how it is made. N.Y., Tudor, 1960.

ZORN, ANDERS LEONARD, 1860–1920

Asplund, Karl. Anders Zorn, his life and work. London, Studio, 1921.

_____Zorn's engraved work; a descriptive catalogue. Trans. by Edward Adams-Ray. Stockholm, Bukowski, 1920.

Servaes, Franz. Anders Zorn. Bielefeld, Velhagen, 1925. 2 ed.

ZUCCARI, FEDERICO, 1530–1609

Zuccari, Federico. Scritto d'arte. Ed. by Detlef Heikamp. Florence, Olschki, 1961.

ZULOAGA, IGNACIO, 1870–1936

Hispanic Society of America. Five essays on the art of Ignacio Zuloaga. N.Y., Hispanic Society, 1909.

ZURBARÁN, FRANCISCO, 1598–1662

Calzada, Andres M. Estampes de Zurbarán. Barcelona, Canosa, 1929.

Gaya Nuño, Juan A. Zurbarán. Barcelona, Aedos, 1948.

Kehrer, Hugo. Francisco de Zurbarán. Munich, Schmidt, 1918.

Soria, Martin S. Francisco Zurbarán. N.Y., Phaidon, 1953.

Index

Note: Vowels modified by an umlaut (e.g. ä) are listed as if spelled ae, oe, ue. Names beginning with the prefix M' and Mc are listed as if spelled Mac.

A

AALTO, ALVAR, 119
ABBEY, EDWIN AUSTIN, 119
Abbot, Edith R., 71
Abell, Walter, 9
Ackerman, James S., 9, 169, 175
Ackerman, Phyllis, 114
Adam, Leonhard, 13
ADAM, JAMES, 119
ADAM, ROBERT, 119
Adama van Scheltema, Frederick, 35, 45
Adams, Adeline V. P., 146, 154
Adams, Henry, 53
Adhémar, Hélène, 201
Adhémar, Jean, 77, 91, 98, 137, 151, 197
Adriani, Gert, 142
AERTSEN, PIETER, 119
Aeschlimann, Erardo, 1
Agard, Walter R., 63
Agnello, Giuseppe, 29
Agostinelli Tozzi, M. T. Marciano, see Marciano-Agostinelli Tozzi, M. T.
Akurgal, Ekrem, 25
Alazard, Jean, 157
Albers, Anni, 114
ALBERTI, LEONE BATTISTA, 119
Albright, William F., 25
Alcala, Rafel Lainez, see Lainez Alcala, Rafel
Aldred, Cyril, 15
Alex, William, 23

Alexander, William, 50
Alexandre, Arsène, 101, 122, 155, 171
Alfons, Sven, 45
Algoud, Henri, 114, 145
Alibert, François P., 180
ALLEGRI, ANTONIO, see CORREGIO
Allen, John R., 29
Allende-Salazar, Juan, 199
Allesch, Gustav J. von, 175
ALLORI, ANGELO, see BRONZINO, AGNOLO
Allsop, Bruce, 50
ALLSTON, WASHINGTON, 119, 120
Alpatov, Mikhail V., 45
ALTDORFER, ALBRECHT, 120
Altena, Johan Q. van Regteren, see Regteren-Altena, Johan Q. van
ALTICHIERI, ALTICHIERO, 120
AMADEO, GIOVANNI ANTONIO, 120
American Art Directory, 1
Amsterdam. Rijksmuseum. Kunsthistorische Bibliotheek, 1
Ananoff, Alexandre, 127, 145
Ancona, Paola d', 1, 41, 81, 82
Anderson, Lawrence L., 108
Anderson, William J., 16, 58
Andrade, José M. Pita, see Pita-Andrade, José M.
Andrae, Walter, 24
ANDREA DEL CASTAGNO, see CASTAGNO, ANDREA DEL

ANDREA DEL SARTO, see SARTO,
    ANDREA DEL
ANDREA DEL VERROCCHIO, see
    VERROCCHIO, ANDREA DEL
ANDREA DELLA ROBBIA, see ROBBIA,
    ANDREA DELLA
ANDREA DI CIONE, see ORCAGNA,
    ANDREA
Andrews, Frederick H., 25
Andrews, Wayne, 61
Androuet du Cerceau, Jacques, 53
Angeli, Diego, 171
ANGELICO, FRA, 120
ANGERS, PIERRE JEAN DAVID D',
    see DAVID D'ANGERS, PIERRE JEAN
Angulo Iñiguez, Diego, 43
Annuaire International des Beaux-Arts, 3
Annuario Bibliografico di Archeologia, 1
Annuario Bibliografico di Storia dell'
    Arte, 1
Antal, Frederick, 9, 82, 146, 155
ANTELAMI, BENEDETTO, 120
Anthony, Edgar W., 29, 111
ANTONELLO DA MESSINA, 121
Apollinaire, Guillaume, 71
ARCA, NICCOLÒ DELL', see BARI,
    NICCOLÒ DELL'
Archer, William G., 25
ARCHIPENKO, ALEXANDER, 121
Arents, Prosper, 187
Argan, Giulio C., 71, 120, 126, 129
Arias, Paolo E., 16
Armand, Alfred, 67
Arms, John T., 99
Armstrong, Walter, 146, 161, 181, 183,
    194, 197
Arnason, H. Harvard, 130
Arndt, Paul, 16
Arnheim, Rudolf, 9
Arnold, Hugh, 106
Arnold, Thomas W., 25, 26
ARNOLFO DI CAMBIO, 121
Aronson, Joseph, 103
ARP, HANS, 121
Arslan, Wart, 122
Art Index, 1

Arthaud, J., 27
Artz, Frederick B., 29
Ashby, Thomas, 16, 20
Ashmole, Bernard, 16, 17
Ashton, Leigh, 23
Asplund, Karl, 204
Athey, Isabella, 195
Aubert, Marcel, 38, 53, 64, 106
Auquier, Phillippe, 180
Aurelj, Antonietta M. Bessone, see
    Bessone Aurelj, Antonietta M.
Aurenhammer, Hans, 6
AVERLINO, ANTONIO, see
    FILARETE
Avery, Clara L., 108
Ayrton, Michael, 155
Azcárate, José M. de, 46
Aznar, José Camon, see Camon Aznar,
    José

B

Babelon, Jean, 64, 108, 111, 151, 178,
    197
BACCHIACCA, see UBERTINI,
    FRANCESCO
Bacci, Mina, 177
Bacci, Pèleo, 181
Bachhofer, Ludwig, 23, 25
BACICCIO, see GAULLI, GIOVANNI
    BATTISTA
Bacon, Edward, 13
Bacou, Roseline, 181
Badawy, Alexander, 15
Badt, Kurt, 132, 139, 193
Baier-Fütterer, Ilse, 65
Baikie, James, 17
Baker, Charles H. C., 80, 84, 137, 162
Baker, Hollis S., 103
Balcarres, Lord, see Crawford, David
    A. E. L.
Baldass, Ludwig von, 120, 126, 143, 148,
    165, 169
Baldinucci, Filippo, 124
BALDOVINETTI, ALESSO, 121
Baldry, Alfred L., 170

BALDUNG, HANS, 121
Ballo, Guido, 82, 125
Baltrusaitis, Jurgis, 101
BANCO, NANNI DI, see NANNI DI BANCO
Bange, Ernst F., 65
Banti, Anna, 164
BARBARELLI, GIORGIO, see
    GIORGIONE DA CASTELFRANCO
BARBARI, JACOPO DE', 121
Barber, Edwin A., 112
Barbier de Montault, Xavier, 6
BARBIERI, GIOVANNI FRANCESCO,
    see GUERCINO, IL
Barbour, F. W. M. Maxwell, see Maxwell-
    Barbour, F. W. M.
Bardi, Pietro M., 43
Bargellini, Piero, 148, 151
BARI, NICCOLÒ DA, 121
Barker, Virgil, 89
BARLACH, ERNST, 122
Barnes, Albert C., 76
Barocchi, Paola, 35, 187
BAROCCI, FEDERIGO, 122
Baroni, Costantino, 67, 127
BAROZZI, GIACOMO, see VIGNOLA
Barr, Alfred H., 47, 71, 168, 177
Barry, Alfred, 122
BARRY, CHARLES, 122
BARTOLO, TADDEO DI, see TADDEO
    DI BARTOLO
BARTOLOMMEO, FRA, 122
Bartsch, Adam von, 91
BARYE, ANTOINE LOUIS, 122
Baschet, Jacques, 114
BASSANO, JACOPO, 122
Bassi, Elena, 130
Bastelaer, René van, 128
BASTIDA, JOAQUIN SOROLLA Y, see
    SOROLLA Y BASTIDA, JOAQUIN
Bastlund, Kurt, 191
Baston-Dreyfus, Philippe, 136
Bataille, Georges, 13
Batchelder, Ernest Allen, 9
Battaglia, Silvia de Vito, see Vito
    Battaglia, Silvia de
Battisti, Eugenio, 134, 149

Bauch, Kurt, 182
Baud-Bovy, Daniel, 135
Baudelaire, Charles, 9, 139
Baudi di Vesme, Alessandro, 91
Baudicour, Prosper de, 91
Baum, Julius, 29, 30, 53, 58, 190
Baur, John I. H., 47, 89, 129
Bautier, Pierre, 195
Baxter, Sylvester, 59
BAYER, HERBERT, 122
Bayley, Frank W., 135
Bazin, Germain, 72, 135, 169
BAZZI, GIOVANNI ANTONIO, see
    SODOMA, IL
Beam, Philip C., 9, 156
Beard, Alice, 107
BEARDSLEY, AUBREY, 122
Beaupré, Charles Mauricheau, see
    Mauricheau-Beaupré, Charles
BEAUX, CECILIA, 123
Beazley, John D., 16, 17
Becherucci, Luisa, 179
Becker, Felix, 5, 92
Becker, Hanna L., 120
Beckett, Ronald B., 135, 155, 162
BECKMANN, MAX, 123
Beckwith, John, 25, 30
Beenken, Hermann T., 39, 65, 143
Beerbohm, Max, 186
Beets, Nicholas, 165
Behne, Adolf B., 92
Behrendt, Walter C., 50
Bell, Clive, 9, 71, 76
Bell, Edward, 50
Bell, Malcolm, 108, 129
BELLINI, GENTILE, 123
BELLINI, GIOVANNI, 123
BELLINI, JACOPO, 123
BELLOTTO, BERNARDO, 123
BELLOWS, GEORGE WESLEY, 124
Benavides Rodríguez, Alfredo, 59
BENEDETTO DA MAIANO, 124
BENEDETTO DI PARMA, see
    ANTELAMI, BENEDETTO
Bénédite, Léonce, 133, 136, 143, 168,
    171

Benesch, Otto, 35, 78, 92, 120, 182
Bénézit, Emmanuel, 1
Benkard, Ernst, 130, 190
Benois, Aleksandr N., 87
Benoist, Luc, 64
Benoit, François, 50
BENTON, THOMAS HART, 124
Benz, Richard E., 39
Beraldi, Henri, 98
Berchem, Marguerite van, 111
Bercken, Erich von der, 82, 196
Berenson, Bernard, 9, 82, 92, 130, 165,
  190
Berger, Ernst, 74
Berger, Klaus, 92, 148, 182
Berjano Escobar, Daniel, 172
Berlin. Staatliche Kunstbibliothek, 101
Berliner, Rudolf, 101
BERNARD, JOSEPH, 124
Bernays, Hermann Uhde, see Uhde-
  Bernays, Hermann
Bernet Kempers, August J., 26
Bernheimer, Richard, 9
BERNINI, GIOVANNI LORENZO, 124
Bernouilli, Johann J., 17
Bernt, Walther, 84, 92
BERRUGUETE, PEDRO, 124
Bersier, Jean E., 99
Berti, Luciano, 168
BERTOLDO, GIOVANNI DI, 124
Beruete y Moret, Aureliano de, 88, 151,
  199
Besnard, Albert, 161
Besson, George, 192
Bessone-Aurelj, Antonietta M., 1
BETTI, BERNARDINO, see
  PINTURICCHIO
Bettini, Sergio, 122
Bevan, Bernard, 60
Beyen, Hendrik G., 167
Beyer, Klaus G., 107
Bezold, Gustav, 55
Bhattacharyya, Benoytosh, 26
Biagi, Luigi, 165, 181
Bianconi, Piero, 145, 165
Biddle, Edward, 195

BIDDLE, GEORGE, 125
Bieber, Margarete, 17
Biehl, Walther, 67
Bier, Justus, 184
Bigelow, Francis H., 109
Binder, M. J., 153
BINGHAM, GEORGE CALEB, 125
Binyon, Laurence, 23, 26, 80, 125, 126,
  150
Bird, Paul, 160
Birren, Faber, 195
Bittner, Herbert, 160
Blake, Vernon, 92
BLAKE, WILLIAM, 125
Blanc, Charles, 182, 200
Blanc, Louis, 109
Blashfield, E. H., 199
Blashfield, E. W., 199
Blegen, Carl W., 17
Bliss, Douglas P., 96
Bloch, Raymond, 16
Blochet, Edgar, 26
Blomfield, Reginald T., 53, 56
Blum, André, 76, 96, 167
Blunt, Anthony, 38, 41, 92, 125, 166,
  174, 180, 191
Boardman, John, 17
Boas, Franz, 13
Boas, George, 17, 136
Boase, Thomas S. R., 40
BOCCIONI, UMBERTO, 125
Bock, Elfried, 92, 93
Bode, Wilhelm von, 41, 65, 68, 84, 104,
  124, 126, 128, 142, 153, 182
Bodkin, Thomas, 199
Bodmer, Heinrich, 131, 136, 163
Boeck, Wilhelm, 177, 198
Boeckler, Albert, 30
Boehn, Max von, 71, 102, 124, 148, 183
Boerschmann, Ernst, 23
Boethius, Axel, 17
Boggs, Jean S., 138
BOILLY, LOUIS LÉOPOLD, 125
Boinet, Amédée, 30
BOLOGNA, GIOVANNI DA, see
  GIOVANNI DA BOLOGNA

Bolton, Arthur T., 119, 193
Bolton, Theodore, 89
Bombe, Walter, 125, 176
Bond, Francis, 56
BONDONE, GIOTTO DI, see GIOTTO
    DI BONDONE
BONFIGLI, BENEDETTO, 125
BONHEUR, ROSA, 125
Boni, Albert, 111
BONINGTON, RICHARD PARKES, 125
BONNARD, PIERRE, 126
Bonnefoy, Yves, 171
BONVICINO, ALESSANDRO, see
    MORETTO, IL
Bony, Jean, 53
Bordona, Jesús Domínguez, see
    Domínguez Bordona, Jesús
Borenius, Tancred, 80, 82, 182
Born, Wolfgang, 89
Borovka, Grigorii I., 14
BORROMINI, FRANCESCO, 126
Bòrroni, Fabia, 1
Borsook, Eve, 82
BOS, CORNELIS, 126
BOSCH, HIERONYMUS VAN AKEN,
    126
Boschetto, Antonio, 164, 190
Boskovic, Durde, 30
Bosschère, Jean de, 168
Bossert, Helmuth T., 17, 101
Bothmer, Dietrich von, 17
Bottari, Stefano, 121, 153
BOTTICELLI, SANDRO, 126, 127
BOUCHER, FRANÇOIS, 127, 194
Bouchot, Henri, 76, 130
Bouchot-Saupique, Jacqueline, 130, 152
Boudaille, Georges, 177
BOUDIN, EUGÈNE, 127
BOURDELLE, ÉMILE ANTOINE, 127
Bouret, Jean, 187
Bourget, Pierre, 167
BOUTS, DIERCK, 127
Bouvy, Eugène, 137
Bovy, Adrien, 88
Bovy, Daniel Baud, see Baud-Bovy,
    Daniel

Bowie, Henry P., 23
Bowie, Theodore R., 23, 201
Bowra, Cecil M., 17
Brackett, Oliver, 104, 133
Bradley, John William, 1
Brainerd, G. W., 44
Braive, Michel F., 111
BRAMANTE, DONATO, 127
BRANCUSI, CONSTANTIN, 127
Brandi, Cesare, 82, 149
BRANGWYN, FRANK, 127
Branner, Robert, 50
BRAQUE, GEORGES, 127, 128
Brauer, Heinrich, 124
Braun, Joseph, 6, 109
Breasted, James H., 30
Bredius, Abraham, 43, 182
Breeskin, Adelyn D., 132
Bréhier, Louis, 6, 30, 38
Brest, Jorge Romero, see Romero
    Brest, Jorge
Breton, André, 36
BREUER, MARCEL, 128
Breuil, Henri, 13
Breuning, Margaret, 180
Bridenbaugh, Carl, 154
Brière, Gaston, 65
Briganti, Giuliano, 177, 203
Briggs, Martin Shaw, 26, 50
BRILL, MATTHÄUS, 128
BRILL, PAUL, 128
Brinckmann, Albert E., 35, 55, 58, 63,
    201
Brinton, Selwyn J. C., 146
Brion, Marcel, 36
Brion-Guerry, Liliane, 132
Briquet, Charles M., 2
Britten, Frederic J., 101
Britton, John, 56
Brizio, Anna M., 36
Brockwell, Maurice W., 143
Brommer, Frank, 17
Bronstein, Léo, 120, 151
BRONZINO, AGNOLO, 128
Brooke, Iris, 102
Brooks, Charles M., 150

Brooks, Van Wyck, 192
BROSSE, SALOMON DE, 128
Broulhiet, Georges, 154
BROUWER, ADRIAEN, 128
Brown, Bolton, 99
BROWN, FORD MADOX, 128, 186
Brown, Frank E., 17
Brown, Gerard B., 40, 155
Brown, Milton W., 36, 89
Brown, Percy, 26
Brownell, Baker, 50
Brownell, William C., 38
BRUEGHEL, JAN, 128, 129
BRUEGHEL, PIETER, 128, 129
Bruhn, Wolfgang, 102
Bruhns, Leo, 128
BRUNELLESCHI, FILIPPO, 129
Brunn, Heinrich, 17
Brunov, Nikolai I., 45
Bryan, Michael, 2
Buchanan, Donald W., 76
Buchheim, Lothar G., 123
Buchner, Ernst, 190
Buckley, Wilfred, 107
BULFINCH, CHARLES, 129
Bulfinch, Ellen S., 129
Bum, Lili Fröhlich, see Fröhlich-Bum,
    Lili
Bunim, Miriam S., 30
Bunt, Cyril G. E., 45, 109
Bunting, Bainbridge, 61
BUONARROTI, see MICHELANGELO
BUONINSEGNA, DUCCIO, see DUCCIO
    DI BUONINSEGNA
Burchard, Ludwig, 187
BURCHFIELD, CHARLES, 129
Burckhardt, Jacob C., 41, 50, 187
Burckhardt, Rudolf F., 134
Burger, Fritz, 79, 161, 175
Burger, Willy, 65, 84, 202
Burgess, J., 27
BURGKMAIR, HANS, 129
Burke, Joseph, 155
Burkhard, Arthur, 129, 152
BURNE-JONES, EDWARD, 129
Burne-Jones, Georgiana M., 129

BURNHAM, DANIEL HUDSON, 130
Burr, Grace H., 104
Burroughs, Alan, 89, 170
Burton, William, 112
Bury, Adrian, 203
Buscaroli, Rezio, 168, 169
Busch, Günter, 123
Busch, Harald, 63
Buschiazzo, Mario J., 59
Buschor, Ernst, 17
Bushell, Stephen W., 23
Bushnell, Geoffrey H. S., 112
Butler, Alfred J., 26
Butler, Howard C., 30
Buxton, David, 59
Byne, Arthur, 60, 104, 109
Byne, Mildred Stapley, 60, 104, 109
Byron, Robert, 30
Byvanck, Alexander, 13

C

Cabreras, Narciso Sentenach y, see
    Sentenach y Cabreras, Narciso
Cabriada, Agustin Ruiz, see Ruiz
    Cabriada, Agustin
Cabrol, Fernand, 6
Cadafalch, José Puig y, see Puig y
    Cadafalch, José
Caflisch, Nina, 165
CAGLIARI, PAOLO, see VERONESE,
    PAOLO
Cahen, Gustave, 127
Cahill, Holger, 47, 202
Cahill, James, 23
Caillaux, Henriette, 137
Cairns, Huntington, 9
Calabi, Augusto, 96
CALDER, ALEXANDER, 130
CALLOT, JACQUES, 130
Calmette, Joseph L. A., 188
Calvert, Albert F., 173
Calzada, Andres M., 205
CAMAINO, TINO DA, see TINO DA
    CAMAINO

CAMBIO, ARNOLFO DI, see ARNOLFO
   DI CAMBIO
Camesasca, E., 3
Camón Aznar, José, 60, 152, 199
Campbell, Joseph, 29
Canaday, John, 37
CANALE, ANTONIO, 130
CANALETTO, see CANALE, ANTONIO
CANOVA, ANTONIO, 130
Cantinelli, Richard, 124, 138
Canton, Francisco J. Sanchez, see
   Sanchez Canton, Francisco J.
Canuti, Fiorenzo, 176
Capart, Jean, 15
CARAVAGGIO, MICHELANGELO,
   130, 131
Carli, Enzo, 82, 140, 149, 169, 196
CARPACCIO, VITTORE, 131
CARPEAUX, JEAN-BAPTISTE, 131
Carpeaux, Louise Clement, see Clement-
   Carpeaux, Louise
Carpenter, Rhys, 9, 13, 17
CARRA, CARLO, 131
CARRACCI, AGOSTINO, 131
CARRACCI, ANNIBALE, 131
CARRACCI, LUDOVICO, 131
Carré, Louis, 109
Carreres, Carlos Sarthou, see Sarthou
   Carreres, Carlos
CARRIÈRE, EUGÈNE, 131, 132
Carrington, Fitz Roy, 96
CARRUCCI, JACOPO, see PONTORMO,
   JACOPO
Carson, Julia M., 132
Cartwright, Julia, 171
Cary, Elisabeth L., 172, 186, 202
Casotti, Maria Walcher, see Walcher-
   Casotti, Maria
CASSATT, MARY, 132
Casson, Stanley, 17, 63
Cassou, Jean, 133, 139, 157
CASTAGNO, ANDREA DEL, 132, 198
Castelfranchi Vegas, Liana, 41
CASTELFRANCO, GIORGIONE DA,
   see GIORGIONE DA CASTELFRANCO
Castiglione, Baldassare, 35

Cattaneo, Irene, 186
Cattani, George, 167
Cavalcaselle, Giovanni B., 82, 85, 181,
   197
CAVALLINI, PIETRO, 132
Cazalis, Henry, 182
Cecchi, Emilio, 82, 140, 149, 164
CELLINI, BENVENUTO, 132
Cendali, Lorenzo, 124
Cennini, Cennino, 74
CENNO DI PEPI, see CIMABUE,
   GIOVANNI
Cerceau, Jacques Androuet du, see
   Androuet du Cerceau, Jacques
Ceroni, Ambrogio, 171
Cescinsky, Herbert, 104
CÉZANNE, PAUL, 132, 133, 166
Chabrun, Jean F., 185
Chaffers, William, 109, 112
CHAGALL, MARC, 133
Chamberlain, Arthur B., 155, 186
Chamberlin, Mary W., 2
Chambers, Frank P., 9
Chamot, Mary, 103
Chamoux, François, 17
CHAMPAIGNE, JEAN BAPTISTE DE,
   133
CHAMPAIGNE, PHILIPPE DE, 133
Champion, Claude, 190
Chanin, Abraham, 146
Chantelou, Paul F., 124
Charbonneaux, Jean, 17
CHARDIN, JEAN-BAPTISTE SIMÉON,
   133
Charensol, G., 124
Charleston, R. J., 112
Charteris, Evan E., 190
Chase, George H., 63
CHASE, WILLIAM MERRITT,
   133
CHASSÉRIAU, THÉODORE, 133
Chastel, André, 41
Chatelet, Albert, 76
Chavagnac, Xavier R. M., 112
CHAVANNES, PIERRE PUVIS DE, see
   PUVIS DE CHAVANNES, PIERRE

Chavez, Austin Velazquez, see Velazquez, Chavez, Austin
Cheney, Sheldon, 9, 37, 71
Chesterton, Gilbert K., 202
Chevreul, Michel E., 74
Chicago. Art Institute. Ryerson Library, 2
Chiesa, Angela Ottino della, see Della Chiesa, Angela Ottino
Childe, Vere Gordon, 13, 26
Chipiez, Charles, 14
CHIPPENDALE, THOMAS, 133
CHIRICO, GIORGIO DE, 134
Choay, Françoise, 162
Christ-Janer, Albert, 189
Christensen, Erwin O., 13, 101
Christie, Archibald, 101
Christie, Grace, 114
Christoffel, Ulrich, 39
CHURCH, FREDERIC EDWIN, 134
Churchill, Sidney J. A., 109
Cicognara, Leopoldo, 2
CIMA DA CONEGLIANO, GIOVANNI BATTISTA, 134
CIMABUE, GIOVANNI, 134
CIONE, ANDREA DI, see ORCAGNA, ANDREA
Cirici-Pellicer, Alexandre, 46
Cladel, Judith, 185
Clapham, Alfred W., 50, 56
Clapp, Frederick M., 179
Clark, George N., 35
Clark, Kenneth M., 50, 71, 145, 163, 182
Clasen, K. H., 50
CLAUDE LORRAIN, 134
Clausse, Gustave, 189
Clemen, Paul, 40, 43
Clément, Charles, 148, 150
Clément-Carpeaux, Louise, 131
Climent, Carlos Fages de, see Fages de Climent, Carlos
CLOUET, FRANÇOIS, 134
CLOUET, JEAN, 134
Clouzot, Étienne, 111
Clouzot, Henri, 109, 114
Coburn, W., 200

Codrington, Kenneth deB., 26
COECKE, PIETER, 134
Cogniat, Raymond, 92, 147
Cohn, William, 23
Colacicchi, Giovanni, 179
Colas, René, 53, 54, 102
Colasanti, Arduino, 147
Coletti, Luigi, 134, 196
Colgate, William G., 38
Colin, Paul, 96
Collingwood, Robin G., 9
Collins, George R., 147
Collison-Morley, Lacy, 41
Colnaghi, Dominic E., 2
COLOMBE, MICHEL, 134, 135
Columbia University. Avery Architectural Library, 2
Colvin, Howard M., 2
Colvin, Sidney, 144
Comanducci, Agostino M., 2
Combe, Jacques, 126
Conant, Kenneth J., 50
Condit, Carl W., 61
CONEGLIANO, GIOVANNI BATTISTA CIMA DA, see CIMA DA CONEGLIANO, GIOVANNI BATTISTA
Connick, Charles J., 107
Conrat, Erika Tietze, see Tietze-Conrat, Erika
CONSTABLE, JOHN, 135
Constable, William G., 71, 80, 130, 144, 203
Contenau, Georges, 30
Conway, William M., 45, 141, 143, 148
Cook, Dorothy E., 103
Cook, Herbert F., 149
Cooke, Hereward L., 92
Coomaraswamy, Ananda K., 26, 29
Cooper, Douglas, 162, 194, 197
COPLEY, JOHN SINGLETON, 135
Coquiot, Gustave, 183, 197
Cornelius, Charles O., 104
Cornell, Henrik, 45
Cornette, Arthur J. J., 84
COROT, JEAN-BAPTISTE-CAMILLE, 135

Corpus Vasorum Antiquorum, 17
Corpus Vitrearum Medii Aevi, 107
CORREGGIO, ANTONIO ALLEGRI, 136
Cortissoz, Royal, 89, 138, 154, 160, 189
CORTONA, PIETRO DA, see PIETRO DA CORTONA
COSIMO, PIERO DI, see PIERO DI COSIMO
COSIMO TURA, see TURA, COSIMO
Cossío, Manuel B., 9, 152
Costa, Felix da, 88
Costa Torres, Raul, 59
Costantini, Vincenzo, 42
COTMAN, JOHN SELL, 136
Cotterell, Howard H., 109
Coulton, George G., 30
COURBET, GUSTAVE, 136
Courboin, François, 96
Courthion, Pierre, 134, 136, 137, 139, 142, 157, 180, 187
Covarrubias, Miguel, 43
Cowdrey, Bartlett, 173
Cox, John C., 56
Cox, Trenchard, 35, 145
Cox, Warren E., 112
COZENS, ALEXANDER, 136
COZENS, JOHN ROBERT, 136
CRAM, RALPH ADAMS, 136
CRANACH, LUCAS, 136
Crawford, David A. E. L., 68, 140
CREDI, LORENZO DI, see LORENZO DI CREDI
Crespelle, Jean-Paul, 76
Cresson, Margaret F., 146
Creswell, Keppel A. C., 26
Crichton, George H., 68
Cripps, Wilfred J., 109
CRIVELLI, CARLO, 137
Croce, Benedetto, 10
CROME, JOHN, 137
Cronin, William V., 184
Crosby, Sumner M., 54
Crossley, Frederick H., 67
Crous, J. W., 17
Crowe, Joseph A., 82, 85, 181, 197

Crowfoot, J. W., 50
Cruttwell, Maud, 167, 179, 184, 192, 200
Cumming, David, 99
Cummings, Charles A., 58
Cummings, Paul, 2
Cundall, Herbert M., 80
Cundall, Joseph, 96
Cunill, Josep Gudiol i, see Gudiol i Cunill, Josep
Cunynghame, Henry H., 103
Čurchin, Milan, 169
Curjel, Hans, 121
CURRY, JOHN STEUART, 137
Cursiter, Stanley, 80
Curtis, Atherton, 125
Curtius, Ludwig, 13, 17
Cushion, J. P., 112
Cust, Anna M. E., 108
Cust, Lionel H., 142
Cust, Robert H. H., 132, 193

D

Dacier, Émile, 96, 189, 201
DADDI, BERNARDO, 137
Daglian, Philip B., 81
Daix, Pierre, 177
Dale, S. S., 116
DALI, SALVADOR, 137
Dalli Regoli, Gigetta, 164
DALOU, AIMÉ JULES, 137
Dalton, Ormonde M., 30
Daly, Cesar, 51
Damase, Jacques, 142
Damon, S. Foster, 125
Danckert, Ludwig, 112
Daremberg, Charles V., 18
Dark, Sidney, 175
Dauberville, Henry, 126
Dauberville, Jean, 126
DAUBIGNY, CHARLES-FRANÇOIS, 137
Daulte, François, 192
DAUMIER, HONORÉ, 137, 138
Daun, Berthold, 194, 201
Daux, Georges, 18

Davenport, Cyril J. H., 71, 96
Davenport, Millia, 102
David, Henri, 192
DAVID, JACQUES-LOUIS, 138
DAVID D'ANGERS, PIERRE JEAN, 138
DAVIES, ARTHUR BOWEN, 138
Davies, Gerald S., 68, 148, 153
Davies, Randall, 150, 186
DAVIS, STUART, 138
Dawson, Nelson, 109
Day, Lewis F., 107
Dayot, Armand P. M., 133, 200
Debes, Dietmar, 101
Déchelette, Joseph, 13
Decker, Hans, 42
Decker, Heinrich, 65
DEGAS, HILAIRE GERMAIN EDGAR, 138, 139, 172
Degener, Frederik Schmidt, see Schmidt-Degener, Frederik
Degenhart, Bernhard, 92, 178
Dehio, Georg G., 40, 55
Deknatel, Frederick B., 173
Delacre, Maurice, 93, 142, 169
DELACROIX, EUGÈNE, 139
Délaissé, L. M. J., 30
Delen, Adrien J. J., 93, 96
Delevoy, Robert L., 85
Della Chiesa, Angela Ottino, 165
DELLA ROBBIA, see ROBBIA
Delogu, Giuseppe, 58, 68, 82, 93, 169
Delteil, Loÿs, 96
DeMazia, Violette, 76
Demotte, Georg J., 114
Demus, Otto, 111
DEMUTH, CHARLES HENRY, 139
Denis, Maurice, 166
Denucé, Jean, 128
Deonna, Waldemar, 18, 66
DERAIN, ANDRÉ, 139, 140
Desborough, Vincent R. d'A., 18
Deschamps, Paul, 64, 65
Descharnes, Robert, 185
Deshoulières, François, 54
DESIDERIO DA SETTIGNANO, 140

Desjardins, Abel, 149
Desparmet Fitz-Gerald, Xavière, 151
Destrée, Joseph, 150
Destrée, Jules, 182, 202
Deusch, Werner R., 79
Deutscher Verein für Kunstwissenschaft, 2
Devigne, Marguerite, 65
Dewald, Ernest T., 82, 164
Dewey, John, 10
Dickens, Guy, 18
Dickinson, G. Lowes, 18
Dickinson, Helena A. S., 79
Diderot, Denis, 76
Didron, Adolphe N., 6
Diehl, Charles, 30
Diehl, Gaston, 168
Dieterle, Jean, 135
Diez, Ernst, 26, 27, 111
Digby, Adrian, 112
Dilke, Emilia F. S., 96, 104
Dilley, Arthur U., 114
Dillon, Edward, 107, 113
Dimier, Louis, 77, 93, 180
Dinsmoor, William B., 18
Diringer, David, 71
Dirks, Rudolf, 203
Dobson, Austin, 155
Dockstader, Frederick J., 43, 47
Dodgson, Campbell, 141
Doering, Heinrich Ubbelohde, see Ubbelohde-Doering, Heinrich
Doering, Oskar, 40
Doerner, Max, 74
Dörries, Bernhard, 93
Dohme, Robert, 55
Domenech Gallissa, Rafael, 193
DOMENICHINO, 140
Donínguez Bordona, Jesús, 88
DONATELLO, 140
Donati, Lamberto, 97
Donati, Ugo, 165
DONATO DI NICCOLO DI BETTO BARDI, see DONATELLO
Dorbec, Prosper, 187
Dorival, Bernard, 71, 77, 132

Dorner, Alexander, 122
Dorra, Henri, 191
DOSSI, DOSSO, 140
DOU, GERARD, 140
DOUANIER, LE, see ROUSSEAU,
  HENRI JULIEN FELIX
Doughty, O., 186
Douglas, Frederic H., 47
Douglas, Robert Langton, 120, 163, 177
Dow, George Francis, 47
Dowd, David, 138
Downes, William H., 156, 190
Downing, Antoinette F., 61
Drake, Maurice, 6, 107
Drake, Wilfred, 6, 107
Drepperd, Carl W., 47
Drexler, Arthur, 23, 185
Drey, Franz, 137
Dreyfous, Maurice, 137
Dreyfus, Carle, 104
Dreyfus, Philippe Baston, see Baston-
  Dreyfus, Philippe
Drioton, Étienne, 15
Drost, Willi, 79, 142
Drucker, Michel, 183
Dube-Heynig, Annemarie, 159
Du Bois, Guy P., 156, 192
Dubray, Jean P., 131
DUBUFFET, JEAN, 140
Dubuisson, A., 125
Ducati, Pericle, 16, 18
DUCCIO DI BUONINSEGNA, 140, 149
DUCHAMP, MARCEL, 141
Du Columbier, Pierre, 38, 151
Dülberg, Franz, 85
DÜRER, ALBRECHT, 141
DUFY, RAOUL, 142
Dugdale, William, 56
Dumesnil, A. P. F.,Robert, see Robert-
  Dumesnil, A. P. F.
Dumesnil, Henri, 197
Dunlap, William, 47
Duparc, Arthur, 182
Du Peloux de Saint Romain, Charles, 2,
  38
Dupont, Jacques, 30

Duret, Théodore, 136, 150, 166, 183,
  197, 202
Durrieu, Paul, 85
Dussler, Luitpold, 97, 123, 124, 178, 181,
  192
Duthuit, Georges, 71
Dvořák, Max, 42, 129
DYCK, ANTHONY VAN, 142

E

EAKINS, THOMAS, 142
EARL, RALPH, 142
Earle, Alice M., 102
Eastlake, Charles L., 74
Eberlein, Harold D., 61, 104, 113
Ebersolt, Jean, 30, 51
Eckstädt, George Vitzhum von, see
  Vitzhum von Eckstädt, George
Ede, Harold S., 97
Edgell, George H., 52, 61, 83
Édouard-Joseph, René, 2
Edwards, Iowerth E. S., 15
Edwards, Ralph, 105
Egger, Hermann, 154
Eggers, George W., 124
Einem, Herbert von, 146
Einstein, Carl, 37, 127
Eisen, Gustav, 107
Eisler, Max, 158
Elias, Julius, 164
Eliasberg, Alexander, 60
ELSHEIMER, ADAM, 142
Elst, Joseph J., 85
Elster, Hanns M., 191
Emiliani, Andrea, 128
Emmons, Robert, 192
Encyclopedia of World Art, 2
Encyclopédie Photographique de l'Art,
  10
Enggass, Robert, 147
Enlart, Camille, 39, 54
Ensko, Stephen G. C., 109
ENSOR, JAMES, 142
EPSTEIN, JACOB, 142
Erben, Walter, 133

Erhard, Hermann, 161
ERLACH, JOHANN BERNHARD
  FISCHER VON, see FISCHER VON
  ERLACH, JOHANN BERNHARD
ERNST, MAX, 143
Erréra, Isabelle, 2
Escher, Konrad, 83
Escherich, Mela, 121, 152, 203
Escholier, Raymond, 77, 139, 152
Escobar, Daniel Berjano, see Berjano
  Escobar, Daniel
Esdaille, Katharine A. M., 67, 187
Estrada, Genaro, 151
Ettinghausen, Richard, 27
Evans, Arthur J., 18
Evans, Joan, 30, 39, 40, 54, 101, 109
Evans, Ralph M., 74
Evers, Hans G., 187
EYCK, HUBERT VAN, 143
EYCK, JAN VAN, 143

F

FABRIANO, GENTILE DA, see GEN-
  TILE DA FABRIANO
Fabriczy, Cornelius von, 68
Fages de Climent, Carlos, 145
Faille, J. Bernard de la, see La Faille, J.
  Bernard de
FALCONET, ÉTIENNE MAURICE, 143
Falk, Bernard, 187
Falke, Otto von, 104, 114
FANTIN-LATOUR, IGNACE HENRI
  JEAN THÉODORE, 143
Fantin-Latour, Victoria D., 143
Faraday, Cornelia B., 114
Farbman, Michael S., 87
Fasola, Giustina N., 145, 179
Faure, Élie, 10, 131, 139, 168
Fechheimer, Hedwig, 15
FEININGER, LYONEL, 143
FEKE, ROBERT, 143
Feld, Stuart P., 89
Félibien, André, 180
Félice, Roger de, 104, 105
Fels, Marthe de, 171

Fenaille, Maurice, 114
Fenollosa, Ernest F., 23
Ferguson, John C., 23
Fergusson, James, 27, 51
Fergusson, John D., 80
Fernández, Justino, 43, 175
Ferrari, Enrique Lafuente, see Lafuente
  Ferrari, Enrique
FERRARI, GAUDENZIO, 144
Ferrari, Giulio, 109
Ferrari, Oreste, 148
FEUERBACH, ANSELM, 144
Feulner, Adolf, 66, 105
Ffoulkes, Constance J., 109, 144
Fiedler, Konrad, 10
Fielding, Mantle, 2, 97, 195
Fierens, Paul, 43, 85, 162
Fierens-Gevaert, Hippolyte, 85, 158
FIESOLE, MINO DA, see MINO DA
  FIESOLE
Figgis, Darrell, 125
FILARETE, 144
Filov, Bogdan D., 27
Finberg, Alexander J., 198
Finberg, H. F., 198
FINI, TOMMASO, see MASOLINO DA
  PANICALE
FINIGUERRA, TOMMASO, 144
Fiocco, Giuseppe, 83, 131, 149, 153,
  167, 179, 200
FIORENZO DI LORENZO, 144
Firdausi, 27
Fischel, Oskar, 97, 181, 197
Fischer, Josef L., 107
Fischer, Otto, 23, 79
FISCHER VON ERLACH, JOHANN
  BERNHARD, 144
Fitch, James M., 61, 152
Fitz-Gerald, Xavière Desparmet, see
  Desparmet Fitz-Gerald, Xavière
FLAXMAN, JOHN, 144
Flechsig, Eduard, 141
Fleischer, Robert, 18
Fleming, Gordon H., 186
Fleming, John 119
Flemming, Ernst R., 115

Flemming, Willi, 122
Fletcher, Banister, 51
Flexner, James T., 89, 135
Flipo, Vincent, 54
Florence. Kunsthistorisches Institut.
    Bibliothek, 3
Florisoone, Michel, 77, 166
Focillon, Henri, 10, 30, 31, 37, 178, 182
Foerster, Otto H., 127
Fokker, Theodore H., 85
Fokker, Thomas, 35
Folnesics, Hans, 129
Fontainas, André, 39
Fontaine, Georges, 113
Foote, Henry W., 143, 193
FOPPA, VINCENZO, 144
Foratti, Aldo, 130, 131
Ford, Brinsley, 203
FORLI, MELOZZO DA, see MELOZZO
    DA FORLI
Forman, Henry C., 61
Forrer, Leonard, 3
FORTUNY, MARIANO, 145
Fossi Todorow, Maria, 178
Foster, Joshua J., 3
FOUQUET, JEAN, 145
Fourcaud, Louis de, 188
Fourreau, Armand, 172
Fowler, Harold N., 18
Fraenckel, Ingeborg, 190
Fraenger, Wilhelm, 126
FRAGONARD, JEAN-HONORÉ, 145
Francastel, Pierre, 149
FRANCESCHI, PIETRO DI
    BENEDETTO DEI, 145
FRANCESCO DI GIORGIO MARTINI,
    146
FRANCESCO DI STEFANO GIUOCHI,
    see PESELLINO
FRANCIA, 146
Francovich, Géza de, 120
Frank, Edgar B., 109
Frankenstein, Alfred V., 153
Frankfort, Henri, 27
Frankfort, Henriette A. Groenewegen,
    see Groenewegen-Frankfort, Henriette A.

Frankl, Paul, 31, 51
Frary, Ihna T., 158
Fredeman, William E., 80
Frederiks, Johann W., 109
Freedberg, Sydney J., 83, 176, 190
Freeden, Max H. von, 31
FRENCH, DANIEL CHESTER, 146
French, Hollis, 110
French, Mary F., 146
Freund, Gisèle, 111
Frey, Carl, 169
Frey, Dagobert, 35, 58, 169
Friedländer, Max J., 71, 72, 85, 93, 97,
    120, 129, 136, 141, 164, 165
Friedländer, Walter F., 77, 83, 130, 134,
    180
Friedrich, Carl J., 35
FRIEDRICH, CASPAR DAVID, 146
Fritzsche, Hellmuth A., 123
Fröhlich-Bum, Lili, 157, 176
Fromentin, Eugène, 85
Fry, Roger E., 10, 23, 80, 132, 168, 191
Fuchs, Eduard, 137
Fürst, Viktor, 203
FÜSSLI, JOHANN HEINRICH, see
    FUSELI, HENRY
Fütterer, Ilse Baier, see Baier-Fütterer,
    Ilse
Furness, S. M. M., 161
Furst, Herbert, 97
Furtwängler, Adolf, 13, 18
Furumark, Arne, 18
FUSELI, HENRY, 146
Fyfe, David T., 18

G

Gabelentz, Hans von der, 122
GABO, NAUM, 146
GABRIEL, JACQUES ANGE, 146
Gadd, Cyril J., 27
Gaillard, Émile, 189
Gaillard, Georges, 69
GAINSBOROUGH, THOMAS, 146, 147
Galassi, Giuseppe, 68, 111
Galetti, Ugo, 3

Gallatin, Albert E., 123
Gallissa, Rafael Domenech, see
  Domenech Gallissa, Rafael
Gamba, Carlo, 123, 126
Ganay, Ernest de, 162
Gantner, Joseph, 40, 203
Ganz, Paul, 88, 93, 155, 203
Gardner, Albert Ten Eyck, 69, 72, 89
Gardner, Alfred H., 56
Gardner, Arthur, 54, 65, 67
Gardner, Ernest A., 18
Gardner, Helen, 10
Gardner, John S., 110
Gardner, Percy, 18
Garlick, Kenneth, 161
Garner, Thomas, 56
Garnier, Édouard, 107
Garrett, Jane N., 48
Garrett, Wendell D., 48
Garrison, Edward B., 83
Garrison, J. J., 12
Garwood, Darrell, 203
Garzarolli-Thurnlackh, Karl, 93
Gascoyne, David, 37
Gassier, Pierre, 151
GAUDENS, AUGUSTUS SAINT, see
  SAINT-GAUDENS, AUGUSTUS
GAUDI, ANTONIO, 147
GAUGUIN, PAUL, 147
Gauguin, Pola, 147
GAULLI, GIOVANNI BATTISTA, 147
Gaunt, William, 10, 199
Gauss, Charles E., 77
Gaya Nuño, Juan Antonio, 46, 199,
  205
Gayet, Albert J., 31
Gazier, A. L., 133
GEERTGEN TOT SINT JANS, 147
Geffroy, Gustave, 171
Geiger, Benno, 93, 166
Geisberg, Max, 97
Geiser, Bernhard, 177
Geist, Sidney, 127
GELDER, ARENT DE, 147
Gelder, Jan G. van, 93, 199
Geldzahler, Henry, 89

GELLEE, CLAUDE, see CLAUDE
  LORRAIN
Gengaro, Mario L., 35
GENTILE DA FABRIANO, 147
George, Waldemar, 93, 154, 166
GÉRICAULT, JEAN-LOUIS ANDRÉ
  THÉODORE, 148
Germain, Alphonse, 134
Gernsheim, Helmut, 112
GÉRÔME, JEAN-LÉON, 148
Gerson, Horst, 43, 160
Gerstenberg, Kurt, 184
Gerstinger, Hans, 31
Gestoso y Perez, José, 199
Gettens, Rutherford J., 74
Gevaert, Hippolyte Fierens, see Fierens-
  Gevaert, Hippolyte
Geymüller, Heinrich von, 58
GHIBERTI, LORENZO, 148
GHIRLANDAIO, DOMENICO, 148
Giacometti, Georges, 157
GIACOMO DA PONTE, see BASSANO,
  JACOPO
Giedion, Siegfried, 51, 184
Giedion-Welcker, Carola, 63, 121, 127,
  177
Gielly, Louis J., 181
Giesecke, Albert, 178
Gieure, Maurice, 128
Giglioli, Giulio Q., 16
Gilchrist, Agnes E. A., 194
Giles, Herbert A., 23
GILL, ERIC, 148
Gillet, Louis, 201
GIORDANO, LUCA, 148
GIORGIONE DA CASTELFRANCO,
  148
GIOTTO DI BONDONE, 149
GIOVANNI DA BOLOGNA, 149
GIOVANNI DA FIESOLE, see
  ANGELICO, FRA
GIOVANNI DA MILANO, 149
GIOVANNI DI PAOLO, 149
Giovannoni, Gustavo, 189
GIRARDON, FRANÇOIS, 149
Girouard, Mark, 193

GIRTIN, THOMAS, 150
Gischia, Léon, 39
GISLEBERTUS, 150
Gissing, Alfred C., 157
GIULIO ROMANO, 150
Glaser, Curt, 79, 97, 136, 155, 173
Glazier, Richard, 101, 114
Gleizes, Albert, 37
GLEYRE, MARC CHARLES GABRIEL,
    150
Glück, Gustav, 35, 129, 142, 187
Glück, Heinrich, 27
Gnoli, Umberto, 83, 176
Gnudi, Cesare, 30, 121
Godefroy, J., 55,
Godefroy, Louis, 175
Godfrey, Walter H., 56
Göbel, Heinrich, 115
Goering, Max, 79, 83, 153
GOES, HUGO VAN DER, 150
Goetz, Hermann, 27
Goffin, Arnold, 178
GOGH, VINCENT VAN, 150
Golding, John, 72
Goldscheider, Ludwig, 10, 16, 18, 123,
    140, 148, 150, 152, 163, 170, 182,
    200
Goldschmidt, Adolph, 79, 108
Goldsmith, Elizabeth E., 6
Goldstein, Franz, 3
Goldwater, Robert J., 10, 72, 147
Golzio, Vincenzo, 31, 42
Gombosi, György, 172, 176, 194
Gombrich, Ernst H., 10, 35
Gómez-Moreno, Manuel, 60, 69
Gómez Sicre, José, 86
Goncourt, Edmond de, 77, 180, 201
Goncourt, Jules de, 77
Gonse, Louis, 65
Goodenough, Erwin R., 18
Goodhart-Rendel, Harry S., 56
Goodrich, Laurence B., 142
Goodrich, Lloyd, 47, 142, 156, 170,
    192, 202
Goodwin, Philip L., 59
Goris, Jan A., 187

GORKY, ARSHILE, 151
GOSSAERT, JAN, 151
Gotch, John A., 56, 57, 158
GOUJON, JEAN, 151
Gould, Cecil, 83
Gowans, Alan, 61, 72
Gower, Ronald C. S., 161, 186, 203
GOYA Y LUCIENTES, FRANCISCO
    JOSÉ DE, 151
GOYEN, JAN VAN, 151
GOZZOLI, BENOZZO, 151
Grabar, André, 31
Grabar, Igor, 87
Gradmann, Erwin, 88, 93
Graefe, Julius Meier, see Meier-Graefe,
    Julius
Graham, J. C., 144
Graham, Robert P. Howgrave, see
    Howgrave-Graham, Robert P.
Grant, Maurice H., 80
Grant, Michael, 31
Grappe, Georges, 145, 185
Grassi, Luigi, 124
Grautoff, Otto, 180
Graves, Algernon, 3, 41, 184
Gray, Basil, 23, 27, 97
Gray, Christopher, 37
Graziosi, Paolo, 13
Great Britain. Royal Commission on the
    ancient and historical monuments, 57
GRECO, EL, 151, 152
Green, Samuel M., 47
Greenberg, Clement, 171
Greene, Theodore M., 10
Greig, James, 181
GREUZE, JEAN-BAPTISTE, 152
Grey, Roch, 187
Griaule, Marcel, 13
Gribble, E. R., 104
GRIEN, HANS BALDUNG, see
    BALDUNG, HANS
Griffin, James B., 48
Grimschitz, Bruno, 154
Grinnell, Isabel H., 18
GRIS, JUAN, 152
Grivot, Denis, 150

Groce, George C., 3
Grodecki, Louis, 51, 107, 108
Groenewegen-Frankfort, Henriette A., 15
Grohmann, Adolf, 25
Grohmann, Will, 37, 158, 159
Grolier, Gaston A., 112
Gromort, Georges, 58, 146
Gronau, Georg, 123, 136
Groot, Cornelis Hofstede de, see
    Hofstede de Groot, Cornelis
GROPIUS, WALTER, 152
GROS, ANTOINE-JEAN, 152
Gros, Gabriel J., 198
Groslier, Bernard P., 27
Grossman, Fritz, 129
GROSZ, GEORGE, 152
Grousset, René, 23
GRUEN, HANS BALDUNG, see
    BALDUNG, HANS
Grüneisen, Wladimir de, 31
GRÜNEWALD, MATTHIAS, 152, 153
Gruyer, François A., 145
GUARDI, FRANCESCO, 153
GUARINI, GUARINO, 153
Gudiol i Cunill, Josep, 72, 88
Gudiol y Ricart, José, 46, 157
Gudlaugsson, Sturla J., 195
GUERCINO, IL, 153
Guérin, Marcel, 138, 147, 166
Guerrero, P. E., 130
Guerry, Liliane Brion, see Brion-Guerry,
    Liliane
GUIDI, TOMMASO, see MASACCIO
GUIDO DA SIENA, 153
Guiffrey, Jean, 77, 133, 180
Guiffrey, Jules, 115, 162
GUILLAUMIN, JAN B. A., 166
Gunnis, Rupert, 3
Gurney, Oliver R., 14
Gutheim, Frederick, 119, 204

H

Haack, Friedrich, 37, 191
Habich, Georg, 68
Hackin, Joseph, 23

Hadeln, Detlev von, 93, 130, 196, 197
Haesaerts, Paul, 142
Haftmann, Werner, 72
Hagen, Oskar F. L., 40, 46, 89, 93, 153
Haggar, Reginald C., 113
Hague, Marian, 116
Hahnloser, Hans R., 201
Hale, Philip L., 200
Hale, R. T., 200
Hall, Donald, 172
Hall, H. van, 3
Hall, Harry R. H., 19
Hallays, André, 176
Halm, Philipp M., 66
HALS, FRANS, 153
Hamann, Richard, 10, 31, 79, 182
Hamberg, Philip G., 19
Hamerton, Philip G., 97
Hamilton, George H., 45, 166
Hamilton, John A., 31
Hamlin, Alfred D. F., 102
Hamlin, Talbot F., 51, 61, 161
Hammond, William A., 3
Hancke, Erich, 164
Handcock, Percy S. P., 14
Hanfmann, George M. A., 19
Hannover, Emil, 45, 113
Harada, Jiro, 23
Harcourt-Smith, Simon, 14
Hardie, Martin, 80
HARDOUIN-MANSART, JULES, see
    MANSART, JULES HARDOUIN
Hare, Richard, 45
HARNETT, WILLIAM, 153
Harnoncourt, René d', 47
Harper, J. Russell, 76
Harris, Enriqueta, 88
HARRISON, PETER, 154
Harrisse, Henry, 125
Hart, Charles H., 195
Hartlaub, Gustav F., 168
HARTLEY, MARSDEN, 154
Hartt, Frederick, 150, 170
Harvey, John D., 57
Harvey, John H., 31
Haseloff, Arthur E. G., 68

Haskell, Francis, 35
HASSAM, CHILDE, 154
Haupt, Albrecht, 54, 60
Hausenstein, Wilhelm, 120, 123, 131, 138, 149
Hauser, Arnold, 10, 72
Hautecoeur, Louis, 54, 150, 161
Hauttmann, Max, 31
Hauvette, Henri, 193
Havard, Henry, 105, 110
Havell, Ernest B., 27
Hawes, Charles H., 19
Hawes, Harriet A., 19
Hawley, Walter A., 115
Hayden, Arthur, 97
Hayes, Bartlett H., 73
Hayes, William C., 15
Hayter, Stanley W., 99
Head, Barclay V., 19
Heath, Dudley, 72
HEEMSKERK, MARTIN VAN, 154
Hege, Walter, 19, 21
Hegemann, Hans W., 196
Heikamp, Detlev, 204
Heinemann, Fritz, 123
Heise, Carl G., 79
Hekler, Anton, 19
Held, Julius, 187, 188
Hell, Hellmut, 31
Hell, Vera, 31
Hellens, Franz, 195
Helm, MacKinley, 86, 167, 175
Hempel, Eberhard, 40, 55, 126, 175
Henderson, Philip, 173
Hendy, Philip, 123, 168
Henkel, Max D., 93, 98
HENRI, ROBERT, 154
Henry, Françoise, 40, 41
Herbert, John A., 72
Herbert, Robert, 10
Hermanin, Federico, 178
Herzfeld, Ernst E., 27
Hess, Hans, 143
Hess, Jacob, 35
Hess, Thomas B., 160
Hevesy, André de, 121

Heydenreich, Leonard H., 163
Heynig, Annemarie Dube, see Dube-Heynig, Annemarie
Hibbard, Benjamin H., 124
Hildebrand, Adolf, 10
Hildebrandt, Edmund, 39
Hildebrandt, Hans, 37
HILDEBRANDT, JOHANN LUCAS VON, 154
HILER, HILAIRE, 154
Hill, George F., 19, 63, 68, 178
Hilles, Frederick W., 184
Hind, Arthur M., 97, 155, 167, 178, 182
Hind, Charles L., 189
Hinks, Roger P., 31, 130
Hipkiss, Edwin J., 48
Hispanic Society of America, 193, 205
Historic American Buildings Survey, 61
Hitchcock, Henry-Russell, 51, 57, 61, 184, 204
Hoag, John D., 27
HOBBEMA, MEINDERT, 154
Hobson, Robert L., 23, 112
Hodin, J. P., 159
HODLER, FERDINAND, 154
Höver, Otto, 110
Hoff, August, 162
HOFFMAN, MALVINA CORNELL, 155
Hoffmann, Edith, 159
Hofmann, Friedrich H., 113
Hofmann, Theobald, 181
Hofstede de Groot, Cornelis, 85, 182
HOGARTH, WILLIAM, 155
HOLBEIN, HANS, 155, 156
Holloway, Edward S., 105
Hollstein, F. W. H., 97
Holman, Louis A., 99
Holme, Charles, 45, 98
Holme, Geoffrey, 45, 98
Holmes, Charles J., 75, 135, 181
Holt, Elizabeth G., 10
Holt, Rosa B., 115
Holweck, Frederick G., 6
HOMER, WINSLOW, 156
Honey, William B., 23, 107, 112, 113

HONNECOURT, VILLARD DE, see
  VILLARD DE HONNECOURT
HONTHORST, GERRIT VAN, 156
HOOCH, PIETER DE, 156
Hoogewerf, Godefridus J., 85, 191
HOPPER, EDWARD, 156
Hoppin, Joseph C., 19
HOPPNER, JOHN, 157
Horne, Herbert P., 127
Horst, Carl, 55
HOUDON, JEAN-ANTOINE, 157
Hourticq, Louis, 149
Housser, F. B., 76
Houston, Mary G., 102
Houvet, Étienne, 54
Howarth, Thomas, 165
Howgrave-Graham, Robert P., 54
Hubbard, Eric H., 75, 93, 99
HUBER, WOLF, 120
Hubert, Jean, 31, 54
Hudnut, Joseph, 51
Hueffer, Ford Madox, 128
Huelsen, Christian, 154
Hürlimann, Martin, 16, 53, 153
Hugelshofer, Walter, 93
HUGUET, JAIME, 157
Huish, Marcus B., 19
Huizinga, Johan, 31
Hulst, Roger A. d', 115, 187
HUNT, WILLIAM HOLMAN, 157
Hunter, George L., 104, 105, 115
Hunter, Sam, 77, 89
Huntington, David C., 134
Huntley, George H., 189
Hustin, Arthur, 197
Huxley, Aldous L., 151
Huxtable, Ada L., 174
Huyghe, René, 72, 93
Hymans, Henri,S., 43, 172

I

Immerzeel, Johannes, 3
Ingersoll-Smouse, Florence, 176, 200
Ingholt, Harald, 28

INGRES, JEAN-AUGUSTE DOMINIQUE,
  157, 158
Iñiguez, Diego Angulo, see Angulo
  Iñiguez, Diego
INNESS, GEORGE, 158
International Directory of Arts, 3
Internationale Bibliographie der
  Kunstwissenschaft, 3
Internationales Kunst-Adressbuch, 3
Inventaire Génerale des Richesses d'Art
  de la France, 39
Inverarity, Robert B., 48
Ireland, John, 155
Ironside, Robin, 80
Irwin, David, 41
Isham, Samuel, 89
ISRAELS, JOZEF, 158
Ivins, William M., 91, 99

J

Jackson, Charles J., 110
Jackson, Thomas G., 51
Jacobsen, Emil, 193
Jacobsthal, Paul, 32
Jacobus de Varagine, 6
JACOPO DE BARBARI, see BARBARI,
  JACOPO DE
JACOPO DELLA QUERCIA, see
  QUERCIA, JACOPO DELLA
Jaffe, Hans, 37
Jakovsky, Anatole, 72
James, Macgill, 90
James, Philip, 172
Jameson, Anna B., 6
Jamot, Paul, 77, 138, 161, 162, 166, 180
Janer, Albert Christ, see Christ-Janer,
  Albert
Janis, Sidney, 89
Janneau, Guillaume, 107
Janson, Horst W., 10, 140
Jantzen, Hans, 32, 66
Jaques, Renate, 115
Jeanneret, Pierre, 162
JEANNERET-GRIS, CHARLES
  ÉDOUARD, see LE CORBUSIER

Jedlicka, Gotthard, 88, 129, 197
JEFFERSON, THOMAS, 158
Jenyns, Soame, 24
Jewell, Edward A., 77, 187
Jiménez-Placer, Fernando, 46
Jiminez, José Lopez, see Lopez Jiminez,
    José
JOHN, AUGUSTUS, 158
Johnson, Ada M., 110
Johnson, Charles, 75, 80
Johnson, Philip C., 51, 185
Johnston, Edward, 72
Jones, Edward A., 110
JONES, EDWARD BURNE, see BURNE-
    JONES, EDWARD
JONES, INIGO, 158
Jones, Owen, 102
JONGKIND, JOHAN BARTHOLD, 158
JORDAENS, JAKOB, 158
Joseph, René Édouard see Édouard-
    Joseph, René
Joubin, André, 139
Jouin, Henri A., 138, 161
Jourdain, Margaret, 105
Joyant, Maurice, 197
Joyce, Thomas A., 43, 44
Judson, Jay R., 156
Jullian, René, 68
Jullien, Adolphe, 143
Jullienne, Jean de, 201
Justi, Ludwig, 149, 159

K

Kähler, Heinz, 19
Kaftal, George, 7
Kahn, Gustave, 127, 143, 191
Kahnweiler, Daniel-H., 72, 152, 177, 201
Kallen, Horace M., 10, 11
Kallir, Otto, 190
Kampfer, Fritz, 107
KANDINSKY, WASSILY, 158, 159
Kar, Chintamoni, 27
Karlinger, Hans, 32, 66
Kasper, Karl, 55
Kates, George N., 24

Katzenellenbogen, Adolf, 32
Kaufman, Edgar, 204
Kaufmann, Carl M., 32
Kaufmann, Emil, 52
Kehrer, Hugo, 205
Kelby, William, 48
Kelemen, Pál, 44, 48
Keller, Harald, 179
Keller, Luzius, 178
Kelly, Francis M., 103
Kempers, August J. Bernet, see Bernet
    Kempers, August J.
Kendrick, Albert F., 115
Kendrick, Thomas D., 41
Kennedy, Edward G., 202
Kennedy, Ruth W., 121
Kenny, John B., 113
Kent, William W., 176
Kepes, Gyorgy, 11
Kerfoot, John B., 110
Kerr, R., 51
Kessler, J. H. H., 147
Kettell, Russell H., 105
Keynes, Geoffrey L., 125
Khandalavala, Karl, 29
Kidder, Alfred V., 48
Killanin, Michael M., 159
Kimball, S. Fiske, 35, 52, 62, 158, 165
KIRCHNER, ERNST LUDWIG, 159
Kitson, Sydney D., 136
Kitzinger, Ernst, 32
KLEE, PAUL, 159
Klein, Robert, 42
Kleinclausz, Arthur J., 192
Kleinschmidt, Beda, 32
Klingender, Francis D., 37
KLINGER, MAX, 159
Klipstein, August, 160
Klumpke, Anna, 125
Knackfuss, Hermann, 40, 142, 170, 197,
    199
Knapp, Fritz, 122, 167, 170, 176, 177,
    190
Knappe, Karl Adolf, 141
KNELLER, GODFREY, 159
Knittle, Rhea M., 107

Knuttel, Gerhardus, 128
Koch, Carl, 121
Koechlin, Raymond, 24, 108
Koegler, Hans, 156
Koehler, Mathilde Meng, see Meng-
  Koehler, Mathilda
Koehler, Sylvester R., 141
Köhler, Wilhelm R. W., 32
Koepf, Hans, 55
Kohlbach, Rochus, 63
KOKOSCHKA, OSKAR, 159
KOLBE, GEORG, 159
KOLLWITZ, KÄTHE SCHMIDT, 160
Kondakov, Nikodim P., 32, 87
KONINCK, PHILIPS, 160
Konody, Paul G., 175
Konrad, Martin, 66
KOONING, WILLEM DE, 160
Koop, Albert J., 24
Korn, Rudolf, 159
Kouwenhoven, John A., 48
Kowalczyk, Georg, 63
Kraay, Colin M., 19
Kraeling, Carl H., 52
KRAFFT, ADAM, 201
Kramer, Hilton, 160
Kramrisch, Stella, 27
Krautheimer, Richard, 52, 148
Kriegbaum, Friedrich, 170
Kristeller, Paul, 98, 167
Krommes, Rudolf H., 122
Kubler, George, 11, 46, 48, 59
Kühn, Herbert, 13
Kühn, Paul, 159
Kühnel, Ernst, 27, 117
Künstle, Karl, 7
Kuh, Katharine, 37, 162
Kuhn, Alfred, 63
Kuhn, Charles L., 66, 79, 88
KUHN, WALT, 160
Kuile, E. H. ter, 43
KULMBACH, HANS SUESS VON, 160
Kunoth, George, 144
Kuo, Hsi, 24
Kurth, Betty, 115
Kurth, Willi, 141

Kurz, Otto, 4
Kusenberg, Kurt, 187

L

LACHAISE, GASTON, 160
Ladendorf, Heizn, 190
La Faille, J. Bernard de, 150
LA FARGE, JOHN, 160
Lafenestre, G. E., 145
LaFollette, Suzanne, 48
Lafond, Paul, 126, 138, 173, 184, 199,
  202
Lafuente Ferrari, Enrique, 88, 199
Lainez Alcala, Rafel, 124
Lamb, Winifred, 19
Lambert, Élie, 60
Lambotte, Paul, 85
Lami, Stanislas, 4
Lampérez y Romea, Vicente, 60
Lancour, A. Harold, 4
LANCRET, NICOLAS, 160
Landsberger, Frantz, 35
Lane, Arthur, 19, 28, 113
LANE, FITZ HUGH, 160
Langberg, Harald, 60
Lange, Kurt, 15
Lankheit, Klaus, 68
Lantier, Raymond, 39
Lapauze, Henry, 157, 161
Laprade, Jacques de, 191
Laran, Jean, 131, 136, 180
LARGILLIÈRE, NICOLAS DE, 160
Larkin, Oliver W., 48, 138, 173
Lassaigne, Jacques, 71, 85, 88
Lasteyrie du Saillant, Robert C., 54
LA TOUR, GEORGES DUMÉSNIL DE,
  161
LATOUR, IGNACE HENRI JEAN
  FANTIN, see FANTIN-LATOUR,
  IGNACE HENRI JEAN THÉODORE
LA TOUR, MAURICE-QUENTIN DE,
  161
LATROBE, BENJAMIN, 161
Lauer, Philippe, 76
Laufer, Berthold, 24

Laughlin, Ledlie I., 110
LAURANA, FRANCESCO, 161
Laurie, Arthur P., 19, 75, 182
Laurin, Carl, 46
LAUTREC, HENRI MARIE RAYMOND
DE TOULOUSE, see TOULOUSE-
LAUTREC, HENRI
Lauts, Jan, 121, 131, 148
Lavagnino, Emilio, 42, 132
Lavallée, Pierre, 93, 94, 99, 127, 139,
145, 175, 202
Lavalleye, Jacques, 11, 165
Lavedan, Pierre, 11, 54
Laver, James, 77, 98, 103, 202
Lawrence, Arnold W., 19
LAWRENCE, THOMAS, 161
Leach, Bernard, 113
LEAL, JUAN DE VALDÉS see VALDÉS
LEAL, JUAN DE
LeBas, Georges, 131
Lebel, Robert, 141
LE BRUN, CHARLES, 161
LE BRUN, MARIE LOUISE
ÉLISABETH VIGÉE, 161, 162
Leclercq, Henri, 32
Leclère, Tristan, 133, 185
Lecomte, Georges C., 131
LE CORBUSIER, 162
LEDOUX, CHARLES NICHOLAS, 162
Lee, Sherman E., 24
Lees-Milne, James, 119
Lefrançois, Louise P., 39, 65
Léger, Charles, 136
LÉGER, FERNAND, 162
Lehmann, Edgar, 55
Lehmann, Phyllis, 19
Lehmann, Walter, 44
LEHMBRUCK, WILHELM, 162
Lehnert, Georg H., 115
Lehrs, Max, 98
Leipnik, F. L., 98
Lejard, André, 115
Leloir, Maurice, 103
LELY, PETER, 162
Lem, F. H., 13
Lemoisne, Paul A., 77, 138

Lemonnier, Camille, 85, 169, 194
Lemonnier, Henry, 39, 152
LE NAIN, ANTOINE, 162
LE NAIN, LOUIS, 162
LE NAIN, MATHIEU, 162
Lenning, Henry F., 37
Lenormant, François, 63
LE NÔTRE, ANDRÉ, 162
Lenygon, Francis, 105
LEONARDO DA VINCI, 163
Leporini, Heinrich, 94, 98
Leroquais, Victor, 72
Leroy, Alfred, 77, 78, 156
Leroy, Gregoire, 142
LESCAZE, WILLIAM, 163
Leslie, Charles R., 135
LE SUEUR, EUSTACHE, 163
Letarouilly, Paul M., 58
Lethaby, William R., 32
Leurs, Stan, 43
Levey, Michael, 72, 83
Levi, Doro, 111
Lewis, George C., 115
Lexow, Einar Jacob, 46
LEYDEN, LUCAS VAN, see LUCAS
VAN LEYDEN
Leymarie, Jean, 72, 86, 126, 135
Licht, Fred S., 63
LIEBERMANN, MAX, 164
Liebreich, Aenne, 192
Lieure, J., 130
Lilienfein, Heinrich, 136
Lilienfeld, Karl, 147
Limay, Paul Ratouis de, see Ratouis de
Limay, Paul
Lindblom, Andreas A. F., 87
Lindsay, Jack, 198
Lindwell, Bo, 45
Linton, Ralph, 13
Lipman, Jean H., 89
Lipperheide, Franz J. von, 103
LIPPI, FILIPPINO, 164
LIPPI, FILIPPO, 164
Lippmann, Friedrich, 98, 141
Lippold, Gertrude, 123
Litchfield, Frederick, 105, 113

Little, Frances, 115
Lloyd, Nathaniel, 57
LOCHNER, STEFAN, 164
Lockwood, Luke V., 105
Locquin, Jean, 175
Lohse, Bernd, 63
Londi, Emilio, 121
London, Kurt, 45
Long, Basil S., 80
LONGHI, PIETRO, 164
Longhi, Roberto, 83, 145
Longhurst, Margaret H., 108
Loosli, Carl A., 154
Lopez Jiminez, José, 193
Lopez Pegna, Mario, 16
Lopez Rey, José, 199
Loran, Erle, 132
Loreau, Max, 140
Lorenz, Paul, 127
LORENZETTI, AMBROGIO, 164
LORENZETTI, PIETRO, 164
LORENZO, FIORENZO DI, see
     FIORENZO DI LORENZO
LORENZO DI CREDI, 164
LORENZO MONACO, 164
LORRAIN, CLAUDE, see CLAUDE
     LORRAIN
Lossky, Vladimir, 87
Lothrop, Samuel K., 44
LOTTO, LORENZO, 164, 165
Lotz, Arthur, 115
Lotz, Wolfgang, 200
Lowrie, Walter, 32
Lowry, Bates, 11, 52
Lozoya, Juan C., 46
LUCA SPINELLI, SPINELLO DI, see
     SPINELLO ARETINO
Lucas, Alfred, 15
Lucas, Edward V., 119
LUCAS VAN LEYDEN, 165
Luckiesh, Matthew, 75
Ludwig, Allen I., 69
Lübke, Wilhelm, 50
Lüdecke, Heinz, 136
Lüthgen, Eugen, 66
Lugt, Frits, 4, 91

LUINI, BERNARDINO, 165
Lukomskii, Georgii K., 87, 200
Lullies, Reinhard, 19
Lumsden, Ernest S., 99
Lundberg, Erik, 60
Luporini, Eugenio, 129
Lurçat, Jean, 115
Luthmer, Ferdinand, 105
Lutze, Eberhard, 194
Lyons, Islay deCourcy, 28

M

Mabbott, Maureen C., 163
Mabee, Carleton, 173
MABUSE, see GOSSAERT, JAN
McCallum, Ian R. M., 62
McCausland, Elizabeth, 154, 158
McClellan, Elisabeth, 103
McClure, Abbot, 104
McComb, Arthur K., 83, 128
McCurdy, Edward, 163, 181
McDermott, John F., 125
MacDonald, George, 19
MacDonald, William L., 20, 52
Macfall, Haldane, 123
MacGibbon, David, 57
McInnes, Graham, 38
MACINTIRE, SAMUEL, 165
MacIver, David Randall, see Randall-
     MacIver, David
Mack, Gerstle, 132, 136, 197
Mackail, John W., 172
Mackay, Ernest J. H., 28
McKay, William, 157
McKearin, George S., 107
McKearin, Helen, 107
Mackenzie, Donald A., 7
MCKIM, CHARLES FOLLEN, 165
McKinney, Roland J., 142
MACKINTOSH, CHARLES RENNIE,
     165
Maclagan, Eric R. D., 68
McMahon, Amos P., 48
Macquoid, Percy, 105
MacTavish, Newton, 38

MADERNO, CARLO, 165
Madsen, Stephen T., 37
MAES, NICOLAES, 166
MAGNASCO, ALESSANDRO, 166
Magne, Émile, 180
Magni, Giulio, 35
MAGRITTE, RENÉ, 166
Magurn, Ruth S., 188
Mahon, Dennis, 35
Mahr, Adolf, 32
MAIANO, BENEDETTO DA, see
    BENEDETTO DA MAIANO
Maillard, Élisa, 157
MAILLOL, ARISTIDE JOSEPH
    BONAVENTURE, 166
Maiocchi, Rodolfo, 144
Maison, Karl E., 138
Maiuri, Amedeo, 20
Major, Howard, 62
Malaguzzi-Valeri, Francesco, 120, 183
Mâle, Émile, 7
Malingue, Maurice, 147, 157, 171
Mallett, Daniel T., 4
Malraux, André, 11, 151
Manatta, J. I., 22
Mancini, Girolamo, 119
Mander, Carel van, 86
MANET, ÉDOUARD, 166, 172
Mankowitz, Wolf, 113
MANSART, FRANÇOIS, 166
MANSART, JULES HARDOUIN, 167
Mansbridge, John, 52
MANSHIP, PAUL, 167
MANTEGNA, ANDREA, 167
MANZÙ, GIACOMO, 167
Marabottini, Alessandro, 149
MARC, FRANZ, 167
Marcais, Georges, 28
Marceau, Henri, 188
Marcel, Pierre, 77, 161
March, Benjamin, 113
Marchini, Giuseppe, 189
Marciano-Agostinelli Tozzi, M. T., 193
Maret, Jacques, 138
Mariani, Valerio, 121
Marillier, Henry C., 186

MARIN, JOHN, 167
MARIS, MATTHEW, 167
MARIS, WILLEM, 167
Markham, Violet R., 39
Marle, Raimond van, 7, 83, 149, 168
Marlier, Georges, 134, 172
Marmottan, Paul, 125
Marquand, Allan, 185
Marquet de Vasselot, Jean J., 103, 110,
    116
Marquina, Ignacio, 59
Marshall, John H., 28, 44
Martin, Camille, 42, 54
Martin, Fredrik R., 28, 116
Martin, Henry M. R., 78
MARTIN, HOMER DODGE, 167
Martin, Kurt, 121
Martin, Wilhelm, 140, 194
MARTINI, FRANCESCO DI GIORGIO,
    see FRANCESCO DI GIORGIO
    MARTINI
MARTINI, SIMONE, 168
Marx, Camille Roger, see Roger-Marx,
    Camille
Marx, Claude Roger, see Roger-Marx,
    Claude
Maryon, Herbert, 63
MASACCIO, 168
Masai, François, 80
Maseras, Alfonso, 145
Maskell, Alfred, 63, 108
MASOLINO DA PANICALE, 168
Mason, Eudo C., 146
Maspero, Gaston C. C., 15
MASSYS, QUENTIN, 168
MASTER of FLÉMALLE, 143, 202
Mather, Frank J., 48, 72, 83, 167
Mathey, Jacques, 166
MATISSE, HENRI, 168
MATTEO DI GIOVANNI, 168
Matthey, Werner von, 45
Mattingly, Harold, 20
Matz, Friedrich, 20
Mau, August, 20
Mauclair, Camille, 145, 152, 171, 180,
    198

Mauricheau-Beaupré, Charles, 39
Maurois, André, 138
Maxwell, Herbert E., 186
Maxwell, William Stirling, see Stirling-
    Maxwell, William
Maxwell-Barbour, F. W. M., 98
Mayer, Anton, 128
Mayer, August L., 68, 69, 88, 94, 151,
    152, 173, 184, 199
Mayer, Ralph, 75
Mayne, Johathan, 150
Mayor, A. Hyatt, 178
MAZZOLA, FRANCESCO, see
    PARMIGIANINO
MAZZUOLI, FRANCESCO, see
    PARMIGIANINO
Meder, Joseph, 94, 141
Medioni, Gilbert, 44
Meeks, Carroll V., 58, 62
Meier, Michael, 153
Meier-Graefe, Julius, 37, 132, 138, 150,
    183
Meiss, Millard, 78, 83, 167
Meissner, Franz H., 196, 200
MEISSONIER, JEAN LOUIS ERNEST,
    168
Mekhitarian, Arpag, 15
Mellaart, J. H. J., 94
Meller, Simon, 66, 201
Mellerio, Andre, 182
Mellquist, Jerome, 48
MELOZZO DA FORLÌ, 168, 169
MEMLING, HANS, 169
MENDELSOHN, ERICH, 169
Mendelsohn, Henriette, 140
Meng-Koehler, Mathide, 203
Menzel, Heinz, 20
Merin, Peter, 40
MERISI, MICHELANGELO, see
    CARAVAGGIO, MICHELANGELO
Merrifield, Mary P., 75
Mesnil, Jacques, 168
MESSINA, ANTONELLO DA, see
    ANTONELLO DA MESSINA
MEŠTROVIĆ, IVAN, 169
MEUNIER, CONSTANTIN, 169

Meyer, Franz, 102, 133
Meynell, Alice C., 190
Michel, André, 11, 127, 180
Michel, Émile, 154, 183, 188, 195
Michel, Paul H., 78
MICHELANGELO BUONARROTI, 169,
    170
Micheli, Géneviève, 80
Michelis, P. A., 32
Middeldorf, Ulrich A., 181
MIES VAN DER ROHE, see ROHE,
    LUDWIG MIES VAN DER
Migeon, Gaston, 24, 28, 116
Milanesi, Gaetano, 42
MILANO, GIOVANNI DA, see
    GIOVANNI DA MILANO
MILLAIS, JOHN EVERETT, 170
Millais, John G., 170
Millar, Eric G., 80, 81
Miller, Alec, 63
Miller, Dorothy C., 90
MILLER, KENNETH HAYES, 170
Miller, Margaret, 159
MILLES, CARL, 170
Millet, Gabriel, 7, 28, 32
MILLET, JEAN-FRANÇOIS, 171
Millon, Henry A., 52
Mills, John W., 64
Minamoto, Hoshu, 24
Mindlin, Henrique E., 59
Minghetti, Aurelio, 113
Minns, Ellis H., 20
MINO DA FIESOLE, 171
Miquel, Salvador Sanpere y, see Sanpere
    y Miquel, Salvador
Mireur, Hippolyte, 4
MIRÓ, JOAN, 171
Mock, Elizabeth, 62
MODIGLIANI, AMADEO, 171
Moes, Ernst W., 153
Moholy-Nagy, László, 37
Moir, Alfred K., 131
Molinier, Émile, 102
Molmenti, Pompeo G., 131, 172, 196
Molsdorf, Wilhelm, 7
MONDRIAAN, PIETER CORNELIS, 171

MONET, CLAUDE, 166, 171
Mongan, Agnes, 94, 157, 204
Monro, Isabel S., 103
Monroe, Harriet, 186
Montault, Xavier Barbier de, see
  Barbier de Montault, Xavier
Monti, Raffaele, 190
Monzó, Elías Tormo y, see Tormo y
  Monzó, Elías
Moore, Charles H., 52, 57, 130, 165
Moore, Hannah H., 107, 116
MOORE, HENRY SPENCER, 172
Moore, Robert E., 155
MORALES, LUIS DE, 172
Morassi, Antonio, 196, 197
Moreau, Adrien, 172
MOREAU, JEAN MICHEL, 172
MOREAU, LOUIS GABRIEL, 172
Moreau-Nélaton, Étienne, 134, 135, 137,
  139, 158, 166, 171
Moreau-Vauthier, Charles, 148
Moreno, Manuel Gómez, see Gómez-
  Moreno, Manuel
Moret, Aureliano de Beruete y, see
  Beruete y Moret, Aureliano de
MORETTO, IL, 172
Morey, Charles R., 32, 111
Morgan, Charles H., 124
Morgan, John H., 194
MORISOT, BERTHE, 166, 172
Morley, Lacy Collison, see Collison-
  Morley, Lacy
Morley, Sylvanus G., 44
MORO, ANTONIO, 172
Morris, Frances, 116
MORRIS, WILLIAM, 172, 173
Morrison, Hugh, 62, 195
MORSE, SAMUEL FINLEY BREESE,
  173
Mortari, Luisa, 194
Moschini, Vittorio, 123, 153, 164
Mosel, Christel, 174
Moss, Henry S. B., 32
Motherwell, Robert, 73
Mottram, Ralph H., 137
MOUNT, WILLIAM SIDNEY, 173

Mras, George P., 139
Muchall-Viebrook, Thomas W., 94
Müller, Hermann A., 4
Müller, Theodor, 66
Müntz, Eugène, 33, 116, 181
Münz, Ludwig, 129, 183
Mulk-Raj, Anand, 28
Mumford, John K., 116
Mumford, Lewis, 48, 62
MUNCH, EDVARD, 173
Muñoz. Antonio, 42, 126, 130, 165, 173,
  199
Munro, Thomas, 11
Munsell, Albert H., 75
Muratov, Pavel P., 33, 87
MURILLO, BARTOLOMÉ ESTEBAN,
  173
Murray, Linda, 4
Murray, Margaret A., 15
Murray, Peter, 4
Murrell, William, 139
Murtha, Edwin, 167
Museums Directory of the U.S. and
  Canada, 4
Muther, Richard, 73
Myers, Bernard, 11, 73, 79, 87
Mylonas, George E., 20

N

Nacenta, Raymond, 78
Nadeau, Maurice, 73
Naef, Hans, 157
Nagel, Charles, 105
Nagler, Georg K., 4
Nagy, László Moholy, see Moholy-Nagy,
  László
NAIN, LE, see LE NAIN
NANNI DI BANCO, 173
NASH, JOHN, 173
Nash, Joseph, 57
NASH, PAUL, 173
Natanson, Joseph, 108
NATTIER, JEAN MARC, 174
Neal, Ambrose, 105, 110
Neil, William, 11

Neilson, Katharine B., 164
Nélaton, Étienne Moreau, see Moreau-
    Nélaton, Étienne
NERVI, PIER L., 174
Netherlands. Rijksbureau voor
    Kunsthistorische Documentatie, 4
Neugebauer, Rudolf, 116
Neuhaus, Eugen, 48
Neumeyer, Alfred, 133
NEUTRA, RICHARD J., 174
Neuweiler, Arnold, 88
New York Historical Society, 3
New York. Metropolitan Museum of Art.
    Library, 4
Newcomb, Rexford, 52
Newhall, Beaumont, 112
Newton, Eric, 11, 73
NICCOLO DA FOLIGNO, 174
Nicholson, Alfred, 134
Nicodemi, Giorgio di, 185
NICOLA D'APULIA, see PISANO,
    NICOLA
Nicolas, Raoul, 88
Nicolson, Benedict, 196
NIEMEYER, OSCAR, 174
Nierendorf, Karl, 159
Nijhoff, Wouter, 98
Nikolenko, Lada, 198
Nilsson, Martin P., 20
NITHART, MATHIS GOTHART, see
    GRUENEWALD, MATTHIAS
Nocq, Henry, 110
NOLDE, EMIL, 174
Nolhac, Pierre de, 127, 145, 162, 174,
    185
Nordenfalk, Karl, 31
Nordensvan, Georg G., 46
Nørlund, Poul, 46
Norton, Frederick H., 113
NÔTRE, ANDRÉ LE, see LE NÔTRE,
    ANDRÉ
Novotny, Fritz, 36, 133
Nuño, Juan Antonio Gaya, see Gaya
    Nuño, Juan Antonio
Nutting, Wallace, 105, 106
NUZI, ALLEGRETTO, 174

O

Oakeshott, Walter F., 81
Odom, William M., 106
Oelsner, G. H., 116
Oertel, Robert, 164
Offner, Richard, 83
O'Hara, Frank, 179
Oikonomides, A. L. N., 18
Ojetti, Ugo, 83
Okakura, Kakuzo, 24
O'KEEFFE, GEORGIA, 174
Okkonen, Onni, 46
Oldenbourg, Rudolf, 188
Olmer, Pierre, 106
Olsen, Harald, 122
Olson, Ruth, 146
Omont, Henri A., 33
Oppé, Adolf P., 94, 136, 155
ORCAGNA, ANDREA, 174
Orlandi, Stefano, 120
ORLEY, BERNAERT VAN, 174
ORME, PHILIBERT DE L', 174
OROZCO, JOSÉ CLEMENTE, 175
ORPEN, WILLIAM, 175
Ortolani, Sergio, 179
Osborn, Henry Fairfield, 13
Osborn, Max, 36, 98
Osmaston, Francis P. B., 196
OSTADE, ADRIEN VAN, 175
OSTADE, ISAAC VAN, 175
Ostby, Leif, 87
Ostini, Fritz von, 196, 198
Ostwald, Wilhelm, 75, 102
Oswald, Friedrich, 55
OUDRY, JEAN-BAPTISTE, 175
Ouspensky, Léonide, 87
Ozzola, Leandro, 186

P

Paatz, Walter, 33, 36
Paccagnini, Giovanni, 168
Pacchioni, Guglielmo, 131
Pach, Walter, 37, 158, 183
PACHER, MICHAEL, 175

Pagani, Carlo, 58
Paine, Robert T., 24
PALLADIO, ANDREA, 175, 176
Palliser, Fanny M., 116
Pallottino, Massimo, 16
Pallucchini, Rodolfo, 83, 123, 153, 177,
    178, 200, 201
Palm, Erwin W., 59
PALMA, GIACOMO, 146, 176
Palol, Pedro, 47
Pane, Roberto, 175
Pannier, Jacques, 128
Panofsky, Erwin, 11, 33, 36, 54, 66, 86,
    141, 163
PAOLO, GIOVANNI DI, see GIOVANNI
    DI PAOLO
PAOLO DI DONO, see UCCELLO, PAOLO
Papadaki, Stamo, 162, 174
Papini, Roberto, 146
Pariset, François G., 161
Park, Lawrence, 195
Parker, Barbara N., 135
Parker, Karl T., 94, 130, 156, 202
PARMIGIANINO, IL, 176
Pascal, Georges, 160
Passanti, Mario, 153
Passavant, Johann D., 91, 174, 181
Pastor, Willy, 159
Pataky, Dénes, 79
PATER, JEAN-BAPTISTE JOSEPH, 176
Pater, Walter, 36
Paton, James M., 20
Pauli, Gustav, 37, 164
Paulson, Ronald, 155
Pauly, August F. von, 13
Payne, Humfry, 20
Pazaurek, Gustav E., 107
Peacock, Carlos, 135
PEALE, CHARLES WILLSON, 176
Pearson, Hesketh, 202
Peet, Thomas E., 13
Pegna, Mario Lopez, see Lopez Pegna,
    Mario
Peirce, Hayford, 33
Pelka, Otto, 108
Pellicer, Alexandre Cirici, see Cirici-
    Pellicer, Alexandre

Pendlebury, John D. S., 20
Penkala, Maria, 113
Pennell, Elizabeth R., 98, 202
Penrose, Roland, 177
PEPI, CENNO DI, see CIMABUE, GIO-
    VANNI
Pepper, Stephen C., 11
Percival, MacIver, 116
Perez, José Gestoso y, see Gestoso y Perez,
    José
Perls, Klaus G., 145, 201
PERRAULT, CLAUDE, 176
Perrot, Georges, 14
PERUGINO, 176
PERUZZI, BALDASSARE, 176
PESELLINO, 176
Peter, John, 52
Peterdi, Gabor, 99
Pethebridge, Jeanette E., 116
Petrides, Paul, 198
Petrie, William M. F., 15
PEVSNER, ANTOINE, 146, 177
Pevsner, Nikolaus, 11, 41, 52, 79, 153
Peyre, Roger R., 195
Pfannstil, Arthur, 171
Pfuhl, Ernst, 20
Philippowich, Eugen von, 108
Philipson, Morris, 163
Phillipps, Evelyn M., 178
Phillips, John G., 113
Phillips, John M., 110
Phythian, J. E., 158
PIAZZETTA, GIOVANNI BATTISTA, 177
Picard, Charles, 20
PICASSO, PABLO, 177
Picton, Harold W., 40
PIERO DELLA FRANCESCA, see FRAN-
    CESCHI, PIETRO DI BENEDETTO DEI
PIERO DI COSIMO, 177
PIERO DI LORENZO, see PIERO DI COSIMO
PIETRO, SANO DI, see SANO DI PIETRO
PIETRO DA CORTONA, 177
PIETRO DI BENEDETTI DEI FRAN-
    CHESCHI, see FRANCESCHI, PIETRO
    DI BENEDETTO DEI
PIGALLE, JEAN-BAPTISTE, 177, 178
Piggott, Stuart, 13

Pigler, A., 7
Pijoán y Soteras, José, 9, 11
Pilcher, Donald, 57
Pillement, Georges, 69, 184
PILON, GERMAIN, 178
Piltz, Georg, 66
Pinder, Wilhelm, 55, 66
Pinto, M., 44
PINTURICCHIO, 178
PIOMBO, SEBASTIANO LUCIANI, 178
PIRANESI, GIOVANNI BATTISTA, 178
PISANELLO, 178
PISANO, ANDREA, 178
PISANO, GIOVANNI, 179
PISANO, NICOLA, 179
Pisetzky, Rosita L., 103
PISSARRO, CAMILLE JACOB, 179
Pissarro, Ludovic R., 179
Pita-Andrade, José M., 47
Pittaluga, Mary, 164, 168, 196, 198
Place, Charles A., 129
Placer, Fernando Jiménez, see Jiménez-
    Placer, Fernando
Planché, James R., 103
Planiscig, Leo, 68, 140, 148, 185, 186, 200
Platner, Samuel B., 20
Platz, Gustav A., 55
Plaut, James S., 159
Plenderleith, Harold J., 75, 99
Plietzsch, Eduard, 196
Pliny, 11
Plommer, William H., 20
Plon, Eugène, 132
Podreider, Fanny, 116
POLLAIUOLO, ANTONIO, 179
Pollen, John H., 4, 110
POLLOCK, JACKSON, 179
Pollock, Peter, 112
Ponente, Nello, 73
Ponten, Josef, 183
PONTORMO, JACOPO DA, 179
Poortenaar, Jan, 100
Pope, Arthur, 75
Pope, Arthur U., 28
Pope-Hennessy, John, 68, 73, 83, 120,
    132, 140, 149, 181, 190, 198
Popham, Arthur E., 94, 136, 163

Popp, Hermann, 55
Porada, Edith, 28
PORDENONE, GIOVANNI ANTONIO,
    179
Portalis, Roger, 98, 145
Porter, A. Kingsley, 33, 58, 69
Portoghesi, Paolo, 126
Pospisil, Maria, 166
Posse, Hans, 136
Post, Chandler R., 63, 64, 88
Pottier, Edmond, 20
Poulsen, Fredrik, 16
POUSSIN, NICOLAS, 180
Pradel, Pierre, 134
Pratt, Richard A., 62
Praz, Mario, 7
PRENDERGAST, MAURICE BRAZIL,
    180
Price, Frederic N., 138, 188
Prideaux, Sarah T., 98
Priest, Alan, 116
PRIMATICCIO, FRANCESCO, 180
Primitifs Flamands, Les, 86
Prior, Edward S., 57, 67
Procacci, Ugo, 168
Proske, Beatrice, 69
Proskouriakoff, Tatiana A., 44
Prown, Jules, 135
PRUD'HON, PIERRE-PAUL, 180
PUGET, PIERRE, 180
Pugin, Augustus C., 33
Puig y Cadafalch, José, 60
PUVIS DE CHAVANNES, PIERRE, 172,
    180
Puyvelde, Leo van, 43, 86, 94, 142, 188

Q

QUERCIA, JACOPO DELLA, 181
Quintavalle, Armando O., 176

R

Racinet, Auguste, 102, 103
Racz, Istyan, 46
Radin, Paul, 14

RAEBURN, HENRY, 181
Rafols, José F., 47
RAIBOLINI, FRANCESCO, see FRAN-
CIA
Raj, Anand Mulk, see Mulk-Raj, Anand
Ramsay, John, 113
Ramsdell, Roger W., 104, 113
Randall-MacIver, David, 16, 20
Ranke, Hermann, 15
RAPHAEL, 181
Raphael, Max, 14
Rathbun, Mary C., 73
Ratouis de Limay, Paul, 94
Raval, Marcel, 162
Rave, Paul O., 4, 79, 196
Rawlinson, William G., 198
Raynal, Maurice, 73, 121
Read, Helen A., 154
Read, Herbert E., 11, 34, 37, 64, 73, 107,
172, 173
Rearich, Janet Cox, 179
Reath, Nancy A., 116
Réau, Louis, 7, 39, 45, 73, 77, 78, 143,
157, 177, 201
Redgrave, Richard, 81
REDON, ODILON, 181, 182
Redslob, Edwin, 60
Régamey, Raymond, 180
REGNAULT, HENRI, 182
Regoli, Gigetta Dalli, see Dalli Regoli,
Gigetta
Regteren-Altena, Johan Q. van, 95
Reifenberg, Benno, 123
Reilly, Paul, 57
Reinach, Salomon, 20, 21, 73
Reis, José Maria dos, 87
Reis Santos, Luiz, 61
Reitlinger, Henry S., 95
Reitzenstein, Alexander, 66
REMBRANDT HERMANSZOON VAN
RIJN, 182, 183
Rendel, Harry S. Goodhart, see Goodhart-
Rendel, Harry S.
Renders, Émile, 143, 202
RENI, GUIDO, 183
RENOIR, PIERRE AUGUSTE, 185

Répertoire d'Art et d'Archéologie, 4
RETHEL, ALFRED, 183
Rewald, John, 73, 126, 132, 133, 139,
147, 166, 167, 179, 183, 191
Rey, José Lopez, see Lopez Rey, José
Rey, Raymond, 33
Rey, Robert, 138, 150
Reymond, Marcel, 68, 185, 200
Reynolds, Graham, 81, 95, 135
Reynolds, James, 175
REYNOLDS, JOSHUA, 183, 184
Rhodes, Daniel, 113
Riat, Georges, 188
RIBERA, JUSEPE, 184
Ricart, José Gudiol y, see Gudiol y
Ricart, José
Ricci, Corrado, 58, 83, 123, 136, 169,
178
Ricci, Elisa, 7, 116
Rice, David T., 14, 28, 33, 45
Rice, Norman L., 169
Rice, Tamara, 45
Rich, Daniel C., 139, 174, 187, 191
Rich, Jack C., 64
Richards, James M., 52
Richardson, Albert E., 57
Richardson, Edgar P., 11, 90, 120
RICHARDSON, HENRY HOBSON, 184
Richardson, John, 128
Richter, George M., 132, 149
Richter, Gisela M. A., 21
Richter, Hans, 73
Richter, Jean P., 163
Rickert, Margaret, 81
Ridder, André de, 133
Riegle, Alois, 12, 21
RIEMENSCHNEIDER, TILMAN, 184
RIGAUD, HYACINTHE, 184
Riis, Poul J., 16
Rinaldis, Aldo de, 84, 168
Ring, Grete, 78
Ritchie, Andrew C., 64, 81, 139
Richter, Hans, 73
Rittich, Werner, 55
RIVERA, DIEGO, 184
Rivière, Georges, 183

Rivière, Henri, 139
Rivoira, Giovanni T., 21, 28, 58
Robaut, Alfred, 135, 139
Robb, David M., 12, 73
ROBBIA, ANDREA DELLA, 184, 185
ROBBIA, GIOVANNI DELLA, 184, 185
ROBBIA, LUCA DELLA, 184, 185
Robert, Carl, 21
ROBERT, HUBERT, 185
Robert-Dumesnil, A. P. F., 91
Roberts, William, 157, 186
Robertson, Donald, 52
Robertson, Donald S., 21
Robertson, Martin, 21
Robinson, David M., 14
ROBUSTI, JACOPO, see TINTORETTO,
    IL
Rocheblave, Samuel, 39, 78, 178
Rodenwaldt, Gerhart, 19, 21
RODIN, AUGUSTE, 185
Rodman, Selden, 191
Rodriguez, Alfredo Benavides, see
    Benavides Rodriguez, Alfredo
Roeder, Helen, 7
Roethlisberger, Marcel, 134
Roger-Marx, Camille, 98
Roger-Marx, Claude, 91, 158, 182
Rogers, Frances, 107
ROGERS, JOHN, 185
Rogers, Meyric R., 106, 170
ROGER VAN DER WEYDEN, see
    WEYDEN, ROGER VAN DER
Roh, Franz, 86
Rohault de Fleury, 7
ROHE, LUDWIG MIES VAN DER,
    185
Rolfs, Wilhelm, 161
Romagnoli, Fernanda, 174
Roman, Joseph, 184
ROMANINO, GIROLAMO, 185
ROMANO, GIULIO, see GIULIO
    ROMANO
Romea, Vicente Lamperez y, see
    Lamperez y Romea, Vicente
Romero Brest, Jorge, 87
ROMNEY, GEORGE, 186

Roof, K. M., 133
Roos, Frank J., 12, 62
Rooses, Max, 86, 158, 188
Roosval, Johnny, 46
ROOT, JOHN WELLBORN, 186
ROSA, SALVATORE, 186
Rosenberg, Adolf, 175, 181, 183,
    188, 195, 196, 202
Rosenberg, H., 37
Rosenberg, Jakob, 12, 43, 136, 183,
    188, 190
Rosenberg, Marc, 110
Rosenblum, Robert, 37
Rosenhagen, Hans, 198
Rosenthal, Léon, 98
Ross, Denman W., 75
Ross, Edward D., 15, 28
Ross, Thomas, 57
ROSSELLINO, ANTONIO, 186
ROSSELLINO, BERNARDO, 186
ROSSETTI, DANTE GABRIEL, 186
Rossetti, William M., 186
ROSSI, GIOVANNI ANTONIO, 186
Rossi, Giovanni B. de, 33
ROSSO, IL, 187
Rostovtsev, Mikhail I., 21, 28
Roth, Alfred, 52
Rothe, Hans, 151
Rothenstein, John, 41, 81
Rothschild, Edward F., 38
Rothschild, Lincoln, 64
Rotonchamp, Jean de, 147
ROUAULT, GEORGES, 187
ROUBILLIAC, LOUIS FRANÇOIS, 187
Rouchès, Gabriel, 122, 131, 163, 180,
    181, 190
Rourke, Constance M., 48, 192
ROUSSEAU, HENRI JULIEN FÉLIX, 187
Rousseau, Henry, 65
ROUSSEAU, PIERRE ÉTIENNE
    THÉODORE, 187
Roussel, Jules, 65
Roux, Marcel, 96
Rovinskii, D. A., 183
Rowland, Benjamin, 12, 24, 28, 29, 157
ROWLANDSON, THOMAS, 187

Rowley, George, 24, 164
Roy, Maurice, 39
Royal Institute of British Architects.
  Library, 4
RUBENS, PETER PAUL, 187, 188
Rubissow, Helen, 45
Rudder, Arthur de, 156
RUDE, FRANÇOIS, 188
Rudolph, Richard, 24
Rudrauf, Lucien, 139
Ruhmer, Eberhard, 120, 197
RUISDAEL, see RUYSDAEL
Ruiz Cabriada, Agustín, 151
RUIZ Y PICASSO, see PICASSO, PABLO
RUSH, WILLIAM, 188
Rushforth, Gordon M., 137
Russell, Archibald G. B., 153
Russell, John, 128, 143, 191
RUYSDAEL, JACOB ISAACSZOON
  VAN, 188
RUYSDAEL, SALOMON VAN, 188
RYDER, ALBERT PINKHAM, 188
Ryerson, Margery, 154
Rykwert, J., 119

S

Saalman, Howard, 52
SAARINEN, ELIEL, 189
Sabartes, Jaime, 177
Sabatini, Attilio, 179
Sachs, Eleanor B., 116
Sachs, Paul J. 91, 94, 95
Sack, Eduard, 196
Saglio, André, 106
Saglio, Edmond, 18
Saillant, Robert C. Lasteyrie du, see
  Lasteyrie du Saillant, Robert C.
Saint, Lawrence B., 106
SAINT-AUBIN, GABRIEL JACQUES DE,
  189
SAINT-GAUDENS, AUGUSTUS, 189
Saint-Gaudens, Homer, 189
Saint Romain, Charles Du Peloux de,
  see Du Peloux de Saint Romain, Charles
Sakanishi, Shio, 24

Sakisian, Armenag, 29
Saladin, Henri, 28
Salaman, Malcolm C., 92, 98, 203
Salazar, Juan Allende, see Allende-
  Salazar, Juan
Salerno, Luigi, 186
Salis, Arnold von, 36
Salmi, Mario, 68, 145, 168, 197, 198
Salverte, François de, 106
Salvini, Roberto, 64, 111, 134, 149, 203
Sanford, Trent E., 59
Sanchez-Canton, Francisco J., 151
SANGALLO, ANTONIO DA, 189
SANGALLO, GIULIANO DA, 189
Sangiorgi, Giorgio, 116
SANO DI PIETRO, 189
Sanpaolesi, Piero, 129
Sanpere y Miquel, Salvador, 88
SANSOVINO, ANDREA, 189
SANSOVINO, JACOPO, 189
Santayana, George, 12
Santos, Luiz Reis, see Reis Santos, Luiz
Santos, Reynoldo dos, 47
SANZIO, GIOVANNI, 189
Sapori, Francesco, 189
SARGENT, JOHN SINGER, 190
Sarthou Carreres, Carlos, 61
SARTO, ANDREA DEL, 190
Sartoris, Alberto, 52
Sarvig, Ole, 173
SASSETTA, 190
Sauerlandt, Max, 66
Saunders, O. Elfrida, 41, 81
Saupique, Jacqueline J. Bouchot, see
  Bouchot-Saupique, Jacqueline
Sauvage, Marcel, 201
Savage, George, 113
SAVOLDO, GIOVANNI GIROLAMO, 190
Saxl, Fritz, 41, 67
Scavizzi, Giuseppe, 148
Schädler, Alfred, 67
Schäfer, Heinrich, 24
SCHÄUFELEIN, HANS LEONHARD,
  160
Schapiro, Meyer, 133, 150
Schardt, Alois J., 167

Scharf, Alfred, 164
Schéfer, Gaston, 133, 172
Scheffler, Wolfgang, 110
Schéle, Sune, 126
Scheltema, Frederick Adama von, see
  Adama von Scheltema, Frederick
Schendel, Arthur F. E. van, 95
Scherer, Valentin, 141
Schiavo, Armando, 170
Schiefler, Gustav, 159, 173, 174
SCHIELE, EGON, 190
Schiller, Gertrud, 7
Schilling Edmund, 95, 156
Schleinitz, Otto J. W. von, 157, 202
Schliemann, Heinrich, 21
Schlosser, Julius, 4, 148
SCHLÜTER, ANDREAS, 190
Schmalenbach, Werner, 14, 191
Schmarsow, August H., 143, 168, 169,
  189
Schmeckebier, Laurence E., 87, 137, 169
Schmid, Frederic, 75
Schmid, Heinrich A., 156
Schmid, Max, 183
Schmidt, Erich F., 29
Schmidt, George, 89
Schmidt, Hugo, 97
Schmidt, Max, 44
Schmidt, Robert, 108
Schmidt-Degener, Frederik, 128, 194
Schmitt, Otto, 40
Schmitz, Hermann, 106, 116
Schmutzler, Robert, 38
Schneider, Arthur von, 131
Schnier, Jacques P., 70
Schoder, Raymond V., 21
Schoeller, André, 135
Schönberger, Arno, 36, 67
Schoenberger, Guido, 153
Schöne, Wolfgang, 127
SCHONGAUER, MARTIN, 190
Schoolman, Regina L., 95
Schottmüller, Frida, 64, 106, 120
Schrade, Hubert, 164, 184
Schreiber, William L., 98
Schubring, Paul, 42, 58, 69, 84, 120, 140

Schudt, Ludwig, 131
Schuette, Marie, 116
Schutz, Anton, 4
Schwabacher, E., 151
Schwabe, Randolph, 103
Schweinfurth, Philipp, 87
SCHWIND, MORITZ VON, 191
SCHWITTERS, KURT, 191
SCOREL, JAN VAN, 191
Scott, Geoffrey, 12
Scott, Robert G., 102
Scranton, Robert L., 21
Scully, Vincent, J., 21, 52, 61, 204
Seailles, Gabriel, 132
Sears, Clara E., 90
Secker, Hans F., 184
Sedlmayr, Hans, 55, 144
Seeger, Georg, 201
Seele, K., 16
Segard, Achille, 151, 193
SEGHERS, HERCULES PIETERSZ, 191
Segy, Ladislaw, 14
Seidlitz, Woldemar, 24
Seitz, William, 171
Sekler, Edward F., 204
Seligman, Germain, 191
Seligmann, H. J., 167
Sellers, Charles C., 176
Seltman, Charles T., 21
Selz, Jean, 201
Selz, Peter, 38, 79, 140
Sensier, Alfred, 171
Sentenach y Cabreras, Narciso, 88
Serra, Luigi, 140, 181
SERT, JOSÉ LUIS, 147, 191
Serullaz, Maurice, 95, 138
Servaes, Franz, 159, 204
Servolini, Luigi, 121
Sesonske, Alexander, 12
SETTIGNANO, DESIDERIO DA, see
  DESIDERIO DA SETTIGNANO
Seuphor, Michel, 64, 171
SEURAT, GEORGES PIERRE, 191
Seymour, Charles, 54, 64, 69
Seznec, Jean, 36, 77
SHAHN, BEN, 191

Sharp, Dennis, 52
Shaw, James B., 153
Shearman, John, 190
SHEELER, CHARLES, 192
Sherman, Frederic F., 188
Shewring, Walter, 148
Shirley, Andrew, 125, 135
Sichel, Pierre, 171
SICKERT, WALTER RICHARD, 192
Sickman, Laurence, 24
Sicre, José Gomez, see Gomez Sicre, José
Sievers, Johannes, 119
SIGNAC, PAUL, 139, 192
SIGNORELLI, LUCA, 192
Silcock, Arnold, 24
Silsby, Wilson, 100
SILVA Y VELÁQUEZ, DIEGO
   RODRÍGUEZ DE, see VELÁZQUEZ
   DIEGO RODRÍGUEZ DE SILVA Y
Simmons, Pauline, 116
SIMONE MARTINI, see MARTINI,
   SIMONE
Simpson, Frederick M., 52
Simson, Otto von, 33
Singer, Hans W., 4, 100, 141, 183
Singh, Madanjeet, 29
Singleton, Esther, 106
Sinibaldi, Giulia, 164
SINT JANS, GEERTGEN TOT, see
   GEERTGEN TOT SINT JANS
SIQUEIROS, DAVID ALFARO, 192
Sirén, Osvald, 24, 25, 149, 163, 164
SISLEY, ALFRED, 166, 192
Sitwell, Sacheverell, 40, 42, 57, 67
Sizer, Theodore, 197
Slater, John H., 98
Slatkin, Charles E., 95
Slive, Seymour, 43, 183
SLOAN, JOHN, 192
Sloane, Joseph C., 78
SLUTER, CLAUS, 192
SMIBERT, JOHN, 193
Smith, Bernard, 81
Smith, Chetwood, 185
Smith, Earl B., 15, 33
Smith, George E. K., 55, 60

Smith, Harold C., 110
Smith, Robert C., 44
Smith, Simon Harcourt, see Harcourt-
   Smith, Simon
Smith, Solomon C. K., 136, 137
Smith, Vincent A., 29
Smith, William, 22
Smith, William S., 15
Smouse, Florence Ingersoll, see Ingersoll-
   Smouse, Florence
Smyth, Craig H., 73
SMYTHSON, ROBERT, 193
SOANE, JOHN, 193
Soares, Ernesto, 98
Sobotka, Georg, 64
Soby, James T., 38, 73, 90, 121, 134,
   137, 152, 159, 166, 171, 187
SODOMA, IL, 193
Soehner, Halldor, 36
Solá, Miguel, 44
SOLARIO, ANDREA, 193
Solon, Louis M. E., 114
Sonn, Albert H., 110
Soper, Alexander C., 24, 25
Soria, Martin S., 46, 87, 205
SOROLLA Y BASTIDA, JOAQUIN, 193
Soteras, José Pijoán y, see Pijoán y
   Soteras, José
SOUTINE, CHAIM, 193
Spagnesi, Gianfranco, 186
SPAGNOLETTO, LO, see RIBERA
   JUSEPE
Spahn, Annemarie, 176
Spargo, John, 114
Sparrow, Walter S., 127
Spearing, Herbert G., 14
Speltz, Alexander, 102
Spielmann, Heinz, 175
Spiers, R. P., 51
Spinden, Herbert J., 44
SPINELLI, SPINELLO DI LUCA, see
   SPINELLO ARETINO
SPINELLO ARETINO, 194
Springer, Anton, 12
Springer, Jaro, 191
STAËL, NICOLAS, 194

Stange, Alfred, 56, 80
Statham, Henry H., 52
Stauffer, David M., 99
Stechow, Wolfgang, 36, 86, 188
Steegmann, John, 36, 184
STEEN, JAN HAVICKSZ, 194
Stefănescu, Ioan D., 73
STEFANO DI GIOVANNI, see SASSETTA
Stegmann, Carl M., 58
Stein, Gertrude, 177
Stein, Mark Aurel, 29
Steinbart, Kurt, 168
Steindorff, George, 15, 16
Steingraber, Erich, 111
Steinitz, Kate T., 191
Steinmann, Ernst, 148, 170, 178
Steinweg, Klara, 174
Sterling, Charles, 73, 78
Sternberg, Harry, 100
STEVENS, ALFRED, 194
STEVENS, ALFRED GEORGE, 194
Stevenson, Robert A. M., 188
Stewart, Cecil, 33, 53
Stirling-Maxwell, William, 47
Stix, Alfred, 95
Stoddard, Whitney S., 54
Stokes, Hugh, 151
Stokes, Margaret M., 33
Stoll, Robert, 57
Stone, Lawrence, 67
Story, Sommerville, 185
STOSS, VEIT, 194
Stotz, Charles M., 62
Stout, George L., 74, 75
Strang, William, 100
Strange, Thomas A., 106
Stratton, Arthur, 56
STRICKLAND, WILLIAM 194
Strong, Donald E., 22
Strong, Eugénie S., 22
Stroud, Dorothy, 193
STROZZI, BERNARDO, 194
Strzygowski, Josef, 33, 34, 45
STUART, GILBERT, 194, 195
Stubbe, Wolf, 92, 122
Stubblebine, James H., 153

Sturgis, Russell, 53
Suger, Abbot, 54
Suida, Wilhelm, 127, 163, 181, 197
Sullivan, Edward, 73
SULLIVAN, LOUIS HENRY, 195
SULLY, THOMAS, 195
Summerson, John N., 57, 158, 173, 193
Supino, Igino B., 132, 149, 164
SUSTERMAN, JUSTUS, see SUTTER-
    MANS, JUSTUS
SUTTERMANS, JUSTUS, 195
Sutton, Denys, 95, 185, 203
Swarbrick, John, 119
Swarzenski, Georg, 95, 179
Swarzenski, Hanns, 34, 73
Sweeney, James J., 14, 73, 130, 138, 147,
    172
Sweet, Frederick A., 90, 132
Swift, Emerson H., 34
Swillens, P. T. A., 200
Swindler, Mary H., 14
Sybel, Ludwig von, 34
Sydow, Eckart von, 14
Sylvester, David, 172
Symeonides, Sibilla, 195
Symonds, John A., 42, 170
Symons, Arthur, 125
Sypher, Wylie, 12, 36, 38
Szittya, Emil, 193

T

Tabarant, Adolphe, 166, 179, 198
Tabor, Margaret E., 7
TADDEO DI BARTOLO, 195
Taft, Ada B., 195
TAFT, LORADO, 64, 70, 195
Taft, Robert, 112
Taki, Sei-Ichi, 25
Tallmadge, Thomas E., 57, 62
Tarbell, Frank B., 22
Tatlock, Robert R., 47
Tattersall, Creasy E. C., 115, 116
TATTI, JACOPO, see SANSOVINO,
    JACOPO
Taullard, Alfredo, 44, 106

Taut, Bruno, 53
Taylor, Harold M., 57
Taylor, Henry O., 34
Taylor, Joan, 57
TENIERS, DAVID, 195
TERBORCH, GERARD, 195, 196
TERBRUGGHEN, HENDRIK, 196
Tériade, E., 162
Ternois, Daniel, 130
Terrasse, Antoine, 126
Terrasse, Charles, 78, 178
Tervarent, Guy de, 8
Testori, Gianni, 168
Thelen, Heinrich, 126
Theophilus, 34
THEOTOCOPOULOS, DOMENICO, see
  GRECO, EL
Theunissen, André, 106
Thieme, Ulrich, 5
Thiery, A., 169
Thode, Henry, 170, 196
THOMA, HANS, 196
Thomas, Stanley, 41
Thompson, Daniel V., 76
Thomson, David C., 78, 167
Thomson, William G., 117
Thorn, C. Jordan, 111, 114
Thornbury, George W., 198
Thorpe, William A., 108
THORVALDSEN, BERTEL, 196
Thuillier, Jacques, 76
Thurnlackh, Karl Garzarolli, see
  Garzarolli-Thurnlackh, Karl
Tibol, Raquel, 192
TIEPOLO, DOMENICO, 196
TIEPOLO, GIOVANNI BATTISTA, 196
Tietze, Hans, 95, 120, 141, 196, 197
Tietze-Conrat, Erika, 95, 141, 167
Tigler, Peter, 144
Tikkanen, Johan J., 46
TINO DA CAMAINO, 196
TINTORETTO, IL, 196
Tipping, Henry A., 57
Tischner, Herbert, 14
TITIAN, 197
Toch, Maximilian, 76

Toda, Kenji, 25
Todorow, Maria Fossi, see Fossi Todorow,
  Maria
Toesca, Elena, 179
Toesca, Ilaria, 178
Toesca, Pietro, 42, 84, 168
Toft, Albert, 64
Tolnay, Charles de, 95, 126, 129, 143,
  170
Toor, Frances, 44
Tormo y Monzó, Elías, 47
Torres, Raul Costa, see Costa Torres,
  Raul
Toscano, Salvador, 44
Totten, George O., 44
TOULOUSE-LAUTREC, HENRI, 197
Tourneux, Maurice, 161
Toussaint, Manuel, 44, 59
Tovell, Ruth M., 86
Towndrow, Kenneth R., 194
Toynbee, Jocelyn M. C., 22
Tozzi, M. T. Marciano Agostinelli, see
  Marciano-Agostinelli Tozzi, M. T.
Trapier, Elizabeth du Gué, 152, 184, 199
Traquair, Ramsey, 34
Treves, Marco, 10
Tristram, Ernest W., 80, 81
Trivas, Numa S., 153
Troescher, Georg, 12, 78
Trowell, Margaret, 14
TROYON, CONSTANT, 197
Trübner, Jörg, 189
TRUMBULL, JOHN, 197
Tsountas, Chrestos, 22
Tsuda, Noritake, 25
Tuckerman, Henry T., 48
TURA, COSIMO, 197
TURNER, JOSEPH MALLARD
  WILLIAM, 197, 198
Turner, Reginald, 58
Turner, Richard A., 84
Tyler, Royall, 33

U

Ubbelohde-Doering, Heinrich, 44
UBERTINI, FRANCESCO, 198

UCCELLO, PAOLO, 198
UHDE, FRITZ VON, 198
Uhde, Wilhelm, 43, 150
Uhde-Bernays, Hermann, 144
Underwood, Paul A., 34
UNESCO, 5, 12
Updike, Daniel B., 92
Upjohn, Everard M., 12, 198
UPJOHN, RICHARD, 198
UTRILLO, MAURICE, 198
Uzanne, L. G., 130

V

Vaccarino, Paolo, 173
Vaillant, Annette, 126
Vaillant, George C., 44, 48
VALDÉS LEAL, JUAN DE, 199
Valentiner, Wilhelm R., 43, 64, 138, 153, 156, 159, 166, 183, 196
Valeri, Francesco Malaguzzi, see Malaguzzi-Valeri, Francesco
Valotaire, Marcel, 138
VANBRUGH, JOHN, 199
Vandeputte, H., 142
VAN DE VELDE, JAN, see VELDE, JAN VAN DE
VAN DER ROHE, LUDWIG MIES, see ROHE, LUDWIG MIES VAN DER
VAN DER WEYDEN, ROGER, see WEYDEN, ROGER VAN DER
Vandier, Jacques, 16
VAN DYCK, ANTHONY, see DYCK, ANTHONY VAN
VAN EYCK, see EYCK
VAN GOGH, VINCENT, see GOGH, VINCENT VAN
VAN GOYEN, JAN, see GOYEN, JAN VAN
VAN HEEMSKERK, MARTIN, see HEEMSKERK, MARTIN VAN
VAN LEYDEN, LUCAS, see LUCAS VAN LEYDEN
Van Millingen, Alexander, 34
VANNUCCI, PIETRO, see PERUGINO
VAN ORLEY, BERNAERT, see ORLEY, BERNAERT VAN

VAN OSTADE, see OSTADE
VAN RIJN, REMBRANDT HERMANS-ZOON, see REMBRANDT HERMANS-ZOON VAN RIJN
VAN RUYSDAEL, see RUYSDAEL
Vantoura, André, 95
VANVITELLI, GASPARE, see WITTEL, GASPAR VAN
VAN WITTEL, GASPAR, see WITTEL, GASPAR VAN
Vanzype, Gustave, 194
Varenne, Gaston, 127
VASARI, GIORGIO, 199
Vasari Society, 95
Vasselot, Jean J. Marquet de, see Marquet de Vasselot, Jean J.
Vaughan, Malcolm, 140
Vauthier, Charles Moreau, see Moreau-Vauthier, Charles
Vavalà, Evelyn S., 84
VECCHIO, PALMA, see PALMA, GIACOMO
VECELLI, TIZIANO, see TITIAN
Vegas, Liana Castelfranchi, see Castelfranchi Vegas, Liana
VELÁZQUEZ, DIEGO RODRÍGUEZ DE SILVA Y, 199
Velazquez Chavez, Austin, 87
VELDE, JAN VAN DE, 199
VENEZIANO, DOMENICO, 198
Venturi, Adolfo, 42, 84, 178, 179, 192, 200
Venturi, Lionello, 12, 74, 84, 127, 131, 149, 187
Verga, Ettore, 163
Verlet, Pierre, 117
VERMEER, JAN, 199, 200
Vermeule, Cornelius C., 12, 22
Vermeule, Emily, 22
Vermeulen, Frans, 56
VERNET, CARLE, 200
VERNET, HORACE, 200
VERNET, JOSEPH, 200
Verneuil, Maurice P., 170
VERONESE, PAOLO, 200
VERROCCHIO, ANDREA DEL, 200
Vertue, George, 81

Vesme, Alessandro Baudi di, see Baudi di
    Vesme, Alessandro
Viebrook, Thomas W. Muchall, see
    Muchall-Viebrook, Thomas W.
Vienna. Österreichisches Museum für
    Kunst und Industrie, 117
Vieyra, M., 14
VIGNOLA, 200, 201
VILLARD DE HONNECOURT, 201
VINCI, LEONARDO DA, see
    LEONARDO DA VINCI
Viollet-le-Duc, Eugène E., 53, 55, 106
VISCHER, PETER, 201
Vito Battaglia, Silvia de, 136
Vitruvius Pollio, 53
Vitry, Paul, 65, 135, 151, 167
Vitzhum von Eckstädt, George, 137
VIVARINI, ALVISE, 201
VIVARINI, ANTONIO, 201
VIVARINI, BARTOLOMMEO, 201
VLAMINCK, MAURICE DE, 201
Volbach, Wolfgang, F., 34, 111, 117
Volhard, Hans, 151
Voll, Karl, 86, 169
Vollard, Ambroise, 133, 139, 183
Vollmer, Hans, 5
Voss, Hermann G. A., 84, 95, 120
Voyce, Arthur, 45, 60
Vries, Ary B. de, 200

W

Waagen, Gustav F., 41
Wace, Alan, 22
Wackernagel, Martin, 56
Waern, Cecilia, 160
Waetzoldt, Wilhelm, 141, 156
Wahl, J. B., 186
Walcher-Casotti, Maria, 201
Waldberg, Patrick, 74, 166
Waldmann, Emil, 38, 185, 197
Waley, Arthur, 25
Walker, John, 90
Walker, R. A., 122
Wallace, David H., 3, 185
Walpole, Horace, 81
Ward, Thomas H., 186

Ward, William H., 55
Wark, Robert, 184
Warner, Langdon, 25
Warner, Ralph, 86
Wasmuth, Gunther, 53
Waterhouse, Ellis K., 81, 84, 147, 184
Waterman, Thomas T., 62
Waters, William G., 69, 145
Watkins, Lura, 108, 114
Watrous, James, 96
Watson, Forbes, 132
Watson, Walter C., 61
WATTEAU, JEAN-ANTOINE, 201, 202
WATTS, GEORGE FREDERICK, 202
Watts, Mary S., 202
Waugh, Evelyn, 186
Wauters, Alphonse J., 174
Weale, William H. J., 143
Webb, Geoffrey, 58, 204
Webber, Frederick R., 8
WEBER, MAX, 202
Weber, Siegfried, 144
Weber, Wilhelm, 99
Webster, Thomas B. L., 22
Wedmore, Frederick, 99, 203
Weege, Fritz, 16
Wehle, Harry B., 90, 173
Weibel, Adèle C., 117
Weigelt, Curt H., 84, 140, 149
Weigert, Hans, 40
Weigmann, Otto A., 191
Weinberger, Martin, 96, 170
Weintraub, Stanley, 123
Weisbach, Werner, 36, 47, 176
Weise, Georg, 61, 69
Weismann, Elizabeth W., 69
Weissman, Adriaan W., 56
Weitenkampf, Frank, 99
Weitzmann, Kurt, 34, 74, 108
Weizsäcker, Heinrich, 142
Welcker, Carola Giedeon, see Giedeon-
    Welcker, Carola
Weller, Allen S., 146
WENGENROTH, STOW, 202
Wenham, Edward, 111
Werner, Alfred, 122, 141, 171
Werth, Léon, 180

Wescher, Paul R., 89, 145
Wessel, Klaus, 34
Westheim, Paul, 162
Westlake, Nat H. J., 108
Wethey, Harold E., 59, 88, 152
Wettergren, Erik, 46
WEYDEN, ROGER VAN DER, 202
Wheatley, Henry B., 155
Wheeler, Anne B., 135
Wheeler, James R., 18
Wheeler, Monroe, 187
Whinney, Margaret D., 41, 67
WHISTLER, JAMES ABBOT McNEILL,
    202, 203
Whistler, Laurence, 199
Whitaker-Wilson, Cecil, 204
White, John, 34, 42
Whitehill, Walter M., 48, 61
Whiting, Gertrude, 117
Whitley, William T., 81, 147, 195
Whitman, Alfred, 99
Whittemore, Thomas, 34
Whittick, Arnold, 53, 169
Who's Who in American Art, 5
Who's Who in Art, 5
Wickhoff, Franz, 22
Wiele, Marguerite van de, 175
Wight, Frederick S., 90
Wilber, Donald N., 29
Wild, Angenitus M. de, 76
Wildenstein, Georges, 133, 145, 158, 160,
    161, 166, 172
Wilder, Elizabeth, 44
Wilenski, Reginald H., 38, 64, 78, 81, 86
Wiles, Bertha H., 69
WILIGELMUS, 203
WILKIE, DAVID, 203
Wilkinson, J. V. S., 51
Willets, William, 25
Willey, Basil, 36
Williams, Hermann W., 173
Williams, William C., 192
Williamson George C., 2, 74, 120, 146,
    157, 165, 176
Willich, Hans, 59, 201

Wilm, Hubert, 64, 67
Wilmerding, John, 160
Wilpert, Josef, 34, 111
Wilson, Cecil Whitaker, see Whitaker-
    Wilson, Cecil
Wilson, Ralph P., 29
WILSON, RICHARD, 203
Winchester, Alice, 89
Winckelmann, Johann J., 14
Wind, Edgar, 36
Windels, Fernand, 14
Wingert, Paul S., 13, 14, 48, 204
Winkler, Friedrich, 80, 86, 96, 141, 150,
    160, 165, 202
Winzinger, Franz, 96, 120
Wissler, Clark, 49
Wissowa, Georg, 13
With, Karl, 25
Witte, Fritz, 40
WITTEL, GASPAR VAN, 203
Wittgens, Fernanda, 144
Wittkower, Rudolf, 41, 42, 59, 124, 131, 170
WITZ, KONRAD, 203
Wölfflin, Heinrich, 12, 36, 42, 141
Wolfe, Bertram D., 184
Wollin, Nils G. A., 46
Woltmann, Alfred F. G. A., 156
WOOD, GRANT, 203
Wood, T. Martin, 129
Woodall, Mary, 147
Woodforde, Christopher, 108
Woolley, Charles L., 29
World Collector's Annuary, 5
Worringer, Wilhelm, 12, 16, 34, 76
WREN, CHRISTOPHER, 203, 204
WRIGHT, FRANK LLOYD, 204
Wright, Olgivanna L., 204
Wu, Nelson I., 25
Wulff, Oskar K., 34, 45
Wurzbach, Alfred, 5
Wycherley, R. E., 22
Wyckoff, Alexander, 49
WYETH, ANDREW, 204
Wyler, Seymour B., 111

Y

Yalouris, N., 16
Yashiro, Yukio, 25, 127
Year's Art, The, 5
Young, G. M., 20
Young, George F., 42
Yriarte, C. E., 145
Ysendyck, Jules J., 43

Z

Zaidenberg, Arthur, 12
Zampetti, Pietro, 122, 137, 165
Zarnecki, George, 67, 150
Zeitler, Rudolf, 38
Zerner, H., 42

Zervos, Christian, 14, 22, 38, 142, 152, 168, 177
Zevi, Bruno, 53, 170
Zieseniss, Charles U., 122
Zigrosser, Carl, 99, 160
Zimmer, Heinrich R., 29
Zimmermann, Ernst H., 74, 202
ZORACH, WILLIAM, 204
ZORN, ANDERS LEONARD, 204
Zorzi, Giangiorgio, 176
Zschietzschmann, Willy, 13
ZUCCARI, FEDERICO, 204
Zucker, Paul, 74
Zürcher, Richard, 59
ZULOAGA, IGNACIO, 205
ZURBARÁN, FRANCISCO, 184, 205
Zwanziger, W. C., 140